Impacts and Influences

This book was sponsored by the Acton Society.

The Acton Society Trust is an independent non-profit-making organization set up in 1948 with charitable status. It takes its name from the nineteenth-century historian, Lord Acton. The Society has carried out or sponsored many research projects in social and economic fields. A list of the resulting publications is available from the Acton Society, 9 Poland Street, London W1V 3DG (01 437 8954).

Impacts and Influences

Essays on media power in the twentieth century

Edited by James Curran, Anthony Smith and Pauline Wingate

Routledge
Taylor & Francis Group

LONDON AND NEW YORK

First published in 1987 by
Methuen & Co. Ltd
11 New Fetter Lane, London EC4P 4EE

Reprinted 2004 by Routledge,
11 New Fetter Lane, London EC4P 4EE

Transferred to Digital Printing 2004

Published in the USA by
Methuen & Co.
in association with Methuen, Inc.
29 West 35th Street, New York NY 10001

British Library Cataloguing in Publication Data

Impacts and influences: essays on media
power in the twentieth century.
1. Mass media—Social aspects
I. Curran, James   II. Smith, Anthony, 1938–
III. Wingate, Pauline
302.2'34   HM258
ISBN 0–416–00602–7
ISBN 0–416–00612–4 Pbk

Library of Congress Cataloging in Publication Data

Impacts and influences.
Includes bibliographies and index.
1. Mass media—Great Britain—History—20th century.
2. Mass media—Influence.
3. Mass media—Social aspects—Great Britain—History—20th century.
I. Curran, James. II. Smith, Anthony, 1938–
III. Wingate, Pauline. IV. Acton Society Trust.
P92.G7146 1987   302.2'34'0941   86–23813
ISBN 0–416–00602–7
ISBN 0–416–00612–4 (pbk.)

Contents

List of illustrations

Tables

Figures

Contributors

Tony Aldgate is Lecturer in History at the Open University.

D. G. Boyce is Reader in the Department of Political Theory and Government at University College Swansea.

David Cardiff is Principal Lecturer in Media Studies at the Polytechnic of Central London.

David Chaney is Senior Lecturer in Sociology at the University of Durham.

James Curran is Head of the Department of Communications at Goldsmiths' College, University of London.

David Dayan is a member of the Faculty of the Annenberg School of Communications at the University of Southern California.

Philip Elliot was Senior Research Fellow at the Centre of Mass Communication Research, University of Leicester.

Simon Frith is Senior Lecturer in Sociology at Warwick University.

Deian Hopkin is Lecturer in History at the University College of Wales, Aberystwyth.

Tom Jeffery is a civil servant.

Elihu Katz is Professor of Sociology at the Hebrew University of Jerusalem.

Keith McClelland is Lecturer in History at Bulmershe College of Higher Education, Reading.

Geoff Matthews teaches communications studies at Trent Polytechnic.

Gill Murphy is teaching at Hadley County Infants School, Telford, Shropshire.

Richard Paterson is Television Projects Officer at the British Film Institute.

Nicholas Pronay is Senior Lecturer in History at the University of Leeds.

Paddy Scannell is Senior Lecturer in Media Studies at the Polytechnic of Central London.

Roger Silverstone is Reader in Sociology in the Department of Human Sciences, Brunel University.

Anthony Smith is Director of the British Film Institute.

Pauline Wingate is the former organizer of the Acton Society press group.

Introduction

It is almost impossible to make any statement about the media of communication without offering an implied model or theory of how information exercises influence. Listen to any contemporary politician arguing about such diverse topics as film or video censorship, education reforms, the de-regulation or regulation of broadcasting, the sharing out of election time, the subsidizing of the film industry, the privatization of telecommunications or any other of the scores of issues which arise in the course of the normal annual public agenda, and you will be able to detect the operations of one or more of a score of theories of media influence which have accumulated over the last century or more. Each theory carries the impact of a different academic or professional specialism. Like Keynes's politician who is the prisoner of defunct economists, ours is the captive of decaying doctrines offered over the years by philosophers, historians, sociologists, semioticians, psychologists, journalists.

In astrology 'influence' refers to an ethereal liquid which acts upon the character and destiny of people. In the media – the modern mechanical ones in particular – society has come profoundly, and partly unconsciously, to accept a source of perpetual and partially inexplicable power. Almost any event or social phenomenon today which is not easily explicable by other means is casually ascribed to the 'effects' of newspapers, video, television, the cinema. Tastes and crazes, swings of electoral opinion, standards of personal behaviour, moral qualities, fashions in clothing, nutrition, music, habits of speech, all have come popularly to be believed to be the subjects of mysterious manipulative operations on the part of the media.

These casual ascriptions beg a number of questions about the processes of influence. How is media influence exerted? Are the media merely one of a nexus of influences? How important are the media in relation to these other influences?

These are familiar questions which researchers, particularly during the 1940s, 1950s and 1960s, concentrated upon. Their work provided a useful antidote to a simplistic and still widely held belief in the omnipotent power of the media. But, as has been frequently pointed out, their negative appraisals of media influence were based on a restricted and inadequate conceptualization of media effects.[1] Much of this early work also suffered from an exclusive concentration upon the transmission of media influence without considering on whose behalf influence was being exerted.

Attempts have been made during the past fifteen years to make good these shortcomings. But, instead of a new consensus emerging, divergent and indeed totally contradictory views about the place of the media in society, and the degree of influence it radiates, have emerged in the rapidly expanding literature on the subject. Some argue, for example, that the mass media successfully engineer support for the social order among the subordinate classes by the way in which they 'construct' reality.[2] Others argue that media influence is essentially a circulatory process in which the media both reflect and reinforce social norms.[3] This cleavage – and it is only one of a number of sharp differences that have emerged – has been predicated on a number of further differences about the extent of hierarchical controls within media organizations, how communicators respond to external pressures, the degree of real autonomy they enjoy and, ultimately, the structure of power within society.

In this volume, we are attempting to offer a kind of anthology of alternative views of the media, their place and influence within society. Our contributors examine a heterogeneity of events and developments in twentieth-century British history, and each study embodies, in varying degrees of explicitness, one (or sometimes more) of the available models. Together they provide, we hope, for students and general readers, a picture of the range of ways in which press, cinema, radio and television can be seen as having wielded power in the course of this century.

The editors are not arguing for any single or immutable model: they do, however, believe that it is no longer acceptable to view the media as autonomous institutions – as, so to speak, free, floating, independent satellites beaming down influences on mass publics. The media need to be relocated in the context of the competing social forces that determine the disposition and trajectory of media influence. The interplay of these social forces decisively shapes the character of media organizations, their evolving technologies, and the symbolic content they transmit. No less important, they also structure the values and predispositions that audiences bring to the media which crucially affect, in turn, the extent to which they are influenced by what they view, listen to and read.

The historical perspective of this book has enabled many contributors to situate the media more fully in their political and social context than is generally the case in communications research. Some of these essays also provide a more illuminating and complex understanding of the interaction between media institutions and gradually evolving social and political processes than would have been possible through analysis based on one-off social surveys and small-sample laboratory experiments. Taken together, these chapters indicate the usefulness of historical enquiry – an as yet underdeveloped discipline in mass communications research.

We hope that this book will also stimulate greater interest in the media among modern historians by illuminating different ways in which mass communications have contributed to the development of modern British society. Most general historical accounts pay scant attention to the media except as source material (often over-respectfully handled) while most historical studies of the media are narrowly focused institutional accounts little concerned with the media's wider social, cultural and political influence. In attempting to address these wider issues, we have been forced therefore to rely more on social scientists than on historians. If we mount a similar enterprise in some ten years' time, it would be satisfying to reverse this balance.

Notes

1 See, for instance, Todd Gitlin, 'Media sociology: the dominant paradigm', *Theory and Society*, 6 (1978); M. Gurevitch, T. Bennett, J. Curran and J. Woollacott (eds), *Culture, Media and Society*, London, Methuen, 1982; Denis McQuail, *Mass Communication Theory*, Beverly Hills , Sage, 1983, for alternative surveys of communications research as it has developed.
2 S. Hall, J. Clarke, J. Critcher, T. Jefferson and B. Roberts, *Policing the Crisis*, London, Macmillan, 1978.
3 John Whale, *The Politics of the Media*, London, Fontana, 1980 (rev. edn).

Part 1

Media and public opinion

Introduction

The relationship between the mass media and public opinion has been conceptualized in a variety of ways. According to classic liberal theory, the media are representative institutions which expose governments to the full blast of public opinion. Another research tradition sees this influence as flowing mainly in the other direction, with governments skilfully using the media to manage public opinion. Other commentators offer a more complex model in which the media are viewed as an arena in which a plurality of political opinions and social values, derived from a variety of influences, is contested or negotiated. This model, in turn, is presented in different forms with one influential school claiming that most media are structurally linked to the dominant power bloc in British society.

Each of the chapters in this section contributes explicitly or by implication to this debate. Thus Deian Hopkin's opening essay illustrates the way in which small-circulation publications can sustain minority opinions which subsequently gain a growing number of adherents. His central theme is that the seemingly marginal publications of the left in the early years of this century helped to develop opposition to the imperialist consensus of Edwardian Britain not so much by proselytizing the middle ground of public opinion as by intellectually re-equipping radical activists. The radical press helped socialists to grope through the fog of contemporary jingoism to arrive at a more radical understanding of what was happening in South Africa. This process was a faltering and uncertain one in which some radical papers idealized the Boers (while ignoring the plight of black South Africans), only half assimilated the critiques of imperialism advanced by radical economists like J. A. Hobson and never fully resolved the contradictions between supporting the idea of empire and supporting the Boers. But by providing a forum for debate and self-education, the radical press laid the foundation for the subsequent development of a more successful anti-imperialist movement after the South African War.

Tom Jeffery and Keith McClelland provide another example of the way in which the press can articulate and also shape the views of a section of society by making sense of what is happening in the world. They argue that the *Daily Mail* both gave expression to and helped to mobilize a conservative stratum within the middle class during the 1920s. It championed what it called 'the new poor' within the middle class, initiated political campaigns against government spending and organized labour, and provided a coherent and persuasive definition of reality that encouraged the regrouping of political forces around a platform of anti-socialist, national unity. But during the 1930s, the paper moved further to the right and its view of the world began to diverge from the social experience and political perspectives of increasingly affluent, middle-income homes. As a consequence, the paper became, according to Jeffery and McClelland, merely a minority voice of the middle class.

Nicholas Pronay provides an interesting insight into how governments have used the media to engineer a change in public opinion. Senior ministers, he argues, were deterred by fear of public reaction from accelerating the rearmament programme as much as they would have liked to have done after 1933. The breakdown of the élite consensus over foreign policy, and the increasing autonomy of the press and BBC, made it difficult to engineer a change of public attitudes. In the end, ministers came to rely mainly on newsreel companies to mobilize the British people in support of rearmament, principally by reinvoking the themes of anti-Hun, First World War propaganda.

George Boyce analyses the attempts of press barons to make politicians toe their editorial line. As Northcliffe's henchman put it, 'ministers should do the bidding of a Press which claims to be the voice of the people'. But Boyce argues that proprietors patrolled the corridors of power without ever determining political decision-making because most politicians viewed them with distrust as outsiders. Press magnates helped to set agendas, shape public preferences, influence public policy. But the power they sought eluded them because they were never able to supplant political parties as the central levers of political authority.

In the concluding essay of this section, James Curran also contends that the press has exercised only limited influence. Indeed, he argues that the popular press attack on the Greater London Council (GLC), though initially successful, ultimately backfired and helped the GLC to rally public support behind it. The GLC's counter-offensive was also aided by the more positive coverage it received from broadcasting media, its skilful advertising and grassroots campaigns and a nationwide shift in political orientations.

1

Socialism and imperialism: the ILP press and the Boer War

Deian Hopkin

The South African War, fought over three exhausting years between the armies of Britain and the burgher commandos of the two Boer republics of Transvaal and the Orange Free State, was a cathartic experience for Britain.[1] British military power was revealed to be terribly vulnerable and its governing élite to be disunited over both the declaration and the conduct of the war. It was an emotional war; a great deal of xenophobic patriotism was displayed in the press and in the streets. Anyone who opposed the war came to be known as a pro-Boer, defined by Joseph Chamberlain, the member of the government most directly involved in the diplomatic exchanges which led to the war, as

> one who thinks the Boers have been right from beginning to end and who thinks the British government and, of course, the country have been wrong, and who believes every scandalous libel against the honour of British soldiers and British officers, who repudiates with scorn every accusation against Boer generals or Boer statesmen.[2]

The press played a central role in the preparations for war and in marshalling the case both for and against the war. Recently, one historian has persuasively argued that Lord Milner, the British government's chief negotiator in South Africa after 1897, made calculated use of the press in his attempts to outmanoeuvre the leaders of the Boer republics, even to the extent of arranging for the appointment of his supporters as editors of key South African newspapers in order to influence the course of events.[3] Contemporaries were quick to point to the connection between Cecil Rhodes, whose ambitions for British hegemony in South Africa were seen by many as largely responsible for the poor relations between Britain and the Boer republics, and certain newspapers and journals both in Britain and overseas.[4] When the war eventually broke out, so ferociously was the debate joined that at least one eminent editor, H. W. Massingham, was dismissed from his post simply for opposing the government.[5] Denied access to many newspapers, the opponents of the war organized elaborate propaganda campaigns through leaflets and pamphlets.[6] Eventually, a group of leading anti-war Liberals, under the leadership of David Lloyd George and financed by George

Cadbury, the Quaker chocolate manufacturer, purchased a majority holding in the *Daily News*, hitherto a leading pro-war newspaper. Ironically, the vendor of the shares was Henry Oppenheim, a member of one of the leading South African financial syndicates, on whose behalf many contemporaries felt the war had been fought.[7]

Among the most active opponents of the war was the Labour movement, still in its political infancy. The leading political wing of the movement at this time was the Independent Labour Party (ILP), whose leader, Keir Hardie, became one of the most determined critics of the war.[8] In the absence of support from the majority of Fleet Street, moreover, the tiny but active ILP press was one of the few voices persistently to oppose the war. What sort of opposition did it offer? What kind of arguments did it advance? And what impact did it have?

In 1899 the ILP had been in existence for six years. As yet it had no Members of Parliament, though the party's effective leader, Keir Hardie, was shortly to be returned as MP for Merthyr Tydfil. Despite the apparent failure at the 1895 general election and its relatively small size, it was an enthusiastic and energetic party, largely composed of young men and women and with an active membership scattered throughout Britain, often holding significant positions in local government and in the trade union movement. Some of this energy was reflected in the publication of newspapers and periodicals.[9] Apart from the ILP's official monthly, the *ILP News*, and its semi-official weekly, the *Labour Leader*, which was owned and edited by the party's chairman, Keir Hardie, local branches themselves published a number of weeklies and monthlies. Although it is difficult to be precise about these local publications, largely because copies of many of them have not survived or are incomplete, there were sixteen published at one time or another in 1899, several of which had been running for several years. The distribution was uneven, as was the distribution of the ILP itself; most of the papers were published in the north of England, in a band extending from Liverpool to Newcastle. Several papers came to an end in 1899, possibly before the war had even started, and two of the best-known, the *Bradford Labour Echo* and the *Rochdale Labour News*, were discontinued within six months of the start of the war. Eight new papers were begun during the next two years, in areas where there had been no ILP paper previously, such as Finsbury, Chelsea, Cardiff and Swansea, but none lasted longer than a year or two. Only two local ILP papers, the *Pendlebury Pioneer* and the *Blackburn Labour Journal*, were published throughout the period 1899 to 1902 and the former was discontinued between 1901 and 1903. The national ILP papers, however, continued publication throughout these years. One other paper, the *Clarion*, was not so much an ILP paper as a weekly paper read by many members of the ILP. The *Clarion* was launched well before the ILP came into existence, and was the voice and property of the remarkable Robert Blatchford, a supreme journalist and quixotic politician, who ploughed his own unique furrow in the Labour movement.

The importance of the ILP is that it became, within a very short time, one of the key elements in the Labour Party, formed as an alliance of socialists and trade unionists in 1900 at the height of Boer War agitation. While the trade unions provided much of the organizational and financial impetus for the new party, the ILP provided both its effective leadership and much of its inspiration. Certainly the policies which were eventually to form part of the Labour Party's fighting programme from 1906 onwards arose from the debates within the ILP itself. At the 1901 conference of the Labour Representation Committee (LRC), for example, the main motions opposing the South African War and the policies of imperialism which, it was argued, had led to the war, were proposed in the name of the ILP and agreed to unanimously.[10]

If the Jameson Raid came as a surprise to an unwary British public, the political debates of the ensuing three years, the accusations and counter-accusations over the role of Chamberlain in the conspiracy and the mounting tensions in the relations between the Kruger government and Britain's representative in South Africa, Lord Milner, helped to alert the British press to the possibility of war and to prepare the public for its outbreak. Few wars in recent history have been so well signposted. Four months after the war began, at least one anti-war committee was reporting its first six months' work.[11] The political issues over which the war was ostensibly fought were rehearsed throughout the three years prior to its actual outbreak. Both sides were visibly girding their loins: Milner to resolve the apparently irreconcilable differences between the Colonial Office and the increasingly entrenched Kruger administration; J. A. Hobson and other Liberal intellectuals to resist 'Milnerism' and its underlying impetus.[12]

Long before the outbreak of war, the Labour press had been paying increasing attention to the political problems of South Africa. In part this had been stimulated by the Jameson Raid which, more than any other event, focused attention both on the prospect of war and on possible causes. In addition, a number of socialists had emigrated to South Africa in recent years, part of a tide of emigration which was stimulated both by depression in Britain and the expansion of the goldfields in the Rand. As a result, the ILP press, for example, obtained regular reports from correspondents in South Africa, giving details of life in the Transvaal and reactions to the unfolding political crisis. From 1898 onwards the *Labour Leader* published regular dispatches from its own Johannesburg correspondent, 'Kopjes', together with frequent letters from emigrants. The *Rochdale Labour News* published articles from a roving correspondent, Joe Dyson, in Cape Colony and Natal, and the *Bradford Labour Echo* published dispatches from Harry Smith. Early in 1899 an ILP branch was formed in Johannesburg and there were promises of regular reports.[13] Beyond the ranks of the party, the ILP press was keenly aware of the work of radical and Liberal critics of imperial policy both in Britain and in South Africa itself. As early as March 1896, Isabella Fyvie Mayo gave an account in the *Labour Leader* of the attempts of the

South African radicals, the Cronwright-Schreiners, to establish a Progressive Party in opposition to Cecil Rhodes, and Olive Schreiner's novel, *Trooper Peter Halkett*, a ferocious attack on British imperial policy, was reviewed as soon as it appeared in 1897.[14] The work of J. A. Hobson, shortly to become one of the best-known critics of the economic aspects of imperial policy, was commended in the *Keighley Labour Journal* at least a year before the war began, while the *Labour Leader* ran interviews with prominent political critics of imperialism, such as Thomas Bayley, the radical Liberal MP for Chesterfield.[15] It would be wrong to suggest, therefore, that the Labour press was tardy in its response to the South African War or that it failed to develop a view.[16] It is true, however, that in the early days the view was amorphous and often undeveloped. From late 1899 onwards, however, the socialist press rapidly developed a coherent critique of the causes of the war, albeit strongly influenced by the developing critique of the anti-war movement more generally.

In the early phase, before the final crisis of summer 1899, the main thrust of the criticism of Britain's South African policy had been directed at individual politicians and the ambitions of the traditional *bêtes noires* of the Labour movement, the aristocracy and the English establishment. For example the *Labour Leader* had expressed some distaste at Cecil Rhodes's 'land-stealing' activities well before the Jameson Raid.[17] But from 1896 onwards the volume and vehemence of the criticism mounted. The *ILP News* was convinced as early as May 1897 that 'the Government has made up its mind to fight the Boers'.[18] Comparisons were made between the leaders of both sides, usually in terms of villains and heroes. An editorial in the *Labour Leader* in January 1899 declared that Cecil Rhodes may have been acting 'from the purest motives', but that he was being used by 'impecunious aristocrats . . . and sordid speculators'.[19] The paper's South African correspondent concluded that Rhodes owed his position 'to his wonderful insight into the human heart, and an almost magnetic sympathy', though he was in no doubt that Rhodes's greatest fault was his ambition.[20] In this respect, Rhodes was less villainous than Chamberlain who was usually seen to be consumed by personal ambition and prompted, moreover, by his family's commercial and industrial interests.[21] Occasionally, however, even Chamberlain was presented as the unwitting creature of 'the English Elysée' and the inevitable aristocratic cabal, including members of the royal family.[22] When the war finally came, the mask of indulgence was dropped and the language deteriorated accordingly. Overnight, Cecil Rhodes became 'a confirmed drunkard – a dipsomaniac' with a special refrigeration plant in Kimberley to keep his 'copiously flowing' champagne cool.[23] Chamberlain's stock descended even lower, and he was finally proclaimed a drug addict.[24] Milner got off rather more lightly, dismissed as an 'insolent puppy', though on one occasion he was being compared unfavourably with a 'savage chief'.[25] Their associates were given kinder treatment in order to intensify the guilt of Chamberlain, Milner and Rhodes. As late as January 1900, the *Labour Leader* absolved the Cabinet of blame, insisting that Salisbury, Hicks

Beech and Devonshire were totally ignorant of 'bagman' Chamberlain's machinations.[26]

By contrast with the opprobrium heaped on the English establishment and its leaders, there was a tendency throughout the ILP press to idealize the Boer. In this sense, the ILP press was genuinely pro-Boer. 'Most of the Outlanders', pronounced Arthur Zemo in the *Rochdale Labour News*, 'went to Boer-land with greedy hearts . . . to plunder.'[27] There they found, according to Kopjes in the *Labour Leader*, 'the country where the rights of labour are most respected and where the capitalist has the least power in proportion to his wealth'. Kopjes continued by outlining a vision of a socialist society in deepest Transvaal with the mouth-watering prospect of a nationalized transport system, free libraries, public telephones and municipal markets. In the Transvaal, he concluded, the black natives enjoyed a better life 'than the white slaves of urban England'.[28] Even the voteless workman of the Transvaal was, according to Marxian in the *Labour Leader*, 'better off than in some parts of manhood suffrage America'.[29] Moreover, as W. Hills wrote in an account of the operations of Joubert's Transvaal commando against the Makatese tribes of Magatoland, the British government should beware of underestimating the Boers; like Cromwell's Ironsides, their religious zeal gave them unexpected advantages over their opponents. Even if defeat was inevitable, the obstinate resistance of the burghers 'fighting for their hearths and homes and aided by a thorough knowledge of the country, would mean that England would have to wade [*sic*] its sovereignty over the Republic through seas of blood'.[30] Even as the war was breaking out in South Africa, the *Labour Leader* was publishing souvenir photographs of Kruger and Joubert.

Not every ILP paper or correspondent was so uncritical of the Boers or so convinced of the case against war. The most famous example of socialist support for the war was Robert Blatchford; an ex-soldier, Blatchford's patriotism was deep-rooted and endured throughout his life. In the months before the outbreak of war, however, other ILPers had their doubts. In particular, the *ILP News*, the official organ of the ILP, struck an independent note under the editorship of Russell Smart. When it first appeared in 1897 it shared the widespread radical condemnation of the 'cover-up' of the complicity of the Colonial Office in the Jameson Raid. In June 1898, however, it began to shift its ground. While condemning the 'jingo press' for its attempts to force public opinion to accept the necessity of a war in the Transvaal the paper added:

> We have little sympathy with the Boer who has perpetrated atrocities on the natives only rivalled by the English of the Chartered Company.[31]

In January 1899 the shooting by the Johannesburg police of a British citizen who had killed a man in a brawl, an incident which sparked off a wave of protest among the Uitlanders and led directly to their petition to the British government demanding enfranchisement and wider civil rights, prompted a vigorous response from the *ILP News*.

The latest action of the Transvaal police in shooting an apparently harmless citizen almost necessitates British intervention. There is little doubt the clemency exercised by the Gladstone government after our defeat at Majuba Hill – one of the noblest episodes in our foreign policy – has been ill appreciated. They have construed our forebearance based on the consciousness of overwhelming strength as fear of Boer prowess.[32]

When the war finally erupted at the end of October, Smart expressed his wish that the Boers might be quickly defeated so that there would be peace.[33] By the end of the year he was back in the mainstream of ILP attitudes to the war and even took a lead in condemning the opinions of Fred Brocklehurst, a fellow member of the ILP's National Administrative Council, who maintained his advocacy of a quick victory.[34] By January 1900, Smart had been replaced as editor by Bruce Glasier, shortly to become the chairman of the ILP, who took a more conventional line.

The local ILP press was more equivocal. The majority of long-standing local papers, notably the *Bradford Labour Echo*, the *Rochdale Labour News*, the *Keighley Labour Journal* and the *Blackburn Labour Journal*, was staunchly behind its national leaders in condemning the war. The Bradford and Rochdale papers ceased publication within six months of the advent of the war, but the Blackburn paper continued to attack government policy and to publicize anti-war activities. Other papers were less enthusiastic. The *Pendlebury Pioneer*, while giving some coverage to the anti-war case, also reprinted A. M. Thompson's editorial in the *Clarion*, which urged a British victory in the interest of peace.[35] Some ILP newspapers were reluctant to discuss the war at all, perhaps reflecting the depths of division in their own ranks or the extent of patriotism in their own localities. *Finsbury*, for example, was launched when interest in the war had reached a peak in the weeks after the relief of Mafeking, but the editor adamantly refused to discuss the war. He pointed to the greater level of casualties in the railway industry and drew attention to the fact that while the British press was obsessed with events in South Africa, a famine had been raging in India and the British public had been singularly parsimonious in response to an appeal for relief funds for what was after all a major part of the very British empire which they sought to uphold in Africa.[36] Throughout 1900 neither the *Liverpool Labour Chronicle*, the *Manchester Social Reformer* nor the *Chelsea Pick and Shovel*, all significant local ILP papers, made any mention of the war, while a correspondent to the *Woolwich and District Labour Notes* was driven to ask why the paper was ignoring events in South Africa.[37] Other papers which expressed strong views in the early part of the war seemed to lose interest, notably the *ILP News*, which hardly made any mention of the war throughout 1901 and the early part of 1902, at a time when the Liberal press, and the *Labour Leader* with it, was conducting a vigorous campaign against the use of dum-dum bullets, the policy of farm burning and the maintenance of concentration camps.

Running parallel with the simple explanations, based on juxtaposing individuals and personal factors, was a more profound analysis both of the cause and character of the war. Long before the war some sections of the ILP press had been paying attention to a new critique of imperialism, which shifted the focus of the explanation from politics to economics. The ILP and its press developed at a time when the empire played a less conspicuous part in British domestic politics than it had done in the decade immediately preceding. During the period up to 1896 no incident had an impact on British politics comparable with Gordon's death in the Sudan or the Majuba Hill débâcle.[38] In his three years in Parliament between 1892 and 1895, for example, Keir Hardie did not ask a single question on the empire or even on foreign affairs, although this was characteristic of the lack of interest shown in such matters by Lib-Lab MPs.[39] The Jameson Raid changed all that. At first, as we have seen, the explanation centred on personalities and politics, but gradually the emphasis changed. In July 1897 the *Labour Leader* published its first serious examination of the principles underlying imperial expansion. The article drew attention to an editorial in the *Daily Chronicle* published on the occasion of Queen Victoria's Diamond Jubilee, which had proclaimed the mission of the British race amongst the people of the world. This, the *Labour Leader* article claimed, was nothing more than a screen for commercial enterprise.

> Every socialist will see through all this rhetoric and fine writing about honour and glory and law and justice. He knows that it simply means NEW MARKETS and nothing more; that the whole bombastic business is just a glorification of commercialism . . . . These pioneers, of whose heroism we have heard so much, we know for the advance agents of a shoddy commercialism, opening a way with their bayonets and paving it with dead bodies, for the shoddy goods of British capitalism to follow. Trade follows the flag, and trade is production for profit.[40]

In all probability the article, signed FH, was written by the radical propagandist Frederic Harrison, who produced a large number of pamphlets on the same subject during the Boer War.[41] The argument was familiar enough. The claim that British colonial activity was accompanied by increased trade and commercial activity was widely accepted in the late nineteenth century and had been given currency among British socialists by William Morris.[42] Its echoes could be heard well into the Boer War itself, but by that time another interpretation had begun to emerge in radical circles. A young liberal economist, J. A. Hobson, who had been advocating protection and imperialism as a way of countering underconsumption and declining living standards at home, came to the conclusion that imperialism was in fact a direct product of underconsumption in so far as the inability of the British working class to buy the surplus product of industry forced capitalists to find customers abroad.[43] Far from being an instrument for protecting the domestic market, tariffs and protectionism were part of the armoury of an imperialist capitalism which sought above all to protect the financiers and their investment. Hobson argued that the newly acquired markets were unprofitable, but that the efforts to establish them led inevitably to militarism and international conflict. In this respect, and in his subsequent claim that free trade did not diminish the national income even while other countries continued to pursue protectionism, Hobson was following the well-established tradition of Cobdenism.[44] Where he differed was in arguing that trade did not necessarily lead to continued prosperity. Hobson also identified groups of financiers who, he claimed, were largely responsible for encouraging the imperialist policies of the British government, notably in South Africa.[45]

Hobson's arguments appealed to socialists for two reasons. His early articles suggested a general explanation which argued that it was the maldistribution of domestic incomes, and the absence of adequate social reform, which was the tap-root of imperialism.[46] Secondly, Hobson soon discovered evidence of particular financial and capitalist activity which fitted well with the socialist propensity towards a 'conspiracy theory'; after all, socialists engaged in public political activity required the enemy to have a name and address. In late 1900 Hobson was sent by the *Manchester Guardian* to South Africa to report on the war and from there wrote a clutch of articles which attributed the pre-war crisis in the Transvaal to the ambitions and speculative activity of international finance houses, such as Beit, Wehrner & Co., and their interest in overthrowing the Kruger administration in order to break the Dutch and German monopolies in dynamite and railways, which tended to keep the costs of the mining industry high.[47]

Hobson gave sharp definition to a thesis which had been current in socialist circles for some time beforehand. In the early 1890s an American property developer and socialist journalist, Gaylord Wilshire, who spent some four years in Britain largely in the company of Fabians and Social Democrats, began to argue that international tension was directly related to the development of monopoly capital, and in particular the financial trusts.[48] There is evidence that Wilshire's ideas profoundly influenced the work of J. A. Hobson after 1900, and although it is difficult to show an equally direct influence on the development of socialist ideas, it is likely that Wilshire's years in London and the north of England may have sown some seeds. Certainly, the Social Democratic press had begun to discuss the role of international capitalism in the development of overseas policy some time before Hobson's original article published in the *Contemporary Review* in 1898. As early as 1896 socialist writers had begun to attribute colonial activity to finance capitalism.[49] They had evidence for so doing. The small-scale panning activities of gold prospectors in the Transvaal goldfields had been transformed by the mid-1890s to large-scale, capital-intensive, deep-level mining, the first of which, the Geldenhuis Deep, began crushing operations late in 1895. It was this which brought Beit, Wehrner & Co. and their associates, Eckstein & Co., and several similar groups, into prominence in the South African economy.[50]

The ILP press seized avidly on J. A. Hobson's work, though the editors used it selectively.[51] His articles were reprinted, usually without comment, and it is doubtful whether anyone in the ILP press fully understood his arguments, especially the central thesis of *Imperialism* which was published in 1902. His claim, made in 1898, that the empire was actually unprofitable was given little emphasis in ILP papers. Instead his identification of the economic motive for imperialism, represented by ILP journalists either as the crude lust of individual financiers or as the product of capitalism *per se*, provided them with a sufficient condemnation of imperialism in itself. Indeed, despite Hobson's detailed claim that colonies were unprofitable, leading journalists in the ILP press continued to speculate on the amount derived from imperialism. In one of the most elaborate articles on the subject, published in the *Labour Leader* in December 1899, S. G. Hobson rhapsodized on the money England made from the empire.[52] Much of his argument was confused, a number of terms were used indiscriminately – 'unregulated markets', 'wealth' and 'capital', for example – and there was a number of serious statistical fallacies in the article. Yet in a very tenuous way, S. G. Hobson was anticipating his namesake, J. A. Hobson, and his economic model of imperialism, when he declared that exploitation of foreign markets was due to the 'overcapitalisation of home industries'. More importantly, S. G. Hobson stressed a crucial distinction between 'the natural expansion of a race such as ours with its special intellectual and physical characteristics' and what he termed 'Military Imperialism' by which Britain was 'taxed with a giant army and a leviathan navy not from any high-flown sentiment of a national vision but as an insurance policy upon our world trade'. Like many of J. A. Hobson's own arguments in this period, S. G. Hobson's article owed much to established liberal thinking in its opposition to military spending, but unlike Cobden, the two Hobsons saw the expansion of trade as the danger.

One aspect of J. A. Hobson's arguments struck a chord in the ILP press. Some historians have detected a strong streak of anti-Semitism in his dispatches from South Africa when he ferociously attacked the influence of Jewish financiers in the Rand.[53] It had been long understood that most of the capital for the developing gold industry had been raised on the European money markets by well-connected Jewish families. Without descending to the generalized hostility towards Jews characteristic of the work of Arnold White and Joseph Bannister, some socialist papers had indulged in what could only be called mild anti-Semitism. In August 1896, for example, *Justice* had attributed the deteriorating political situation in South Africa to the influence of Jewish capitalists and the Jewish-owned press. The editorial stressed that

> though we admire many Jews . . . there is nevertheless a great deal to be urged against them . . . . They are exceedingly purse proud when wealthy, very arrogant, very unscrupulous and very clannish.[54]

When the paper suggested in September 1899 that the Transvaal was only being seized 'in the interests of Messrs Rhodes, Beit, Rothschild, Eckstein, Oppenheimer, Israel, Solomons and Company', there was an immediate and angry response from a large number of readers, after which the paper moderated its tone.[55] By this time the cry had been taken up by some sections of the ILP press, in particular the *ILP News*. In its editorials in the closing months of 1899 the Rand Jew was planted firmly in the corridors of influence in Britain:

> It is worth noting . . . that the most prominent of the Jingo organs are owned and financed largely by stalwart patriots whose names have curiously foreign terminations and whose features seem to indicate that they are of the circumcision. In whatever walk of life the Jew adopts he generally becomes pre-eminent and the stock-exchange Jew is no exception. He is the incarnation of the money idea and it is no exaggeration to say that the Jew financier controls the policy of Europe.[56]

By 1900, J. A. Hobson had given flesh and blood to these generalized accusations in his book *The South African War*. Some of his articles on the subject in the *Speaker* were reprinted in the *Labour Leader* and his accusations were often repeated elsewhere in the ILP press.[57]

Many ILP journalists, among them S. G. Hobson, were equivocal in their treatment of imperialism. Even where they were resolute in their opposition to current imperial policy, they did not challenge the idea of empire. Even Keir Hardie, for example, believed that the empire could be justified on a number of grounds and that Britain had a responsibility to civilize the world in order to restrain the uncontrolled power of exploitive capitalism which, significantly, was blamed as much on foreigners as capitalists. To this extent the disturbing streak of anti-Semitism in much of the criticism of Rand finance houses was as much anti-alien as anti-Jewish. For many ILPers, Hardie among them, feared for the existence of the empire itself. In January 1900, Hardie wrote:

> Russia wants us out of India, France [wants us] out of Egypt and Germany [wants us] out of Africa. With the entire British army locked up, and our last gun with it, it only needs these three powers to agree and the Empire goes to pieces like a pack of cards. By ending the war this at once becomes impossible, the Empire would be saved and national honour redeemed.[58]

A week earlier the *Keighley Labour Journal* had despaired at the declining prestige of Britain and openly expressed its fears for the continued existence of the empire.[59] Even if these are construed as alarmist arguments addressed to an audience known to be apprehensive at the military failures of the British army over the previous weeks, the idea of Britain's moral responsibilities to the rest of the world, embodied in the empire, was widely understood and accepted in ILP circles. In a series of articles in the *Ethical World* in 1898 Ramsay MacDonald had outlined a case for a paternalistic educational programme in the tropical countries, designed to rationalize the practices and customs of 'people of low civilisation' and to assist their development.[60] S. G. Hobson's ideas of trusteeship were simpler and more direct; he demurred at the new imperialism because it stood in the way of 'the humanitarian administration of subject races'. Keir Hardie even postulated the idea of a federation of English-speaking peoples which would 'police the whole world'.[61] That such ideas, and indeed the underlying assumption about the virtue of Empire, were left unchallenged is some evidence of their acceptance within the ILP. The ILP press was usually quick enough to seize on dissenters within its ranks. Moreover, many leaders of the party, Hardie and Philip Snowden among them, remained members of the Fabian Society even after it was clear that the majority of the society was imperialistic in the broadest sense. Significantly when S. G. Hobson had moved a motion at the society's meeting in December 1899 condemning the war, an important proviso had been attached to his motion supporting the expansion of empire 'only in so far as it may be compatible with the expansion of that higher social organisation which this Society was founded to promote'.[62] In this sense there was little difference between those ILP members of the Fabian Society who opposed the Boer War and those who subscribed to the views of the Fabian pamphlet, *Fabianism and Empire*, which was the society's official endorsement of contemporary colonialism. The debate was over practice not principle. The indictment was of imperialists not empire. In particular, J. A. Hobson's writings appealed to the ILP because he named names and moreover provided a vivid torch by whose light opponents of the war, desperate to avoid the charge of unpatriotic activity, might illuminate the crepuscular corners of politics to reveal the real traitors, those who 'destroy the Empire to put dividends in their own pockets'.[63] Keir Hardie published, with great relish, rumours of royal involvement in South African financial circles, and dwelt at considerable length on allegations that Joseph Chamberlain's family firm stood to make enormous profits from naval and military contracts.[64] Such exposés in the *Labour Leader* were constantly juxtaposed with revised casualty rates to show how high a price the British working class was paying for the capitalists' war.[65] At the same time Hardie was often prepared to indemnify 'authentic' imperialists; when Mafeking was relieved Hardie praised Baden-Powell's courage and resourcefulness.[66]

This ambivalence goes deeper. Trade union and socialist leaders in the late nineteenth century tended to apply the 'capitalist' explanation of imperial expansion only when it affected white subjects in Britain's colonies. The oppression of the Boers, and even the exploitation of the Uitlander working class, could be equated with the oppression of trade unionists in Britain itself. Later on, for example, the introduction of indentured Chinese labour into South Africa was seen more as a threat to the livelihood of white miners than as a moral issue in its own right.[67] Besides, where capitalism was less obvious, as in much of the rest of tropical Africa, socialists saw less to criticize. The ILP press, in particular, was reluctant to apply to tropical Africa the right to self-government it so readily offered the Boers. Kopjes even went so far as to explain why 'natural law', which determined the degree and quality of cultural and ethnic differences between races, insisted on separate treatment of white and black, adding that the natives were reasonably well treated in the bargain.[68] Self-interest was never far below the surface. Referring, at the height of the Boer War, to the famine in India the *Keighley Labour Journal* crudely stated that

by good government India might be made one of the richest countries in the world and one of the greatest markets for British goods. It is a foolish policy to kill the goose that might go on laying golden eggs.[69]

If socialists were not altogether surprised by the behaviour of capitalists and politicians, they were disappointed by the behaviour of the working class. The most disturbing feature of the South African War for the ILP and its press was the public response to it.[70] If the men clamouring for war were capitalists, they were readily supported by 'the section of the working class who take their opinions ready made from the sporting press'.[71] Some ILP papers had had few illusions to begin with. During the wave of public protests over the Jameson Raid, the *Keighley Labour Journal* had declared knowingly:

> The attack of jingoism from which we have been suffering is a pregnant illustration of the temper and ignorance of the British working man. Something was said in this journal a week or two ago that the most sickening phase of the industrial question is to see the masses kiss and hug their chains. And this so-called patriotism exhibited by the masses during these war scares is another illustration of this sad fact.[72]

In March 1899, moreover, the *Woolwich and District Labour Notes* railed against the workers who got 'rampant about an Empire that will not afford him the common rights of man'.[73] Nevertheless when war began the situation became much worse. The *Keighley Labour Journal* spoke of 'war fever' in the district.[74] The editor of the *Bradford Labour Echo* blamed the 'hatred, envy and malice' displayed by the average Briton as the product of 'declamatory music hall singers', or as Keir Hardie put it 'the brainless inanities of the music hall'.[75] As the war continued and violence against opponents of the war increased, especially after the British military recovery of early 1900, so the ILP press became more bitter and disillusioned. In March 1900, Keir Hardie readily admitted in the *Labour Leader* that

> the war is the most popular war ever waged by England. Mobs of working men nightly invade and smash up public meetings held in the interests of peace and assault the speakers with sticks and stones.[76]

That month the offices of the *Labour Leader* in Glasgow were attacked by a mob who ransacked the building.[77] A large number of ILP meetings were broken up in other parts of the country; at a Bradford ILP meeting a dead cat thrown at the chairman was the cue for a riot which it took 120 police to control.[78] Keir Hardie himself was in personal danger on several occasions. The strain of ceaseless campaigning against the heavy tides of patriotism shows through in some of his editorials and his frustration at the behaviour of his countrymen emerges in stark metaphors: the 'mulish British workman', fanned into excitement by Kipling's 'brass-band poetry' and the 'atrocity-mongering' of the 'drunken jailbirds' of Fleet Street in defence of an empire 'built on a foundation of oppression and cemented by greed'. In contrast, the idealization of the Boers reached new, even ridiculous, heights; they were 'Nature's gentlemen – courageous, humane and chivalrous', who had come to occupy a 'higher type of civilisation than any to which Europe has yet attained' and whose leaders would take their place in the history of freedom movements alongside William Tell, Owain Glyndwr and William Wallace. While Britain, ruled by a 'putrid mass of corruption at Westminster', had introduced 'gin and scrofula in every quarter of the globe', the Boers, consumed with religious ardour, had lived 'good and true lives'. Even in war, the Boers remained compassionate despite all the horror and suffering which they faced; even their Mauser bullet was 'the most humane bullet ever used in actual warfare'.[79]

Hardie's contempt for the 'jingoistic' British working class is characteristic of his deep-rooted fear that the working class generally was prone to be led astray by unscrupulous men. In his view, for example, the Uitlander working class had been misled to the point where it expressed grievances it did not feel and sought a franchise it did not want.[80] In 1900, possibly because of some personal strain after the illness of his daughter and the deaths of both his parents within an hour of each other, Hardie's pessimism reached new depths. In 1902, with the celebrations for the ending of the war in full swing, Hardie gave vent to his frustration with ill-concealed anger.

There is nothing under the sun so depressing as a London mob in holiday mood. It has not one redeeming feature. Stunted in physique, haggard in look, dressed without taste in flaming shoddy, it rolls along. Its apparent light-heartedness is the outcome of mere vacuity. Here he is celebrating a great victory, and not one in fifty of those who roll along blowing hideous noises from paper trumpets has bone or muscle enough to fit entrance to the army. As for brain power, I prefer not to attempt to describe it . . . . And these are the making of the men and women who are to be the fathers and mothers of the next generation of Londoners. Be merciful, O God.[81]

The South African War presented the emerging socialist movement in Britain with its first great political challenge. There had been occasions in the past, notably during the Trafalgar Square riots of 1886 and the great dock strike of 1889, when the socialists were clearly at odds with the establishment. What was different about the Boer War was that, for a time at least, it appeared as though the leaders of the socialist movement were at odds with their own supporters. It is difficult in this period to use electoral behaviour as a barometer since, as recent work has shown, so many members of that class to which the Labour Party appealed were in any case disenfranchised.[82] A study of jingo crowds and of recruitment, however, has revealed that the working class was as likely to be against the war as for it, but that there was a serious absence of political leadership.[83] It is difficult, however, to estimate the impact of the Labour press. For one thing it was a fragile press, with a small readership; the circulation of the most widely read paper can be counted in a few thousands. It is difficult to know, therefore, what impact the campaigns of the *Labour Leader* against concentration camps or farm burning had on a wider public after the first-hand reports of Emily Hobhouse and others began to appear after mid-1901.[84] Recognizing that the pro-Boers were generally unpopular, there is nevertheless no evidence to suggest that it was their stand against the war that caused so many local ILP papers to cease publication in these years. The Social Democratic Federation, for example, maintained a vigorous campaign against the war, stressing even more strongly the capitalist dimension, but its press remained more or less intact throughout the war, albeit on an even smaller scale than the ILP. The four local papers which were being published in 1899, for example, were all going strong in 1902 when the war ended.

The greatest impact the ILP press had was within the ILP itself. It may be argued that political newspapers – that is, newspapers published by and on behalf of political parties – perform three functions: to broadcast the party's programme and proselytize the public, to perform a number of organizational functions such as acting as a notice-board for party activities and as a channel between different sections of the party, and to provide a platform for the local and national leaders of the party.[85] The ILP press performed all these functions during the war, especially the *Labour Leader*, which acted as a focus for all the party's activities. But in addition the ILP press altered the perception of the party itself. By rehearsing the arguments, by giving space to a wide spectrum of anti-war opinion, and by locating a coherent critique of the war, the press helped to raise the awareness in the ILP of the long-term problems of the empire and its relation to the domestic condition of Britain. If there was little discussion of imperial matters before the South African crisis, the topic became significantly more important thereafter. After 1906, in particular, the interest of leaders of the ILP, and of its press, turned to other parts of the empire. Keir Hardie, who had already displayed some interest in Indian affairs, paid his first visit to the subcontinent in 1907 and thereafter published his own plans for reform.[86] It was in this period that Ramsay MacDonald began to develop more fully his ideas on international moral responsibility towards subject peoples.[87] The growing interest of Labour MPs in the subject is reflected in a dramatic change in the number and content of speeches made in the House of Commons, even allowing for the great increase in the actual number of Labour MPs after 1906. Between 1906 and 1914 the Labour Party in Parliament developed something approaching a colonial policy and the ILP played a central part in this. It was a slow, gradual process. The South African War exposed the ambivalence of the ILP towards Britain's foreign relations and revealed how insecure its policies were once they were addressed to problems outside domestic issues. This uncertainty emerges clearly in the press. It was Keir Hardie himself who expressed most clearly the underlying fear that the real issue at stake was not empire itself but 'the stability of British political life'. As the British army was being routed in Magersfontein, Stromberg and Tugela in December, with Mafeking, Kimberley and Ladysmith threatened, and as Durban and the soft underbelly of Cape Colony became exposed to attack, Hardie uttered a veritable *cri de coeur*:

On what rotten foundation must this great Empire of ours be built that it can be thus shaken by a handful of untrained farmers.[88]

Notes

I am very grateful to Dr John Davidson for his comments and advice on an earlier draft of this paper.

1 A valuable recent account of the war which examines a variety of different aspects, economic, social, political, as well as military, is P. Warwick (ed.), *The South African War*, London, 1980. The most comprehensive recent survey of the war itself is Thomas Pakenham, *The Boer War*, London, 1979.

2 *Hansard*, vol. 89, HC Deb., 4s., 18 February 1901, cols 425–6. See J. Dillon's passionate reply, *Hansard*, vol. 89, HC Deb., 4s, 26 February 1901, cols 1234 ff.

3 A. N. Porter, 'Sir Alfred Milner and the press, 1897–99', *Historical Journal* (*HJ*), XVI, 2 (1973), 323–39. The argument is developed at greater length in the same author's *The Origins of the South African War: Joseph Chamberlain and the Diplomacy of Imperialism*, Manchester, 1980.

4 J. A. Hobson, *How the Press was Worked before the War*, South African Conciliation Committee Pamphlets, no. 14, London, 1899.

5 A. F. Havinghurst, *Radical Journalist: H. W. Massingham*, London, 1974.

6 Over 2000 pamphlets were produced during the war, largely by anti-war groups: J. S. Galbraith, 'The pamphlet campaign on the Boer War', *Journal of Modern History*, XXIV, 2 (1952), 111–26.

7 Peter Rowland, *Lloyd George*, London, 1975, p. 150.

8 The most recent biography of Keir Hardie is Kenneth O. Morgan, *Keir Hardie: Radical and Socialist*, London, 1975. See especially chapter VI.

9 See Deian Hopkin, 'The newspapers of the ILP, 1893–1906', unpublished Ph.D. thesis, University of Wales, 1981. Virtually all extant copies of ILP national and local papers can be consulted in the microfilm collection at the Hugh Owen Library, University College of Wales, Aberystwyth.

10 *Report of the First Annual Conference of the Labour Representation Committee*, London, Hammersmith Reprints, 1967, p. 20.

11 Report of six months' work of the Transvaal Committee, 1 February 1900, quoted in Stephen Koss (ed.), *The Pro-Boers*, Chicago, 1973, p. 4.

12 See Eric Stokes, 'Milnerism', *HJ*, V, 1 (1962), 47–60. G. H. Le May even called it 'Sir Alfred Milner's War': *British Supremacy in South Africa, 1899–1907*, Oxford, 1965. This idea is challenged, however, in Shula Marks and Stanley Trapido, 'Lord Milner and the South African state', *History Workshop Journal*, 8 (1979), 50–80, which examines the central role of the mining companies in the political crisis. See also Shula Marks's review article, 'Scrambling for Africa', *Journal of African History* (*JAH*), 23 (1980), 97–113.

13 *Labour Leader* (*LL*), 8 July 1899, 212.

14 *LL*, 14 March 1896, 93; 27 February 1897, 66.

15 *Keighley Labour Journal* (*KLJ*), 1 October 1898; *LL*, 12 June 1897, 197.

16 This is the clear implication of Koss, op. cit. See also A. Davey, *The British Pro-Boers 1877–1902*, Cape Town, 1978. Richard Price is dismissive of the Labour view which, he argues, was generally shallow and inadequate: *An Imperial War and the British Working Class: Working-Class Attitudes Reactions to the Boer War*,

1899–1902, London, 1972, pp. 71, 237. Henry Pelling describes Keir Hardie's views in particular as 'so extreme as to be slightly absurd': *Origins of the Labour Party, 1880–1900*, 2nd edn, Oxford, 1965, p. 189. Bernard Porter, on the other hand, reveals the considerable depth of the Labour view on empire in *Critics of Empire: British Radical Attitudes to Colonialism in Africa, 1895–1914*, 1968, pp. 127 ff; hereafter cited as *Critics of Empire*. See also his chapter, 'The pro-Boers in Britain', in Warwick (ed.), op. cit., pp. 239–57. A detailed local study of imperial attitudes is M. D. Blanch, 'Nation, Empire and the Birmingham working class 1899–1914', unpublished Ph.D. thesis, University of Birmingham, 1975.

17 *LL*, 25 August 1894, 8.

18 *ILP News (ILPN)*, May 1897, 1.

19 LL, 7 January 1899, 6. See also *Rochdale Labour News (RLN)*, January 1899, 3.

20 *LL*, 30 April 1898, 147.

21 For example: *LL*, 18 November 1899, 365; 29 September 1900, 310; 6 October 1900, 315; 13 October 1900, 323; 17 November 1900, 365; 24 November 1900, 371; 1 December 1900, 381.

22 *LL*, 31 March 1900, 100.

23 *LL*, 4 November 1899, 347.

24 *LL*, 10 August 1901, 254.

25 *LL*, 23 September 1899, 301.

26 *LL*, 20 January 1900, 20.

27 *RLN*, December 1899, 3.

28 *LL*, 23 April 1898, 130; 20 August 1898, 278.

29 *LL*, 5 August 1899.

30 *LL*, 22 April 1898, 127.

31 *ILPN*, June 1898, 1. For a similar view, see Joe Dyson's article in *Bradford Labour Echo (BLE)*, 30 September 1899, 3.

32 *ILPN*, January 1899, 2.

33 *ILPN*, November 1899.

34 *ILPN*, February 1900, 5; April 1900, 5; May 1900, 4–5; June 1900, 3. See also *LL*, 10 March 1900, 77; 24 March 1900, 91.

35 *Pendlebury Pioneer (PP)*, December 1899, 5.

36 *Finsbury*, May 1900.

37 *Woolwich and District Labour Notes*, December 1899, 2.

38 See, for example, R. J. Hind, *Henry Labouchere and the Empire, 1880–1905*, London, 1972, pp. 169–79.

39 For a discussion of the voting record and public statements of Labour MPs, see L. B. Simpson-Holley, 'The attitude of Labour Members of Parliament towards the empire, 1895–1914; unpublished Ph.D. thesis, University of Southampton, 1971.

40 *LL*, 17 July 1897, 234.

41 See, for example, Frederic Harrison, *The Boer Republics*, South African Conciliation Committee Pamphlets, no. 21, London, 1900.

42 Gladstone, in 1878, maintained that 'Empire is greatness; leagues of land are empires . . . trade follows the flag': *Nineteenth Century*, IV September 1878, 393. Chamberlain claimed that finding new markets was a major activity of both Foreign and Colonial Offices: speech to Birmingham Chamber of Commerce, November 1896, quoted in Porter, *Critics of Empire*, p. 47.

43 The political dimension of Hobson's ideas is discussed in J. Allett, *New Liberalism: The Political Economy of J. A. Hobson*, Toronto, 1982. See also

Porter, *Critics of Empire*, pp. 168 ff. For Hobson's own evaluation see his autobiography, *Confessions of an Economic Heretic*, London, 1938.

44 The place of Hobson in the liberal tradition is considered in P. J. Cain, 'J. A. Hobson, Cobdenism and the radical theory of economic liberalism, 1898–1914', *Economic History Review (Econ. H.R.)*, 31 (1978), 565–84; and J. A. Hobson, 'Finance capitalism and imperialism in late Victorian and Edwardian England', *Journal of Imperial and Commonwealth History*, 23, iii (1985). See the comment by P. F. Clarke and the rejoinder by P. J. Cain in *Econ. H.R.*, 34 (1981), 308–16. Excellent evaluations of Hobson in relation to later critics of imperialism, such as Hilferding and Lenin, have been written by Norman Etherington: 'Reconsidering theories of imperialism', *History and Theory*, XXI, 1 (1982), 1–36; 'Theories of imperialism in Southern Africa revisited', *African Affairs*, 81 (1982); and *Theories of Imperialism, War, Conquest and Capital*, London, 1984.

45 J. A. Hobson, *The War in South Africa: Its Causes and Effects*, London, 1900.

46 J. A. Hobson, 'The economic taproot of imperialism', *Contemporary Review*, August 1902, 219–32.

47 Recent research tends to reinforce the view that the gold-mining companies played a key role in the politics leading to the war. See, for example, A. Jeeves, 'The Rand capitalists and the coming of the South African War, 1896–99', *Canadian Historical Papers*, 1973, 61–83; D. Denoon, 'Capitalism and capitalists in the Transvaal in the 1880s and 1890s', *Historical Journal*, XXIII, 1 (1980), 111–32. See also the recent work by Van-Helten: 'Mining and imperialism', *Journal of Southern African Studies*, VI, 2 (1980), 230–5; 'Empire and high finance, South Africa and the international gold standard, 1890–1914', *JAH*, 23 (1982), 529–48. For Rhodes's part see C. Newbury, 'Out of the Pit; the capital accumulation of C. Rhodes', *Journal of Imperial and Commonwealth History*, 10 (1981).

48 For Wilshire's career see H. R. Quint, 'Wilshire's magazine', in J. R. Conlin (ed.), *The American Radical Press, 1880–1960*, Westport, 1974, vol. I, pp. 72–81. For his contribution to the theory of imperialism, see N. Etherington, *Theories of Imperialism*, chapter 2.

49 *KLJ*, 26 January 1896.

50 A brief general survey of the development of gold-mining in the Transvaal is given in P. Richardson and J. J. Van-Helten, 'The gold-mining industry in the Transvaal, 1886–1899', in Warwick (ed.), op. cit., pp. 18–36.

51 His 'Capitalism and imperialism in South Africa' (*Contemporary Review*, January 1900) was recommended in *LL*, 20 January 1900, 19, and *KLJ*, 13 January 1900, 3. See also *LL*, 15 December 1899, 397; 24 February 1900, 60; 3 March 1900, 67; and see *RLN*, April 1900.

52 *LL*, 14 December 1899, 396.

53 Harvey Mitchell, 'Hobson revisited', *Journal of the History of Ideas*, July 1965, 398–404. Colin Holmes, 'J. A. Hobson and the Jews' in Colin Holmes (ed.), *Immigrants and Minorities in British Society*, London, 1978, esp. pp. 137–41.

54 *Justice*, 26 August 1899.

55 *Justice*, 9 September 1899. See the replies in the issues of 23 September, 7 October and 21 October 1899.

56 *ILPN*, October 1899.

57 'For whom are we fighting?', *LL*, 23 December 1899, 404.

58 *LL*, 27 January 1900, 28.

59 *KLJ*, 30 December 1899; 20 January 1900.

60 *Ethical World*, 5 November 1898, 19 November 1898. The argument was

developed in 'The propaganda of civilization', *International Journal of Ethics*, XI, 4 (1901).

61 *LL*, 17 February 1900, 52.

62 A. M. McBriar, *Fabian Socialism and English Politics, 1884–1918*, Cambridge, 1962, p. 121.

63 *LL*, 31 March 1900, 100. The Duke of Fife, son-in-law to the Prince of Wales, was singled out for particular mention.

64 *LL*, 29 September 1900, gives a list of the shareholders of Kynocks, the munitions firm, identifying members of Chamberlain's family.

65 For example *LL*, 22 December 1900, 404; 29 December 1900, 412.

66 *LL*, 6 May 1900, 163.

67 See, for example, Keir Hardie's speeches: *Hansard*, vol. 119, HC Deb., 4s., 19 March 1903, cols 1251–2; *Hansard*, vol. 120, HC Deb., 4s., 24 March 1903, cols 113–15.

68 *LL*, 20 August 1898, 278.

69 *KLJ*, 7 April 1900.

70 M. D. Blanch, 'British society and the war', in Warwick (ed.), op. cit.

71 *LL*, 14 October 1899, 324.

72 *KLJ*, 26 January 1896.

73 *Woolwich and District Labour Notes*, March 1899.

74 *KLJ*, 30 September 1899.

75 *Bradford Labour Echo*, 14 October 1899, 2; *LL*, 23 December 1899, 403.

76 *LL*, 31 March 1900, 100.

77 *LL*, 10 March 1900, 77.

78 *LL*, 31 March 1900, 100.

79 This compilation is taken from a large number of articles by Hardie in the *Labour Leader*. A typical example is *LL*, 14 July 1900, 220.

80 *LL*, 25 May 1901, 162.

81 *LL*, 7 June 1902, 179.

82 R. McKibbin, H. C. G. Matthew and J. A. Kay, 'The franchise factor in the rise of the Labour Party', *English Historical Review*, XCI (1976), 732–52, and the subsequent debate in later issues of that journal.

83 Price, op. cit., esp. chapter IV.

84 Emily Hobhouse's account was published in *LL*, 12 October 1901, 235. See also *LL*, 14 December 1901, 396; 4 January 1902, 3. The first lengthy article on the use of 'dum-dum' bullets was in *LL*, 30 June 1900. Atrocity stories were given in *LL*, 6 December 1900, 381; 22 December 1900, 405; 12 January 1901, 11.

85 For a discussion of the socialist press more generally in this period see Deian Hopkin, 'The socialist press in Britain, 1890–1910', in G. Boyce, J. Curran and P. Wingate (eds), *Newspaper History from the Seventeenth Century to the Present Day*, London, 1977, pp. 294–306.

86 Keir Hardie, *India: Impressions and Suggestions*, London, 1909.

87 Ramsay MacDonald, *Labour and the Empire*, Rutherford, 1907.

88 *LL*, 23 December 1899, 403.

A world fit to live in: the *Daily Mail* and the middle classes 1918–39

Tom Jeffery and Keith McClelland

Introduction

Richard Maddison lived with his family in a house he owned in the London suburb of Lewisham. He worked in the City as a clerk in the Moon Insurance Company and devoted his spare time to cycling and membership of the Special Constabulary. Holding decided ideas upon what was good for his family, Britain and the empire, he was a stiff, awkward, spiritually and morally crabbed man. Many of the ideas he held upon the wider world were at one with the *Daily Trident*, a paper he had adopted on the day of its first publication in 1896, in preference to the *Morning Post*:

> the *Daily Trident* was Richard Maddison's only companion, of like mind with himself, in his house. It shared his inner life. Its pages, particularly the articles on the English countryside, bicycling, gardening, fishing and other sports and games, made him feel that he enjoyed a full life as he read . . . in the train to and from London Bridge, keeping the best of them for the armchair at night, together with the first pipe of the day.[1]

The *Daily Trident* was, in fact, the *Daily Mail* thinly disguised and Richard Maddison the fictional creation or autobiographical memorialization of Henry Williamson, author of *Tarka the Otter*, chronicler and philosopher of English fascism and a firmer friend of Sir Oswald Mosley than the *Daily Trident* was ever to be. Williamson's portrait of Maddison and the *Daily Trident*, and his identification of the lower middle class with the *Mail*, is the quintessence of an image that continues to resonate throughout writing on the history of both the press and the lower middle class. The *Mail* is seen as the paper of the lower middle class and, by no means the same thing, the values of the lower middle class as those of the *Mail*.

But is this an accurate representation of the relationship between the *Mail* and its readership between 1918 and 1939? In exploring the question we shall do two things. First, we shall look at the composition of the *Mail*'s readership, in terms of class, age and sex, and chart the major feature of the paper's history in the period, its relative decline. Whether or not the paper was a commercial success, whether or not it could sustain its market share and continue to sell the right kind of reader to the advertisers, was crucially dependent upon creating, maintaining and reworking that community of sentiment in which a reader could recognize her- or himself in the world of the paper. Second, therefore, we explore that world and the associations and dissonances between it and that of the *Mail*'s readers.

1

In May 1921 the *Daily Mail* celebrated its silver jubilee. There was much to celebrate: the *Mail* was not only the largest-selling daily newspaper in Great Britain but in the world. A confident, dynamic paper, it was sure of its ability to interpret the apparent chaos of the post-war period to an anxious middle class and of its ability to create a world which would be fit for that class to live in. On Sunday, 1 May 1921, 7000 guests congregated at Olympia to rejoice in the achievement of the 'world's record net sale' of 1,365,000 copies a day, to give thanks for the 'prosperity of the enterprise and its workers' and to beseech God to continue to grant

> thy servant Alfred . . . health and strength, wisdom and power . . . that he may continue to serve his time and generation, holding ever aloft the torch of imperial faith, and guiding aright the destinies of this great Empire.[2]

Fifteen months later, on 14 August 1922, Alfred Harmsworth, Lord Northcliffe, architect of the *Mail*'s success since its foundation in 1896, died insane in a guarded rooftop hut in Carlton Gardens.[3] His death coincided with the peak of the *Mail*'s success: in December 1921 the paper had been selling 1,750,000 copies a day; in the course of 1922 sales rose to 1,784,313. Yet, as the figures in Table 2.1 show, by 1939 the *Mail*'s circulation was the same as in 1921. But over the period the aggregate circulation of metropolitan morning newspapers had doubled, from nearly 5.5 million to over 10.5 million copies a day, and the numbers of people reading newspapers had also greatly expanded.

The relative stagnation and, eventually, absolute decline of the *Mail* was presided over by Northcliffe's brother and heir, Viscount Rothermere. The Harmsworths had held unrivalled sway over the popular press: they had owned and closely controlled the only two daily papers with circulations above 1 million, the *Mail* and the *Daily Mirror*, with the former exceeding the latter by 500, 000 copies a day in 1921. In the 1920s, under Rothermere's control, the *Mail* at first maintained its circulation at 1,750,000 and then, after 1926, began to creep towards 2 million. But during that period two new rivals emerged, Beaverbrook's *Daily Express* and, in the latter part of 1929, the newly commercialized *Daily Herald*. In 1929–30, the *Mail*'s circulation peaked at 1,950,000 and in 1931 was passed by both the *Express* and the *Herald*. It then fell into absolute decline. During the 1930s the aggregate sales of metropolitan morning newspapers grew by 23 per cent but the circulation of the *Mail* declined by 17 per cent. Moreover, although

Table 2.1 Circulation of metropolitan morning newspapers, 1921–39
(in thousands)

	Year[1]						% Change		
	1921	*1925*	*1930*	*1935*	*1937*	*1939*	*1921–30*	*1930–39*	*1921–39*
Daily Mail	1,533[2]	1,743	1,845	1,719	1,580	1,533	+ 20	− 17	—
Daily Express	579	850	1,693	1,911	2,329	2,546	+ 192	+ 50	+ 340
Daily Herald	211	350	1,082	2,000	2,000+	1,850	+ 413	+ 71	+ 777
Daily News	300	570⎱	1,400[3]	1,345	1,324	1,299	—	− 7	—
Daily Chronicle	661	949⎰							
Daily Mirror	1,003	964	1,071[4]	950	1,367[7]	1,571	+ 7	+ 47	+ 57
Daily Sketch	835	850	1,013[5]	750	850[8]	750	+ 21	− 26	− 10
Daily Telegraph	180	125	90[6]	461⎱	637[9]	737	− 50	—	—
Morning Post	50	70	132	120⎰			+ 164		
The Times	113	190	187	183	192	204	+ 65	+ 9	+ 80
Total	5,465	6,661	8,513	9,439	10,279	10,500+[10]	+ 56	+ 23	+ 92

Sources: A. P. Wadsworth, 'Newspaper circulations 1800–1954', *Manchester Statistical Society Transactions*, IV, 1954–5; Colin Seymour-Ure, 'The press and the party system', in G. Peele and C. Cook (eds), *The Politics of Reappraisal 1918–1939*, London, Macmillan, 1975, table 10.4, p. 237; Political and Economic Planning, *Report on the British Press*, London, PEP, 1938; *Report of the Royal Commission on the Press*, PP, Cmnd 7700, London, HMSO, 1947–9; W. A. Belson, 'The British press', mimeo, n.d.

Note: These figures should be treated with caution as neither full nor wholly accurate figures are available. Nevertheless, they illustrate the central trends of circulation.

[1]Full year except where otherwise stated.

[2]Annual average; the *Mail*'s circulation rose from 1.3 million to 1.75 million during 1921.

[3]The combined circulation of the *Daily News* and the *Daily Chronicle* was about 1.6 million preceding amalgamation in 1930 as the *News Chronicle*.

[4]December 1929; a figure for June 1930 of 1.3 million was also published.

[5]Last six months of 1930.

[6]October 1929; circulation rose to 175,000 in December 1930, when the price of the *Telegraph* was reduced from 2*d* to 1*d*.

[7]Last six months.

[8]Estimated.

[9]October–December 1937; at the time of their amalgamation the circulation of the *Telegraph* was 535,000, of the *Morning Post* 117,000.

[10]Including estimated daily sale of the *Daily Worker*.

circulation recovered during the war and in the late 1940s, eventually reaching the 2 million mark, the *Express* was then pushing towards 4 million. As a final irony, and as if confirming the collapse of the commercial and journalistic acumen of the house of Harmsworth, the *Daily Mirror*, sold by Rothermere in 1935 and subsequently restyled by Bartholomew and Cudlipp, passed its former stable-mate on the eve of war in 1939.

That the *Daily Mail* began to lose in the circulation battles of the 1930s was a crucial factor in its history: but sheer size of circulation was not all. Circulation performed two, connected, functions: it provided revenue directly and it produced it indirectly by providing an advertising medium. In the inter-war period it became clearer to newspaper owners and advertisers

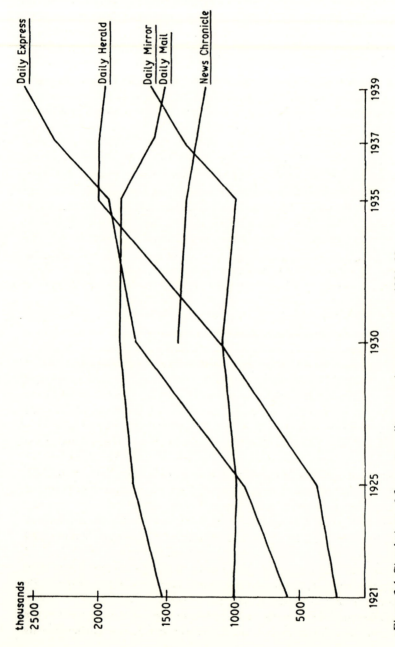

Figure 2.1 Circulations of five metropolitan morning newspapers, 1921–39

alike that there was no simple, unified market, that purchasing power varied from area to area, from class to class, and that purchasing was largely carried out by women. It was also clear that considerable care was needed if advertising was to reach its consumer targets; advertising effort might be dissipated if it was directed through a medium with a large circulation but one concentrated among working-class men living in depressed areas. On the other hand, there might be much to be gained by advertising in a smaller circulation medium if it had a considerable impact on relatively affluent women. Of course, none of this was necessarily new to owners or advertisers; but increasingly sophisticated marketing theory gave new precision to advertising techniques, especially in the field of media selection. It was in this context that newspaper readership surveys were developed.

Those surveys are of major importance for historians in that they allow an assessment of the performance of individual papers, in so far as they give an insight into the balance between the maximization of circulation and the maximization of impact upon differentiated consumer groups. They also allow the analysis of the profile of a newspaper's readership, in terms of class, age, sex and regional distribution. In this chapter we have used three of these surveys: the pioneering one carried out by H. G. Lyall in 1928, *Press Circulations Analysed*, the only survey conducted while the *Mail* was still in its supremacy; the survey carried out by Lyall in conjunction with the Institute of Incorporated Practitioners in Advertising (IIPA) in 1934, *An Analysis of Press Circulations*; and the most sophisticated survey of the inter-war period, *A Survey of Press Readership*, carried out by Mark Abrams for the IIPA in 1939.[4]

The 1928 survey set out to discover 'what the less well-to-do, those who have not a middle-class income, but have many buying habits in common with the well-to-do, viz. the lower middle class, read . . . [and] . . . what . . . the working classes read'. The survey purported to show the proportion of families, not individuals, in certain class groups, in certain areas and nationally, who saw, not bought, a wide variety of publications, ranging from national newspapers to monthly magazines. The social class of respondents was assessed by interviewers who were asked to evaluate 'buying capacity – plus social outlook'. Slum and 'very poor' areas were not covered and, most damagingly, the sample was not weighted for class; as a result, figures for newspaper 'penetration' of the population as a whole must be omitted. Still, when all qualifications are made, the survey reveals a number of points of considerable interest (Table 2.2).

It suggested that the *Daily Mail* was unrivalled in its claims upon the middle class: nationally, 37 per cent of established middle-class families, and in London nearly 50 per cent, saw the paper. Further, the *Mail*'s lead extended across all classes in the country as a whole, although it was pressed more closely among the working class by the *Daily Express* and the *Daily Chronicle*. In London, however, the picture was different. Save for among the established middle class, its lead was less secure, with, in particular, the *Express* and, to a lesser extent, the *Chronicle* and *Mirror* challenging its

Table 2.2 Metropolitan morning newspapers: percentage penetration of three class groups, London and Great Britain, 1928 (*Figures are rounded.*)

	London			Great Britain		
	Middle class	Lower middle class	Working class	Middle class	Lower middle class	Working class
Daily Mail	49	30	15	37	26	14
Daily Express	25	26	14	20	17	10
Daily Herald	1	6	9	1	3	5
Daily Chronicle	7	19	25	5	9	10
Daily News	4	8	2	4	7	7
Daily Mirror	15	18	12	12	10	7
Daily Sketch	11	10	10	11	8	5
Daily Telegraph	13	4	1			
Morning Post	15	2	—			
The Times	19	2	—			
Westminster Gazette	4	6	6			

Source: adapted from *Press Circulations Analysed*, 1928.

penetration of the lower middle class. Among the working class the *Chronicle* overtook the *Mail* and the *Express* was close to equalling it. The *Daily Herald*, soon to launch a severe challenge within the lower-middle- and working-class markets, remained an uncommercialized Labour paper at this stage.

Table 2.2 also illustrates the continuously uneven development of a national press in Britain and the disparity between London and the rest of the country. The most notable example is the *Daily Chronicle*, significantly more successful in London than elsewhere. But it was generally the case that there was a higher penetration of all classes by each newspaper in London than nationally. However, the *Mail*, the leading daily, the unrivalled leader among the middle classes, could, more so than any of its competitors, also lay serious claim to being a truly 'national' newspaper.

The Lyall/IIPA survey of 1934 (Table 2.3) marked a considerable methodological advance (although its title, *An Analysis of Press Circulations*, is slightly misleading). The survey did not cover the country as a whole but concentrated on newspaper penetration of a number of towns, which were then aggregated to form regional groups, the South-East, Greater London (the Metropolitan Police District), the West Midlands, The North-West and the West Riding of Yorkshire; slum areas were still excluded. However, this survey weighted the 22,500 households for class and the characteristics of each class were spelt out in advance, although accurate categorization depended upon the interviewer's judgement. The primary criterion employed in defining social class was the number of rooms occupied by a family, although interviewers were asked to take into account the family's apparent social standing and purchasing power. Families who occupied eight or more rooms, employed a servant and were of 'sufficient cultural standard' were allocated to class A; here the main breadwinner would earn £600 or more a year. In class B were families of clerks, small shopkeepers and the like, earning between £5 and £12 a week, living in small villa-type houses of six or seven rooms and who had the 'social and buying outlook of class A but without class A incomes'. Class C consisted of those living in five or fewer rooms and who were of 'essentially working-class character'.

The readership figures in Table 2.3 reflect the developments in circulation we have already seen. The survey suggests that the narrowness of the new *Daily Herald*'s victory in the circulation wars of the early 1930s was as nothing compared to its clear victory in terms of readership. With penetration ranging from 19 per cent of households in the North-West to 29 per cent in the South-East, the *Herald* far outstripped its rivals. The regional disparities evident in 1928 show up again in 1934: in London and the South-East the *Mail* had slipped some way behind the *Express*, the *Herald* and the *News Chronicle* but outside these areas it held up reasonably well and in terms of overall penetration in each area it retained second place by some margin from the *Express* and *Chronicle*.

However, what continuing advantage the *Mail* had, rested almost entirely upon its success among the middle and lower middle classes. In the working

Table 2.3 Metropolitan morning newspapers: total penetration of classes A, B and C in five regions, 1934

(*Figures are rounded percentages.*)

	The South-East				Greater London			
	Class				Class			
	A	B	C	Total	A	B	C	Total
Daily Mail	32	22	9	13	30	20	9	13
Daily Express	26	24	14	17	27	24	13	17
Daily Herald	5	18	34	29	6	19	36	29
News Chronicle	12	20	23	22	13	22	24	22
Daily Mirror	20	13	9	10	21	13	10	10
Daily Sketch	12	9	7	8	12	9	8	8
Daily Telegraph	22	7	1	4	24	7	2	4
Morning Post	11	2	—	1	9	1	—	1
The Times	12	1	—	1	14	—	—	1

	West Midlands				The North-West			
	Class				Class			
	A	B	C	Total	A	B	C	Total
Daily Mail	35	31	8	14	46	34	9	15
Daily Express	22	18	8	11	11	14	9	10
Daily Herald	5	12	27	23	3	11	22	19
News Chronicle	9	15	9	10	8	9	9	9
Daily Mirror	16	9	3	4	8	4	1	2
Daily Sketch	12	8	3	4	13	8	3	4
Daily Telegraph	12	2	—	1	10	2	—	1
Morning Post	4	1	—	—	5	1	—	—
The Times	5	—	—	—	8	1	—	—

	The West Riding of Yorkshire			
	Class			
	A	B	C	Total
Daily Mail	41	36	9	13
Daily Express	9	12	7	8
Daily Herald	2	10	24	21
News Chronicle	4	9	9	8
Daily Mirror	7	3	1	2
Daily Sketch	8	5	3	2
Daily Telegraph	12	3	—	1
Morning Post	3	—	—	—
The Times	6	—	—	—

Source: adapted from *An Analysis of Press Circulations*, 1934.

class the *Herald* was far more popular everywhere, reaching 36 per cent of working-class households in Greater London as against the *Mail*'s 9 per cent, and 27 per cent in the West Midlands as against the *Mail*'s 8 per cent. With the exception of the *Express* in the West Riding, the two other popular papers, the *Express* and the *Chronicle*, performed as well or better than the *Mail* everywhere. But in the provincial middle classes the *Mail*'s lead was decisive: nowhere outside London did it reach less than 30 per cent of middle- or lower-middle-class households, while in the North-West the paper was seen in 46 per cent of established middle-class homes, a statistic which prompts speculation on the relationship between this success and the activity of the British Union of Fascists in the area during 1934. Yet in the South-East and especially in Greater London, with their generally younger, more prosperous and more consumer-oriented populations, the *Mail* was slipping badly: only among the established middle class did the *Mail* lead and the margin by which it did so was minimal compared with its provincial performance. Among the lower middle class of Greater London the *Mail* had fallen behind the *Express* and the *News Chronicle* and was on a par with the Labour *Daily Herald*. Finally, so far as penetration is concerned, in terms of overall performance the *Mail*'s main rivals were the other mass circulation popular dailies, the *Express*, the *Herald* and the *Chronicle*, with the *Express* and the *Herald* having the edge by 1934. If the *Mail* was to retain a place as *a* leading if not *the* leading paper it could do so only by becoming increasingly dependent upon clear success among the middle classes. Yet even here a new rival was emerging. In 1930 the *Daily Telegraph* cut its price from 2*d* to 1*d*, the same as the *Mail*'s, and new readers flowed in. By 1934 the *Telegraph* was reaching 24 per cent of Greater London's established middle-class homes, challenging the *Express*'s 27 per cent and the *Mail*'s 30 per cent.

One of the major innovations of the 1934 survey was its introduction of 'duplication' tables which show the extent to which one paper's readers also read another, or others. The extent of duplication was dependent upon two main factors: the degree to which a paper provided sufficiently comprehensive coverage for its readers, and the class within which it was predominantly read. So, as Table 2.4 shows, the pictorial papers, especially the *Daily Sketch*, tended to be read in combination with others, especially among the middle class where they were strongest but also among the working class. *The Times*, *Morning Post* and *Telegraph*, while comprehensive in their scope, also tended to be read alongside other papers, again especially within the middle class where they were overwhelmingly based. But, in contrast, the popular papers, all of which attempted to be comprehensive in their coverage, tended to be more 'independent'. Thus 50 per cent of *News Chronicle* class A readers read no other daily paper, compared with the 28 per cent of *The Times* class A readers and the 13 per cent of *Sketch* class A readers. However, within the established middle class the *Daily Mail* was the least 'independent' of the popular papers, an ill omen so far as advertising was concerned.

But when the *Daily Mail* readers *did* read another paper, which was it likely to be, and what proportion of the readers of other papers also read the *Daily Mail*? The answer to the first part of the question, the extent to which the *Mail* was 'duplicated *by*' other papers, was, of course, heavily dependent upon the circulations of those papers: the larger the competitor's circulation the more likely was it that *Mail* readers would see it. So, what is more

Table 2.4 Sole readership: percentage of readers seeing this paper only, by class, 1934

(*Figures are rounded percentages.*)

	Class		
	A	B	C
Daily Mail	42	68	73
Daily Express	48	62	72
Daily Herald	45	68	80
News Chronicle	50	66	74
Daily Mirror	20	38	59
Daily Sketch	13	34	48
Daily Telegraph	36	49	54
Morning Post	36	40	50
The Times	28	42	25

Source: An Analysis of Press Circulations, 1934.

enlightening is the extent to which the *Mail* 'duplicated *on*' its rivals. In Table 2.5 'duplicated by' is given by reading the columns horizontally, 'duplicated on' by reading them vertically.

It is evident from these figures that the *Mail* was most strongly duplicated by the *Daily Mirror*, Rothermere's other London daily, while the other major popular papers, the *Express*, *Chronicle* and *Herald*, took broadly similar shares of the *Mail's* readership. It is also evident that, as would be expected, the political and social character of the papers was reflected in these duplication figures. Thus the working-class and Labour *Daily Herald* took far more of the *News Chronicle's* readers than of the *Mail's*. Similarly, the *Herald* duplicated fewer readers of the *Telegraph*, *Post* or *The Times* than any of its rivals, while the liberal, middle-class *Chronicle* took a substantial proportion of *Times* readers but markedly fewer of the right-wing *Morning*

Table 2.5 Duplication among metropolitan morning newspapers, all classes, 1934

(expressed as percentages)

	Daily Mail	Daily Express	Daily Herald	News Chronicle	Daily Mirror	Daily Sketch	Daily Telegraph	Morning Post	The Times
Daily Mail	—	8·3	6·1	7·3	9·4	6·8	3·8	1·3	1·3
Daily Express	6·4	—	9·3	7·7	7·8	6·8	3·0	0·7	0·6
Daily Herald	2·7	5·4	—	9·2	4·5	4·5	0·8	0·05	0·2
News Chronicle	4·3	5·9	12·1	—	5·8	5·4	1·3	0·3	0·4
Daily Mirror	11·7	12·6	12·5	12·1	—	7·7	4·3	2·2	2·0
Daily Sketch	11·1	14·3	16·6	14·9	10·1	—	5·3	1·5	2·0
Daily Telegraph	13·7	13·9	6·4	8·2	12·4	11·8	—	1·6	3·7
Morning Post	17·2	11·1	1·4	5·7	23·1	11·9	5·9	—	7·3
The Times	16·3	10·2	5·8	9·0	20·0	15·1	12·8	7·0	—

Source: An Analysis of Press Circulations, 1934.

Post's. In contrast, the *Mail* took the largest share of *Morning Post* and *Times* readers, at least compared with the *Express*, *Chronicle* and *Herald*, and it and the *Daily Mirror* between them were seen by 40 per cent of *Morning Post* readers and 36 per cent of *Times* readers.

The IIPA's 1939 *Survey of Press Readership* was the most sophisticated exercise of its kind carried out in the inter-war period. Directed by Mark Abrams and executed by the London Press Exchange, the survey differed from its predecessors in one vitally important respect. Where previous surveys had analysed *household* readership, this one concentrated on *individuals*, which allowed age and sex to be introduced. Further, the results were presented in such a way as to allow the assessment not only of the competitive readership performance of newspapers but also of their statistical profile, irrespective of circulations. Over 43,000 interviews, weighted for class, sex, age and region, were conducted. Four classes were delineated and the interviewers were required to assess both the overall status of the household and the occupation and earnings of individual respondents. The classes were defined according to the following:

Class	Earnings £ a year	Type of dwelling	Domestic service	Children's education	Ownership of telephone	car
A	£500+	House in more expensive suburbs	Yes	Private or 'good' secondary school	Yes	Yes
B	£250–£499	Buying a house on mortgage	Occasional	Secondary school	Probably not	Perhaps
C	£126–249	Small house or flat	No	Elementary school	No	No
D	£125 and below	Older terraced house or tenement	—	—	—	—

Class B included young professional, executive and higher clerical civil servants; older bank and insurance officials; key workers in certain trades.
Class C included skilled workers; semi-skilled in some protected jobs (e.g. London Passenger Transport Board); shop assistants; junior black-coated workers.
Class D included semi- and unskilled workers.
Note: Those living in the worst slum areas were again excluded.

The results were presented in three volumes, the first looking at Great Britain as a whole, the second at ten marketing areas and the third at particular towns and cities. Figures for London were presented separately, with the area being defined, on marketing premises, as 'transport London', an area which took in the 1930s 'sunbelt', the most economically advanced and the youngest areas of the South-East, including parts of Kent, Surrey, Sussex, Hertfordshire, Buckinghamshire and Bedfordshire.

As Table 2.6 shows, the *Daily Express* had assumed a commanding lead by the end of the 1930s, with the *Herald* retaining second place and the *Mirror*, now free of the deadening hand of the Rothermere organization, in third; and although the difference may be statistically insignificant, the *Daily Mail* had been edged into fifth place by the *News Chronicle*. In the highly significant 'London' market, the *Mail* was doing even worse. Here the *Mirror* had already made an extraordinary impact, reaching 27 per cent of individuals and far outstripping the *Express*, *Herald* and *Chronicle*. The *Mail* languished: with a 9 per cent share of the market it was equalled by the *Daily Telegraph* (recently merged with the *Morning Post*) and nearly equalled by the *Daily Sketch*, a paper which had made little previous impact.

Table 2.6 Metropolitan morning newspapers: penetration, Great Britain and 'London' by sex, age and class, 1939

(*Figures are rounded percentages.*)

	Total G.B.	London	Sex: G.B. Male	Female	Class: G.B. A	B	C	D	Age: G.B. 14–24	25–44	45–64	65+
Daily Mail	10	9	10	11	24	18	9	6	8	9	13	13
Daily Express	21	18	23	18	23	26	22	16	19	22	21	16
Daily Herald	17	19	19	15	4	9	19	19	16	17	18	12
News Chronicle	11	18	12	9	11	13	11	9	8	11	12	11
Daily Mirror	12	27	13	12	12	13	13	11	16	13	10	7
Daily Sketch	5	8	4	5	9	7	5	3	4	5	5	5
Daily Telegraph	4	9	5	4	28	12	2	1	3	5	5	6
The Times	1	2	1	1	9	2	—	—	1	1	1	1

Source: IIPA, *Survey of Press Readership*, 1939.

The 1939 survey revealed other unmistakable signs of a newspaper in serious decline. First, the *Mail*'s performance among the working class was notably poor compared with all its major rivals. Second, and more significantly, while the paper continued to reach substantial proportions of the established middle and lower middle classes, it now held the lead in neither group: among the lower middle class the *Express* was the clear leader, and among the established middle class, long the *Mail*'s preserve, the *Telegraph* now dominated. In the 'London' middle classes the *Mail* was doing particularly badly: with a 15 per cent share of the lower-middle-class market it lagged behind not only the *Express* but also the *Mirror*, *News Chronicle* and *Telegraph*, whilst among the established middle class the *Telegraph*, seen by 47 per cent of class A Londoners, held a position akin to that which the *Mail* had held in 1928. Moreover, a further sign of decline was that the *Mail*'s greatest impact was on older people: it ranked fifth in the younger age groups, third in the 45–64 group, second in the 65+ group. It was strongest of all among middle-aged and middle-class women and elderly and lower-middle-class women: it reached 27 per cent of class A women aged

45–64, compared with the *Telegraph*'s 26 per cent and the *Express*'s 19 per cent and 27 per cent of class B women aged 65 and over, compared with the *Express*'s 19 per cent and the *Telegraph*'s 13 per cent. Here was a paper being subjected to a particularly acute market squeeze, from the well-established but continuously expanding *Daily Express* across the board, from the new, sensationalist *Daily Mirror* among the London young and from the growing *Daily Telegraph* among the London middle classes. The *Mail*'s claims to leadership rested now only upon its continuing impact on elderly, provincial, middle-class women.

These conclusions are strongly reinforced by Table 2.7. Women formed a larger proportion of the readership of the *Mail* than of any other paper, save for the *Daily Sketch*; these and the *Mirror* were the only papers with predominantly female readerships. In terms of class, the *Mail* was a good deal less working-class than the other popular papers, including the *Daily Mirror*, but less exclusively middle-class than *The Times* or the *Telegraph*. In terms of age, the *Mail*'s readership was older than that of any other paper except for *The Times*: only 30 per cent of the *Mirror*'s readers were over 44, 36 per cent of the *Express*'s and 38 per cent of the *Herald*'s, but 48 per cent of *Mail* readers were in this age bracket. Finally, the *Mail*'s readership was very largely provincial. Though this was also true of the *Express*, the region with the largest share of its readership (outside the South-East) was Scotland, which took 16 per cent compared with only 5 per cent of the *Mail* readership.[5] The readership of all the other metropolitan papers (with the partial exception of the *Daily Herald*) was heavily concentrated in the prosperous South-East, none more so than the *Telegraph* and the *Mirror*.

Table 2.7 Metropolitan morning newspapers: statistical profile by sex, age and class of readership, 1939

(*Figures are rounded percentages.*)											
	% of readers in in S.E. England	Sex		Class				Age			
		Male	Female	A	B	C	D	14–24	25–44	45–64	65+
Daily Mail	32	46	54	12	28	41	19	17	36	36	12
Daily Express	31	53	47	6	20	48	27	20	44	29	7
Daily Herald	36	53	47	1	8	52	39	20	42	31	7
News Chronicle	52	55	45	5	19	48	28	17	40	33	10
Daily Mirror	64	48	52	5	16	44	30	29	42	24	6
Daily Sketch	50	44	56	9	24	43	23	18	39	33	10
Daily Telegraph	61	51	49	30	42	21	7	13	42	34	11
The Times	53	55	45	47	32	15	6	12	33	41	14
Sample	32	47	53	5	16	45	34	22	40	29	9

Source: IIPA, *Survey of Press Circulations*, 1939.

It is evident that between the wars the *Mail*'s history was one of decline, even among the middle classes that lay at the core of the paper's readership. But the paper certainly continued to appeal to a significant section of the middle classes: what that section was and how the paper created and re-created a distinctive relationship between itself and its readers we now go on to explore.

2

> When the traditional rhetoric of a newspaper flows in the same direction as the emergent experience of social change, the convergence, in terms of confidence, mastery of language and presentation, inner assurance, is striking. When such convergence does not take place, the newspaper seems to go to pieces: the central organising core is not there.[6]

Though written of another paper in another period, this captures much of the inter-war history of the *Daily Mail*: the paper began to encounter major problems at the point at which its rhetoric and middle-class experience of social change began seriously to diverge. However, to put it like this immediately presents a difficulty: just as it is necessary to avoid assuming that the *Mail* was simply a 'middle-class newspaper', so too it is necessary to avoid the too easy assumption that the middle class was homogeneous, with a uniform 'culture'. The assumption is prevalent in the historiography evident in this succinct, though ultimately misleading summary:

> Throughout the past fifty years such men [white-collar workers] remained, pinching and resentful, a sullen army of the suburbs and massive supporters of right-wing and anti-labour newspapers and politicians.[7]

In fact, there were widely differing middle-class responses to the social and political challenges of the inter-war period. The *Daily Mail* spoke to and for only one section of the class: it did not speak for white-collar trade unionists in the years immediately following the First World War; it did not speak for the pacifist, low-church middle class; still less did it do so for those involved in the anti-fascist campaigns in the crisis of the coming of war.[8] Moreover, as the figures above suggest, the *Mail*'s rhetoric found a response in an increasingly narrow section of the middle class as the period progressed.

Still, having said this, some generalizations can and must be made. Most importantly, a major characteristic of the inter-war period was the establishment of a framework of stability for the middle class, especially between 1921 and 1936.[9] In the construction of stability two elements were crucial. First, the middle class escaped the worst effects of the depression which, for the working class, was the overarching experience of the time. In good part this was due to the lasting nature of the salary agreements achieved, directly or indirectly, by white-collar trade union pressure in 1919 and 1920. In the deflation of the early 1920s salaries held up much better, in general, than did working-class wages. Second was anti-working-class social and political pressure. This was not necessarily in contradiction with white-collar unionism, at least so far as individuals were concerned, but the *Daily Mail* imagined that its readers were firm and active adherents to such a stance. The middle class was seen to be the popular beneficiary of a right-wing, post-war settlement. If that settlement was won, economically, by 1922, in terms of trade union and political power the battle continued throughout the decade and it was orchestrated by, among others, the *Daily Mail*.

The rhetoric of the *Mail* had one central theme, the need to establish 'national unity' or to regain that sense of unity with which, it supposed, the war had been won. But unity was not, could not be, all-inclusive: 'the nation' was defined by exclusion as well as inclusion. For since the war a new enemy had arisen: in its external form, as Bolshevism, and internally, by association, as the political and industrial organizations of the working class. Whereas some papers were prepared to admit moderate labour leaders to the political nation and others were willing to negotiate on a wide range of political and industrial issues with 'progressive' trade union leaders, the *Daily Mail* was firmly opposed to the organized labour movement and the 'alien creed' of socialism in whatever form.

For the *Mail* the middle class and the nation were one. In its heyday in the early 1920s the *Mail* was addressing an imagined and idealized version of the middle class, drawing it into the political nation while aligning it against the organized working class. The immediate post-war period was, for the majority of the middle classes, a period of difficulty, for some even one of severe crisis. 'The Middle Class is at its wits' end', wrote one commentator, 'and, being at the end of its own wits, it naturally imagines that the world must be at an end also. It does not take kindly to the march of recent events.'[10] Over and above the emotional distress and social dislocation resulting from the war, both deeply disturbing, the largely unorganized middle class faced inflation, industrial action by the working class, a severe housing crisis and the apparent destruction of a pre-war world which, with illusory hindsight, looked like Arcadia. Those organized at work secured some measure of protection against inflation, as much in later years as at the height of the crisis, while those with small businesses could and did pass on inflation to their customers. But for the unorganized, the retired and those on fixed incomes, the post-war world was one of crisis and confusion. This the *Mail* sought to resolve through massaging the self-concern of the middle class and, in a longer perspective, by delivering a world fit for the middle class to live in.

The rhetoric addressed a broad audience: if tea-drinking, pen-pushing civil servants were beyond the pale, women clerical workers were not. But there lay, inside a wide penumbra, a core audience, composed of male clerical workers in the private sector, like 'Richard Maddison', the retired, the widowed and the servant-employing middle-class woman at home. Such people were championed in the *Daily Mail* as the 'New Poor'.

The *Mail*'s campaign on behalf of the New Poor is an example of direct, unmediated and undisguised address to its middle-class audience. In the autumn of 1919, while the advertising columns offered 'inexpensive' frocks from Harrods at £4 14s 6d and £5 10s 0d and the readers were captivated by stories such as 'Hunt For Ugly Woman – One Without Teeth Not Hideous

Enough', the paper's journalists, bolstered by a stream of letters, bewailed the plight of the middle class:

> Trying to keep up the appearance of living in middle-class comfort and actually living in penury, scraping and saving to make both ends meet, fearful lest the next knock at the door may mean the unforeseen expense, in utter dejection over a doctor's or dentist's bill – such is the chronic state of many who are, perforce, the New Poor. The New Poor is a vast, silent and increasing section of the community. Economic pressure has ruthlessly forced new recruits into its ranks. Every day shows how rates, taxes and other financial burdens are widening the circle.[11]

There were, said the paper, many kinds of New Poor: widows and dependants living on fixed pensions, authors, actors, musicians and artists, doctors and, 'the saddest of all cases', the clergy.[12] They could economize by living in cheaper houses, if any were available, by employing fewer servants, sending their children to cheaper schools, buying cheaper clothes and eating less nutritious foods. But there were

> signs that the New Poor were coming close to the end of their tether. Labour, they point out, is being looked after by a tame Government apprehensive of its power. The great commercial class can look after itself. The professional man – the New Poor Man – and the New Poor Woman – these complain that they have no one to look after them. They cannot strike and they cannot threaten, though they are worse off today than in the war's darkest days.[13]

'Their case', declared the *Mail*, 'needs a spokesman':[14] the paper was more than willing to undertake the task.

Letters poured into Carmelite House from 'Mother of Two', 'Grateful', 'Heartbroken and Weary' and 'Justice'. An ex-officer wrote that he could not afford to marry on his income of £200 a year and prospects of not more than £350–£400. It was a theme which the *Mail* readily picked up.

> The income which sufficed in 1914 is utterly insufficient now. The man in his twenties who has been brought up for professional and business life, cannot suddenly become a mechanic or an artisan, living as he lives. He must continue to earn his living in the way for which he has been trained, and the income he earns is now not enough to keep a wife and children, in the manner customary among middle class people.[15]

At the same time the working class no longer came to heel. 'A Mother' wrote:

> Life is a continual round of annoyances. The tradesmen despise the middle class woman who calculates in pence: servants and charwomen dislike to work in what they call 'mean' places. Yet how can a woman be otherwise than 'mean' when she lives in constant anxiety that she will not be able to pay her way, and in constant annoyance because her house is shabby and ill-kept? And now I am faced with the greatest tragedy of all – a fourth child.[16]

The *Mail*'s correspondents yearned for pre-war certainties but the paper itself recognized that any solution to the post-war crisis had to encompass an acceptance of change. Bewailing the reluctance of working-class women to return to domestic service, the paper constantly encouraged the authorities to ensure that such women should not draw unemployment benefit when the middle classes were crying out for cheap domestic labour. At the same time it gave great emphasis to the need for labour-saving, efficient, domestic gadgetry designed for the new conditions in which the middle classes found themselves. But change of this kind could only come gradually for a New Poor whose chief difficulty was

> the newness of their hardship and their inability to change, as if by magic, all their conventions, their methods of living . . . . Could their world be made afresh by a wave of the Wizard's Wand the New Poor would need little sympathy. Smaller houses built on labour saving principles, communal nurseries, laundries and baby schools, a different system of education, a different scale of social values, would make life on reduced means no less pleasant than before the war. But the New World is not here. The inconvenient, expensive house must be kept on, for no better lodgings can be found; the same standard of dress and conduct is expected; and it is impossible to defer the education of the children until times improve, for the years lost now can never be made good.[17]

But if the New World and the post-war settlement were to be secured, then the middle classes had to be enrolled in the fight against inflation. That meant, effectively, fighting against the overweening demands of the organized working class. With rhetorical exaggeration the *Mail* called upon the middle classes to face the enemy, though it tacitly admitted that the fate of the middle classes would be determined by others:

> [The middle class is] now composed of shabby, threadbare men and ill-dressed, half-starved women living in conditions in which there is no prospect of improvement. The only hope is that before this class is crushed – as it was crushed in the declining days of the Roman Empire – the tendency to reduce production may be stopped. The recent rise in wages cannot be accompanied by a fall in prices unless the output of goods is greatly increased. If the worker could be touched with compassion for the New Poor he might yet save them and benefit himself by augmenting his output.[18]

The problems posed by middle-class apathy were recognized by Sir Archibald Salvidge, writing to complain that those in Liverpool, where he was Conservative organizer, would not vote in municipal elections:

> Unless this anaemic condition is swiftly cured the time is not far distant when the prosperous middle class man will look up from his rubber of bridge or pause in his round of golf and discover that he no longer counts in the destinies of his country, and when that day dawns the middle and upper classes will have gone under because they did not deserve to survive.[19]

Still, the *Daily Mail* did its best to rouse the middle classes. The anonymous author of the regular Saturday column, 'Letter from an Englishman', wrote in a sharper tone than had been used hitherto on the subject. 'If the middle classes, which are now combining, submit to the despotism of the lower class, they will have only themselves to blame'. They should be more strongly united than ever before 'because they share a poverty which has been imposed upon them by the State [and] . . . are determined to seek their own salvation without aid of the State'. But the State 'tells the middle classes that they must pay higher and higher rates and taxes that the children of the lower class may have food and education and medical attendance lavished upon them for nothing'. Their duty was clear: they must 'take pride in belonging to the middle classes' for

> we are stronger and more open minded than heretofore, and if only we concert to organise our strength and to discuss political affairs with our open minds, we need not fear the prospect of being ground down under the heel of our enemies.[20]

In this rhetoric the middle classes and England were as one, sharing the same desires and the same enemies. Moreover, there was an organization which could give body to that simulacrum, the Middle Classes Union (MCU), formed in March 1919. Through the summer and autumn of the year the MCU gained strength and enjoyed the backing of the *Daily Mail*. Indeed, in November 1919 the MCU sent its 'heartfelt thanks to Viscount Northcliffe for the unsolicited fashion in which his newspapers are championing the cause of the middle classes'.[21] By the time prices began to fall and the organized working class was in retreat the MCU had become little more than the mouthpiece of disaffected diehard politicians and their acolytes. By 1922, with its name changed to the National Citizens Union, the organization had become an anti-Semitic, obsessively anti-Bolshevik fringe body and maintained that role through the 1930s when it lent its support to European fascist regimes. But briefly in 1919 and 1920 the MCU was a populist organization of the reactionary sections of the middle class. It had a substantial membership, branches throughout the London suburbs and regular meetings publicized by its friends in Fleet Street and the suburban press. In a statement published in the *Mail*, Kennedy Jones, Northcliffe's collaborator in the days of the *Evening News* and now an MP, defined both the constituency and aims of the MCU. The middle class was composed of 'all unorganised citizens who come between the federated manual worker on the one hand and the smaller but almost equally powerful class who stand for organised capital'. He argued that unity between the classes was essential:

> The Labour agitator is against the co-operation of all classes. He wants one class only. The Middle Classes Union is out to tell the working man that such a policy will end in his own destruction, that the share-holder is essential, that individual initiative, the taking of risks, boldness, inventiveness and organisation, are also all-important, and that without these the manual worker is of little account. We are organising for our own protection, preparing a big stick so that it can be used with vigour and effect if necessary.[22]

The 'big stick' which Kennedy Jones and the MCU were preparing was, of course, a strike-breaking organization. Their attitude was very much in accord with that of the *Mail*. If, at times of relative 'industrial peace', the paper carried labour news that was not overtly hostile, its tone became increasingly shrill when faced with action by the organized working class. The railway strike of September and October 1919 provides an example.

As in the *Mail*'s campaign over the New Poor, the railway dispute presented, at first, an opportunity to berate the government for failing to fulfil its responsibilities to 'the nation'. Negotiations had dragged on since February when, the *Mail* claimed, the impression had been given that wages would be levelled upwards. However, by the autumn the issue had not been settled and a strike loomed, a state of affairs attributable to the government:

> The Government have largely brought this menace upon themselves by the utterly unjustifiable delay in settling the question, and it is clear that the Board of Trade has utterly misjudged the situation.[23]

But once a strike was called the *Mail*'s rhetoric of anti-socialist national unity came to the fore. Suddenly the dispute was an issue of the nation versus 'revolution'. This 'ruthless and unjust' strike was 'against the public . . . an attempt to starve the country into submission . . . [a] blow at the nation's heart'. While the trade unions did have a legitimate place, so long as they stuck to the business of negotiating over wages and the like, they had no right to step beyond this role: a strike was an attempt to 'destroy the Government of the country by force'. While so engaged trade unionists were analogous to the enemy, to the Germans during the war:

> The pretence made by Mr Thomas and Mr Cramp that they are fighting 'to prevent trade unionism from being destroyed' is very much like the pretence that was dinned into our ears during the past five years that the Germans were fighting a defensive war against the aggression of Great Britain and France. It is not made in good faith and it is made to deceive honest men.[24]

But when the strike was over the *Mail* again adopted a more conciliatory approach. Mr Thomas could be thanked for showing that a national strike could not work. Moreover, working men should realize that they did possess the means of social and political change in that they were vested with rights, as individual citizens, within the sovereign people. This conferred upon them a legitimate power which striking could only destroy:

> Industrially the working man's future is in his own hands. In politics also he is the master of his destiny. The Parliamentary vote can give him any political or social change he really desires. He can establish or abolish any institution that pleases or offends him. But he cannot establish or abolish anything by a national strike, because the people of this country will not submit to it.[25]

The 'people of this country' were, of course, the middle classes whom the *Mail* sought to mobilize in defence of the nation. During the strike the paper had called for volunteer help on motor transport, in the Special Constabulary and as wireless operators, and had urged its readers to 'fight for the life of the Community' at the same time as trying to instil a spirit of stoicism in the face of irritating and troublesome difficulty. 'How to Walk' proclaimed the *Mail* in September, followed by advice on 'Wet Weather Walking' and 'Cycling in Heavy Traffic'.[26]

The appeal to the nation was met by the *Mail*'s readers, for many of whom the notion had become common coinage. Delivered by the leader column one morning, the rhetoric came pounding back on the letters page the next:

SIR, The railway strike is a direct challenge to the nation and a blow aimed at every man, woman and child in the United Kingdom. Will the Government give us a chance to meet the challenge, or shall we always be at the mercy of any organised section which has the power to withdraw a vital public service? All of us who work perform some service for our fellows. Let us all refuse to serve the strikers. WIMBLEDON.[27]

One way in which the middle class could refuse to serve the strikers was, the *Mail* claimed, by refusing to pay the high rates of tax imposed by the wastrel coalition government. Indeed, Rothermere was later to claim that the most distinctive and consistent feature of the paper was its attitude to public spending, the great bulk of which it regarded as sheer waste. The demand for 'cheap government' had a long and diverse history. In the *Mail*'s case it was central to the negotiation of the post-war settlement and to the definition of the political nation. In its campaign against waste, which included supporting 'Anti-Waste' candidates in elections, the *Mail* was constantly asserting the claims of the middle class against labour, the government and big business.[28] But the primary focus of its attack was the government for 'until expenditure is reduced prices cannot fall' and 'if the Government wished to allay social unrest they must take a strong hand in grappling with high prices'; otherwise there would be 'fresh trouble in every quarter' and particularly from labour for 'labour will demand more, as it is already demanding large increases in wages'. The government had to 'face the trusts . . . the simple question today is whether the Government are going to control the price-makers or whether the price-makers will be allowed to control the Government'. However, the government would only understand the necessity for a reduction of its expenditure, and hence of prices, when it recognized that the middle classes were suffering inordinately. The *Mail* urged the government to respond to that discontent which the paper detected and sought to orchestrate, especially by appealing to and articulating the disquiet among middle-class women, who were 'not going to sit still and see their homes broken up'. Once again the *Mail* could claim that it had found the previously unexpressed voice and had amplified it:

We are glad to see evidence in the recent debates [in Parliament] that the women are acting upon the advice given to them in the *Daily Mail* and are sending post cards to their members urging them to put down every form of waste. There is an ample field for their efforts.[29]

3

By 1922 the post-war settlement was beginning to take shape. Prices were falling, the most severe challenges from the labour movement had been overcome and the political foundations of Conservative domination had been laid. Of course, there was much to be done to consolidate the right-wing settlement. But throughout the 1920s, in furthering this cause, the *Mail* continued to draw upon the rhetoric set up in the crucial years of 1918–22. This entailed the constant recourse to the theme of anti-socialist national unity: if anything, this became more insistent during the 1920s, in part because of the increasing strength of the Labour Party in Parliament, in part because of the personal obsessions of Rothermere. The most grotesque and infamous example was the publication of the 'Zinoviev letter' in 1924 but this was only one, albeit dramatic, display of the *Mail*'s stance. The victories of 1926 – the defeat of the General Strike – and of 1931 – the election of the National government and the near-decimation of the parliamentary Labour Party in the panic of that year – were everything that the *Mail*, its idealized readers and, in great measure, those sections of the middle class that it spoke for had dreamt of.[30] So far as its diehard middle-class readers were concerned, the rhetoric of the *Daily Mail* had flowed in the same direction as their emergent experience of social change. Anti-socialist national unity and stability had been established. What is remarkable is that the *Daily Mail* failed to recognize this. In the 1930s the *Mail* acted as though the right-wing middle-class world was as politically unstable as it had been in the immediate post-war years. The parliamentary destruction of Labour and the defeats and emasculation of the trade union movement had not produced stability: only fascism, or an injection of it, could produce true stability. In the 1930s the rhetoric flowed on, diverging ever further from all but a section of the *Mail*'s readership, a readership which was always a minority of the middle class as a whole.

The *Mail*'s rivals were better attuned to middle-class experience in the 1930s. The emphasis of the *Daily Express* on escape, enjoyment and consumption became far more attractive than the staid approach of the *Mail* to things domestic, its advocacy of drastic political action and its doom-laden reiteration of the necessity to rearm. As it became clearer, from about 1936, that war was approaching, the *Mail*'s rhetoric ironically diverged even further from the experience of social change. For as Mass-Observation found in its studies of public opinion, there were two predominant reactions: one was a desire to 'fly from the facts' into fantasy, to horoscopes, to prayer, to any form of escape. This mood was articulated by the *Daily Express* with its slogan, 'There Will Be No War'. The other reaction was a desire to 'face the facts', to participate in the common struggle of the democracies (and, until August 1939, the USSR), against fascism, either to prevent war or, if war came, to ensure that it was anti-fascist.[31] The *News Chronicle*, more than any other paper appealing to the middle class, articulated this reaction. In doing so it played some part in formulating a radically new version of the rhetoric of national unity, a version which effectively cut away the ground upon which the anti-socialist national unity rhetoricians had stood. The external threat was now identified as fascism rather than Bolshevism, the internal threat as fascism's active friends and the appeasers. Among such was the *Daily Mail* which could, in the course of the 1930s, be identified as a threat to stability and an enemy of 'the people's England'.

The support of Rothermere and the *Daily Mail* for fascism is well known. The paper was, as Richard Griffiths has recently written, 'the only major British daily to take a consistently pro-Nazi line'.[32] Its support for fascism both extended beyond Germany and pre-dated the rise of Nazism. The paper had spoken in glowing terms of Mussolini throughout the 1920s and celebrated ten years of his dictatorship as 'the greatest evolution of the last decade of world history . . . that regeneration of the national genius of Italy', a development 'traceable to the visualisation of a single mind'.[33] Fascism, in Italy as elsewhere, was portrayed as the bastion of hope against the Bolshevik menace. During the Spanish Civil War the *Mail*'s correspondent, Harold Cardozo, filed reports whose laudatory commendation of the fascists was matched only by those received from G. Ward Price. The tone frequently verged on the hysterical; the content was accurately depicted by Orwell: 'the *Daily Mail*, amid the cheers of the Catholic clergy, was able to represent Franco as a patriot delivering his country from hordes of fiendish "Reds" '.[34]

In its support for fascism, many of the themes of the *Mail*'s rhetoric evident since 1918 were drawn in, above all its persistent association of Bolshevism with any 'illegitimate' working-class activity at home. Thus the Belfast riots of the unemployed in October 1932 or the hunger marches in England in the same period were attributed to 'Communist Plots' and the 'Reds'. The *Mail* also continued to attack the government; it welcomed the formation of the National government in so far as it had meant the defeat of the Labour Party but it none the less found the government insufficiently 'National'. It had abrogated its responsibilities in seeming to give away India, in handing over Ceylon to a 'coloured democracy' and in failing to give adequate support to the RAF. The *Mail* called for a modernized, invigorating system of government which would replace both the outmoded system of parliamentary government and the 'Old Gang' politicians who ran it. For alternatives Rothermere turned to Germany and Italy where there had been a 'gigantic revival of national strength' whose force derived from 'youth triumphant'. Domestically, British politics needed that same kind of national spirit. Yet this did not entail a simple remodelling of British politics upon fascist lines. Rothermere and the *Mail* welcomed Nazism as the proper solution for Germany yet were suspicious of its international repercussions. It was essential to build British air defences, not for aggressive purposes but so that Germany would be forced to direct its attentions to the east, to the destruction of Bolshevism.[35] Domestically and internationally Rothermere's espousal of fascism was a significant break with the *Mail*'s past and the most important instance of the radical inconsistency which characterized the newspaper during the 1930s. For since its foundation the *Mail*'s rhetoric had emphasized unswervingly two themes, nationalism and anti-socialism, the former couched in terms of anti-Germanism, the latter in terms of an affirmation of parliamentarism. For thirty-five years the paper had told its readers, 'they'll cheat you yet those Junkers', and that the ballot box was a sure defence against socialism. Now the paper poured scorn upon Parliament and praise upon Germany.

Temporarily Rothermere found a vehicle for his vision in the British Union of Fascists (BUF). In Britain, youth had, for generations, been allowed to run to waste. But the blackshirt movement offered the opportunity for the young to 'break the stranglehold' which the Old Gang politicians had on the nation's affairs. At the next general election, Rothermere wrote, there would be a 'pronounced swing either to Right or Left' and therein lay great possibilities for national regeneration:

> At this next vital election Britain's survival as a Great Power will depend on the existence of a well-organised Party of the Right, ready to take over responsibility for national affairs with the same directness of purpose and energy of method as Mussolini and Hitler have displayed . . . . That is why I say Hurrah for the Blackshirts! . . . Hundreds of thousands of young British men and women would like to see their own country develop that spirit of patriotic pride and service which has transformed Germany and Italy. They cannot do better than seek out the nearest branch of the Blackshirts and make themselves acquainted with their aims and plans.[36]

There can be little question that the *Mail* had some effect as a recruiting agent for British fascism, not least among the middle class. In Lancashire, for example, the activities of the BUF were reinforced by the *Mail*; in Leeds the great majority of the local BUF branch, numbering about 2000 by mid-1934, were middle class and drawn in by Rothermere's campaign.[37] Yet the *Mail's* support for the BUF, which was severely moderated after the violence displayed by the fascists at Olympia in June 1934, is indicative of the shifts and growing uncertainties in the paper's relationship to its readers. In the campaign over the New Poor, for instance, the *Mail* had spoken directly to and, it imagined, out of the middle class: here it claimed to speak for a largely undifferentiated 'youth'. It still imagined that its predominantly middle-class readers yearned for stability but it no longer spoke as if the middle class could be mobilized in a campaign, except in so far as individuals could and should be politically engaged as fascists. This uncertainty, this movement away from majority middle-class opinion, had its effects on circulation and readership. As Colin Brooks, Rothermere's factotum, wrote, the consequence of Rothermere's attempts to use the *Mail* as an instrument of his pro-fascist meddling was not only to lose readers but to render the paper increasingly boring.[38] As Mass-Observation later found, the *Mail's* readers were 'the least politically interested of all the Conservative readerships'.[39] Moreover, the circulation battles of the early 1930s purchased readers by free gifts rather than political persuasion yet the *Mail* did little to hold these fickle newcomers. Politically extreme yet typographically and visually bland, it could not match the presentational flair of the *Express* or the *Mirror*.

If in its political expression the *Mail* was increasingly diverging from middle-class social experience, it remained in accord with it in some measure in its continuing emphasis upon the domestic world. Yet here again the paper was losing coherence. There are tensions, even competing voices, within most newspapers. In the *Mail* these can be seen in the polarity of, on the one hand, its assumption of the need for 'hard', even violent, political solutions and, on the other, its depiction and celebration of a domestic world fit for the middle classes to live in. In the early 1920s the calls for national unity sought to bring order to a world of economic, social and moral uncertainty: when all was in flux the diverse aspects of middle-class existence could be framed in an apparently coherent whole. But by the 1930s the *Mail* floated between an already achieved social stability and the vision of a new, vigorous social and political order. Its celebration of the home, particularly in its annual 'Ideal Home' exhibitions, stood in stark contrast to the political world it depicted. F. E. Gordon, organizer of the exhibition in 1937, recalling 'twenty-one years of making ideal homes' wrote that

> the late King George V, most home-loving of monarchs, once said: 'The foundations of the nation's glory are set in the homes of the people.' These are memorable words, full of a profound truth – and they may well stand as a motto for the great undertaking which is the Ideal Home Exhibition.[40]

Two years later, the exhibition was taken as showing that 'the interest of the nation in its homes and gardens' displayed a commendable steadfastness in the face of 'international worries'.[41]

At the centre of this world stood the middle-class woman, particularly the middle-aged and the elderly middle-class woman living in the provinces, the bedrock of the *Mail*'s readership. The paper was full of appeals to her – both through the editorial columns, and the pages on fashion, beauty and home hints, and through the advertising columns. It assumed that such a woman was not the near-penurious victim of 1919 but the relatively affluent consumer of the 1930s, filling her mortgaged house with the essential labour-saving devices made necessary by the absence of domestic servants. One aspect of the *Mail*'s vision of 1919 was fulfilled. This side of the *Mail* certainly did reflect middle-class experience of social change. But juxtaposed to the *Mail*'s politics, it also draws attention to the disintegration of the paper's world. Unlike the *Express* and the *Chronicle*, the *Mail* could not even pretend to internal coherence. By the end of the 1930s it was simply one confused, minority, voice of the middle class.

Notes

We are especially grateful to W. D. McClelland, Bill Greenslade and members of the London Group for their help in the preparation of this chapter.

1 Henry Williamson, *Donkey Boy*, London, Macdonald, 1952, p. 46.
2 *Daily Mail* (hereafter *DM*), 2 May 1921.
3 Hugh Cudlipp, *The Prerogative of the Harlot. Press Barons and Power*, London, Bodley Head, 1980, p. 137.
4 Care is needed in the use of these surveys, based as they were on different and developing statistical approaches. However, there is a greater degree of continuity between each of these surveys than between other surveys of the inter-war period – for example, that carried out by Repfords Ltd in 1932, or the Advertising

Association survey of 1936 which was used by Political and Economic Planning.

5 The *Scottish Daily Express* was arguably a separate newspaper.

6 A. C. H. Smith *et al.*, *Paper Voices: The Popular Press and Social Change*, London, Chatto & Windus, 1975, p. 245.

7 E. J. Hobsbawm, *Industry and Empire*, Harmondsworth, Penguin, 1969, p. 277.

8 For some evidence of middle-class involvement in anti-fascist activities, which tends to confirm the divergence of middle-class behaviour from the accepted imagery, see, *inter alia*, E. J. Hobsbawm, 'Gli intellettuali e l'antifascismo', in E. J. Hobsbawm *et al.* (eds), *Storia del marxismo*, III, ii, Turin, G. Einaudi, 1981, pp. 443–90.

9 A fuller account than can be given here would take into account necessary qualifications. These would include: the rationalization of routine white-collar work affecting some women clerical workers in the 1930s; unemployment among the middle cass, though neither new nor widespread, undoubtedly induced a sense of insecurity among those who were not directly affected; wage cuts made in the worst years of the slump but which were largely restored by the mid-1930s; the persistent problems of the marginal *petit bourgeoisie* and those who relied upon dividends for income.

10 R. Dimsdale Stocker, *What's Wrong with the Middle Classes*, London, Cecil Parker & Hayward, 1919, p. 14.

11 *DM*, 23 October 1919.

12 ibid., 18 and 21 October 1919.

13 ibid., 18 October 1919.

14 ibid., 20 October 1919.

15 ibid., 1 November 1919.

16 ibid.

17 ibid., 6 November 1919.

18 ibid., 27 October 1919.

19 ibid., 6 November 1919.

20 ibid., 29 November 1919.

21 ibid., 27 November 1919.

22 ibid., 29 November 1919.

23 ibid., 25 September 1919.

24 ibid., 2 October 1919.

25 ibid., 6 October 1919.

26 ibid., 27 September, 1 and 2 October 1919.

27 ibid., 30 September 1919.

28 Rothermere's *Daily Mirror* and *Sunday Pictorial* led the anti-waste campaign, as Rothermere himself, with Horatio Bottomley at his side and his son Esmond in Parliament, led the Anti-Waste League; but Northcliffe's *Mail* was not slow to follow. In this, as in all other Harmsworth campaigns, it is important to bear in mind their dual purpose: personal spite and short-term political intrigue were never far from the surface. But, as we have seen with the railway strike of 1919, while political capital would be wrung from any incident, the moment incident became crisis the Harmsworth press would lead the anti-socialist forces as ranks were joined: short-term gain was not confused with long-term vision. The same applies to Rothermere's feud with Baldwin when, having hounded the Conservative leader during 1929 and 1930, the *Mail* and all Rothermere's papers joined the anti-Labour, pro-National clamour in the summer of 1931. That Rothermere broke ranks thereafter and attacked the National government and Baldwin as crypto-

socialist was indicative of Rothermere's lack of judgement and of the *Mail*'s decline.

29 *DM*, 1 and 5 March, 13 April 1920.

30 See Rothermere's preface to *The Economic Crisis Foretold by the Daily Mail 1921–1931*, London, Associated Newspapers, 1931, p. 2: 'The *Daily Mail*'s predictions have been fulfilled with a completeness that is now recognised by all. In supporting the National Government, which it largely helped to bring into existence, it will use the same outspoken frankness which . . . has always marked its treatment of vital public affairs.'

31 Tom Harrisson and Charles Madge, *Britain by Mass-Observation*, Harmondsworth, Penguin, 1939, passim.

32 Richard Griffiths, *Fellow Travellers of the Right: British Enthusiasts for Nazi Germany 1933–39*, London, Constable, 1980, p. 163.

33 G. Ward Price, 'Mussolini's ten years of triumph', *DM*, 28 October 1932.

34 George Orwell, *Homage to Catalonia* (1938), Harmondsworth, Penguin, 1966, p. 48.

35 For a discussion of Rothermere's policy see Paul Addison, 'Patriotism under pressure: Lord Rothermere and British foreign policy', in G. Peele and C. Cook (eds), *The Politics of Reappraisal 1918–1939*, London, Macmillan, 1975.

36 *DM*, 15 January 1934.

37 Griffiths, op. cit., p. 107.

38 Colin Brooks, *The Devil's Decade*, London, Macdonald, 1948, pp. 147–8.

39 *The Press and Its Readers. A report prepared by Mass-Observation for the Advertising Service Guild*, London, Art & Technics Ltd, 1949, p. 80.

40 *DM*, 30 March 1937.

41 ibid., 8 May 1939.

3

Rearmament and the British public: policy and propaganda

Nicholas Pronay

The successes and failures of British foreign policy during the 1930s, and within it the question of Britain's military preparations, have been some of the most debated historical topics since the opening of the records of the Cabinet under the 'thirty years rule' in the late 1960s. The main issues and constraints upon policy which they revealed was identified almost at once, in 1971, by Professor Michael Howard in his Ford Lectures, subsequently published as *The Continental Commitment*.[1] By now, it must surely rank as one of the most remarkable historical surveys in our times, alike for its insights, the durability of its main conclusions and its style. Professor Howard suggested that there were six main factors, the interplay of which determined the Cabinet's policies in respect of rearmament. Five of these have since been treated in detailed monographs, largely confirming and amplifying his own conclusions. The six factors suggested by Professor Howard were: (1) the role of economic considerations in general and that of the Treasury in particular; (2) unrealistically high assessments of the destructive power of aerial bombardment; (3) fears about collapse of morale and social unrest in Britain as a consequence of the bombing of the civilian population; (4) the melancholy way in which the possession of a vast empire came to weigh on the mind of the Cabinet as a constraining and enervating factor rather than as a source of confidence; (5) the undemanding and dispirited performance of the army chiefs in planning, and above all pressing, for the creation of a substantial modern army capable of taking on Germany on land.[2]

The sixth factor indentified by Professor Howard was the impact of what the Cabinet assumed to have been the 'state of public opinion', coupled with the conviction that, in the circumstances of Britain in the 1930s, public opinion *had* to be a first consideration for the government. There is much evidence *inter alia* in some of the subsequent monographs, especially on the development of the air force, underlining Professor Howard's original identification of the Cabinet's views about public opinion as a major factor, while other writers have taken a more sceptical view of its role. A fuller consideration of this issue seems overdue.

There are two distinct but, of course, related issues involved: first, the role which the Cabinet's *perceptions* of public opinion in relationship to rearmament had played in shaping their policies; second, what Cabinet members believed they could and did do about *changing* public opinion in order to allow them, as they saw it, to implement such steps as they recognized ought to be taken. Although these two aspects were interrelated and in the final stages they interacted, for the sake of clarity they can be best treated separately, at least in the initial phases of the policy. Once the Cabinet began to take steps to change the mind of the public, then members' perception of how far their efforts might have succeeded at each point came to be a factor in itself.

The story of the impact of the perceptions of public opinion on the rearmament policies during the 1930s begins with that of rearmament itself, and runs parallel with each successive stage. It needs to be set against the evolution of the policy as a whole. A brief recapitulation of the principal stages is unavoidable if sense is to be made of the part which perceptions of public opinion played in the tortuous process by which the Cabinets of the 1930s failed in both of their alternative yet parallel lines of policy about rearmament. The policy of going for aerial rearmament in earnest but only for a show rearmament overall failed to deter Hitler either from a foreign policy by threats or from going to war as soon as he felt ready. When he did go to war, the alternative policy, also pursued eventually, real rearmament, was also shown to have failed to prepare British forces to be able to fight Germany effectively on land, or Japan by sea. The one area where the Cabinet's policies might have proved successful, namely in preparing the country to defend itself against an aerial knock-out blow at the outset by a German strategic bomber-force, was not put to the test because Germany had no intention of conducting the war by strategic bombing and did not choose to build up such a force at all. The waste of scarce resources involved in preparing first and foremost for a war to be fought by strategic bombing was itself one of those aspects of the whole sad story in which the Cabinet's perceptions of and attitude to public opinion played a part. What was not a failure, however, was the preparation of the public to be ready to go to war when asked and to stand up stoically and determinedly to the morale-sapping consequences of an unending series of military and naval defeats during the first eighteen months of the war.

Our story therefore begins after the Cabinet had decided in the autumn of 1933 that, in view of the trends in Japan and Germany, it had become necessary to lift the 'ten year rule' – that the armed forces should work on the assumption that they need not be ready to fight a war with a major power within ten years at any time – and had instructed the Chiefs of Staff to prepare a plan for a gradual programme of rearmament. A special committee, called the Defence Requirements Committee, was established to co-ordinate the work of defining the military needs of the country. The committee consisted of the Chiefs of Staff and of the 'permanent heads' of the Foreign Office and the Treasury. It worked under the chairmanship of the Cabinet Secretary whose duties, *ex officio*, included keeping up to date the country's military and civilian contingency plans, known as the 'War Book'. After long consideration, this committee of professional experts recommended, at the beginning of 1934, the institution of a planned expansion and modernization scheme.[3] It was, perhaps, unduly modest in scope and the costs were underestimated.[4] But it was designed to lay the foundations for rebuilding overall British military capacity for fighting a modern war, should war come, with Germany, Japan or possibly Italy, these being the only countries which could possibly be expected to resort to war in the foreseeable future. The navy would acquire a fortified and garrisoned base in Singapore and would be generally modernized, including provision of naval air power. The army would be re-equipped and expanded to be able to provide an armoured and mechanized, if compact, expeditionary force, to be ready at the outbreak of hostilities to oppose a German onslaught on the Low Countries, and would be backed up in the longer run by a restored Territorial Army. In the air, a metropolitan air force would be developed capable of operating against countries possessing modern aircraft and anti-aircraft defences, as distinct and in addition to its operational needs against rebellious tribesmen in its previous role as the empire's aerial policeman. In short, the professional advisers of the government proposed that Britain should embark on a programme of a gradual and balanced rearmament which would develop the three services, the navy, the army and the air force, on a co-ordinated and complementary basis.

In May 1934 the Cabinet got down to what amounted to the starting definition of its programme of rearmament, initially based on the submission of the Chiefs of Staff through the Defence Requirements Committee. After a series of discussions, however, it was an alternative memorandum prepared by the (civilian) Chancellor of the Exchequer, Neville Chamberlain, which came to form the basic framework of the rearmament programme. The policy of a co-ordinated rebuilding of services was replaced by that of a deterrent, strategic, air force. The Cabinet took the view that while a slow development of the navy, the least neglected of the services in any case, presented little difficulty, there could be no question of building up the army to provide an expeditionary force capable of fighting on the continent. The reasons for this decision were neither strategic nor military, indeed the services were not even asked to consider the proposal. It was a decision by the Cabinet alone, a political decision by a cabinet of civilians which completely overruled professional advice in a matter of vital national interest.[5]

All the members of the Cabinet whose views are recorded, either in the ministerial committee which discussed the issues in detail or in the Cabinet itself, took the same view – in a nutshell, that no matter what the strategic considerations might have been, they thought that the public would simply not stand for any building up of the army, or any move which implied that the campaigns of Flanders and Passchendaele might one day be refought. Neville Chamberlain felt that 'even if no public mention was made of an Expeditionary Force, expenditure on the Army . . . bulks so large in the total so as to give rise to the most alarmist ideas of future intentions and commitments'.[6] He believed that the only practical approach, given the state of public opinion, was that the government should give 'overriding priority to measures which the public would understand and approve – those directly related to the defence of the United Kingdom'.[7] He argued that before any building up of the army could possibly begin, there must come the establishment of a large air force, which is a manifestly defensive arm, protecting the people at home. He hoped that it would also act as a powerful token of British determination, and thus deter Germany from proceeding towards warlike policies. Accordingly, he, as the Chancellor of the Exchequer, the minister principally mindful of the expense of it all, nevertheless proposed that instead of the fifty-two squadrons actually asked for by the Royal Air Force, it should in fact be provided with eighty, while the requirements of the army should be cut to less than half. These proposals met with universal agreement. In fact it was Lord Londonderry, whose Air Ministry was given this unexpected bonus, who was the least enthusiastic, though naturally he concurred, remarking that he regarded the proposals as 'better designed for public consumption than for real utility'. The minister for the army, Lord Hailsham, agreed that 'it would be a big mistake to make any declaration' (concerning the intention to build up the army at the present time) because he felt that a 'good deal of education was required and to come out with the programme now would have a very alarming effect on opinion generally'.[8] Stanley Baldwin, in practice the most powerful member of the 'National government' of Ramsay MacDonald, had already argued at an earlier stage the prior need for a 'campaign of public education' about rearmament. As far as this proposal was concerned, he felt that 'from the political point of view it was necessary to do something to satisfy the semi-panic conditions which existed now about the air force'.[9] Baldwin concluded: 'At present the public were not in the least familiar with the position and he thought that it was time that they were made aware of what the position really was. Only when these fundamental things had been explained to the people and they understood might it be possible to lead them on.'[10]

As far as the diplomatic measures forming the foreign policy component of rearmament were concerned, namely that Britain should declare that it would resist by force any attack on Belgium, the same kind of considerations came into play. After a lengthy discussion, Baldwin explained that the reason why he felt that no such declaration concerning Belgium should be made was that 'he anticipated that the government would announce a considerable air programme and it was impossible to conceal that we were also considering the rectification of deficiencies in other defence services. If on the other hand we were to make a declaration of our intention to use force if necessary, for the preservation of Belgian independence, the political effect might well be serious.'[11] What he meant by 'political effect' he had already made clear to Robert Vansittart who as Permanent Under-Secretary of the Foreign Office and a member of the Defence Requirements Committee had for some time been pressing for effective military *and* diplomatic rearmament. Baldwin feared that it would lead to an electoral landslide against the government which, he added, 'would let in a Socialist government who would give you no rearmament at all instead of me who does not give you enough'.[12] Chamberlain said much the same, in another discussion, when he explained that if too much were spent on the army 'the government could be turned out and its successor might do nothing at all'.[13]

Thus began the policy which led to the neglect of the British army and the creation of an independent and essentially isolated strategic air arm. It was a policy for which, in the end, Britain paid first with the loss of France and the European allies, and then with the human, material and *moral* devastation, not to mention the crippling diversion of scarce resources, involved in the doctrine and practice of strategic bombing. The road which led via Dunkirk to Dresden.

Thereafter, the story of the role of perceived public opinion, as recorded in the minutes and papers of the Cabinet and its committees, remained essentially the same. In 1935, the Chiefs of Staff emphasized to the Cabinet that the nettle of the army must be grasped if it was to be rebuilt in time. It was still not too late to make a start, for, however fast Germany's rearmament might have been progressing, it had in fact started from a far lower point than Britain's. Germany, after all, had actually been disarmed in 1918, unlike Britain. Time would run out soon, however, unless a decision to begin the preparations for an expeditionary force were to be put into hand. The Cabinet nevertheless felt that while this was indeed so an electoral mandate would first have to be obtained for rearmament; and that it could only be hoped for on the basis of an *aerial* rearmament programme with as little as possible being said about the army, which in the public mind was identified with the bogey of 'great armaments'. In the election campaign supposedly for a 'mandate for rearmament' Baldwin felt obliged, first, to fudge it altogether by running it behind an appeal to return a 'National' government of 'experienced men at the helm who laid aside their party political differences' as against 'untried experiments' by an inexperienced Socialist party. Second, in all such appeals as he did make for rearmament, he studiously avoided mentioning the army at all.[14]

With the election won, the Cabinet got down to considering the next step which came to be incorporated in the Defence White paper of 1936. The programme now announced was indeed impressive; it aimed for an air force of some 1700 first-line aircraft, including 1000 bombers by September 1939, and a naval building programme which would enable Britain to place a fleet in the Far East adequate to act on the defensive as well as to maintain in home waters a force able to meet the requirements of war with Germany. As before, this was a heavily modified version of the policy actually proposed by the Defence Requirements Committee. As far as the army was concerned, the committee did not even try to propose an 'expeditionary force' again. It recognized that the name was taboo as far as the Cabinet was concerned. However, it did propose what was now called a 'field force' of five fully equipped and mechanized divisions with a follow-up force of twelve territorial divisions. It was to be based on the building up of peacetime reserves and on the development of sufficient capacity in the munitions industry for the maintenance of this force on the continent. The outcome of the deliberations during the winter of 1935 and the spring of 1936, *after* the government had been returned to power with one of the biggest majorities in recent history and at a time which it knew to be the last possible moment for laying the foundations of an effective force capable of opposing the *Wehrmacht*, was summed up by Professor Howard:

> One item still stuck in the throat of the cabinet: the proposals for a Field Force with its train of territorial divisions to take part in a campaign on the continent. The cabinet challenged neither the political nor the military arguments of the Chiefs of Staff: they only said, almost unanimously, that the British public would not stand for it.[15]

In fact there was an even sharper edge to Baldwin's own expression of this view. In the last of the series of meetings specially held to consider the army's future, he said, 'there might well be undesirable political reactions if it were announced that the role of the territorial force would be to take part in a future European war. Public opinion might react violently to such an idea.'[16]

Then came the long-drawn-out discussions over the next revision of the rearmament programme in the light of the darkening international situation, the reoccupation of the Rhineland, Italy's growing attachment to Germany and Japan's ever more aggressive policies in China: the 1937 Defence White Paper. By that time the two to three years' grace during which Germany had a lot of basic catching up to do with a not actually disarmed Britain was expiring, and the military became deeply, and justifiably, worried. In his submission to the ministerial committee the War Minister formally informed its members that the army's condition for facing Germany in the field in the foreseeable future 'was deplorable'. After having had their recommendations referred back to them *three* times by the ministerial committee, the Chiefs of Staff returned the same *unanimous* opinion to the Cabinet: that beginning to prepare the army to be able to fight a continental war had become essential.[17] It could not be left any longer to half-measures either. Recruitment for the regular army as opposed to the air force stood at a very low level, which was hardly surprising since for the last two years the government had been projecting the air force as the service of the future. At the same time, the requirements of building up a massive force of large heavy bombers, as well as capital ships, left insufficient industrial capacity for re-equipping the regular army – at least within the deliberately low-key and peacetime economic and industrial approach adopted by a government convinced that it must not be seen to be diverting resources into 'great armaments'. Only the redevelopment of the Territorial Army and a measure of industrial mobilization could solve the problem. That would require a public declaration of the need for a field force. Once again this was felt by the Cabinet to be 'politically' impossible. Chamberlain reiterated that public opinion in general, and in particular 'the political temper of the people', ruled out any possibility of 'preparations in peacetime for operations in Europe'.[18]

In the end, having failed to shift the Chiefs of Staff away from their blunt declaration of the alternatives, the Cabinet decided to accept the risk that, should the air force fail to deter Hitler from going to war, Britain would not have an army to fight the Wehrmacht, and would have to depend on the French and the air force to sustain the nation in war.[19] The War Office was told that the regular army would be equipped only for police duties in the empire. As for the Territorial Army, the manifold fears of the Cabinet on account of the 'political temper of the people' and the Cabinet's consequent policy were succinctly summarized by the Chief of the Imperial General Staff, General Ironside, in his diary. 'The Cabinet have decided behind closed doors that the Territorial Army is required to keep the peace in England and restore law and order in air raids. They dare not give this out because it would be unpopular.' Any changes in policy, it was felt around the Cabinet table, would have to wait on the 'education of the public'.[20] Given the timetable for the coming of the war in the autumn of 1939, accurately forecast by the Foreign Office, the decisions embodied in the 1937 White Paper had cast the die as far as British military preparedness was concerned.

Thus, at each of the annual revisions of the programme of rearmament, when the decisions were taken which determined the extent and rate of rearmament as well as the relative distribution of resources between the three services, alongside the voices of financial orthodoxy, military narrow-mindedness and Chamberlain's amateur strategies, there were heard agonized voices, like the chorus in a Greek tragedy, trying to appraise what 'the public' or 'the people' would or would not be prepared to accept, for what they might or might not yet have been 'sufficiently ready' or 'educated'. On the record, they appear to have been the decisive voices.

But were they genuine? Were these perceptions of the state of public opinion, and the fears of what the public might do if its 'opinion' and 'temper' were not heeded, a genuine factor in and a constraint on the making of policy? Brian Bond suspected that this was not the case, that 'the politicians invoked "public opinion" in support of whatever policies they wished to pursue'.[21]

Making windows into men's souls, as Queen Elizabeth well knew, is an unsure undertaking, particularly when they are dead. In the case of politicians whose essential craft is the persuasion of others it is especially difficult ever to be sure whether what they presented as their reason for doing or not doing something was indeed what had persuaded them, or whether it was the argument which they thought most likely to succeed – or indeed whether this was the view which they thought it would be most advantageous for themselves to be heard expressing. As far as direct evidence is concerned, in the form of what they confided to their diaries or to confidants in letters or conversations, it seems that the two most important figures in the policy-making process, Chamberlain and Baldwin, were at the opposite ends of the spectrum in the actual weight which they placed on public opinion as a factor.

Chamberlain seems to have been personally convinced that if a large air force were built up and it was merely supplemented by a show force of a small regular army, there would not be a need for a continental fighting force at all. Faced with no prospect of carrying out a successful aerial knock-out blow against Britain, Hitler would not be mad enough (or his generals would not let him if he were) to start a war. In those curious, boastful, soul-baring letters which he wrote to his admiring sisters most Sundays, he claimed that the fateful, and in the time available the irreversible, decision behind the 1937 White Paper 'gave me what I always wanted', with no reference whatever to public opinion considerations or the temper of the people.[22] It seems clear from all we know about Chamberlain that by 1935 at the latest he had indeed developed 'that overweening confidence in his own abilities and that poor opinion, sometimes even contempt, for those of others' which would allow him to take it upon himself to be his own expert in foreign policy, strategy and tactics, as well as finance.[23] More charitably, perhaps, it might be said that Chamberlain was a man dominated to an extent unusual in a politician by strong moral and ethical convictions, and that he held that what the politician believed to be the 'right' policy he should put into practice regardless of popularity. 'General scepticism formed no part of Chamberlain's mental habits and nor did cynicism.' His strength in politics was that, although he worked hard to acquire a mastery of the facts, he arrived at his judgements by making them fit in his own mind the case which his principles had told him *must* be the case. He could therefore see and present a larger picture into which particular policies might fit. He was also possessed of a singular capacity for rationalizing his intuitions for the benefit of persuading others, and perhaps himself too. His view of the place of the views of others in all this was tactical. As he wrote for the readers of *Harmsworth's Encyclopaedia*, anyone aspiring to become a leader should first and foremost have 'the power to distinguish between the essential and the unimportant, the habit of considering all the possible consequences, and the manner in which it may affect the views of others'.[24] With this mixture of qualities, Chamberlain was thus the least likely to be *consciously* guided in a matter of the utmost importance involving some of his deepest feelings and principles by what he took to be 'public opinion'; and the most prone to merely invoke it for browbeating his military advisers into accepting what he had intuitively perceived as the right strategy for achieving the larger aims. In any case, he pressed Baldwin to frankly ask the country for a mandate for a measure of rearmament in 1935. He would have scarcely done that had he thought, as Baldwin did, that the state of public opinion was such that it would be an election loser. All this suggests that for Chamberlain the parading of 'the temper of the people' against the Chiefs of Staff, and his earlier references in cabinet to the strength of public opinion, were largely invocations of a suitable argument and not expressions of a genuine sense of overriding constraint.

Baldwin was at the other extreme. He had an abiding, almost panicky, concern for preserving Britain's consensual parliamentary system. He believed that it was passing through a period of extreme danger, deriving partly from the 'premature' granting of universal franchise and partly from the emergence as the alternative party of government of a Labour Party which rested on a movement with an ambivalent philosophy concerning the choice between parliamentary or extra-parliamentary means for realizing its social and political aims. This was a subject on which he brooded endlessly and on which he held forth continuously both in private and in public. For him, what he took to be the views of the new mass electorate was certainly a central consideration.[25] He was also deeply fearful of the feelings of the industrial working classes and, perhaps naturally for the son of an iron-master, he was conscious of their capacity for reacting violently when their feelings were roused. Underneath the well-cultivated exterior of simplicity and straightforwardness, Baldwin was a much more intellectually sophisticated, ruthless and indeed devious politician than Chamberlain. For Baldwin to allow himself to be consciously swayed by electoral considerations, keeping the party united, not antagonizing sections of the working class and the like posed no moral dilemma. In any case, he personally and philosophically believed that the prime historical task of the moment – for he was also a man with a strong sense of history – and a task for which he felt personally responsible to posterity, was the preservation of Britain's parliamentary system and social peace. Unkindly, it could be added that he perceived that peace best maintained by maintaining also the status quo in social terms.[26] As against that immediate yet historic task, all other considerations, such as putting all the nation's eggs into the basket of aerial warfare in case war should come at some point in the future, carried much less weight.

Baldwin's general views are too well known to justify more space here than a brief recapitulation. The way in which these views, outlined above, fitted together in his mind in respect of what he thought should be his priorities with regard to rearmament, is well illustrated by one of his less well-known 'inimitable little speeches', as J. C. C. Davidson called them, which he frequently made to confidential gatherings of politicians or businessmen of his own party. Replying to the concerns powerfully represented to him by the so-called 'Defence Deputation' led by the most senior figures of the party, Austen Chamberlain, Lord Salisbury and Winston Churchill, in July 1936, and which echoed the views of the Chiefs of Staff, he rounded on them in no uncertain terms.

> Most of you sit for safe seats. You do not represent industrial constituencies; at least not many of you. There was a very strong, I do not know about pacficist, but pacific feeling in the country . . . if you tried to do too much you might . . . have imperilled . . . you might have lost, the General Election . . . the one thing in my mind was the necessity of winning an election . . . . That was the first thing to do in a democracy, the first thing to do.[27]

The evidence, altogether, suggests that, in contrast to Chamberlain, for Baldwin his perceptions of the state of public opinion, and the potentially explosive condition of the Constitution which made heeding it essential, were indeed the imperative considerations.

As far as the other members of the Cabinet were concerned, they were less prone to soul-baring than Chamberlain in his letters or Baldwin in his conversations. There is less direct evidence of what might have been in the depths of their thoughts. Those who have published their memoirs tend to make oblique claims to have been moved by the state of public opinion. But then, these memoirs were written after they had all been dubbed 'the guilty men' in the wake of Dunkirk.[28] It might therefore have been all too tempting for them to say, as Swinton did, subsuming his own personal part in it all, that while it had become

> fashionable . . . to heap all responsibilities for the outbreak of the war on Baldwin and Chamberlain [as] the guilty men who joined in a conspiracy of silence and deception in order to hold onto power . . . reality was that they represented the mood and spirit of the inter-war age, nothing more nothing less.[29]

It was the people of that generation as a whole who were guilty of failing to prepare themselves. Little weight can be placed on these and similar direct statements about the motives of the majority of the Cabinet who sat through the whole process, as distinct from the few who resigned or were removed on account of a matter some way concerned with the Cabinet's policies towards Hitler, such as Duff Cooper or Lord Londonderry. There is certainly nothing to put against the fact that none presented any counter-argument based on strategic and diplomatic considerations against the recommendations from the Chiefs of Staff, as Chamberlain had done, as a reason for rejecting their advice; nor against the fact that none of those whose utterances have been recorded in the minutes of the Cabinet or of the ministerial committees denied that public opinion would be totally unwilling to accept the kind of rearmament which the military experts recommended; nor against the fact that none of them had told Baldwin that their duty lay in taking such steps as were deemed essential for the defence of the realm by those whose expertise it was to define them, irrespective of how people outside, and without being in the possession of the facts and opinions which were known to the Cabinet, might possibly react to the announcement of those steps. We have, in other words, no evidence against accepting their concurring remarks about the overriding need to wait on public opinion, as being honestly held.

Whether the lesser politicians in their heart of hearts really believed that the British people would sweep them away if they did take those steps or only pleaded 'public opinion', thus cannot be decided from what they said then or since. However, good evidence for their real frame of mind is provided by what they actually did in cases where there was no question of either persuading or posturing. Evidence for the concern with which members of the Cabinet as a whole regarded how their policies might strike the public is provided by the extraordinary amount of time they were willing to devote to the form in which matters relating in any way to rearmament were presented to the public. In the case of recruitment, for example, the whole Cabinet settled down to working over the designs and wordings of the posters and notices which were to be placed in the employment exchanges. In the course of the sessions, both Baldwin and MacDonald repeatedly referred to the 'very great political problems' involved in attracting the unemployed to the army by advertising at all in employment exchanges.[30] The Cabinet even went as far as to resolve formally that all officials were to be given a warning that they must make sure that there were no clerical errors in their correspondence in the matter referring to *unemployment* exchanges! The Cabinet further resolved that the notices must be 'small and very discreetly displayed'.[31] These were hardly the sorts of matter on which the Cabinet of the world's largest empire would be spending its time, unless its members had a genuine concern, indeed fear, about the state of public opinion and the temper of their people.

The amount of time devoted to other matters involving the *appearance* of rearmament-related measures tells the same tale. In July 1934 the Cabinet spent a good part of *three* full meetings considering a paper submitted by the Air Raids Precautions Sub-Committee (Organisation), entitled: 'Publicity matters appertaining to passive air defence'. This technical and quintessentially low level matter the Home Secretary felt ought to be a subject of full cabinet discussion and so it was. The Cabinet minutes are so revealing as to justify extended quotation. In the first of the three discussions

> it was suggested that if, at the very moment when we were announcing an increase in the Air Force, the public were asked to take precautions against air raids, an unnecessarily alarmist view of the international situation would be created. From this point of view it was suggested that it would be better to entrust the duty in the first instance to well-informed private individuals rather than to government representatives . . . . It was pointed out that public opinion was already considerably concerned in this matter and that if an announcement was not made by the government in the near future they were liable to be stampeded by a newspaper campaign. (To be decided next week.)[32]

The following week after another discussion it was decided that 'no statement on ARP should be made as part of the general statement on air defence'.[33]

In the third week the subject was discussed again in cabinet. It was argued by Sir Kingsley Wood, who was responsible in the Cabinet for all matters relating to government propaganda and publicity, and who fulfilled the same co-ordinating authority for the Conservative Party, that

> if an announcement were made it should not be left to stand by itself. The mind of the public required to be approached gradually on this question.

At last, the Cabinet concluded on the matter of publicity:

(a) that in the course of his speech in the debate on air defence policy on Monday next, July 30th, the Lord President of the Council should make a statement on the subject of ARP

(b) that the Home Secretary should consider the desirability of following up the statement by a broadcast.[34]

Nine months later, on 29 May 1935, the whole Cabinet again got down to a sentence-by-sentence revision of the *wording* of a circular letter to be sent out by the Home Office to local authorities on ARP, minuting such details as: '*omit* "heavy" air attacks re Fire Services, which should not be "substantially" strengthened' and '*omit* "heavy additions" to police duties'.[35] Taken together with their words, such extraordinary expenditure of time on such minute details of public presentation (in the last case this was merely a circular *letter* to local authorities and not even for general release) leaves little doubt that as far as Baldwin and the majority of the Cabinet was concerned, the state of public opinion was indeed a central consideration. They must have believed too, in their heart of hearts, that the rate at which the public might be brought to accept rearmament needed to be the principal determinant of their decisions concerning rearmament policy.

What, then, did they do about 'educating the public'? This is a question to which the answer, in so far as it has been considered at all, tended to be 'very little if anything at all'. Yet there was a massive change in public opinion, or at least in the perception of it, by both the government and its critics on the other side of the House. Within two years of the White Paper of 1937 when even 'field force' was thought to be a phrase impossible to mention and when conscription was thought to be totally out of the question in the foreseeable future, peacetime conscription was introduced, so was industrial mobilization, opposed all along tooth and nail by the TUC and which involved breaking such taboos of British industrial relations as 'dilution of labour' and 'transfer of labour',[36] and all without any measurable opposition in the country as a whole or in industrial districts. The government claimed to introduce conscription on account of 'public readiness' and the response of the people certainly bore it out. No doubt Hitler's actions had much to do with bringing home to the British people the menace he represented. Nevertheless his actions needed to be portrayed, pointed and focused for the people of Britain in terms of particular policies. And there still remained the question whether for the sake of stopping Hitler from gobbling up 'faraway countries' in the east of Europe the government was justified in preparing a British army, and a conscript army at that, to fight again in the fields of Flanders.

The traditional interpretation of the policies of the government in terms of educating the public with reference to the army, has been summed up in the view that 'whether or not "public opinion" would have responded earlier to the need to meet German aggression by all-out rearmament if given more determined political leadership must remain a matter of speculation. Since the Press was largely Tory it could easily have been prompted to campaign for rearmament.'[37] Although this view represents a common perception, it is not one which would have been endorsed at the time either by the predominantly Tory Cabinet, or by those whose job it would have been to carry out a campaign of 'educating the public'. There had been major changes in the composition and structure of 'public opinion' since that term was coined in the nineteenth century; major changes in the relationship between the press and the government and in the structure of the media in Britain since the period to which that view would have been appropriate.

Indeed by the 1930s an entirely different set of constraints had come to operate on the ability of government to influence the public in the traditional way, and at the same time some new possibilities of considerable potential had also come into being. In order to judge what the government had actually done, we need to look at these changes and to consider first the question of what *could* the government have done to change opinion about rearmament, amongst those sections of the public which the government believed were the critical people who really mattered.

It had long been a normal part of the craft of government in Britain to carry out on occasion a campaign for bringing the public in line with policies the necessity for which had not yet been generally appreciated. There was, indeed, a well-established, even traditional pattern of conducting such campaigns of 'public education'. Traditionally, they consisted of public speeches in the provinces by leading members of the government; apparently private but well-publicized utterances at the meetings of various bodies, clubs and associations by the Prime Minister himself; a cultivation of sympathetic newspaper correspondents and editors amongst the quality press; the delivery of speeches *in* Parliament but at times calculated to reach the quality daily or Sunday press in time for an editor to present them at length next day and the practice of giving him good notice in advance of the substance of a speech to ensure that he would keep space for it and be ready with a prepared editorial for driving home its points. The Midlothian campaign by Gladstone had set this kind of pattern over half a century earlier and it had become something of a ready ritual by the First World War at the latest.

The problem, however, which faced the governments of the 1930s was that this kind of educational process had both become outdated in technique and was quite inappropriate to the problem of rearmament.

The traditional public education campaign was designed to persuade members of the traditional political elite of Victorian and Edwardian England. The problem in the 1930s was that the kind of people who still came to the Free Trade Halls of the cities of the Midlands or attended the county dinners and the like, the old 'educated electorate', were not open to this kind of political debate, or education, over the issue of armaments. They had already made up their minds one way or another about rearmament and had done so with a depth of commitment and passion which was born in the crucible of the First World War. Such beliefs were simply not amenable to the kind of shift which this kind of ordered, rational, hierarchical, public education campaign was designed to bring about. The political elite of Britain was deeply and fundamentally split over rearmament. Rearmament was therefore not an issue where a broad consensus underneath the surface play of party politics in parliament could be reached through this traditional debating process. Whatever the government, its members and supporters might have done, there was no chance in the 1930s for the sort of hitherto typically British solution to a political disagreement which had been so nicely demonstrated in 1909, when the government wanted four battleships and the opposition demanded six, and in the end they compromised on eight.

The fact was that the British political system, parliamentary government resting on a broad consensus amongst a mature and homogeneous elite concerning *aims*, but with rigorous debates over *means*, had essentially broken down even before the rearmament issue came to be faced. It broke down over the unparalleled economic crisis of 1931, when resort had to be made to the dangerous expedient of a 'National government', which masked a fundamental split over aims as well as means. The political, almost spiritual, crisis over whether or not to rearm and consider fighting another European war made permanent the breakdown of the basic consensus over aims. This was the reason why Baldwin believed that rearmament could *only* be carried out through the perpetuation of a National government, and why in 1935 he sought a mandate for a National government as such, rather than for the particular policy of rearmament as Chamberlain had wanted. The informal machinery of consultation beneath the surface of parliamentary debate leading to effective political consensus, and the traditional debating procedures amongst the political elite which went with it, all had to be suspended in 1931 and they remained suspended in effect from 1931 to 1945. Thus we should look in vain for any Midlothian campaign in a new guise being conducted in the country over the issue of rearmament in the 1930s.

The sophisticated relationship between the politicians and the press which developed in the nineteenth century as a part of the system for consensual parliamentary government had also broken down. It was no longer true in the 1930s that because 'the majority of the press was Tory' it could be 'prompted to campaign for rearmament'. Newspaper owners and, as far as their owners permitted editorial independence, newspaper editors, were as deeply divided *and* as deeply committed on this issue as other members of the political decision-making elite. The nature of the relationship had already changed before the 1930s, as a result of the development of financially independent, indeed very wealthy, mass-circulation press empires and the consequent rise of the 'Press Barons'. They saw themselves in a quite different light from the old 'Tory' or 'Liberal' newspaper owner or editor: not as the propaganda arm for the 'interests' represented by the party but as the makers and arbiters of the policies of both party and government. Moreover, as it happened, neither Lord Rothermere nor Lord Beaverbrook was in the least willing to co-operate on any terms except his own with either the party or the government so long as it was led by Baldwin or Chamberlain, for reasons of personal antagonism mixed with thwarted political ambitions. Thus the *Daily Express*, the largest-circulation national daily newspaper for most of the period, and to the acquisition of which by Beaverbrook during the First World War party funds might have contributed, ran a virulent campaign on the slogan 'There Will Be No War This Year or the Next Year' – right up to the outbreak of war. Rothermere's still very powerful *Daily Mail* and its stablemates pursued a confused and contradictory policy alternatively scaring the public with wildly exaggerated figures of German air strength, demanding instant aerial rearmament, or stressing the ultimate inevitability of German dominance. The policy of the *Daily Mail* reflected the confusion in Rothermere's own mind which was perhaps best summed up by Churchill. 'He thinks the Germans are all powerful and that the French are corrupt and useless and the English hopeless and doomed. He proposes to meet this situation by grovelling to Germany. "Dear Germany, do destroy us last!" '[38]

Even the *Daily Telegraph*, which in normal times was close to being the official voice of Conservatism, had so far drifted out of the normal relationship with the party that it not only printed a highly damaging disclosure concerning proposals being debated in cabinet for the 1935 Air Defence Policy statement but so acted that it was felt necessary for the Cabinet formally to decide that 'the Prime Minister [a Labour man!] should see Lord Camrose'.[39]

The *real* position concerning the relationship between the newspapers and the Conservative Party, as distinct from the abiding myth of 'the Tory Press', was described by Sir Joseph Ball, head of the Research Department of the Conservative Party and a personal confidant of Neville Chamberlain, in a secret memorandum to him in the summer of 1938:

> although a number of the national dailies (e.g. *The Times, Telegraph, Daily Mail, Daily Express, Evening News, Evening Standard, Yorkshire Post*, etc.) are nominally supporters of the government, none of them can be relied upon for full continuous and deliberately planned support, to the same degree that our Socialist opponents can count upon the *Herald* [sic] and *Reynold's* and the Liberal opposition on the *Star* and the *News Chronicle*. Indeed, some of them deliberately adopt, from time to time, the role of 'candid' friend (e.g. the *Daily Mail, Evening News, Daily Express* and *Evening Standard* and even the *Daily Telegraph*) but the *Yorkshire Post* since the Eden crisis has adopted a distinctly hostile attitude.[40]

The fact was that while the number of newspapers which in an old-fashioned election campaign would be likely to support the Conservative Party remained large, the influence of the party over their editorial policies had declined, particularly so in the case of the mass-circulation newspapers of Beaverbrook and Rothermere. At the same time the growth of the *Daily Herald*, the official Labour paper without pretensions of independence, and by the late 1930s of the new-style working-class *Daily Mirror* under Guy Bartholomew, with a combined circulation of nearly 4 million, gave the other side a marked advantage. It was, simply, not possible for the government in the 1930s to rely on the daily press for 'educating the public' over the issue of rearmament.

Theoretically, at least, the government should have been in a much better position for 'educating the public' through the medium of radio. Although broadcasting was subject to much more control in fact by the government than has been traditionally held,[41] in respect of rearmament there was only a limited amount that could effectively be done through it. There were two reasons for this, at first sight, surprising position. First, rearmament was recognized as a 'party political issue' where the official opposition had a right to reply to any direct ministerial statement of policy and where the BBC itself was obliged to present a 'balanced' viewpoint. It was an issue about which the opposition had particularly strong views and was therefore watching the BBC for any departure from the obligation of political balance. Therefore any government campaign for educating the public about the need for rearmament would have turned into a debate with all the emotive phrases such as 'great armaments', 'merchants of death' and the rest given substantial airing. That problem might have been overcome at least to some degree by a vigorously populist presentation of the reasons for rearmament and by the skilful and purposive use of programming devices by the BBC. There were, however, serious obstacles to both of these, which also derived from the peculiar institutional form which had been given to broadcasting in Britain.

In the first place, being a monopoly and a public corporation created by royal charter with its board of directors and chairman appointed directly by the government, the BBC was believed abroad to be the voice of the British government, and no amount of protestation on the part of the government was able to change that belief. This did not only apply to ill-educated and ignorant foreigners such as Hitler or Franco who could not be expected to understand some of the finer distinctions of the English-speaking world. As the Washington embassy had explained as early as 1930, 'to the American public the BBC are HMG'.[42] Continuing attempts to maintain abroad the doctrine of BBC independence were not helped by the BBC describing itself in its own publicity as 'The Voice of Britain'. By the mid 1930s the government had to resign itself to the identification of HMG with the BBC as a fact of international life. By 1938 even the wearily formal protestations to the contrary to foreign countries could at times be dropped. In March 1938, for example, Halifax authorized the British ambassador in Berlin to tell Hitler that as a token of the government's desire for creating a friendly atmosphere between the two countries the BBC would cancel a projected and already announced series of talks on German colonies, as requested by Dr Goebbels.[43]

In these circumstances it was not possible to separate what the government said for home consumption, i.e. to present a vigorous case for the need for rearmament based as it would have to be on a statement of its own assumptions concerning German intentions, without at once jeopardizing the attempt to mollify and appease Germany. The price for creating a single, 'national', broadcasting medium in an otherwise pluralistic political system, in the name of making radio the 'integrator of democracy' and 'the educator for citizenship', turned out to be that this wonderfully persuasive medium could not be fully utilized for the single most important 'educational' purpose of the 1930s.

Then there was the second obstacle which made even the most 'unofficial' use of the BBC for purposes of 'educating the public' over the issue of rearmament very difficult. The BBC, having the status of a national institution which its royal charter and monopoly had conferred upon it, attracted a personnel from far higher up the social scale than an ordinary 'radio station' would have been able to draw, for example in the pluralistic broadcasting system of the United States. The BBC glittered with the sons and daughters of the political and social establishment. They were also amongst the most highly educated young men and women of the upper echelons, who joined the BBC in preference to entering politics or the Civil Service because they were possessed of more rather than less of the generally high quota of idealism and moral sensitivity amongst the inter-war generation. They thus tended to be soft-centred and rather 'pink' in sympathies, like those of their kind who joined the British Documentary Movement. William Greenway of the Foreign Office referred to the 'BBC "superior" mentality . . . the *Manchester Guardian* attitude among the all-wise young gentlemen of Broadcasting House'.[44] They tended to abhor war and were singularly out of tune with war preparations in general, and in particular with encouraging the public to harden its heart. Reith himself was well aware of this and in 1937, under increasingly persistent proddings from Conservative Central Office, not only admitted that 'it was true that nearly nine in every ten in the BBC are Left,' but also promised that 'the administration is doing everything in its power to draft in more of the Right to balance'.[45] Such a declaration of good intentions by Reith in his fifteenth year at the BBC begged the question: 'Who appointed the nine?' It is hardly surprising that, by then, Central Office was doubtful whether Reith himself could be trusted ever to 'balance' his establishment. Sir Joseph Ball, who headed the remarkably efficient and wide-ranging intelligence service of Central Office as well as its propaganda operations, came to be so unconvinced by Sir John Reith's promises that he formally advised Chamberlain that, drastic as he recognized such a step to be, the only answer was for the government to remove Reith from the BBC.[46] Two weeks after receiving this proposal Chamberlain told Reith that 'in the national interest' he must move to Imperial Airways. Whether this was a mere 'coincidence' must remain a conjecture for no reasons for that decision appear to be recorded in Chamberlain's papers, or in Reith's diary.[47]

Whether as a result of indirect 'promptings' or by more direct means, or by 'coincidence', there *were* significant changes in BBC personnel after the rearmament programme, and the need for 'educating the public', became government policy. The founding figures of Hilda Matheson, Fielden and Siepmann, all of the 'soft/left' attitude of mind and personal sympathies, moved out of the positions of editorial control which they had occupied. In 1935 Sir Charles Carpendale, a vice admiral and no pacifist, became Deputy Director and John Coatman, a tough regular officer of the Indian Police, became head of the now independent 'News' division. In the particularly sensitive field of 'Talks' where 'balance' was much monitored by the Labour Party, S. A. Voigt took over the coverage of Germany from Vernon Bartlett. Unlike Bartlett, Voigt was *persona non grata* in Nazi Germany and was hounded by German agents even in Paris. His appointment to the BBC was welcomed by some British officials as being a step towards informing the public 'how serious the European situation is'.[48] His broadcast in March 1935 concerning the large scale of German rearmament caused considerable concern in left circles and marked the beginning of a slow and cautious change in the BBC's 'Talks'.

Nevertheless, as long as Reith remained in charge of the BBC the government had to proceed with great circumspection in trying to use the medium of broadcasting for 'educating the public', even within the constraints imposed by its constitutional position at home and its 'voice of Britain' image abroad. As soon as Reith was gone, matters changed. As far as the 'Talks' part of BBC output was concerned, less than two weeks after Reith's successor took office in October 1938, the government felt safe enough actually to summon to Downing Street Sir Richard Maconachie, Controller of Programmes, and in the most direct fashion but not on record, through the mouth of the Cabinet Secretary, to 'request' the staging of a discussion on National Service 'which would help to clear the public mind of the vague and woolly ideas prevalent on the subject.[49] There was now sufficient confidence in the new leadership to leave the choice of speakers to the BBC. They chose L. S. Amery and Lord Snell, who did the required job very well indeed.

The utility of 'Talks' for educating the public was, however, limited. It was most obviously bound by the rule of 'balance' and the reality of 'balance' could be readily measured, and thus policed, by the opposition through the choice of the speakers selected by the BBC. Furthermore, 'Talks' was by definition a programme device specially oriented towards the educated. It was assiduously listened to by the very intelligentsia who principally held soft/left attitudes and who were also quick to detect any 'propaganda', particularly if it was against their views. More significant may have been the conduct of news broadcasting after Coatman's appointment. For news is the balance of reported facts, and therefore, as Sir John Reith himself so succinctly put it, 'news is the shock-troops of propaganda' – if it is used for that purpose. For reasons which have never been satisfactorily explained, however, the scripts of BBC news broadcasts for the 1930s have not been, apparently, preserved in the corporation's archives. Thus it is impossible to form a judgement as to what might have been done by the medium of news-broadcasting in the service of rearmament education.

The position of the government in respect of the other new medium, film, was paradoxical. Unlike broadcasting, film was neither a state monopoly nor subject to any public service obligations, nor was it supervised by a government-appointed board of governors. Yet in practice, it was over the cinema in general and the newsreels, 'the animated newspapers', in particular, that the government had both real control to exclude counter-propaganda and real influence for conducting 'education' campaigns of its own.

By the 1930s a skilfully constructed and sophisticatedly conducted system of censorship had developed under the British Board of Film Censors (BBFC) which could, and did, take care of any anti-rearmament or 'peace' propaganda. Constitutionally, the BBFC was an anomaly. Its operating costs were paid by the cinema trade itself from the fees which the BBFC charged for 'examining' the films submitted. Not being in receipt of funds provided by Parliament, as a private body it was not supposed to be subject to questions in the House. On the other hand its president was 'nominated' by the Home Secretary. This was essentially the same arrangement which operated in the case of the 'D' notices in respect of the press (and also since 1912), where it was the Press Proprietors' Association which paid the operating costs as well as the salary of the official in charge who was, however, 'nominated' by the Director of Military (or Naval) Intelligence. Except that, unlike the BBFC, the existence of 'D' notices was not officially admitted until 1963. The BBFC had a much more political rather than a 'security' role; it had more power in peacetime, and was more than ready to use it.[50] Between 1929 and 1936, film censorship was run by Edward Shortt, formerly Secretary of State for Ireland during the Sinn Fein period at the end of the First World War and Home Secretary in Lloyd George's coalition government. For the rest of our period the BBFC was headed by Lord Tyrrell. Previous to his appointment as President of the British Board of Film Censors, Tyrrell had been successively Head of the News and the Political Intelligence Departments, and then Permanent Under-Secretary of State, at the Foreign Office. After 1936 he held the presidency of the BBFC together with the chairmanship of the British Council. Combining as he did responsibility for both censorship, i.e. negative propaganda, at home, and for positive, 'cultural' propaganda for overseas, he could be said to have come as close as the niceties of the British constitution allowed in peacetime to being a Minister for Propaganda. The board's secretary, Joseph Brooke-Wilkinson, had been in charge of film propaganda to allied and neutral nations in the First World War. During the 1930s he sat on the CID sub-committee concerned with censorship and with the planning of the Ministry of Information, itself a part of the rearmament process.

By pointing to the amount of money which could be saved by not having to recut, reshoot or indeed find as unsaleable finished films to which the board might have 'objections', the BBFC succeeded by 1934 in persuading companies that instead of submitting finished films, they should submit their 'scenarios' before they would start productions. The BBFC could thereafter prevent the making of films altogether on subjects which it regarded as 'undesirable' as well as interfering in detail – down to altering single words in the dialogue at times – in the complex aural/visual way through which a feature film conveys messages to the viewer. The means were therefore there for 'educating' the cinema-going public, which by the mid-1930s reached close on 18 million, by far exceeding the circulation figures (though not altogether the readership) of the national daily press, and of the BBC.

Feature films can help to inculcate in people who habitually and regularly attend the cinema, and for whom reading is not a prime form of wish fulfilment, a *general* outlook through which their attitude to *particular* policies and events may be conditioned. The essential first step in what Vansittart termed 'psychological rearmament'[51] was therefore to keep the cinema screens free from films which portrayed soldiers as the dupes of armaments manufacturers, reckless politicians or a military caste with a vested interest in war, or films presenting army life as tyrannical, dull and futile, and war itself as an *always* unnecessary, *always* avoidable, bloody and futile business. Control of the cinema was essential because it was the only true mass medium in the period. It was the only medium which could reach all: neither literacy nor maturity was needed for coming to 'the pictures', and it was so cheap that some 82 per cent of working-class youngsters, between 8 and 18 years of age, went to the cinema at least once a week. And it was they, the industrial and working class, from amongst whom the recruits for the forces had to come, and who had to be prepared to work in or even move to new armaments industries. It was also their vote collectively, some 70 per cent of the total since 1929, which determined which group of politicians formed the government, unlike in the pre-war days of the limited franchise. Altogether, the cinema was *the* medium for those whose attitude to rearmament could be decisive in a way in which that of the intelligentsia, or of those who in pre-war days formed the 'educated public opinion', could not.

The measure of what the government had done in terms of educating the public which mattered, in the medium through which it could be done, is that after 1935 there was no chance, for all practical purposes, for anyone to reach the mass audience in the public cinemas with films with an anti-rearmament or pacifist message. The BBFC working in co-operation with the trade association of the film distributors, presided over by Albert (later Sir Albert) Clavering, director of the Conservative Party's own film-propaganda organization, saw to that through the application of a cat's-cradle of rules. The BBFC refused to certify for showing, amongst others, films which 'portrayed British officers and forces in disgraceful, reprehensible or equivocal light' or contained 'realistic presentations of the horrors of war', 'conflicts between the armed forces of a state and the populace' and, *Catch 22*, 'the presentation of objectionable propaganda'.[52] The distributors agreed not to handle any film not certified by the BBFC. Sound commercial instinct thereafter combined with more subtle touches on the tiller to ensure a growing supply of suitable films in their place. Why risk money on making films which may get banned and will not be promoted by the distributors? And then there was the new found willingness of some City institutions to pour capital into studios turning out films with the right messages, such as Alexander Korda's London Films.[53] Films take a long time to produce, any change of direction is bound to be gradual in this medium. However, it is a tribute to what was done that by 1937/8 film critics and literary and art reviewers, such as Graham Greene, of the soft/left and anti-war disposition as a rule, were dismayed by the 'militarism and imperialism' of the cinema, or that John Grierson bemoaned the fact that peace stood no chance when the cinema made 'war more exciting than peace', and that its overall effect on the young was to act as 'the recruiting sergeant'.

Feature film is important because it can affect attitudes of mind and one's general outlook, especially amongst the young and the uneducated. However, it cannot be used effectively for presenting specific political arguments, or for feeding to the public a diet of suitably selected and interpreted information, 'facts', about current events which would make appear as reasonable and sensible such particular steps as the government is taking, or intends to take, from time to time. That, the drip-on-the-stone technique, is the *modus operandi* of the *news* media. That is why the news media have so much importance, particularly in countries such as Britain or the USA, in which empirical pragmatism is the dominant philosophy. Deprived of substantial support from the popular press, this made it vital for the government to be able to utilize the cinema newsreels.

The governments of the rearmament period were able to do so for several reasons. First, that although cinema newsreels were free from the obligation to submit their productions to the British Board of Film Censors, this freedom rested upon custom only and it was clearly understood that the government could have chosen to ignore it if the newsreel companies behaved 'irresponsibly'. To put the newsreels under the BBFC was of course the last thing the government would have wanted to do as a certificate of censorship would have reduced the credibility and therefore the effectiveness of the medium. But it made it clear to the companies, from time to time, that it would certainly do so if the alternative was to see this medium being used against it.[54] Unlike the newspapers, the newsreels had thus a legal sword suspended above their heads which ruled out any *Daily Mirror* style 'Publish and Be Damned' heroics against the government of the day. Moreover, should the government be driven to such a drastic step because of the activities of any one of the newsreels, it would have no choice but to remove the customary protection against censorship from *all* the newsreels. Any newsreel editor moved by an heroic impulse was therefore subject to strong restraining pressures from the others.

There were also other means of control available which were, for the government, not the double-edged weapon which censorship would have been. Newsreels, unlike newspapers, depended for much of their news material, the actual news footage, on the active co-operation of various government agencies. To set up cameras in any street or on the 'King's Highway' required police permission. To do likewise in any 'royal park' required the permission of the Commissioners of Works. The importation of any article, such as cans of film, required customs clearance – and a rapid one at that. Not for nothing was it that the newsreel companies invented the label 'NEWSFILM – Useless If Delayed'. All these powers were not only available, but were used from time to time to demonstrate the need to be 'co-operative'. Then, there was the fact which again distinguished newsreels from newspapers – namely that it was not enough merely to produce a newsreel: before it could reach the audience it had to be bought and projected by a cinema. In a competitive market in an entertainment industry any newsreel which could not be absolutely relied on to provide its customers with all the staple items (royalty, the annual calender of the sporting and ceremonial events of British life and politics) would rapidly find that the customers had gone elsewhere.

The actual effectiveness of this plethora of potential means available to the government for putting an uncooperative newsreel company out of business was bravely tested in 1932 by Tom Cummins, the brash, idealistic and young editor of *Paramount News*, the newsreel company which was then a newcomer straight from the freer world of the American news media. The story is instructive. Like the other newsreel editors, Cummins was told by Lord Trenchard, the Metropolitan Police Commissioner, on behalf of the Home Office, that he was not to film the National Unemployed Workers' Movement's Hunger March. Unlike the other editors, Cummins decided not to comply and even resisted the pressure brought on him by all the other editors in a hurriedly arranged meeting for that purpose. Without, of course, a permit from the Office of Works to take cameras into Hyde Park, he had them smuggled in under his cameramen's coats past the policemen at the gates. The resulting film was hailed by *Film Weekly* as 'really graphic and exciting . . . several "close-ups" of mounted police charging the rioters with drawn batons'. Within forty-eight hours, however, *Paramount* learned that it, alone, was denied police permission to film the Lord Mayor's Show, and that that was merely a token of things to come. So, nine days after *Paramount*'s splendid stand for freedom reached the cinemas, its news editor was sitting in the office of the Deputy Commissioner of the Metropolitan Police, having already made a penitential visit to the Home Office. In the words of the customary Scotland Yard 'verbal' record he 'was full of apologies and emphatic that his firm were most anxious to fall in with the views of the authorities on any matters of this kind'. When the 1934 Hunger March arrived in London, and the newsreels were again asked not to cover it, the general manager of *Paramount* rushed off a letter: 'In view of the Commissioner's feelings in this matter we deem it a pleasure to accede to his request.' The police view of it all was summed up in a letter written by the Police Commissioner's secretary to Sir Patrick Gower of Conservative Central Office(!): 'the incident was useful as it made clear to all the newsfilm companies that we could hit them pretty hard if they don't behave nicely'.[55]

By the time therefore the question of how to present the Peace Ballot came up in November 1934, it is not surprising to find that *Universal News*, for example, thought it wise first to consult the Home Office, assuring the official concerned that 'the Editor was quite willing to do whatever the Home Secretary suggested and he would like to know as soon as possible whether the government had any views on the matter'.[56] After the Foreign Office had been consulted, he was told that the government would rather that he did not cover it at all, and the projected story on the Peace Ballot was duly dropped.

In addition to control, the government also had influence with which to convert a negative policy of not hampering rearmament into positive, active and regular support by most of the newsreel companies. In the case of *Gaumont British News* its owner, Isidore Ostrer, had formally agreed in March 1935 'to place the entire organisation of *Gaumont British* and the *Sunday Referee* behind the government'.[57] This was of particular importance because *Gaumont British News* was one of the most widely distributed newsreels. In terms of technical skills of editing, commentary and the use of sound, backed by incomparably the most lavish studio facilities, it was also the most effective. Under E. V. Emmett, both its editor and commentator, *Gaumont British News* produced some of the most brilliant examples of persuasive screen journalism. That is, in the Northcliffe interpretation of 'persuasive journalism', in which for 'persuasive' one might fairly substitute 'propaganda'.

In the case of *British Movietone News* the position was initially less satisfactory. It was jointly owned by Twentieth Century Fox, USA, and Esmond Harmsworth, Lord Rothermere's son, and until 1935 it followed the same 'candid friend' policy as Rothermere's newspapers. For reasons which are not quite clear yet, this changed in the spring of 1935. From then on, operating under its general manager, Sir Gordon Craig, already a leading member of the Conservative and Unionist Film Association, the party's film propaganda organization, its editor in chief (when other pursuits allowed), Sir Malcolm Campbell, who stood as a Conservative candidate in the 1935 general election, and Gerald Sanger, its producer and working editor, who after the Second World War became the Conservative Party's official Films Adviser, *Movietone* worked in complete harmony with the government. Little is known of the political contacts of *British Pathe* beyond the fact that Sir Albert Clavering, the head of the Conservative and Unionist Film Association, and the first man to be knighted for his services to party propaganda in the medium of film in 1936, was a major shareholder and director of it. Whatever may have been the nature of the contacts, if any, the fact is that *Pathe*, which alone, on a good day, could run *Gaumont British* close in persuasive skill, provided as extensive, as solid and as effective propaganda for rearmament as *Gaumont British* itself. Evidence is lacking concerning the remaining two companies, *Universal News* and *Paramount*. In the case of *Universal* only the commentary scripts survive, in the case of *Paramount* from 1935, only the pictures. As the meaning which sound film, particularly newsreel, actually conveys to the viewer is embedded in the careful counterpointing of pictures and words, any conclusions drawn from commentary scripts only or pictures only would be worthless.

The government, then, had both powers of control over all the newsreels, which the newsreels accepted as a fact of life, and positive influence over at least some of them. But it is important to understand the nature of that influence, as it affected the actual people, the editors and other staff, who carried out the pro-rearmament campaigns. Otherwise it would be easy to jump to unwarranted (and insulting) conclusions concerning their role and professional integrity. They acted like a newspaper editor who had a traditional pattern of relationship with an old-type newspaper proprietor who owned, and usually heavily subsidized, his newspapers in order to support a particular party, but who, unlike Northcliffe and his imitators, did not consider himself to be an editor in chief. In such newspapers, including *The Times*, the editor would 'support' the 'interest' of his proprietor with his best professional expertise, because he believed in it himself. If and when his beliefs changed, or those of his proprietor, it would be understood that he went. No man can be, day in day out, effectively, inventively and consistently persuasive about something he does not support *or* in which he does not believe. That is the first rule of committed journalism, of political propaganda and indeed of any other branch of persuasion. Even in advertising it is a rule that the man given the account must believe (or learn to believe) in the product.

Thus when Mr Donald Barrington-Hudson of *Pathe Gazette* pointed out that he 'never received policy direction and was allowed to write his own commentaries', in response to some ill-informed imputations,[58] that was doubtless as true of him at *Pathe* as of the commentator or editor of any other well-run newsreel or of the leader writers of any decent newspaper. He at *Pathe* campaigned for rearmament because he was convinced that it was in the national interest to do so. Whether he would have retained his job had his *convictions* been different from his board's and from Clavering's is another matter. The same applies elsewhere too. For example, *Movietone News* cameramen and other staff, including its excellent picture editor Mr Raymond Perrin, voluntarily gave up many of their evenings and weekends to do *unpaid* work for their party, trundling around with cinema vans, handling projectors, editing films and so forth: because they *were* Conservatives. They worked for *Movietone* because they enjoyed the company, in both senses of the word. Otherwise they might have preferred to work for Edgar Anstey at *March of Time*, for example, or in Grierson's Documentary Movement. It was the job of the *management* in *selecting* its employees to make sure that they would not have to try to become hacks. Hacks can do many things, but they cannot carry conviction. They cannot help sounding flat or false particularly when working under the terrific pressures involved in bringing out a newsreel twice a week. The government fully understood this, equally in respect of newspapers and of newsreels. They never approached, as a rule, *editors*. Any such approach would have been regarded as improper and counter-productive. They always dealt with the *proprietor*, whether it was Lord Camrose or Isidore Ostrer, or where there was a more corporate structure, with the general manager or, in the case of the BBC, the Director General. It was up to the proprietor/management to sort out their own organization and to put into effect whatever had been agreed at the top. Hence the growing distrust of Reith, who in his own confidential dealings with the government always said the right things, and often in an amazingly obsequious manner too, but whose organization seems to have collected the wrong sort of people.

How then was 'educating the public', psychological rearmament, carried out through the mass medium of the newsreel? To understand what the newsreels actually did we need to understand the medium. We should remember, first, that it was a news medium, not a medium of argument, of editorials or 'think pieces', and therefore it communicated through 'news-pegs' – immediate news events. Its prime technique thus was that of the news editor, communicating through the selection, headlining and juxtaposition of (apparently) hard news. Second, it was a 'popular' not a 'quality' medium and therefore it was expected by its 'popular' audience to explain as well as present 'the news'. Like the popular press, of the Northcliffe tradition, it believed in integrating news and views and was thus as much abominated by those journalists who believed in the 'quality' technique of keeping facts and comment for separate pages as it felt a fraternity with those others who were, equally committedly, 'popular' journalists. The five newsreels were not completely alike. They ranged in the details of their techniques from the completely populist *Gaumont* at the one end of the spectrum to *Movietone* at the more 'quality' end. The newsreels were all, nevertheless, closest in the way they operated to Guy Bartholomew's *Daily Mirror*. Like the *Mirror*, they catered principally for the *educationally* 'working-class' section of the people who were happy with the same simple and dramatized treatment of news and the same direct, propagandist, presentation of views as they found in the *Mirror*. Part of that technique perfected by the *Mirror* was to ruthlessly exclude the majority of simultaneously occurring 'news' from each day's edition, concentrating on a few – or even one – news items presented in the most dramatic form possible. Another *Mirror* technique was to deal with interrelated issues and arguments *sequentially*, using whatever news-peg would work the day after, rather than simultaneously, on the same day, in the same issue. In the case of film, of course, the sequential juxtaposition of items was the natural form of the medium itself. And, of course, the key to all news and persuasion media catering for the uneducated mind was to simplify issues into readily comprehensible analogies, within the knowledge and experience of its audience, and to repeat, repeat and repeat again.

The persuasion formula, for it was scarcely an 'argument' in the higher sense of that word, which the newsreels evolved for selling rearmament, was both simple and consistent. It 'argued' that we were rearming because of what was going on in *Germany* since the 'Nazis' took over. That 'Nazi' Germany – never mind what the 'Nazi Party' or its philosophy might mean – was simply the old Germany reborn, and under new management. It was the same old militarist, mass-armed, aggressive Germany of the Kaiser which the audience knew only too well from the pre-war pictures of parades, from the propaganda during the war and, many of them, from experience. Here, before your very eyes, are the same old strutting, aggressive Germans up to their old tricks again; going about international treaties, the rights of their neighbours and the interest of peace in the same old ways as in the days of the Kaiser. Which, common sense tells *us* – never mind the intellectuals, too clever by half – will lead to the same end, another 'Kaiser's war'. If the Germans insist on going on the same old way, they will have to be stopped again the same old way, dreadful as that was. If we don't want to have to face them again as badly prepared as we were in 1914, we have to rearm *now*. And, if we are armed now, that might, just might, bring them to their senses before it is too late, and we *might* avoid war altogether. Furthermore, 'we' again means the old alliance of the British, the French and the Americans, the world's democracies against the militarist Germans. Proof that our government is not imagining things or acting by ulterior motives is provided by the 'fact' before our eyes that the other *democracies* are rearming too. (That they were not in fact doing so, at least in the case of America, could be dealt with by leaving it to the magic of 'the camera which cannot lie' rather than saying it in words to which objection could be raised. As far as the newsreel public was concerned, the audiences *saw* the United States rearming, like Britain, which both helped the 'argument' and gave reassurance.) This persuasion formula was simple enough to strike intellectuals at the time as a fantastic, even mischievous, oversimplification, but when presented through the medium of film, it was persuasive for ordinary people, for it was couched in their mode of thinking.

The formula never varied – like all sound propaganda it strove for the repetition of the same simple points. A good example, typical rather than outstanding, comes from the first period of major effort at 'educating the public' at the time of the 1935 White Paper. This particular example comes from *Movietone*.

On Monday, 8 March 1935, that is timed exactly right to coincide with the publication of the Defence White Paper, which thus also provided the necessary news-peg, came the first part of the campaign, a lead story titled *Is There To Be An Armaments Race?*[59]

Words	*Pictures*
At the new home of the League of Nations in Geneva, the chief news is of nations arming. It is announced that Britain will spend more on armaments.	Palace of Geneva
Why? Because the whole world is arming. Japan demands parity on the sea with Britain and the United States.	Japanese battleships, etc.
She wishes to supplement her great military strength by greater sea power.	
Germany is building aeroplanes, commercial craft, but perhaps convertible. Her right to rearm is being tacitly recognized.	Flight of heavy aircraft in military V formation
With mighty masses of manpower Soviet Russia parades a Red Army, second to none in her history.	Infantry in massed formation on Red Square, etc.
Aeroplanes for Italy, thousands of them lined up in spectacular array. Mussolini has sponsored an air force which challenges comparison with the finest in the world.	Massed ranks of military aircraft as far as the eye can see. Further shots of the same image

Words	Pictures
France maintains her military strength. Trains artillery, mechanizes her powerful army. France demands security and will not disarm.	The familiar, 75 mm, French guns firing; French infantry with machine guns Close up of French tanks advancing
And Britain, long content with dominance on the sea, contemplates bigger estimates for all three services.	*Wipe to* British battleships in line, guns firing
To the army, still the small professional body of tradition, successor to the 'Old Contemptibles', to the Royal Air Force becoming more and more important to Imperial defence, and to the navy also an increase. These are the measures which however reluctant the government in their quandary propose.	British infantry in battledress marching Single line of British Hawker Fury bi-planes (fighters)
Already the United States has faced the same problem but has taken the course which seems now to lie before Britain, an increase in armaments to preserve some defensive ratio with the offensive power of other nations.	American aircraft-carrier's huge deck covered in aircraft followed by a mass flight of American aircraft Picture sequence ends with shots of US aircraft-carrier silhouetted against the sunlight

Two weeks later, over shots of goosestepping, steel-helmeted Germans, came the superimposed title of the next story: *Germany Asserts Right To Rearm.*[60]

Words	Pictures
This is Germany's official day of mourning for her war dead.	
In the Berlin State Opera General Von Blomberg delivers the speech of commemoration. Then the banners are dipped while the song known as the 'Air of the Good Comrade' is played.	Ceremony inside the building
There follows *Deutschland über Alles* sung by the massed assembly with General Goering, Marshal Mackensen and Adolf Hitler in the box of honour.	
The old National Anthem has the old significance today, for Hitler has just proclaimed to the world Germany's intentions openly to rearm.	
The *Reichswehr*, the National Army, now to be extended to half a million men, parades in the Berlin Lustgarten.	*Long shot* of large square filled with troops in field grey uniform drawn up in squares

Words	*Pictures*
Crosses of honour are attached by the Führer to regimental banners of the old Imperial Army. Then Hitler, Mackensen and Goering and Blomberg proceed to the monument of fallen heroes to place the nation's wreaths.	*Medium shot* of Hitler going from regiment to regiment *Exterior shots* of Memorial building; *close up* on Memorial
As the present rulers of Germany emerge from the monument the ex-Crown Prince Willhelm steps forward and salutes the successor of the Hohenzollern.	Crown Prince, wearing pre-war helmet and uniform, salutes; Hitler shakes him by the hand; then Crown Prince raises arm in Hitler salute and steps back into crowd.
The army back to its old pride, goosesteps past its leader who was once a corporal in its ranks.	Regimental flags marching by carried by steel-helmeted troops
Germany proclaims her intention to re-arm, to conscript men into her armed forces. The world may well watch and mark this formidable demonstration of German armed discipline and hope that Germany's aims are as pacific as her leader's utterances declare them to be.	*Cut to* steel-helmeted infantry wearing field uniform marching past in wide ranks *Cross cuts* between Hitler surrounded by generals and steel-helmeted troops marching past

In the next issue came the lead story *British Ministers Leave For Berlin On Peace Mission*[61] which was followed in the next issue by the lead story titled *Berlin People Are Given Realistic Taste Of Air Raid.*[62] For this latter, used partly as a demonstration that British air strength was already putting some wind up the Germans, the newsreels again used German footage covering a theatrically staged ARP exercise in Berlin, complete with black-out, smoke bombs, German civilians scurrying into air raid shelters and so forth. The main message was that 'they' were prepared already for the kind of war which the next one might be. The campaign ran on at regular intervals repeating the same points, for the rest of the year.[63]

The consistent argument that 'the Germans have not changed' despite defeat and a decade of pretence while weak, took many forms. A good example of the analogy technique occurred in the period following the 1936 White Paper. A perfect occasion for it was Hitler's occupation of the Rhineland. This example comes from *Pathe* and involves an intelligent and skilful deployment of those evocative phrases through which the propagandists in the First World War encapsulated for Britain 'the beastly Hun'. Endlessly repeated, elaborated in pictures and posters, phrases such as 'contemptible little army', 'a scrap of paper' and the rest were lodged in the memory of all those who had lived through the war, or who went to school after it. The title of the item was *SCRAPS OF PAPER – German Troops Enter Rhineland.*[64]

Words	Pictures
European statesmen have been staggered by dictator Adolf Hitler's latest move in denouncing the treaties of Versailles and Locarno and turning those safeguards of European peace into nothing more than 'scraps of paper'.	*Close up* of Hitler, in uniform, speaking with arm raised *Mix to* crowd of soldiers and civilians shouting rapturous '*Heil*'
At Versailles it was laid down and at Locarno it was confirmed that Germany was forbidden to take any armed forces into the Rhineland zone and for eighteen years the fortresses of Frankfurt, Koblenz and the other garrison cities on the Rhine have been empty. But gradually under dictator Hitler Germany has been asserting her independence of treaty obligations.	*Cut to close up* of a German bishop and a German cardinal wearing Iron Crosses, shouting '*Heil*' in front of a crowd of SA men [!] *Cut to* two German generals doing same *Quick cuts* of different types of army units marching amongst welcoming crowds Massed tanks in battle formation dashing full speed ahead; close support aircraft; artillery in action
First, she left the League of Nations, then she set about rebuilding her army, navy and air force until today, when her forces play at war and mimic battle and Germany is seen again to be one of the great armed powers of Europe.	*Quick-cut montage* of scenes of mechanized war *Cut to*: Formations of heavy bombers flying straight at the audience

It should be noted that not one of the shots came actually from the footage of the entry of German troops into the Rhineland. It was all 'faked from the library'. The pictures were carefully chosen from previous films of various events. It was indeed a hard-bitten, some might say unscrupulous, use of pictures, each of which hit a chord below the conscious perception of the viewer, designed to punch in the points made verbally. The overall point, which made openly would not have worked, at least in 1936, and would have caused a furore, that the *Germans* were faithless and brutal *people*, always ready to trample underfoot solemnly agreed treaties and defenceless people alike, was brilliantly driven home by synchronizing it with a shock picture. This was the sight of two German clerics in episcopal dress and wearing Iron Crosses apparently 'Heiling Hitler' as he announced that he had just torn up the treaty. (The actual shots of the bishop and the cardinal came from the coverage of a harvest festival![65])

This formula, analogy–argument, was sometimes used in the hard-hitting, shockwave technique as in the previous example. Sometimes it was done in an elegiac and subtle manner, but the argument was consistently the same. A typical example of the soft, elegiac variation of the theme was the following story, again by *Pathe*, which was pushed at the public three days after the memorial services which were held nationwide on the twentieth anniversary of the Battle of Jutland. Uncommonly for *Pathe* the words and the pictures were set over a continuous music track.

Germany's Fleet Puts To Sea.[66]

Words	Pictures
Adolf Hitler remembers the anniversary of Jutland too and makes it the occasion for the first review of the new German fleet. With the dictator aboard the cruiser the fleet steams out of Kiel harbour on a windy overcast day, the fleet that is being built up in the traditions of the old. And the Air Arm flies overhead.	Hitler reviews naval personnel
	Pocket battleship accompanied by destroyers in line abreast
	Sea planes in formation
Each of these new cruisers, pocket battleships and submarines is named after one of the ships of the old Grand Fleet, and each bears a brass plate commemorating the battles fought by its namesake. So today twenty years after Jutland was fought the German Navy is reborn.	German ships in lined formation sailing across screen as black silhouettes
	Screen filled with ships sailing out into the horizon
	Destroyers etc. in line head formation sailing towards the camera
	Story concludes with (repeated) shots of submarines for an extended period with just the music

The music which was played throughout, first counterpointing the words and pictures, then coming up in volume as the long line of U-boats appeared and then running on for a long time after the words stopped and the message of it all was sinking in, was a poignant orchestral arrangement of one of the best-known and most evocative of the hymns of the Church of England: *For Those in Peril on the Sea.*

The propaganda technique used, stereotyping Germany today as but the country of the same old faithless, ruthless, war-mad Huns whom we knew only too well, under new management by the 'dynamic Hitler', was an excellent choice, in every way. It realized the first essential in mass persuasion: building upon the ordinary man's pre-existing knowledge and his mosaic of past feelings, rather than giving him new things to think about, such as what sort of new 'political system' Hitler might be erecting. This was doubly wise when fascism, and totalitarianism in general, were already in the political air and more airing was undesirable. It was also a happy choice for the medium of the film, because film is essentially a medium of stereotypes. The simpler the stereotypes, the better it works. Which is why the cowboy film, or the gangster film, is such a natural genre of the cinema. So is, of course, the costume drama built on people's pre-existing historical stereotypes, such as (amongst the English-speaking peoples) the Protestant sea-dogs *versus* the Catholic Spaniards; Queen Elizabeth and freedom *versus* Philip of Spain and the Inquisition. The stereotype of the militarist German/Hun also happily allowed newsreels to make full use of that vast quantity of film material which Dr Goebbels provided, readily and cheaply, of Nazi rallies and marches. Within this formula, those beautifully shot sequences of masses of uniformed *Germans* (never mind *what* uniforms they were wearing), happily standing in broad squares or stiffly goosestepping, could simply be

used for reiterating over and over again that the Germans were back to their
favourite national activity; were on the march again.

Stereotype propaganda for making people think of 'the Germans' as
inherently war-loving, and hell-bent on war as long as they see a chance of
winning, and of the present German regime as nothing more and nothing less
than yet another war government, which respects nothing but the force of
arms, was only one way in which the newsreels campaigned on behalf of the
government's need to change public perceptions. Campaigns were also run
from time to time in support of specific policy aims of the moment: recruiting
for various branches of the regular forces and the territorials, or the Air Raid
Precautions organizations, for example. The newsreels also played a central
part in the essential task, as the Cabinet saw it, of maintaining the credibility
of the government, presenting it, and its leading members in particular, as
men who shared the feelings of the people about war and shared their
aspirations and concerns, as against the accusations of their left-wing
opponents of its being a cabinet of hard-hearted, capitalist warmongers. The
'Chamberlain – the man of peace' projection was particularly well done,
partly because Chamberlain stinted no effort in working along with the film
people and his film advisers, such as Alexander Korda. It started with a
string of items 'showing' how caring of the needs 'of the family man in this
cinema audience' he was, how homely and simple in their tastes he and his
wife were, which prepared the ground for the central line in 1938: 'Our great
statesman, the man who brought to politics the common-sense point of view
of the man in the street . . . on whose sane judgement we place our hopes
and happiness'.[67] It was gradually turned into the post-Munich line, 'we
know that no man could have done more to save the peace', and finally into
the line of September 1939: 'In this hour, when Europe reverted to the laws
of the jungle . . . in the simple, moving words of our Prime Minister, WE
ARE READY.' All of this was of great importance in the 'education' of the
public to trust the government's motives and its judgement as to whether
rearmament, and what degree and kind of rearmament, had become an
unavoidable necessity, for the safety of *all*.

Perhaps the most striking of these supplementary campaigns for specific
issues was that run for beating down the opposition of organized labour to
industrial mobilization, after the Cabinet's review of the position preparatory
to the 1937 White Paper identified that as one of the major obstacles of the
moment. This campaign produced, amongst others, one of the most brutally
effective pieces of screen propaganda of the inter-war years, from either side
of the channel: E. V. Emmett's *Britain's Rearmament Plan* of February
1937.[68] He first trapped the audience into a shocked state by running some
particularly dreadful 'atrocity footage' from the Spanish Civil War without
the usual end-of-item emotional release for such stuff. Then he used the
discordant music-break trick to plunge the audience straight from it into a
montage of rearmament/factory footage, so fast-cut and with so much
movement that the mind literally reels under the impact of trying to
assimilate so many different images in such a short time. Over it he ran a

soundtrack composed of unfinished sentences, like blank verse, hammering in an association between the words 'rearmament' and 'work' (employment). The running refrain of 'every aeroplane' (or tank or ship, or training establishment or storage depot, etc.) 'means more work; more wages; for more men' on the soundtrack was rammed in by the use of some really dubious cinematic devices, some of which in later times came to be banned in screen advertising as psychologically damaging. One such was cutting in at the refrain point a close-up shot of a steam-hammer striking towards the audience, over which for just a couple of seconds was superimposed in *huge* white letters *MEN WANTED*. The combined impact of the steam-hammer rushing at the viewer as if he were right under it and the sudden blinding of his eyes by large white areas on the screen is really overwhelming. This was classic, brainwashing, 'forced association' technique; for a generation for whom the sign 'Men Wanted' became the symbol of hope, cruelly effective too.

The main thrust, however, the essential core of making people accept rearmament, was the stereotyping of Germans. In the last resort, as the government well knew, it all hinged on whether the British people could be moved from their belief that no people with the experience of the trenches in their memory would ever again be willing to launch another war. Nothing could basically be done until people could be brought to 'think it possible', in Cromwell's phrase, that other human beings in another nation would be willing to do what for them, Englishmen and women, was unthinkable; until they could be so far alienated from the people of Germany as to regard them as fundamentally different from themselves and so come to believe that these creatures, 'the Germans' (or Nazis or Huns), differed so much from themselves that they were really and actually preparing to launch yet another holocaust, for the sake of the (for Englishmen, insane) ambition to dominate the world. It would have been politically and diplomatically impossible for the government, or anyone who could possibly be taken as speaking for the government, such as senior members of the Conservative Party not in office, to present that brutally simple and persuasively commonsensical argument about 'Once a Hun – Always a Hun'. For one thing, Chamberlain, at any rate, could not himself bear to hear it from Vansittart's Foreign Office and insisted that British policy must operate on the hope that it *might* not be true, while preparing for the possibility that it was.[69] The policy of 'appeasing' the Germans (the meaning of which in his mind would be better spelt 'a-peacing') depended on telling the Germans, by words above all but also by deeds, that Britain did *not* regard them as a warrior-people outside the human race. On the contrary, Britain would be willing to forgive and forget the First World War, disown its own propaganda about the 'beastly Hun' during that war and treat them with all the trust and consideration of their own legitimate ambitions and grievances that it would extend to any other fellow nation. For persuading the British people to rearm, to accept 'the whole dreadful paraphernalia of war' in Lansbury's widely quoted phrase, however, *they* needed to be told that the government much suspected that the

Germans *were* likely to prove to be Huns after all. So, at the same time as the government was trying to pacify the Germans by taking their own claims at face value, the British people needed to be convinced that the Germans' claim that they were rearming only because they did not trust the French or other of their neighbours with armies, and for the sake of national pride, might well turn out to have been a deliberate lie, and that they would in fact launch a war the moment their own rearmament programme was ready.

How were these two propaganda processes to be carried out at the same time, in a world where news already travelled instantly, and in a free country where there was nothing to prevent German correspondents or anyone else from popping up and demanding to know just what the government *really* thought of the Germans? In the course of that long, two-day, confidential discussion which Baldwin held with the 'Defence Deputation', made up, as we have seen, by the senior members of the political establishment, he put this dilemma with his usual clarity. In his reply to demands voiced in particular by Sir Edward Grigg, Sir Henry Page Croft and Lord Winterton, that the government must come out openly and 'warn the people that unless they were prepared to defend this country they would lose it', Baldwin agreed about the necessity of 'telling the people truth about Germany'. The question was how it could be done: it 'was not easy when you get on a platform to tell people what the dangers are'. He could see the general line clearly enough. 'I think the one line whereby you can get people to sit up in this country is if they think the dictators are going to attack them.' But he could not think of a way of putting it. Hitler might turn east first, for example. In the circumstances, he challenged them, would *they* be prepared to get on a platform and say 'Germany is arming to fight us'?[70]

To conclude. The evidence leaves little doubt that the Cabinet's reiteration to the Chiefs of Staff that no matter how valid their demands might have been on military grounds, the state of public opinion must be the determining factor, was an expression of genuinely held beliefs. The possible exception is Chamberlain. The evidence also leaves little doubt that the Cabinet genuinely believed that the temper of public opinion 'in the country' (the old definition of 'public opinion' in British politics) and in particular amongst the industrial working classes (for the first time perceived as the potentially decisive political class) was such that the utmost care had to be taken. Their perception of public opinion was indeed a major determinant in making their policy decisions, as Professor Howard suggested, and was not an excuse, as others have surmised. It is also clear that the idea that a little prompting to the press, as in the pre-war and pre-Northcliffe days, was all that would have been needed was no longer a practical proposition in the 1930s. It was a different political world brought into being by the Great War, both in electoral terms within the constitutional framework and in the greater likelihood of unconstitutional or even violent reactions occurring. And, as yet, effective and reliable means for monitoring the state of opinion, either in the mass electorate or specifically amongst the working classes, had not been developed to match the new needs created by the vast expansion of the 'political nation'. The Cabinet had to operate in a fog of guesswork, and that was an additional reason for being careful not to get it wrong. It was also a different world in terms of the media. New technologies, new types of organization and new ways of perceiving what appeared to be happening elsewhere have all come into being. There has indeed been, as Asa Briggs argued, a 'revolution in communications'.[71]

Taken together, the political and the media changes led to a new relationship between the government and the media in which the old and simple ways of press-prompting and speechifying to the (small) electorate were things of the past; especially in the case of an issue of such universal concern and with so much emotion involved as preparations for war was for the generation of the 1930s.

The evidence also supports the view that the Cabinet members not only believed genuinely that the extent, form and stages of rearmament must wait upon 'the education of the public' but that they did embark on it. They did use what was available to them in the new political/media conditions for persuading the public that rearmament had become unavoidable. There was an effective campaign to get people into the frame of mind which legitimated the government's preparing for the unthinkable. The need to carry out a campaign of 'educating the public' and the need to wait on at least some shift of opinion before embarking on a major rebuilding of the forces was a view which was not only shared by the leading figures of the Cabinet but also by the service ministers, and was at least not questioned by the Chiefs of Staff themselves. When in April 1934 the three service ministers put in a joint, three-point demand to the Cabinet to face up to the issues, they

> asked for three decisions after all the postponements . . . (1) a decision in principle that our armaments must be rendered efficient; (2) a decision that the education of the public as to the urgency of making good our worst deficiencies must be taken in hand; (3) a decision enabling the departments concerned to work out in detail the measures required to render the forces fit to fulfil their respective responsibilities.[72]

There is nothing in the evidence to suggest that little was done to carry out the second promise which the agreement of the Cabinet to these demands of the services entailed. By its very nature, propaganda is underhand. Its success depends on getting people to think in ways they have not thought before, and the first requirement of success is that they should not be aware that they are being 'influenced'. At least, there must be no evidence available of its going on. It is inevitable therefore that there should be little direct evidence (though as we have seen there is some) of the government's getting at the media, including those with the maximum propaganda potential, the audio/visual media of radio and film, and especially news-broadcasting and the newsreels, the media for presenting 'news and views' in a non-written form. The real evidence, however, on which to judge the efforts of the government is the fact that there was a continuous barrage of effective, at times brutally and cynically effective, deployment of the power of the cinema, and especially of the newsreel, the only real 'mass medium' at the time. Its great powers of propaganda, especially over the less-educated and younger working-class majority of the people, *were* employed, from 1935 right to the outbreak of war. Most of the newsreels pushed with every means in their armoury, some close to the limit, to engender in the hearts and minds of their audience the attitudes needed: there *was* 'psychological rearmament'.[73] They worked both on the general level, cultivating in people's minds a reason why they had to think of rearming at all (the Hun is on the march again), and in support of the specific, public-opinion-based, constraints of the moment, such as for overcoming the effects on industrial workers of the opposition of the leadership of the trade union movement to industrial mobilization, and to 'great armaments' in general.

Although other media, even the wording of notices in 'employment' exchanges, were given careful attention by the government when they lay within its power to use them, the newsreels' role was central. Partly because it was the only true mass medium, partly because it was the only medium (for a variety of reasons as we have seen) over which the government could exercise effective control, by having both stick and carrot, and on which it could also exert real influence from the top, but chiefly because it alone could solve the government's central problem about having to alarm the public at home into rearming on account of suspected German intentions, while at the same time trying to appease the Germans by appearing to trust them. This indeed was the nub of the matter. People could only be brought to accept the sacrifices involved in rearmament, of hopes and beliefs as much as material cost, if they believed that the Germans were truly preparing for war. On the other hand, if the government came out with that, in modern circumstances, that would foreclose any hope of lowering the temperature, Baldwin's particular art in politics, between the two countries and of talking Germany out of resorting to war. It was here that the existence of a powerful, persuasive and populist medium, a pluralist medium, which in no constitutional or customary way was 'the voice of Britain', could render a uniquely significant service. The mere fact that the newsreels were privately owned and were notably brash and vulgar was a key element; the government could completely and credibly dissociate itself from whatever they said. No government spokesman, elder statesman, semi-official or even 'informed' organ could come out and say, in 1935, 'It looks as if the Germans have found a new Kaiser and are on the march again.' The newsreels could because the government cannot be held responsible for what is being put out by ignorant film-men in a medium which, it could be claimed, should the matter be raised, no one could be expected to take seriously – except the millions of working-class boys and girls, and not a few of their equally ill-educated elders. For the same kind of reasons, the newsreels were also free to press on their audience whatever was thought to be in the national interest, without any regard to the *actual* facts of the moment.

For example, in the spring of 1939, when the propaganda job became to reassure the public that 'we have not left it too late and can face the might of

Germany with confidence', the newsreels alone were free to cheerfully tell the millions in the cinemas that not only was Britain fully prepared, but was also once again backed by the whole force of the same victorious alliance as in 1918 – 'with the common ideal of peace and liberty, the world's democracies are standing shoulder to shoulder against the forces of tyranny and oppression' being *Gaumont*'s version. This 'point' was made after running some extracts from a speech by Roosevelt talking about 'Huns and Vandals' (!) and after showing him again several times looking grim and determined, and over a montage of cross-cut pictures of Nelson's Column wreathed in a poster, 'England Expects that You Will Join Today', and an (old) shot of the Statue of Liberty against the background of New York Harbor, with an armada of ships in it ready to sail. 'Standing shoulder to shoulder' was about as far from the *actual facts* of Anglo-American relations on 20 April 1939 as any of Goebbels' 'big lies'.[74]

There is, of course, no question of the editors of the newsreels being simply ignorant of the diplomatic facts of the time. Not only did their living depend on their being very well informed – how else could they get their camera teams to the spots where something was *going* to happen? – not only were they subscribers to Reuters so that they possessed the same information at any moment as the newspapers, but in 1934 they were asked, and they agreed, that they should consult the Foreign Office before making any statements relating to foreign policy. The News Department of the Foreign Office had a film/newsreel specialist, Roland Kenney, who acted as the FO man towards the newsreel companies, and was available for consultation, via a special telephone number, at any time, day or night.[75] Neville Kearney, formerly of the FO News Department, and who became the head of the Film Department of the British Council in the war, was appointed secretary of the Newsreel Association itself in 1937.[76] There was no lack of contact with the Foreign Office, nor was there ignorance. On the contrary, what we have here is an effective realization of Ludendorff's much-quoted dictum: 'Good propaganda must keep well ahead of actual political events. It must act as the pacemaker to policy, and prepare the public.'

The newsreels could do that because they were not an official agency and because they worked through the emotions. In this mode of operation the actual facts of the moment were less important than the effect on policies in the future which their propaganda might have. That was how they were seen too by the officials whose particular job was to secure, on a day-to-day basis, their services. As Roland Kenney explained to the Vansittart Committee for the Co-ordination of British Publicity Abroad (which led to a subsidy to *Gaumont British News* in the summer of 1938 for distributing suitable British items abroad): 'The newsreel may arouse passions and enthusiasms about contemporary events and thus act immediately – if we may indulge in the jargon of psychology – on the instinctive parts of the mind.'[77]

In peacetime as in war there is a difference between 'white' propaganda ('publicity' in peace) and 'black' propaganda: the first is what is put out by an *accredited* agency of the government and which therefore has to be the 'truth' of the moment, and the second is what must not be traceable back to the government but which equally serves its needs. As in war, there is need for both, if government by consensus rather than coercion is to work. For a free society propaganda is essential. In a tyranny, it is an optional extra. Their being privately owned, their vulgar, commercialized, competitive style were the newsreels' priceless assets which allowed a determined campaign for changing attitudes and outlook towards Germany amongst the great majority to be waged, while official 'white' propaganda could get on with mollifying the Germans at the same time.

The further asset which the majority of the newsreels brought to the vital task of 'educating the public' was that the newsreels had learned how to communicate to those who lacked education. The uneducated had other qualities: numbers, the capacity for physical work and physical violence. For those qualities competed on the one side the armed services, the armaments industries and the National government; and on the other side, all those who hoped to use those same qualities to oppose all that they, together, stood for. It was a competition to win those in society who had the reality of ultimate power, who alone could, if so minded, rule out rearmament or do even worse. It was of vital importance that for their hearts and minds – in that order – the newsreels had campaigned on behalf of the government.

'Propaganda and publicity' is a specialized business. In the wake of the rapid development of both during the First World War, it came to be generally realized that they were best left to professionals. Advertising agencies grew into importance, political parties gradually came to rely on professionals, and by the 1930s the 'publicity officer' (also called the 'information officer' or, as in the Labour Party in the 1920s, 'the propagandist') became an accepted addition to the payroll of government departments, political parties and big business corporations. In the field of propaganda, as distinct from 'publicity', this job was particularly important and carried great responsibility. Its holders needed to know what were the *intended* policies for which the public must be got ready and they had to get the media to do that preparation without letting the cat out of the bag. This was what General Ludendorff called the propaganda function of being 'the pacemaker to policy'. In the sphere of foreign policy this was the job of the news Department (originally designated the 'Propaganda Department') of the Foreign Office. It was through the News Department that newsreel companies received their 'hints' as to what they should say in the national interest (and very firmly what they should *not* say) and it was one of its officials who would visit the BBFC to view a film about which the BBFC needed 'guidance' if its message touched upon matters of British foreign policy. In practical terms it was the News Department which was HMG as far as day-to-day media contact was concerned. It was therefore of considerable importance that the Head of the News Department, Rex Leeper, was an admirer and follower of Vansittart, holding the same pessimistic view about the chances of a peaceful settlement with the Germans and the same urgent view about 'psychological rearmament'.[78] On the rare occasions that members of the Cabinet strayed into a cinema, they were at times worried by the 'alarmist' tone of the newsreels, just as on occasions they were suspicious that News Department 'confidential briefings' to the press were not what they thought they ought to have been. Eventually, Leeper was removed for his handling of the Munich settlement. He became on the outbreak of war Director for Subversive Propaganda (SOE 1). When we talk about the success of the government in enlisting the newsreels' invaluable propaganda powers for rearmament, it is important therefore to bear in mind that we are considering the work of 'the government' as a whole, including its professional officers, rather than specifically ascribing it to the credit of the Cabinet. To use the media was Cabinet policy – precisely how was their experts' job.

It is also important to realize, though perhaps it should not need to be said, that pushing rearmament in the way they did does not mean that it was the newsreel companies' 'policy' to be anti-appeasement, or that they saw rearmament as an alternative 'policy', and least of all that they suffered from or wanted to whip up xenophobia. First, they fully realized that appeasement and rearmament were two parts of the government's overall policy. The alternative policy was 'collective security' and 'no great armaments'. Second, like the government, like most British people, they prayed and hoped that appeasement would succeed and that the material and psychological armaments would not be needed. They were not concerned with 'policy' at all in this matter. It was a matter of national interest, which they accepted was the government's and Parliament's job to define, where to push their own policy ideas would have been 'irresponsible'. In discussing with surviving members of other newsreels *Paramount*'s tendency to step out of line, that was the word which most often cropped up. The newsreel companies acted as patriotic professionals conscious of the power of the medium in their hands and of the duty of responsibility which went with it, just as media men in this country generally did and do act. They also knew the truth of Goebbels' well-known dictum: 'Propaganda does not have a "policy". Propaganda has a "purpose".' The general purpose, as far as their part was concerned, was clear enough and so were the subsidiary purposes which from time to time reached them through 'the proper authorities', whether it be the Comissioner of the Metropolitan Police in domestic or the News Department in matters of foreign policy. They were, in other words, neither hacks nor warmongers in pushing remorselessly the line that 'the Huns are still the Huns' and 'unless Mr Chamberlain can pull off a miracle, we need to be ready to fight them again, and soon'. As responsible patriots they put their expertise to the service of the national interest represented to them by the appropriate officials of the properly elected government, and as good professionals they knew that this was the line most capable of being effectively pushed by their powerful audio-visual and populist medium.

How important that was may perhaps best be illustrated by contrast. The one newsreel company which was the least amenable to being brought into line, perhaps because it was wholly American-owned, was *Paramount*.

Although it could be, and on several occasions was, forcibly prevented from actually going against government policy, such as at the time of Munich, it did not play its part with a will in rearmament propaganda. It was also apt from time to time to 'slip up' and then apologize. Take this example, from the very important moment when Hitler reintroduced conscription. Whereas *Movietone* presented it as 'the successor of Hohenzollern' reviewing the new German army 'back to its old pride' and as the occasion when *Deutschland über Alles* regained its 'old significance', as we have seen, *Paramount* presented it under the title *No Need to Panic* and followed a mere repetition of the announcement from Berlin with an interview with George Bernard Shaw. Shaw's views were perfectly well-known and were therefore, of course, what he would say if asked. So, those of the young working class whose local cinema took *Paramount News* were given the following, with all the force of its coming from a venerable white-bearded sage speaking with all the experience of Shaw's 'Fabian orator' past:

> Well, you may take it from me that the news from Germany is the very best news that we have had since the war. Ever since 1918 we, like all the other powers, have been behaving just as badly as we possibly could. Well now, when Germany fell, they went and they sat on Germany's head and they kept sitting on Germany's head, although it was quite preposterous, quite evident to any sensible person, that they couldn't go on like that forever. Then there came a very intelligent gentleman named Adolf Hitler and he, knowing perfectly well that the powers would not fight, he snapped his fingers at the Treaty of Versailles. Just exactly as if we in England had been in the same position. As if the powers had beaten us and sat on our head. Then the first man who had the gumption to see that we might get up on our legs and defy all those old treaties, he would be the most popular man in England. There can be no peace in the world until there is peace between England, France, Germany, Russia, the United States and all the big powers of the West. Now take that home and think about it and don't be frightened any more about the Germans.[79]

However much closer this may have been to the government's *official* reaction to the reintroduction of conscription, considering the people at whom it was directed this was effective and powerful anti-rearmament propaganda. It was just as effective as the pro-rearmament propaganda presented at the time of the next move, the reoccupation of the Rhineland, by the *Pathe* newsreel *SCRAPS OF PAPER*, or by *Gaumont*'s 'German artillery and infantry are once again marching across the Hohenzollern Bridge into the once peaceful borderland between France and Germany' or by *Movietone*'s newsreel *Germany Resumes 'The Watch on the Rhine'*, with the music to match. We might well contemplate what might have happened if at every turn the government had been up against this sort of propaganda in the medium which reached the working classes. The issue turned on who would win the battle for the hearts and minds. That the government succeeded in getting the support of the newsreels, by whatever means, and that they were willing to put their backs into the job of 'educating' the public to accept the need for preparing for a war, known to be even more horrible than the last, thanks to the bomber, was one of the important and perhaps underestimated achievements of the governments of the 1930s, the 'Devil's Decade'.

The issues brought out by the story of 'public opinion' and of its 'education' for rearmament should be seen in a longer-term perspective too. The need for mounting a campaign to affect basic attitudes of mind in the population as a whole during the 1935–9 period, was followed immediately by the even greater needs of wartime 'morale' and then the needs of social reconstruction in a period of extreme economic difficulties, intermingled with the needs of the cold (i.e. propaganda) war. For more than fifteen years there was no break in the 'education' of the British people via their principal means of relaxation, the 'mass media'. This greatly extended and accelerated that central process in the evolution of Britain in our century which was identified by Keith Middlemas:

> Over and above the relationships between party, industrial institutions and the mass electorate created by universal suffrage, British central government established, during and after the First World War, a direct link with public opinion whose consequences were ultimately as significant as the expansion of suffrage itself.[80]

Notes

1 Michael Howard, *The Continental Commitment*, London, 1972.
2 Economic considerations: G. C. Peden, *The Treasury and British Rearmament, 1932–1939*, Edinburgh, 1979, and R. P. Shay, *British Rearmament in the Thirties: Politics and Profits*, Princeton, 1977. Strategic bombing: B. D. Powers, *Strategy Without Slide Rule*, London, 1976, and H. Montgomery Hyde, *British Air Policy Between the Wars*, London, 1976. Fear of bombing: Uri Bialer, *The Shadow of the Bomber: the Fear of Air Attack and British Politics*, London, 1980. Imperial considerations: N. H. Gibbs, *Grand Strategy* (vol. 1) and S. W. Roskill, *Naval Policy between the Wars* (vol. 2), London, 1976. The army: Brian Bond, *British Military Policy between the Two World Wars*, Oxford, 1980, and P. Dennis, *Decision by Default: Peacetime Conscription and British Defence, 1919–1939*, London, 1972. See also M. Smith, *British Air Strategy Between the Wars*, London, 1982.
3 Defence Requirements Committee Report, PRO CAB 16/109.
4 Professor Howard used the words 'timid' and 'pathetic' to describe the proposals made by the army chiefs (op. cit., pp. 105–6).
5 Brian Bond points out that not only was the decision to press for an expeditionary force unanimous amongst the three service chiefs, but that they proposed that *half* of the total sum asked should be allocated to the army. The Air Chief, Ellington, was himself a strong supporter of an expeditionary force. Bond, op. cit., pp. 198–9.
6 Howard, op. cit., p. 110.
7 Howard, op. cit., p. 111.
8 ibid.
9 Howard, op. cit., p. 109.
10 ibid.
11 Cabinet Minutes, CAB 28(34), 11 July 1934.

12 Keith Middlemas and John Barnes, *Baldwin*, London, 1969, p. 753.

13 Bond, op. cit., p. 207.

14 For a résumé of Baldwin's speeches during the election campaign see Middlemas, op. cit., pp. 865–9. The text of Baldwin's final electoral appeal given through the newsreels, which was both the most concise expression of the government's appeal to the electorate and the one which reached the largest number of people, is seldom cited although it deserves to be better known – as are the circumstances which surrounded its making. For archive film compilation and accompanying literature, see John Ramsden, 'Stanley Baldwin', Inter-British University History Film Consortium, Leeds, 1979, pp. 16–17. See also T. Stannage, *Baldwin Thwarts the Opposition. The British General Elections 1935*, London, 1980.

15 Howard, op. cit., p. 155.

16 Defence Policy and Requirements (Ministerial) Committee, DPR (RR) Minutes, 7th Meeting, 27 January 1936.

17 CAB 53/29 COS 537, Appendix A.

18 CAB 53/29 COS 537, Appendix D.

19 It should be noted that although the Chiefs of Staff had been unanimous in rejecting the idea that a strategic bomber air force could possible provide for British wartime needs, there was a growing minority of senior air officers who were shifting in that direction: see Bialer, op cit., pp. 140–3.

20 R. Macleod and D. Kelly, *The Ironside Diaries, 1937–1940*, London, 1962, p. 79.

21 Bond, op. cit., p. 127.

22 Keith Feiling, *The Life of Neville Chamberlain*, London, 1946, p. 135.

23 Gibbs, op. cit., p. 810.

24 Quoted in David Dilks, *Neville Chamberlain*, vol. 1, London, 1984, p. 421. 'General scepticism formed no part of Chamberlain's mental habits, still less did cynicism'; Dilks, op. cit., p. 410.

25 Cabinet Papers, PREM1/193 Parliamentary Deputation, Transcript, 1935. See Martin Gilbert, *Winston S. Churchill*, vol. 5, London, 1976.

26 Baldwin saw the conflict with Germany, even when war was certain in August 1939, in ideological terms, and equated the menace of 'the ideas of Bolshevism and those propagated by the Nazis and the fascists' fearing that they were like 'dynamite' for blowing 'systems which appear founded on rocks into fragments'. Quoted in N. Pronay, 'The first reality: film censorship in Liberal England', in K. B. M. Short (ed.), *Feature Films as History*, London, 1981, p. 126.

27 PREM1/193, op. cit., cited in Gilbert, op. cit.

28 The term was coined by Michael Foot, Peter Howard and Frank Owen, in their *Guilty Men*, London, 1940.

29 Quoted in Gibbs, op. cit., p. 806.

30 Cabinet Minutes CAB 28(35), 8 May 1935.

31 ibid.

32 Cabinet Minutes, CAB 28(34), 11 July 1934.

33 Cabinet Minutes, CAB 29(34), 18 July 1934.

34 Cabinet Minutes, CAB 30(34), 25 July 1934.

35 Cabinet Minutes, CAB 31(35), 29 May 1935.

36 For these issues, see R. A. C. Parker, 'Economic rearmament, 1936–39: Treasury, trade unions and skilled labour', *English Historical Review*, 96, 1981, 306–43.

37 Bond, op. cit., p. 217.

38 Quoted in Gilbert, op. cit., p. 636. Rothermere's own defence of his newspapers'

policy – H. S. H. Rothermere, *My Fight to Rearm Britain*, London, 1939 –
unwittingly illustrates the points made by Churchill.

39 Cabinet Minutes, CAB 27(35), 15 May 1935.

40 Chamberlain Papers, NC8/21/8, 1 June 1938.

41 See T. J. Hollins, 'The presentation of politics: the place of party publicity,
broadcasting and film in British politics, 1918–1939', unpublished PhD dissertation,
University of Leeds, 1982. See also A. Adamthwaite, 'The British government
and the media, 1937–38', *Journal of Contemporary History*, 18, 1983, 63–72.

42 Quoted in P. M. Taylor, *The Projection of Britain*, Cambridge, 1981, p. 126.

43 Hollins, op. cit., pp. 604–5. Another illuminating instance was the Foreign
Office's request to the BBC to alter the balance and tone of its *news* output in
respect of Spain, because Franco, believing the BBC to be government-controlled,
deduced from the balance and general tenor of BBC news coverage that the
government was hostile to him. Since he was now obviously winning, the
government would not wish him to be driven further into the arms of Mussolini
and Hitler. Reith agreed to modify suitably the coverage of Spain; Hollins, op.
cit., pp. 601–2.

44 Quoted in Hollins, op. cit., p. 561.

45 Quoted in Hollins, op. cit., p. 468.

46 Chamberlain Papers NC8/21/8, partly quoted in Hollins, op. cit., p. 522.

47 Hollins, op. cit., p. 522. Dr Hollins felt that it must have been a coincidence
because the memorandum by Ball is dated 1 June, while it was on 29 May that
Reith had received the first intimation that he might be asked to move. The
memorandum is a formal recapitulation of all the party's existing arrangements
and its position concerning the media of communications, and of the state of all its
various propaganda organizations in view of a possible election the following year.
It is clear from its introduction that it is an *aide-mémoire* and a formalization of
proposals discussed before. There was close, often daily, contact between
Chamberlain and Ball as the head of the Research Department and of the National
Publicity Bureau. Ball was Chamberlain's perhaps closest personal confidant, a
regular guest at his home, to which he did not as a rule invite political associates,
and Chamberlain spent much of his weekend/fishing holidays in Ball's company,
often alone with him. For some other evidence of the highly confidential and close
co-operation between Chamberlain and Ball see also Morris Cowling, *The Impact
of Hitler*, Cambridge, 1975, p. 163, n. 140. Reith had been floating the idea for a
long time that he ought to be promoted, in effect, to some greater responsibility,
without avail. Imperial Airways was not the sort of thing he hoped for.

48 Bryan Howarth, 'The BBC, Nazi Germany and the Foreign Office, 1933–36', *The
Historical Journal of Film, Radio and Television*, March 1981, 53.

49 Hollins, op. cit., p. 539.

50 For a fuller discussion of the operation of censorship see Pronay, 'The first reality',
op. cit.

51 For Vansittart's and also Eden's views about the need for 'educating the public' see
Taylor, op. cit., pp. 185–7. The phrase 'psychological rearmament' probably
originated with Rex Leeper, head of the News Department. See also Gilbert, op.
cit., pp. 725–6.

52 For the rules of the BBFC, see Pronay, 'The first reality', op. cit., pp. 119–21.

53 For Korda's connections with the Conservative Party and feature-film propaganda
plans, see Hollins, op. cit., pp. 338–60.

54 For the operating conditions of newsreels in Britain and their curiously ambivalent

legal and political conditions see N. Pronay, 'British newsreels in the 1930s', part I, *History*, 1971 and part II, *History*, 1972, and N. Pronay 'The newsreels: the illusions of actuality', in P. Smith (ed.), *The Historian and Film*, Cambridge, 1976.

55 This story which was widely known and long remembered in newsreel circles is nicely told and documented from the Metropolitan Police files in Hollins, op. cit., pp. 647–52.

56 Quoted in Hollins, op. cit., p. 653.

57 Agreement between Sir Derwent Hall-Caine on behalf of Ramsay MacDonald and Isidore Ostrer, 21 March 1935, quoted in Hollins, op. cit., p. 677.

58 Letter to *The Times*, 30 November 1977 quoted in Hollins, op. cit., p. 670. The circumstances of this letter were that in 1977 a group of film-journalists made a BFI-sponsored film, *Before Hindsight*. It was in fact a vehicle for a number of disgruntled BBC reporters to air their views in favour of 'committed reportage' as distinct from the normal BBC approach, on such subjects as apartheid in South Africa, and Ulster. James Cameron and Jonathan Dimbleby were amongst them. But the film ostensibly 'analysed' the newsreels' treatment of Nazi Germany and it condemned them for failing to bring home to the public the bestial nature of that regime. *Before Hindsight* was, even by the 'standards' expected, given its origins, an unusually ill-informed and a-historical piece of screen-journalism which deeply offended most surviving newsreel editors, who were accused, amongst other things, of swallowing 'the truth' they knew in deference to the orders of their superiors.

59 *British Movietone News*, vol. 6, no. 300A, 8 March 1935.

60 *British Movietone News*, vol. 6, no. 302A, 21 March 1935.

61 *British Movietone News*, vol. 6, no. 303, 28 March, 1935.

62 *British Movietone News*, vol. 6, no. 303A, 28 March 1935.

63 These were followed on 25 April by *League Adopts French Censure of Germany* and a hard-hitting presentation of Hitler's forty-sixth birthday parade (vol. 6, no. 307A); 23 May, *All Europe Experiments with Anti-Gas Methods* (6/311A); 27 May, *Hitler Speaks in Reichstag* (6/312); 13 June, *German Manœuvres*, in which the same points about the purpose of it all were made again (7/314A); 24 June, *The Anglo-German Naval Agreement*, expressing very qualified hopes (7/316); 1 August, *Germany's New Air Squadrons* (7/321A). Then the same double issue treatment of recruitment first, followed by the reason for it, in September; 19 September, *Britain Stages Biggest Post-War Manœuvres* (7/328A), and 26 September, *Germany Stages Parade of Newly Equipped Army*, which began 'Truth in newsreels: we are presenting these pictures of Germany's new army in array at Nurenberg because it is important that the public should realize the extent of German rearmament' (7/329A). The same pattern of a major two-stage repetition of 'we are rearming – and now you see the reason why' was presented at roughly four-month intervals, with 'drip-on-the-stone' stories in between, during the following two years as well.

64 *Pathe Gazette*, vol. 36, no. 20, 9 March 1936.

65 The picture of the two churchmen happily smiling and raising their hands, taken at a *1933* harvest festival, was used again, at appropriate moments, later on too.

66 *Pathe Gazette*, vol. 36, no. 45, 4 June 1936. It was followed two weeks later by an excellent coverage of *Vivid Demonstration of Britain's Latest Aircraft*, 'We are building these machines for defence only' (36/50), and then by another double presentation: 23 August, *Army Exercises* – a long and very good campaign piece

about the need for mechanizing the British Army (36/68) – followed by *Nazi Congress. Wild Enthusiasm at Nurenberg* which began 'This year, they say, there will be 800,000 pairs of boots standing heel-to-heel waiting for the Führer who shouts: "My life's fight has not been in vain"' (35/75). *Pathe* had already sounded the theme in 1934: 'Just like pre-war days: Mackensen, Hindenberg and Hitler and thousands of troops, marching along the Unter den Linden' (34/16).

67 Allan Beattie, David Dilks and Nicholas Pronay, 'Neville Chamberlain', British Inter-University History Film Consortium, Archive Series 1, 1975, provides a collection of some of these items.

68 *Gaumont British News*, 328, 18 February 1937.

69 Chamberlain called Vansittart's view, that the Germans were conditioned by their historical, cultural and political experience to refight the last war so narrowly lost, 'the bleak and barren policy of the inevitability of war': speech in the House of Commons, 3 October 1938. Neville Chamberlain, *The Struggle for Peace*, London, 1939, p. 324.

70 Cabinet Papers, PREM1/193 Parliamentary Deputation, Transcript, 1935, cited by Gilbert, op. cit., pp. 770–7.

71 Asa Briggs, *The Communications Revolution*, Leeds, 1964.

72 Cabinet Minutes, CAB 23 18(34), 30 April 1934.

73 See also Anthony Aldgate, *Cinema and History: British Newsreels and the Spanish Civil War*, London, 1979, argued that there was very little rearmament propaganda in the newsreels. The argument, however, is frankly, worthless. Dr Aldgate, by looking for 'rearmament stories' in addition to Spanish Civil War coverage, came across only a particular kind of rearmament publicity – such as ARP which was naturally linked to Spanish bombing scenes. By not looking at the German coverage at all, Dr Aldgate has failed to see the 'rearmament' work of the newsreels as a whole. His remarks concerning rearmament in the newsreels were thus based on either ARP publicity stories or on a relatively few items which were overtly titled *Rearmament . . .* or *Armaments . . .* or the like. Since one does not explain *why* the country *should* be rearming in stories showing *how* it is being done, there is little point in generalizing about what the newsreels did or did not do in helping with the rearmament process from such 'rearmament' stories.

74 *Gaumont British News*, 554, 20 April 1939. It also showed a map of Europe with all the 'democratic' countries named, including Scandinavia, while talking about a 'united front'.

75 For Kenney, see Taylor, op. cit., pp. 232–5.

76 For Kearney, who was also much involved in the history of the Documentary Movement, see Paul Swann, 'The British documentary film movement, 1926–1946', unpublished PhD dissertation, University of Leeds, 1979.

77 Taylor, op. cit., p. 233.

78 'With Germany there is nothing for us to negotiate, except our surrender', Leeper wrote to his sister early in 1938. Quoted in Taylor, op. cit., p. 35. For the debate in the FO between the Vansittart school of thought and others and for the background and careers of 'Van's boys' in the News Department, see also N. Pronay, '"To stamp out the whole tradition . . . "', in N. Pronay and K. Wilson (eds), *The Political Re-Education of Germany and her Allies after World War II*, London, 1985.

79 *British Paramount News*, 8281P, 21 March 1935.

80 Keith Middlemas, *Politics in Industrial Society: The Experience of the British System since 1911*, London, 1977, p. 337.

4

Crusaders without chains: power and the press barons 1896–1951

D. G. Boyce

When, on one occasion, Kingsley Martin encountered Lord Beaverbrook in the Savoy, Beaverbrook shouted to him, 'I've got power – you've got power. I've got the power of suggestion to millions.' This provoked Martin into ruminating on the power of the press lords; and he concluded that Beaverbrook's excited cry was justified only if 'influence' were substituted for 'power'. Such power as Beaverbrook enjoyed, Martin believed, only existed when Beaverbrook sought to exercise it behind the scenes, as he did when Lloyd George supplanted Asquith as prime minister in 1916; and it depended on Beaverbrook's connections with Bonar Law, which enabled him to 'pull strings'. But he was quite wrong in thinking that newspapers could wield political power; for, try as he might, Beaverbrook could not foist empire free trade on Britain, nor could he secure the dismissal of Stanley Baldwin from the premiership.[1]

Kingsley Martin's anecdote, and his thoughts on the nature of press power, raise some of the paradoxes involved in any analysis of the power of the so-called 'press barons'. For the barons straddled a period of transition in the history of the British press and its political role, one that offered them two possible avenues of approach in their search for power. Their founding father, Lord Northcliffe, lived in an era when journalists sought to be, and frequently were, the confidants of politicians, cabinet ministers, and even prime ministers; but he also ran a financially independent, mass-circulation newspaper which (he firmly believed) gave him the 'power of suggestion to millions'. The press baron could therefore expect to be admitted to the exclusive club of the late Victorian and Edwardian political world; but he could also act as the populist representative of a 'mass constituency'. The press baron was, therefore, confronted with a dilemma: should he pull or should he push?

Northcliffe's first instinct, despite his later testimony to the contrary, was to pull: to seek to align himself with a British politician and his political cause, rather than act as a species of journalistic rogue elephant. At the turn of the century he hoped for a realignment of parties and a fusion of 'imperialist' forces;[2] but his first really ambitious bid for political power came in 1903, when he sought eagerly to attach himself to Joseph Chamberlain's great tariff reform campaign. He had always admired Chamberlain and his first reaction to Chamberlain's announcement of his new departure at Birmingham in May 1903 was favourable. But when Northcliffe began to examine the public response to Chamberlain's pronouncements, an examination based not on the facile assumption that readers automatically followed their newspaper's point of view, but on the reports of Northcliffe's own 'special agents' or 'ferrets',[3] he discovered that one-fifth of the interviewees had never heard of the scheme, and the rest were hostile. On 15 September 1903 a leader in the *Daily Mail* declared that the policy of taxing foodstuffs, which Chamberlain had admitted would result from his scheme, was doomed to failure: 'the consensus of opinion from all sides is overwhelming'.[4] Chamberlain, however, was advised on 28 September that 'the moment has arrived when if it suited you to make the smallest concession to Harmsworth, so as to save his appearance of consistency, you could put him in your pocket'.[5] But the *Daily Mail* was prepared to make what Leo Maxse called its 'climb down' without any major concession from Chamberlain, possibly because Harmsworth's approach to Lord Rosebery, urging him to lead a free trade counter-attack, was rebuffed with the withering remark that Rosebery was not prepared to accept a policy at the dictation of any newspaper.[6]

It was an unhappy introduction for Northcliffe to the complex world of active politics, a world to whose subtleties and convolutions he was not, as yet, sensitive. For politicians, although they courted the political press, liked to do so on their own terms; and it was this kind of experience that brought the sadder and wiser press lord to seek to reverse the press–politicians relationship and deal with politicians on his, and not their, terms and conditions. 'There's always a comeback', Tom Clarke reported him as saying, 'and in any case, if you subsequently received the same information from other sources, which so often happened, you would be unable to print it without risking a charge of breach of faith.' However, much as Northcliffe grew to dislike politicians, 'ignore them he could not. His dominant news instinct prevented any such folly.'[7]

The contradictions inherent in the position of the press barons are discernible in any attempt to define exactly what a press baron was in the first place. The simple fact that he owned a mass-circulation newspaper was not a sufficient or complete definition: other journalists, such as George Newnes or C. A. Pearson, had in their day owned or edited popular papers – *Tit-Bits* and *Pearson's Weekly*; and the long-running *Lloyd's Weekly News* gained a circulation of 1 million in the year that the *Daily Mail* was founded, and long before the *Mail* ever achieved that figure. But such publications do not fall into the category of press baron newspapers, but rather into what George Newnes called

another kind of journalism which has no such great ambitions. It is content to plod on year after year, giving wholesale and harmless entertainment to crowds of hardworking people, craving for a little fun and amusement. It is quite humble and unpretentious. That is my journalism.[8]

This was very different from the role of the press baron who, as Beaverbrook put it, aimed at bullying the politician into pursuing courses he would not otherwise adopt.[9] The social and economic influence of the non-political popular journalism was, of course, significant; but it was not the kind of direct and obvious consequence of newspaper ownership that the press barons believed in, when a prime minister was toppled, a government reconstructed, a general election won or lost. The most typical press barons – Northcliffe, Beaverbrook, Rothermere – were not simply men who ran popular newspapers; Lord Riddell of the *News of the World* arguably influenced the lives of many individuals, but he did not see his newspaper as an essential part of the political process of the British democracy. The press baron ran a daily, mass-circulation, nation-wide newspaper which sought to exercise power over public opinion for political purposes; his newspaper was the organ, if not of an educated democracy, then of a partially educated democracy.

The mere possession of thousands of readers did not make a press baron, any more than the possession of millions of money made a wealthy man into an entrepreneur. There had to be a desire to use these readers as, in a sense, voters, or at least as members of a vast political audience which could be reached by the printed instead of the spoken word. But just as the press barons were not the only people to possess mass readership papers, so were they not the only newspapermen to seek political power. C. P. Scott, J. L. Garvin, H. A. Gwynne, J. A. Spender, owners or editors of small-circulation, élite, quality journals, all sought to influence the governing classes, and indeed rated themselves as members of these classes, for their newspapers were a means of access to the inner workings of government. Their power depended on an intimate knowledge of the political world, and they had often no hesitation about accepting confidences, political rewards, even political finance, believing these to be perfectly compatible with their independent stance as journalists, as members of the fourth estate. Yet none of the great editors were regarded, or regarded themselves, as press lords, however much a part of the political system they happened to be.

Press barons were not merely the owners of mass-circulation, down-market newspapers; nor were they merely the proprietors of newspapers with political ambitions. In their anatomy, they combined the circulation of a Newnes with the muscle of a Scott; or, at least, they aspired to do so. They were thus something of a curiosity, or, as some alleged, of a monstrosity: they aspired to 'power without responsibility', using their newspapers not as 'newspapers in the ordinary acceptance of the term', but as 'engines of propaganda for their constantly changing policies, desires, personal wishes, personal likes and dislikes', enjoying 'secret knowledge without the general view' and distorting the fortunes of national leaders 'without being willing to bear their burdens'.[10]

The same, however, might be said of Scott or of any 'responsible' journalist: and the main burden of criticism against the press lords was not that they owned mass-circulation newspapers (for which Lord Riddell gained a peerage), nor that they harboured political ambitions (for which Scott received only general praise), but that they combined the two. And, above all, their style was disliked. They not only wanted to accumulate thousands of readers, but they sought to use their platform in a populist and strident manner; and if they got any pieces of information from politicians in the normal way, they tended to use them in an unorthodox way: to shout from the rooftops, instead of conversing in the drawing-rooms.

Were the press barons to be admitted to the late Victorian and Edwardian political club or were they not? And if they were admitted, would they promise to keep the rules? Or, if they were not admitted, would they seek to change the club, maybe even abolish it altogether? This was the dilemma that confronted both politicians and the press barons themselves, for the rise of the press lord coincided with the golden age of the political press in Britain, when, as R. A. Scott-James noted, many London journalists derived their influence from personal involvement in high political circles: Garvin and St Loe Strachey in the Conservatives, Massingham in the 'left wing of the radical party'.[11] Formal press briefings, the distribution of official information, were not the stuff of journalistic life; it was the journalists' participation in the conversation of the people who counted, their role as political brokers, sounding boards and advisers, that made the press feared and respected, and above all, courted, by politicians. Thus the structure of politics at the accession of Northcliffe was one in which the London and provincial press was more highly politicized than at any other time in its existence. It was not surprising, therefore, that Northcliffe should have been regarded as presenting a challenge to the political system: he was a journalist, and to be a journalist was already to be at least half a politician, and, as Newnes put it, to be involved in directing 'the affairs of nations', making and unmaking cabinets, upsetting governments and building up navies.[12] Moreover, British politics in the Edwardian era were still élitist, even though the occasional popular demagogue like Joseph Chamberlain had his day. Chamberlain put his faith in a renewal of the 'Tory Democracy' ideal, hoping to sustain Conservative fortunes through an infusion of strength from a mass base of the industrial working class.[13] A. J. Balfour, a more traditionalist kind of Tory, was relieved to see Chamberlain depart on his tariff reform campaign in 1903, for public campaigning was often the safety valve for errant politicians, taking them into the wasteland of public opinion, and away from where power really resided. So what were politicians of a more conservative mould to make of Lord Northcliffe, who was moving away from their exclusive world and claiming that power resided, or ought to reside, in the very wasteland that Balfour hoped would render Chamberlain harmless? 'Every extension of the franchise', wrote Northcliffe ominously in 1903, 'renders more powerful the newspaper and less powerful the politician.'[14]

Northcliffe consoled himself with the reflection that power was to be found outside the small political world of the Balfours and Asquiths; his power, he remarked to St Loe Strachey in 1904, is a new one and a difficult one for a newspaper owner. Had I published the *Pall Mall Gazette*'s ridiculous nonsense about Russia the other day, there would have been a panic. During the recent small Savings Bank smash, we were inundated with telegrams and letters from bankers all over the country asking us to leave things alone, and we did so, but from one point of view, quite wrongly.[15]

It arose, he went on, from his large readership, which 'magnifies every utterance'; but Northcliffe, like any newspaperman, had to be careful not to get out of step with his readers, and he exaggerated his power to sway public opinion. His violent anti-German propaganda probably contributed to the worsening climate of international relations before 1914; but it was a gross inflation of his importance to claim, as did one of his biographers, that 'next to the Kaiser, Lord Northcliffe has done more than any other living man to bring about the war'.[16]

Nevertheless, it was the outbreak of the war in 1914 that gave Northcliffe his opportunity to seek to make good his claim that he represented the mass public, and that such representation could and should bring with it the exercise of political power. The war, as has been frequently remarked, gave the press its opportunity, for parliamentary criticism of government was, of necessity, muted; but equally important was the fact that in a total war government had to mobilize the public. Northcliffe claimed that his readers were the '1,104,000 Who Know Daily';[17] or what one Liberal critic disparagingly referred to as the 'mobocracy'.[18] But total war required the support, the acquiescence, even the suffering of the mobocracy; and Northcliffe pushed himself forward as the voice of the people. His patriotism, his simple belief in the virtues of the British empire, caught and packaged the mood of the public in the war. Moreover, war created news, and nothing sold newspapers like news. For Northcliffe and the *Daily Mail*, the war was almost a personal crusade, for had not Northcliffe himself predicted the conflict? In 1919, Irene Cooper Willis, in her compilation of the Liberal press's record in the war, listed Northcliffe's victories: the fall of the Liberal government in 1915, the making of the first coalition, the making of the second coalition of 1916, the coming of military conscription, the 'knock-out blow' campaign, all were 'milestones in his triumphal progress, which culminated in the khaki election and the Peace of Versailles'.[19]

This was, however, evidence, not of Northcliffe's power in shaping events, but of his critics' belief in his power to shape events. Other newspapermen were involved in these developments as well; but Northcliffe evolved a particular style, a harassing, loud, merciless public barrage against those members of the government whom he deemed were falling down in their duty to the nation. This might be troublesome in time of peace, but, usually, no more than mildly troublesome. In wartime, however, when emotions were more easily aroused than dampened down, when emotional attacks on public men were less easily brushed off, such a style of journalism might come into its own.

Northcliffe's campaign to have cotton declared contraband provides a model of his journalistic tactics. In July and August 1915 he placed daily insets in the middle of a page in the *Mail* declaring that the government had not yet made cotton contraband, reinforcing them by characteristic headlines:

Will Germany get Cotton during M.P.s' Holidays?

Cotton and Casualties: Every bale of cotton which reaches Germany means either an Allied cripple or a corpse.

A thoroughly bad example: Six weeks for Ministers to go to sleep again.

Cotton!

The Cotton tragedy: will our politicians never act?

Cotton and Death: Queen's Hall meeting, vigorous speech by Lord C. Beresford.

Wasted Lives: victims of the Cotton Crime.

And, finally, the *Mail* was able to report with satisfaction that

the Foreign Office has at last confessed to the Cotton Crime. After denying that Cotton was going to Germany in any quantity, after shuffling on the subject for months, after attacking the Press, and particularly the *Daily Mail*, it has, 13 months too late, declared Cotton Contraband.[20]

This was populism at its most effective; but Northcliffe's power was purchased at a price. For it was clear to politicians that, while other political journalists aspired to join the political system, Northcliffe wanted to beat it; he wanted to be part of it only to displace it. But this was an aspiration that politicians and élitist journalists alike could not, in the long run, condone, for it threatened their joint political world, and their ideas about how political power could and should be shared between each other. It was, after all, the great Liberal editor, A. G. Gardiner, who despised Northcliffe as the arouser of the mobocracy; and it was the great Liberal politician, Lloyd George, who declared that he would 'as soon go for a sunny evening stroll around Walton heath with a grasshopper as to try to work with Northcliffe'.[21] Lloyd George contradicted himself in 1917, when he did try to work with Northcliffe, offering him a post at the Air Ministry, a post which Northcliffe declined because he could 'do better work if I maintain my independence and am not gagged by a loyalty that I do not feel towards the whole of your Administration'.[22] But the mutual suspicion between press lord and politician was important, for it set bounds to the march of Northcliffe's power. Since he was not – after early disappointments – a member of the inner circles of political decision-making, he found it difficult to pick up the kind of gossip, information and inside knowledge that (for example) enabled Lord Beaverbrook to operate so effectively the 'honest intrigue' that precipitated the fall of Asquith in December 1916. It is outside the scope of this chapter to give a detailed account of that complex affair; but the prime movers in the world of journalism were not Northcliffe and what he liked to call his 'unchloroformed' readers, but Beaverbrook (still a political go-between rather than a populist newspaper proprietor), Robert Donald (editor of the quality Liberal paper, the *Daily Chronicle*) and Geoffrey Dawson, editor, it was true, of the Northcliffe-owned *Times*, but a man who, on this as on so many occasions, was using not only his independent judgement, but also his special contacts within the world of high politics.[23] Northcliffe's part was to add his (certainly not inconsiderable) voice to an already quickening barrage of criticism against what his editor, Thomas Marlowe, dubbed 'The Limpets'.

Significant also was the fact that *The Times*, but not the *Daily Mail*, was the recipient of Colonel Repington's famous despatch on the failure of the British offensive on the western front in May 1915, a failure which he attributed to the lack of sufficient quantities of high-explosive shells. And although Northcliffe originally suggested to Sir John French that he should make a 'short and very vigorous statement to a private correspondent' which would 'render the government's position impossible' and 'thus bring public pressure upon the government', he also remarked in passing that this was 'the usual way of making things public in England'.[24] Most certainly it was: and a journalist who did not enjoy this kind of privileged access spoke with correspondingly less authority on political issues. The eighteenth-century method of backstairs intrigue was, on these occasions, more powerful than the eighteenth-century method of storming the closet, which, in Northcliffe's day as in Walpole's, provoked such disgust as to make it a procedure to be used with caution. Northcliffe was reminded of this when, in the middle of the 'shells scandal' crisis, he launched a savage personal attack on Lord Kitchener in the *Daily Mail* which, if anything, strengthened rather than weakened Kitchener's position, and brought the *Mail* hundreds of abusive letters and telegrams and a drop in circulation.[25]

Northcliffe had influence in government circles; but it was influence, not power. Power was still located in the interstices of party politics, despite the unusual conditions created by the war. Once these conditions ended, Northcliffe's attempts to displace the political system, to storm the closet, were demonstrably futile; and in November 1918 this was revealed when Lloyd George told Northcliffe to 'go to hell'.[26] The scourge of governments was himself scourged in April 1919 when Lloyd George launched a fierce attack on Northcliffe in the House of Commons, referring to his 'diseased vanity' and castigating his attempts to influence the peace conference at Versailles by seeking to 'sow dissent between great allies'.[27] 'Sometimes', wrote Tom Clarke, 'I fancied, when he talked to me in his later days, that he was confessing his failure to find what he sought in life; that he was robbed of the happiness of power.'[28]

Northcliffe failed in his supreme ambition because he sought to mould, rather than exploit, the world of high politics, and because his unchloroformed readers were not (as he liked to think) Northcliffe followers. They did not constitute a faithful party following, a set of disciplined voters, a well-organized pressure group. They were, quite simply, newspaper readers, as likely to prove 'grasshoppers' as Northcliffe himself, and with no direct, constant means of exerting power upon government. The *Daily Mail* could embarrass and trouble governments, especially the faltering administration run by Asquith in the first half of the war; but it could not break Lloyd George, nor could it dictate terms to him. Lloyd George believed in the necessity of a good press; but he was able to build up his own newspaper following, through assiduous distribution of honours, through purchase, and by the natural process of flattery that closeness to power seemed to exercise on newspaper men. Northcliffe was too independent, too unpredictable, to prove a comfortable or lasting political ally. Nor could the fall of Lloyd George in 1922 hold out any real comfort to the men of print; for Lloyd George fell because the Conservatives in his coalition decided that it was time to wind up the coalition, before the Prime Minister did to the Tory party what he had done (they believed) to the Liberals. In 1922, as in 1916, a press lord was present in the 'honest intrigue'; but once again he was there as an honest intriguer, not as a populist press baron. And the rising star of Northcliffe's great successor, Lord Beaverbrook, further revealed the limitations of 'press power' now that the unusual conditions of the war were over, and political parties once more held undisputed sway. For, as much as British political parties disliked each other, they disliked press lord interlopers even more, as the career of Lord Beaverbrook and his fellow baron, Viscount Harmsworth, demonstrated.

When Northcliffe was at the height of his prestige in the Great War, Beaverbrook still had not made his name as a press lord. He owned the *Daily Express*, and was beginning to make it his political mouthpiece, but his main entry point into politics was his contact within the Conservative and Unionist party, and especially his influence over Andrew Bonar Law. Indeed, when he did ultimately acquire control of the *Express* in 1916, he kept the final deal – and its date – a secret, because it coincided with his honest political intrigue that helped bring Asquith down: Beaverbrook knew that any hint of his new press venture would earn him obloquy and suspicion, not respect, from the men in power that he was seeking to manipulate, since their dislike of independent newspaper proprietors was widely known.[29] His nervousness was well founded for, after 1917, when it became known that he was in control of the *Daily Express*, he incurred the wrath of the Conservative Central Office on the grounds that, instead of doing the respectable thing, and subsidizing loyal party newspapers, he was putting his money into an independent – and therefore 'irresponsible' – non-party newspaper. And when he accepted, with Northcliffe, Lloyd George's offer to direct British propaganda in February 1918, Bonar Law warned the Prime Minister that 'one of your newspaper barons was too much. Now there are two. Well, you'll hear of this.'[30]

Lloyd George did hear of it, for the government's connections with the newspaper world were made the subject of a heated debate on press freedom in the House of Commons in February and March 1918, when Austen Chamberlain drew attention to the 'uneasiness and suspicion engendered by the new connection' (as it seemed to many of them) which had been established between the government and the press; relations between government and the press were 'always dangerous' (he did not say to whom).[31] Bonar-Law, faced with this challenge, even urged Beaverbrook to resign his seat in the Cabinet.[32]

To be dubbed a press baron, therefore, held as many, and perhaps more, disadvantages as advantages for a man who was in search of political power. Politicians might find such friends were dangerous, even if they were prepared to throw their newspapers behind the politician, as Beaverbrook did for Lloyd George in the general election of December 1918. The structure of politics was altering for the worse, as far as the aspirations of the press lords were concerned; or, to be more exact, they were returning to the more comfortable and familiar world of party politics that Northcliffe had hoped to displace. But it was not only the structure of politics that held out alarming prospects for the would-be press baron; for while politics were once again becoming, so to say, professionalized, so was journalism. After 1918 it was becoming increasingly clear that journalism was less a branch of politics, and more a branch of commerce, as Rothermere acknowledged when, in 1931, he urged Beaverbrook to 'join with us in conducting intensive competition. The newspaper market is far too crowded. There are not enough readers, or advertisers, to go round.'[33] This might seem to play into the hands of the press lord, since Northcliffe's independence had been founded on commercial success. But newspaper proprietors, in the inter-war years, were obliged to work hard at the undignified business of maintaining commercial solvency: closures, mergers, and take-overs were a far from solid foundation for a press lord constituency. Moreover, the separation of the press from party politics, the decline of the political press, the passing of the political generation that had known and, in a sense, accepted that the press had an important political role to play, all left the press baron an isolated figure, vulnerable to the kind of criticism aimed at him by Austen Chamberlain in 1918.

But the press lord still had the theory upon which his behaviour was founded to legitimize his attitude to politicians. Newspapers, wrote Kennedy Jones in 1919,

> derive their strength from the people, and the larger the number of readers the greater is their revenue and their capacity as a megaphone. Ministers are the servants of the people, and therefore, if the argument be carried to its logical conclusion, Ministers should do the bidding of a Press which claims to be the voice of the people.[34]

The press barons could therefore justify their claim that they were as much – perhaps more – a part of the fourth estate as any small-circulation, quality newspaper of the *Westminster Gazette* or *Morning Post* type. They could seek to bend the minister to their will without incurring any criticism that they were acting unconstitutionally. And it was thus armed that Beaverbrook, now, after 1922, unrepentantly a press lord, and Rothermere, Northcliffe's successor by blood, sought (they said) to put the country before party politics, and press for policies that would ensure the economic prosperity of the British people and of the British empire.

Beaverbrook loudly proclaimed that in politics 'I take an independent attitude';[35] but in any case, after 1922, independence was thrust upon him. For the death of Bonar Law deprived Beaverbrook of his special contact on the inside of politics: Lloyd George, Lord Birkenhead, Winston Churchill were now in the political wilderness, and although Churchill, at least, recovered some of the lost ground, he regarded Beaverbrook as too dangerous to associate with in any intimate fashion. No longer was Beaverbrook the go-between, the kingmaker, the confidant of ministers.[36]

For years Beaverbrook had pestered Conservative leaders to proclaim the doctrine of imperial preference, which would involve the taxation of goods imported from non-empire countries. In the 1923 general election – the timing of which he had opposed – he advised voters to vote on the imperial issue, preferring independent candidates to 'narrow-minded' Baldwin Tories; and after Baldwin's defeat he toyed with the idea of a 'centre party', a coalition of moderate men who agreed on imperial preference.[37] The first breakthrough came in March 1924, when Churchill presented himself as an independent against official Conservative and Liberal candidates, on a platform of imperial preference and 'Conservative social reform'.[38] Beaverbrook supported him, and although Churchill did not win the seat, the by-election was the first in a series of running battles between the press lords and Baldwin that were a feature of British politics up to 1932. Beaverbrook worked to impose his will on Baldwin. In May 1925 the *Daily Express* warned that independent Conservative candidates would again 'arise', and that it was quite likely that the *Express* would support them.[39] In 1929 Beaverbrook and Rothermere began seriously to challenge Baldwin. Their timing was good: Labour won power again (though without a clear majority); and Conservatives, restive under Baldwin's leadership, began to seek a more positive programme. The 'trustees of public opinion' displayed their wares before the potential opponents of Baldwin. Had not the *Daily Express*, Beaverbrook insisted, supported the victorious Lloyd George in 1918, and Bonar Law in 1922? Had it not opposed the premature Baldwin dissolution in 1923, and backed the successful Baldwin in 1924? And Rothermere, for his part, had helped increase the Conservative vote in the 1924 election by his use of the 'Zinoviev letter', estimating that the *Mail* by its timely disclosure of the alleged communist interference in British domestic affairs had garnered some one hundred seats.[40]

There seemed every reason for the press lords to believe that the passing of Northcliffe had not marked also the passing of the age of press lord power. But whereas Northcliffe had attempted to displace the political system by his 'mobocracy', Beaverbrook and Rothermere sought to bully the politicians with their own weapon – a new, journalistically inspired political party. On 14 February 1930 Sir Robert Bruce Lockhart noted in his diary that Beaverbrook would 'announce his New Party on Monday, provided Lord Rothermere comes out in favour of food taxes. It is a big venture. He has already £70,000 promised towards his £1,000,000 fighting fund.' A few days later he recorded that the 'United Empire Party' had been launched.[41]

If mutual admiration was the criterion of political power, then Beaverbrook and Rothermere were indeed riding on the crest of a wave. G. Ward Price wrote in Rothermere's *Sunday Pictorial* that the next Conservative leader would be found outside the 'established hierarchy', and that there was no man more likely to succeed Baldwin than Lord Beaverbrook. Beaverbrook responded by describing Rothermere as 'the greatest master of popular opinion'. 'There would be a wonderful transformation here', remarked Rothermere, 'if, by any turn of the wheel of fortune, Lord Beaverbrook should enter within the next year or two 10 Downing Street as its master.'[42]

This was perhaps a little hopeful; but if a press lord could not enter Downing Street, he could at least eject its present occupant. Beaverbrook's new party enrolled some 173,000 members in a fortnight; and, more significant, J. C. C. Davidson noted that the rank and file of the Conservative party was 'seething with uncertainty and unrest'.[43] Baldwin seemed to be on the run almost immediately, for in March 1930 he agreed to a referendum on food taxes, and the discussion of the issue at an imperial conference after the next election. Beaverbrook accepted this commitment, until a month later a new leaflet put out by Conservative Central Office placed on the dominions the onus of making the necessary initiatives. Beaverbrook now rushed from by-election to by-election backing candidates who challenged the official Conservative line; and he asked his readers for further funds for the crusade, threatening that if the Conservatives did not accept empire free trade, he would break up the party.[44]

Baldwin attacked the press lords at what he hoped was their weakest point: their arrogance in claiming to exercise a veto, not only on political policy, but upon the composition of any future Conservative administration; but his internal position was by no means secure. Neville Chamberlain might, after all, play the new Bonar Law to Beaverbrook, and oust the Conservative leader as Bonar Law had ousted the Coalition leaders in 1916 and 1922; for Chamberlain by February 1931 thought that perhaps Baldwin should go.[45] And on 26 February the party's principal agent, Sir Robert Topping, reported that although Lord Beaverbrook had lost ground, there were growing doubts about whether Baldwin could carry the party to victory. He suggested that, in the party's interest, Baldwin should reconsider his position. Chamberlain took the opportunity of showing this memorandum to Baldwin, who considered resigning.[46]

It was ironic, but appropriate, that Baldwin should instead resolve to join battle with the press lords on the very ground that they claimed gave them their right to exert power in British politics: the ground of public opinion, the voters, the constituency. The press lords liked to claim that their readers were, in a sense, their voters, exercising their political rights through the newspaper rather than at the hustings. Northcliffe had claimed this, but his own sampling techniques in 1903 cast doubt upon it. However, before the days of systematic and scientific research into the relationship, it was a thesis incapable of final proof or disproof. But Beaverbrook and Rothermere were running a party political campaign, and, like all party politicians, there came inevitably the moment when they must, however much they disliked the exercise, put their suppositions of support to the test in an election. The election at which the press lords tested their strength against Baldwin was the St George's, Westminster, by-election in March 1931. Baldwin had considered resignation just before this contest, but had been dissuaded. Now he campaigned strongly for the official Conservative candidate, Duff Cooper, against a press lord independent candidate. And while on the stump, he coined the phrase that since 1931 has haunted the would-be seekers of press power: the accusation that the press lords were seeking to exercise 'power without responsibility'.

This the press lords denied: Northcliffe in his day argued that he was more representative of the public – or at least of his readers – than any politician; did he not represent the '1,104,000 Who Know Daily'? The press lord was responsible to his constituency, the readers, not to any politician or prime minister. But political power in Britain could only be achieved through the medium of the political party; and although the press could exercise influence on the political system – and considerable influence at that, through excluding social or political issues from the agenda, through the promotion of issues which were comparatively innocuous, through the shaping of public preferences[47] – it could not by itself take decisions. It could not aspire to displace the political party as the ladder by which men rose and fell, sought and gained or lost office, and, once in office, took and held the levers of government. The press could not displace the system, substitute readers for voters, press proprietors for politicians, and Lord Beaverbrook for the Conservative leader, or future prime minister. Not, that is, unless the press lords could win an election, and demonstrate to the Conservative party that Baldwin must, for the sake of that party, go. But Baldwin's man won the St George's contest; and the defeat of the Beaverbrook–Rothermere candidate demonstrated that, while newspaper sales might rise, support in the shape of a public following remained as elusive as ever. In September 1933 Sir Robert Bruce Lockhart discussed newspapers with one of Beaverbrook's friends, Brendan Bracken. 'Brendan', he noted, 'thinks that Max will be the last of his tribe and that the reign of the great Press Lords is coming to an end.'[48]

Bracken's prophecy might have appeared ill-founded, for Rothermere continued to flourish in the 1930s, seeking still to bully politicians into adopting courses which they would otherwise not adopt. But his interventions were futile. He advocated Italian fascism, seeing Mussolini as a Napoleon of modern times who (coincidentally, like Lord Rothermere himself) 'out of regard of the heavy responsibilities resting upon me . . . have been for some time past a teetotaller and a non-smoker'.[49] This cost him readers, and did not gain him public position, though his advocacy of the revision of the treaty of Trianon in favour of Hungary did bring him an offer of the Hungarian crown (which he felt obliged to refuse).[50] Rothermere fairly bubbled with policies, now against Indian self-government, now for British rearmament.[51] But in so far as his campaigns made any significant impact, it was an impact of a lesser order than that sought by the press barons in their heyday.

Officials in service ministries in the 1930s were grateful for Harmsworth's rearmament theme because it provided some 'wind in their sails', and gave them material to use against their opponents in Whitehall;[52] but this was a far cry from government walls tumbling to the cry of the popular press: for the high priests were, then as always, already inside the citadel of power, not parading outside it blowing journalistic trumpets.

And yet the press lord, but in an altered form, did continue to exist. Fleet Street had its great proprietors, men who accumulated to themselves the control of more and more newspapers, men such as Cecil King, Lord Thompson, Rupert Murdoch. These men were, perhaps, press magnates rather than press barons. Newspapers were too expensive to run simply as political platforms, even if these press men had had the inclination. The 1930s saw the rise of the entrepreneurial proprietors, the Berry brothers, Lord Cowdray's Westminster chain. This did not destroy the hold of Beaverbrook and Rothermere on circulation figures, and in 1948 Beaverbrook led the market with 16 per cent of the overall circulation, and Rothermere was next with 14 per cent.[53] This was soon to be challenged by the new men, Thompson and Murdoch. But even before this era, the style and ambitions characteristic of the press lords were as dead as the political world that gave them birth. Their formal demise might possibly be dated precisely. In May 1940, after the British failure in Norway, Lord Davis (formerly David Davis, a supporter of Lloyd George) wrote to Beaverbrook, whom he addressed as 'dear kingmaker', asking him why he had 'given up [his] job'.

> You did the trick in 1916, and, by getting rid of old Squiff at the right moment, you enabled us to win the war which we should probably have lost if he had remained in office. Now, even more than in 1916, we are up against it, and if the present Prime Minister is allowed to drag us from one disaster to another, we shall end up in queer street. . . . Therefore I humbly suggest that you should plump for Winston.

But Beaverbrook was a more shrewd observer of the workings of political power than was Lord Davis. He acknowledged, in a letter to Lord Castlerosse, that the crisis had come, and although he believed that Chamberlain would not be turned out now, he speculated that if Chamberlain remained in office with such an 'immense volume of disapproval in his own party', then 'he had better retire'. Party was all. 'You can't break every government the same way', he replied to Davis on 7 May. And when he reviewed the fall of the Liberal giants, Asquith and Lloyd George, he noted that the common factor was not the power of the press lord. 'In every case the revolt that broke the government came from within. The same applies this time. Those who try to do it from without are simply wasting their ammunition.' And, appropriately, Beaverbrook went on to demonstrate his own impotence, for on 6 May he came to the government's assistance with an article which dismissed the Norwegian failure as a minor affair, and encouraged Chamberlain to challenge a division in the House of Commons. He played no part in the events that brought Churchill to power; and when he became Minister of Aircraft Production under Churchill, it was the politician who made the king (or at least the king's adviser), and not the other way round.[54]

Of course, the press and politicians could not ignore each other, or go their wholly separate ways, despite the more businesslike concerns of the new men. Politicians needed the press in its traditional role, as a means of communicating with the public, as a sounding board for policies or potential policies; politicians still distributed honours to proprietors, and even offered them jobs, as Harold Wilson did to Cecil King. The professions of journalism and politics still overlapped, as indeed they had always done. But they were no longer synonymous. Above all, press magnates made no claim to displace the politician from his fundamental role as the wielder of power through the use of the political party. It might indeed be said that Northcliffe was the only member of the species who was a press baron by conviction and even Northcliffe's first instinct had been to attach himself to the cause and campaign of a leading British politician, Joseph Chamberlain. Beaverbrook became a press baron because he could find no other outlet for his political ambitions, his fascination with the world of high politics; Rothermere became one because he inherited, by primogeniture, the Northcliffe press empire and the Northcliffe tradition. Neither, as it turned out, was particularly happy or particularly effective with his role; and when the *Daily Express* first printed its celebrated crusader in chains, in October 1951,[55] it unwittingly provided an appropriate epitaph for the age of the press baron. If the press baron could not prosper within the chains and confines of the party political system, it was equally certain that he could not prosper, nor even exist, outside them.

Notes

1 Kingsley Martin, review of Peter Howard's biography of Beaverbrook, in *Political Quarterly*, 36 (1965), 117–18.

2 S. Koss, *The Rise and Fall of the Political Press in Britain*, vol. I, *The Nineteenth Century*, London, Hamish Hamilton, 1981, p. 374.

3 A. M. Gollin, *Balfour's Burden*, London, Anthony Blond, 1965, pp. 84–8.

4 Gollin, op. cit., p. 197.

5 J. Amery, *Joseph Chamberlain and the Tariff Reform Campaign*, London, Macmillan, 1969, p. 297.

6 Amery, op. cit., p. 298; A. P. Ryan, *Lord Northcliffe*, London, Collins, 1953, pp. 93–4; Koss, op. cit., vol. II, *The Twentieth Century*, London, 1984, pp. 20–2, 25.

7 T. Clarke, *Northcliffe in History*, London, Hutchinson, 1950, p. 188; hereafter cited as *Northcliffe in History*.

8 H. Herd, *The Making of Modern Journalism*, London, Allen & Unwin, 1926, p. 14. Newnes was not as 'harmless' as he liked to claim; for his political activities see Koss, op. cit., vol. II, pp. 327–8, 336–7, 344–5.

9 Lord Beaverbrook, *Politicians and the Press*, London, Hutchinson, n.d. [1925?], p. 9.

10 Stanley Baldwin, *The Times*, 18 March 1931; R. Pound and G. Harmsworth, *Northcliffe*, London, Cassell, 1959, p. 516.

11 R. A. Scott-James, *The Influence of the Press*, London, S. W. Partridge, n.d. [1913], p. 213.

12 Herd, op. cit., p. 14.

13 P. Cain, 'Political economy in Edwardian England and the tariff reform controversy', in A. O'Day (ed.), *The Edwardian Age: Conflict and Stability, 1900–1914*, London, Macmillan, 1979, pp. 52–3.

14 Clarke, *Northcliffe in History*, p. 187.

15 Northcliffe to Strachey, 18 November 1904, House of Lords Library, Strachey MSS, S/11/4/16. Feeling against Russia was high after the Russian battle fleet sank some British trawlers in the North Sea in October 1904.

16 T. Clarke, *Northcliffe in History*, p. 71; Koss, op. cit., II, p. 252.

17 I. C. Willis, *England's Holy War*, New York, A. A. Knopf, 1928, p. 172.

18 A. G. Gardiner of the *Daily News*; see Willis, op. cit., p. 245.

19 Willis, op. cit., p. 173.

20 ibid., p. 218.

21 J. M. McEwen, 'The press and the fall of Asquith', *Historical Journal*, 21, 4, 1978, 868.

22 Pound and Harmsworth, op. cit., p. 592.

23 McEwen, op. cit., pp. 863–83; Koss, op. cit., II, pp. 302–3.

24 Pound and Harmsworth, op. cit., p. 475; D. Lloyd George, *War Memoirs*, vol. i, London, Odhams, 1938, pp. 119–22.

25 R. MacNair Wilson, *Lord Northcliffe: a study*, London, Benn, 1927, chapter xxxix; Herd, op. cit., p. 63; Clarke, op. cit., pp. 76–83; Koss, op. cit., II, pp. 278–9.

26 T. Clarke, *My Northcliffe Diary*, London, Gollancz, 1931, pp. 116–17; hereafter cited as *Northcliffe Diary*.

27 Pound and Harmsworth, op. cit., pp. 714–15.

28 Clarke, *Northcliffe in History*, p. 18.

29 Aitken had control over the *Daily Express* as a result of his friendship with the editor, R. D. Blumenfeld; but he did not finally purchase the paper until 14 November 1916 (A. J. P. Taylor, *Beaverbrook*, London, Hamish Hamilton, 1972, pp. 99–100).

30 Taylor, op. cit., p. 140.

31 *Hansard*, vol. 104, HC Deb., 5 s., 11 March 1918, cols 73–9.

32 Taylor, op. cit., p. 141.

33 Quoted in D. G. Boyce, James Curran and P. Wingate (eds), *Newspaper History*, London, Constable, 1978, p. 36.

34 Kennedy Jones, *Fleet Street and Downing Street*, London, Hutchinson, 1919, p. 11.

35 Taylor, op. cit., p. 162; Koss, op. cit., I, p. 18.

36 Taylor, op. cit., pp. 211–12.

37 T. Driberg, *Beaverbrook*, London, Weidenfeld & Nicolson, 1956, pp. 174–5.

38 Taylor, op. cit., pp. 217–21; Driberg, op. cit., pp. 175–6; Koss, op. cit., II, p. 435.

39 Driberg, op. cit., p. 194.

40 Taylor, op. cit., pp. 223–4.

41 K. Young (ed.), *The Diaries of Sir Robert Bruce Lockhart*, vol. i, *1915–1938*, London, Macmillan, 1973, p. 115.

42 Driberg, op. cit., pp. 203–4; Kingsley Martin, 'The influence of the press', *Political Quarterly*, 1 (1930), 159.

43 K. Middlemas and J. Barnes, *Baldwin*, London, Weidenfeld & Nicolson, 1969, p. 564.

44 Driberg, op. cit., pp. 206–7.

45 Middlemas and Barnes, op. cit., pp. 586–7.

46 ibid., pp. 588–9.

47 S. Lukes argues that such influence amounts to a kind of power; see his *Power: a Radical View*, London, Macmillan, 1974, chapters 2–4. But this seems to me too loose a definition.

48 Young, op. cit., p. 225.

49 R. J. B. Bosworth, 'The British press, the Conservatives and Mussolini, 1920–34', *Journal of Contemporary History*, 5, 2 (1970), 173; Koss, op. cit., II, pp. 533–4.

50 H. Cudlipp, *Publish and Be Damned*, London, Andrew Dakers, 1953, pp. 36–8; Lord Rothermere, *My Campaign for Hungary*, London, Eyre & Spottiswoode, 1939, pp. 37–8.

51 Lord Rothermere, *The Daily Mail Blue Book on the Indian Crisis*, London, Associated Newspapers, 1931; *My Fight to Rearm Britain*, London, Eyre & Spottiswoode, 1939; *Warnings and Predictions*, London, Eyre & Spottiswoode, 1939.

52 J. P. Mackintosh, *The British Cabinet*, London, Stevens, 1962, p. 508.

53 G. Murdock and P. Golding, 'The structure, ownership and control of the press, 1914–1976', in Boyce, Curran and Wingate, op. cit., pp. 136–8.

54 Taylor, op. cit., pp. 407–9, 412–13.

55 Taylor, op. cit., p. 601.

5

The boomerang effect: the press and the battle for London 1981–6

James Curran

A number of studies have shown how the press has mobilized public indignation against 'outsider' groups, such as teenage gangs, drug addicts, muggers and football hooligans, and built public support for tougher state action against them.[1] This chapter seemingly fits this general pattern in that it shows how the press campaigned, initially with considerable success, against 'Red Ken' and the Greater London Council (GLC) and prepared the ground for the council's abolition.

But it differs from comparable studies in that it describes an attempt to engineer a moral panic that ultimately failed. On previous occasions, the press had been able to present itself plausibly as a disinterested champion of the people merely giving voice to the widespread indignation which it had helped to create.[2] But in this instance, the press failed to sustain public hostility towards the GLC. Instead of speaking on behalf of the general public, it became transparently clear that much of the press was preaching to a mostly sceptical and unconvinced readership.

This chapter thus illustrates the limits of press power. In some ways it relates to a very special and unusual set of circumstances, and so does not directly challenge the new academic orthodoxy which argues that the media's persuasive power has been greatly underestimated.[3] Nevertheless, it does highlight the importance of certain constraints on the influence of the media which are present, to a lesser or greater extent, in many other situations. To this we shall return at the end of this chapter.

The political legacy

In 1981, the GLC was not a highly regarded institution. To judge from the available data, there was considerable public uncertainty about what the GLC actually did; and County Hall, with its seven miles of corridors and limited direct contact with its constituents, was widely thought to be overly bureaucratic.[4]

The GLC also had a relatively undistinguished record.[5] It was established in 1963 as a scaled-down version of the London County Council. Sandwiched between an interventionist, central state and strong, increasingly assertive borough authorities, the new institution often found its efforts undermined from one or both directions.

Thus the GLC's housing policy was largely undermined by the boroughs. In particular, its strategic aim of transferring families from the crowded inner city slums and rehousing them in the suburbs was fiercely resisted by the outer boroughs. After unsatisfactory partnership arrangements had been attempted with the boroughs, the GLC decided in 1980 to transfer most of its flats and houses to borough control. In effect, the GLC voluntarily relinquished most of its housing management function.

The GLC's performance as a metropolitan planning authority was scarcely more inspiring. It took eleven years to draw up and endorse a development plan for London – a delay that weakened its authority and encouraged many boroughs to resist an all-London planning approach. The GLC was further undermined by the Department of the Environment which overrode the GLC on several major redevelopment projects and tended to side with local boroughs in planning disputes with County Hall.

But if the GLC's strategic planning record was modest, it was none the less a considerable improvement on its see-sawing and ineffective role as a transport authority. The GLC drew up elaborate plans for a huge motorway network in London only for these to be effectively scrapped in 1973. A different plan was then formulated for revolutionizing public transport and increasing its passenger load. But this too was largely jettisoned in the GLC cutbacks of the mid 1970s.

Greater continuity was maintained in the management of education in the Inner London area. But this was run by the GLC in conjunction with the inner boroughs through the Inner London Education Authority (ILEA). Though ILEA was technically a GLC committee, it was in practice a separate entity which operated more or less autonomously.

This disappointing record prompted an increasing number of people, right across the political spectrum, to conclude in the late 1970s that the GLC was an unviable institution which needed either to be strengthened or scrapped. Typical of this growing body of critics was one influential councillor who argued in 1979: 'I feel a great deal of regret that Marshall [chairman of the Inquiry on Greater London, 1978] did not . . . say "Abolish the GLC" because I think it would be a major saving and would have released massive resources for productive use.' He continued, 'I do not believe you need two tiers of local government, and I very much regret that Horace Cutler [leader of the GLC] . . . has not axed the whole appalling show.'[6]

The councillor's name was Ken Livingstone, who was later to become famous for arguing exactly the opposite point of view.[7] But his was not a maverick voice in 1979 and the government's subsequent decision to axe the GLC was not, as many have suggested,[8] an impulsive 'clutching at a straw', born solely out of political spite and a desire to curb high-spending local authorities. Abolition of the GLC had long been on the agenda for good reason.

This raises a puzzling question. Given the low public esteem in which the

GLC had long been held, and the forceful arguments for its dissolution, why did so many people subsequently rally to its defence?

Press onslaught on the GLC

This question becomes even harder to answer in the light of the sustained barrage of press invective against the GLC. Between mid-1981 and mid-1983, every national daily and Sunday newspaper, as well as London's only evening paper, campaigned against the GLC. The one partial exception to this was the *Daily Mirror*, Britain's only Labour daily. Although it joined the crusade against Ken Livingstone, it very occasionally gave supportive coverage to the GLC itself.

After the 1983 general election, there was, as we shall see, a shift in the attitude of some popular papers towards the GLC. Even so, most of the popular press continued to attack the GLC until its closure on 1 April 1986.

The real dichotomy in press coverage of the GLC was not between left and right papers so much as between the quality and popular press. From the start, quality newspapers assessed favourably Ken Livingstone as an 'affable but serious full-time politician',[9] 'a formidable political operator',[10] even 'the likeable leftie',[11] although he also featured in more critical quality papers as a quirky eccentric who was 'naive but sincere'.[12] The quality press never joined the popular press vendetta against him and generally gave space to the GLC's point of view as well as to its critics.[13] Indeed, the *Guardian* and the *Observer* became increasingly sympathetic to the GLC from late 1981 onwards.

This was important because quality newspapers influenced broadcasters' perceptions of the GLC, and encouraged them to develop a different framework for reporting the GLC on TV and radio than that of the popular press. But quality newspapers were not important in relation to total newspaper consumption. They accounted for less than 20 per cent of national newspaper circulation, although their London sales were slightly above the national average.[14]

Genesis of a moral panic

The beginning of the press campaign against the GLC's Labour administration dates back to the election campaign which it won in May 1981. The GLC Tories concentrated their electioneering on attacking the political extremism of their Labour opponents. Their 16-page manifesto referred to Marx, Marxist and Marxists seventeen times. In particular, Ken Livingstone was singled out by them as a sinister 'Robespierre' figure waiting in the wings to supplant the right-wing Labour leader, Andrew McIntosh.[15]

This provided an initial sensitization to themes that the popular press was subsequently to develop. However, popular papers did not respond fully to the Tory GLC campaign at the time; they generally reported rather than endorsed the attacks on GLC Labour candidates and gave only limited space to the GLC election campaign.

After the GLC election, the Labour administration and its new leader, Ken Livingstone, were subjected from time to time to sharp criticism. But Fleet Street's firepower was not fully deployed on these occasions and its sights were not yet trained on 'Red Ken' as a target. In his first two months, Livingstone made a number of controversial speeches of a sort that would later attract banner headline denunciations: some of these were scarcely even reported in the national press.[16]

Two things changed this – the continuing rise of the Labour left and the Brixton riots. The emergence of Bennism as a political force gave rise to concern in Fleet Street that 'left-wing extremists' might gain control of the Labour Party and be elected to national office at a time when the Conservative government was doing badly in the opinion polls. This coincided with the sudden eruption of arson and looting in Brixton, and on a lesser scale in other inner city areas, which provoked widespread fear that public order was seriously threatened by a new generation of bitterly disaffected black and unemployed white youths. These two fears coalesced and found a focus in Ken Livingstone.

For nine months, the news had been dominated by upheavals within the Labour Party. In October 1980, the 'mandatory' reselection of Labour MPs had been confirmed; in January 1981, a specially convened Labour Party conference voted to introduce a new method of electing Labour's leader and deputy leader which gave trade union and party activists the dominant say; in March 1981, the Social Democratic Party was formally launched; in April, Tony Benn announced that he would stand against Denis Healey for the Labour Party's deputy leadership. The dominant press response to these developments was encapsulated in a graphic *Daily Express* summary: 'Why Labour leaders tremble at the relentless advance of Benn's army. Torn apart by the politics of fear.'[17]

Livingstone had already been marked down, in the words of one Fleet Street journalist, as 'a platoon leader of the advance party of Bennite shock troops'.[18] But what elevated Ken Livingstone to the status of a public health warning advertising the perils of Bennism was his role in the Brixton riots. It was from 12 April 1981, not later as John Carvel suggests,[19] that Livingstone came under *sustained* press attack.

Livingstone blamed the Brixton riots on years of neglect, high unemployment and insensitive policing. Among other things, he alleged that the Special Patrol Group behaved like a 'Clint Eastwood, gung-ho, World War II' squad and that Sir David McNee, the Metropolitan Police Commissioner, had racist views. The outrage this provoked was compounded by the GLC's decision shortly afterwards to set up a specialist unit to monitor the police, and to award a grant to a community group to do the same thing in Tower Hamlets.

The official inquiry into the riots later broadly endorsed Livingstone's arguments, though it by no means vindicated all his pronouncements.[20] The establishment of police monitoring units was justified by the GLC on the grounds that the Metropolitan Police should be accountable to the local authority as was the case in all other parts of England: informed scrutiny through monitoring was, the council argued, the best available substitute for local democracy.

But criticism and surveillance of the police were widely judged in the press at the time to be subversive of public order. Livingstone was lambasted in editorials as a 'cheerleader of trouble',[21] who gave 'sympathy to rioters'[22] and was 'actively engaged in a ruthless campaign to . . . destroy good race relations between the police and the community'.[23] The GLC and Livingstone were projected as being aligned with lawbreakers against the forces of law and order.[24] 'Council Gives Cash to Fight Bobbies' was how the *Sun* reported the GLC grant to the Tower Hamlets police monitoring group: the article featured prominently a denunciation by Jim Jardine, chairman of the Police Federation, of 'the political agitators fighting against us' and an inset photograph of a policeman standing in front of a burning building.[25] Similarly, a well-advertised feature by Max Hastings in the *New Standard* was headlined 'How the Left Aim to Handcuff the Police' and was accompanied by a picture of policemen carrying away a rioter with the caption 'In charge – but for how long?' Hastings even went so far as to imply that Livingstone and his friends were proto-revolutionaries who wanted to 'wreck the Tory government – and clearly the riots are useful stepping stones in this direction'.[26]

The symbolic annihilation of Red Ken

Press attacks on Ken Livingstone mounted in a crescendo in the remainder of 1981, and were sustained at a high, though less shrill pitch, for two years thereafter. A clear composite picture of the GLC leader emerged:

'The IRA-loving, poof-loving Marxist' (*Sunday Express*, 27 September 1981)

'A man who through Marxist dogma has become an alien in his own country' (*Daily Mail*, 12 October 1981)

'The most odious man in Britain' (*Sun*, 12 October 1981)

'This man is dangerous' (*Sunday Mirror*, 18 October 1981)

'Not fit to hold office in London or anywhere else' (*Daily Express*, 14 July 1981)

'Who does this monster think he is anyway?' (Lady Falkender's column in the *Daily Mail*, 12 December 1982)

'By turns sinister, unpleasant or merely foolish' (*New Standard*, 13 October 1981)

'This puffed-up crackpot' (*Sun*, 27 July 1983)

'This fathead' (*News of the World*, 7 July 1983)

'This weird creature' (*Daily Mail*, 20 August 1981)

Livingstone's republican views, outspoken support for the 'colonial struggle' in Northern Ireland (though stopping short of an endorsement of violence), uncompromising commitment to gay rights and belief in unilateral nuclear disarmament all put him outside the political consensus, and fuelled press attacks upon him. But a close reading of his articles and speeches, including those directed at restricted or friendly audiences, clearly reveals Livingstone to be a non-Marxist radical in the empirical, libertarian, ethical tradition of George Orwell.[27] Indeed, one of the most striking things about him, given his long immersion in London Labour politics, is how little he appears to have been influenced by formal, theoretical thinking of any kind outside the natural sciences.

But the portrayal of Livingstone as an alien Marxist clearly had a didactic purpose. It was linked to reporting of the GLC's activities as a cautionary tale that highlighted the dangers that lay just round the corner. As the *Daily Mail* succinctly put it, the GLC 'is a grotesque portent of things to come: of what could happen to all of us if we let the New Left misrule Britain tomorrow as they are misruling London today'.[28]

Political deviants

A central theme of this cautionary tale was that the GLC was an unrepresentative, undemocratic body which promoted a fungus growth of politically and morally deviant organizations.

Popular newspapers directly challenged the legitimacy of the GLC on the grounds that Labour councillors had perpetrated what the *Daily Mirror* called 'a deception' on the electorate by making Livingstone leader after rather than before the GLC elections.[29] Livingstone's apologists answered this by saying that newly elected councillors were as entitled as old ones to decide who should lead them; and that the Labour administration's election manifesto was the basis of its democratic mandate. These arguments carried little weight with the popular press.[30] 'The truth which the left will never acknowledge', declared the *New Standard*, 'is that they are operating on a non-existent mandate. Labour won the election under moderate Mr McIntosh.'[31]

The supposedly undemocratic and unrepresentative character of the GLC was further underscored in popular newspapers by labels that defined it as deviant. The GLC was a 'haven for political loons and crackpots', 'a haven for the loony left', its Labour councillors were 'loopy', 'crazy', 'barmy', 'weird', 'round the bend'.[32] The image of the lunatic left was overlaid, in some press reports, with more sinister overtones: the GLC was controlled by a 'coterie of Marxists, Communists and Trotskyites' and 'undemocratic democrats'.[33]

By invoking pathological and anti-democratic images, the popular press provided a tacit framework for understanding the GLC's 'antics': they were the work of subversive or unstable personalities. This last theme was carried to its logical conclusion by the *Daily Mail* when it published clinical assessments of Ken Livingstone by 'three leading psychologists'. One unnamed 'senior woman psychologist' was quoted as saying that 'it is most likely' that his overworked parents did not give him enough attention. 'Probably the only way he could get it was to be a naughty boy – which he still acts like.' Dr Dougal MacKay, principal clinical psychologist at St Mary's Hospital, Paddington, was also reported as saying: 'The desperate need for attention is the hallmark of the hysteric. Mr Livingstone is in the same category as a punk rocker who wears outlandish clothes.'[34]

The named psychologists later protested that words had been put into their mouths: indeed, Dr MacKay went so far as to say that not only did he not make the remarks about Livingstone attributed to him, he did not even know who Livingstone was until he read the article.[35]

The popular press consolidated this impression of political deviancy by representing the GLC as being, in the alliterative phrase of the *Daily Star*, 'a hand-out machine for the feckless and freaky'.[36] Popular newspapers gave prominence to Tory MPs and councillors who protested against contentious GLC grants. These protests were then followed up in some papers by investigative reports which identified atypical grants and projected them in a stereotypical way as hand-outs to 'Queers' Lib' and other 'bizarre minority groups' from the 'lunatic fringe'.[37] The citation of new controversial grants was usually accompanied by the recitation of past controversial ones (notably to the English Collective of Prostitutes and Babies Against the Bomb, a women's peace campaign group) in a catalogue designed to provoke indignation. A succession of newspaper editorials – sometimes conflating negative stereotypes into a single category like 'Black Lesbians Against the Bomb' – articulated this indignation on behalf of the public.[38] This gave rise in turn to protests from members of the general public that often exaggerated already distorted and exaggerated stereotypes. 'The GLC has made London the laughing stock of local government', complained a retired trade union leader, for instance 'by opening its doors to every no-hoper, Marxist trouble-maker, political scrounger, foreign terrorist and sexual pervert who wanted a public handout.'[39]

What was perhaps surprising is that the press did not devote more space to attacking the GLC's grants policy as a Tammany Hall strategy for buying electoral support.[40] This would have come uncomfortably close to home. But the main gravamen of the press campaign was highly misleading: a computer print-out of GLC grants shows that most of its awards went to orthodox groups running crèches, playgroups, community workshops, cultural and sporting activities, and facilities for local community and ethnic associations.[41]

Threat to the majority

The central theme of the press's cautionary tale led to a predictable denouement: the GLC was a threat to the interests of the majority – to their liberty, security, values and pockets.

The 'lunatic fringe' was portrayed as parasites living off ordinary, 'decent' families, and a financial burden undermining businesses and consequently jobs. As the *Daily Mail* put it, 'terroristic rates . . . have produced a rash of bankruptcies and a flight of firms and offices' because 'the militant lesbians, babies for peace . . . and revolutionary "creators" of all kinds have soaked up millions of ratepayers' money'.[42]

The GLC's libertarian policies were also projected in many papers not as a move towards greater tolerance and freedom but as a frontal assault on societal values. When the GLC endorsed through ILEA the right of gay teachers to 'come out', it was reported characteristically by the *Sun* as 'Gay Sirs' Charter to Cuddle at School' and was the subject of an editorial which urged the government to close down the GLC.[43] The *Daily Express* was even more outraged, arguing that the GLC's new policy could rock the very foundations of London's educational system. 'Standards of education may fall relentlessly', thundered its leader. 'Codes of discipline and decent behaviour may hardly exist.'[44] Blamed for subverting traditional sex norms, the GLC was also accused of flaunting sexuality in an offensive way. 'GLC leftwingers', the *Daily Mail* warned, 'are thinking of granting up to £200,000 for a park display showing nude figures, some of them having sex.'[45] Nothing, it seemed, was sacred to what the *Daily Express* called 'the Boy George of local authorities'.[46] According to some newspaper reports of the GLC's anti-heterosexism campaign, the GLC was a threat to the family as a social unit.[47]

GLC leaders were also portrayed as undermining the nation's security. Accused of wanting 'to destroy the police',[48] they were also represented in some papers as political subversives affiliated to our enemies at both home and abroad. Ken Livingstone's opposition to the Falklands expedition was translated by the *Sun* into 'Red Ken Backs Junta'.[49] His decision to speak at a Sinn Fein meeting in Ulster was hailed in the *Daily Star* as 'Red Ken's Trip of Treachery'.[50] Similarly, when Steve Bundred, vice-chairman of the GLC Police Committee, spoke at a 'troops out' rally in Northern Ireland, it was reported as 'Traitor. Leftie Police Boss Boosts IRA.'[51]

The GLC was also represented in some papers as being dominated by left-wing extremists who wanted to destroy the political system. In part, this was implied through the liberal use of the label 'Marxist'[52] but it was also argued explicitly on the grounds that the far left which dominated the GLC 'wanted the street demonstration to replace the ballot box'.[53] Indeed the real assault on the democracy of the country', argued the *Daily Mail*, 'is by the Fascist left, which has now gained a menacing hold on the power structures at union and local level within Mr Ken Livingstone's Labour Party'.[54] The *Sun* was characteristically more blunt and direct: 'Red Ken is about as wedded to the true spirit of liberty as Attila the Hun.'[55] His secret loyalties, suggested another *Sun* leader, condemning the GLC's refusal to implement the government's civil defence plans, really lay elsewhere. 'Where will you be

should the Russian stormtroopers march through the streets of London. . . .
In the streets welcoming them with open arms?[56]

A weakened institution

Initially, repeated press attacks left the GLC badly mauled and battered. In
August 1981, 51 per cent of Labour supporters in the GLC area said that
they did not support Ken Livingstone. The main plank of GLC policy –
London Transport fare reductions financed from the rates – was rejected by
77 per cent. The survey also indicated that, if fresh GLC elections were held,
the newly formed Social Democratic Party would win a majority.[57]

A mid-term poll in April 1983 showed that the Labour administration at
the GLC had recovered some of its lost support. Opponents of its 'Fares Fair'
policy had shrunk to 43 per cent, though they still considerably outnumbered
those in favour (25 per cent); 51 per cent supported the GLC's policy of
making London a nuclear-free zone, with only 25 per cent against.

But support for the Labour administration in April 1983 was still 10
percentage points below that in May 1981. Disapproval of Ken Livingstone
was still widespread: 58 per cent were dissatisfied with the way he was doing
his job compared with 26 per cent who were satisfied. The poll also showed
that there was considerable opposition to those GLC policies which had been
particularly attacked in the press; 51 per cent disapproved of giving 'financial
grants to fringe and minority groups', with only 24 per cent in favour; the
GLC's police accountability proposals were rejected by 50 per cent and
supported by only 27 per cent; 69 per cent also disapproved of the GLC
invitation to Sinn Fein representatives to come to London.[58]

The sheer ferocity of press attacks and their apparently powerful effect on
public opinion demoralized the Labour group. Ken Livingstone subsequently
recalls thinking that 'we had blown it' and that 'we would never be able to
climb back' into popularity.[59] Even after the morale of the Labour group
recovered, some of the staff at County Hall remained deeply discouraged by
persistent press sniping. 'If the "scrap the GLC" brigade are not to make
rapid headway, we must have some worthwhile initiatives soon', complained
the GLC staff journal.[60] Three months later, it returned to the same theme:
the GLC, it warned, 'is continuing to drift . . . towards final disaster'.[61]

The press vendetta against Livingstone even threatened to destabilize his
position as leader of the GLC. Throughout the summer of 1981, there was
growing criticism among Labour councillors that Livingstone's pronouncements on issues unrelated to the GLC were undermining support for the
council and deflecting attention from its achievements. There were also
complaints, not confined to the centre-right of the Labour group, that the
media's focus on Livingstone was undermining the principles of collective
leadership to which many councillors were committed. These resentments
came to a head in October when twenty councillors signed a round robin
letter of protest. Livingstone was at this point in serious trouble since he had
won the leadership only six months before by a margin of ten votes. 'It was

only the lack of an effective challenger', he recalls, 'that made me assume that at the end of the day I would probably survive.'[62] After this crisis had passed, Livingstone's position as leader was secure, although press attacks probably fuelled a minor mutiny in December 1982.[63]

The press crusade against the GLC weakened support for it within the Labour movement. The Labour leader, Michael Foot, publicly blamed the GLC for Labour's disastrous showing in the Croydon North-West parliamentary by-election in October 1981.[64] Neil Kinnock, Labour's future leader, also complained to the press that Livingstone's name 'repeatedly came up during canvassing. . . . The GLC rates also had some effect on the results.'[65] During 1982 and early 1983, many Labour MPs made no attempt to disguise from journalists their belief that the GLC leadership was alienating 'ordinary people' from the Labour Party by irresponsibly turning London into 'an adventure playground' for a 'variety of zany left-wing causes'.[66] During the 1983 general election, Ken Livingstone was politely told that he would not be welcome at the Labour Party's headquarters in Walworth Road.[67]

Thus in May 1983, the GLC seemed marginalized, isolated and vulnerable. All the indications were that it could be closed down with the minimum of fuss.

Campaign for abolition

There had long been a powerful lobby, rooted in the local London boroughs, in favour of closing down County Hall. Events since 1981 had greatly strengthened its hand. Plans were already well advanced for relieving the GLC of control over London Transport, which would further diminish its role. The GLC had also deliberately flouted the government's spending curbs by foregoing all central government funding and raising additional money from the rates. It had thwarted the 'supremacy of parliament' and needed to be brought to heel, its opponents argued, if the government was to show that it was serious in its commitment to fighting inflation. The GLC had even developed pretensions, according to its critics, to becoming an alternative, Marxist parliament with its own 'policies' on defence, peace and Northern Ireland. The metropolitan county councils, all controlled by socialists, were also leading offenders in municipal overspending. Removing 'this unnecessary tier of local government', it was argued, would save money and promote 'better democracy'. Abolition would also be a way of redeeming a twice-repeated Conservative election pledge to reform the rating system.

The press campaign against the GLC was thus only one contributory factor behind the political moves to axe the GLC. Indeed, the press did not play a significant role even in initiating demands for abolition. In 1981, only two newspapers (the *New Standard* and *Sunday Mirror*) called for the GLC to be closed down and they did not press these demands until more than a year later.[68]

But the press attacks on the GLC provided a fertile environment in which an abolition campaign could germinate and develop. The portrayal of the GLC as a threat to the majority contained a veiled call for retribution. The majority was being invited to defend itself by taking action against the GLC. And when this culminated in a concerted move within right-wing circles to close down County Hall, the press offered a helping hand. It gave publicity from September 1982 onwards to calls for abolition from a succession of groups – the London Boroughs Association, twenty-eight London Conservative MPs, the Institute of Directors, the authors of a Social Democratic policy document and the Confederation of British Industry.[69] From December 1982 onwards, newspapers also published a spate of articles and editorials supporting these demands.[70]

The press thus helped to keep up the pressure for abolition, and give the impression that there was a growing bandwagon of popular support behind the campaign. Indeed in January 1983 London Conservative MPs advocated closing down the GLC partly on the grounds that its abolition would be a vote-winner.[71] Margaret Thatcher seems to have shared this opinion: she told the Commons on 5 May 1983, 'there are many people who would find abolition attractive'.

In March 1981, a Cabinet committee (MISC 79) agreed in principle to the abolition of the GLC and the metropolitan county councils without considering in detail how this might be done. This commitment was inserted at the last moment into the Conservative Party manifesto, several days after the election was called, seemingly at the personal behest of Mrs Thatcher.[72] It would be, predicted the *Daily Express*, 'one of her most popular manifesto pledges'.[73]

The underestimation of the GLC

Shortly before this election commitment was made, the GLC commissioned a major survey.[74] This provided a much more complex picture of public attitudes towards the GLC than the simple polls commissioned by the media during the previous two years. Although it added new evidence about the negative aspects of the GLC's public image, it also suggested that the GLC was in a much stronger position than its political isolation suggested.

The survey's most damaging finding was that 78 per cent of Londoners said that they did not know much or knew very little about what the GLC did. The survey also showed that the GLC had an adverse image as an overly partisan bureaucracy which was out of step with its constituents; 72 per cent said that the GLC was 'too concerned with politics', 55 per cent that it was 'too bureaucratic and impersonal' and 52 per cent that it was 'out of touch with ordinary people'. Furthermore, whereas critics of the GLC tended to have clear ideas about what they did not like about it (mainly echoing the themes of the press campaign), supporters tended to be vague, coming out with defensive comments like 'they do their best'.

But the survey also revealed that a very large minority thought of the GLC as a purposive, forward-looking authority committed to the interests of its constituents; 41 per cent agreed that the GLC was 'go-ahead and progressive', 42 per cent that it had 'a clear idea of what it is doing', 44 per cent that it 'acts in the best interests of Londoners'. In each case, these proportions slightly exceeded those who disagreed.

But the most encouraging finding for the GLC was that 55 per cent said that they thought that it did its job well or fairly well, with only 24 per cent saying that it did it badly or fairly badly. However, 89 per cent of those who made a positive assessment opted for the qualified 'fairly well' rather than 'well'. Furthermore, the total number of positive answers was also almost certainly artificially inflated by being in response to a question inserted towards the end of the questionnaire, after respondents had been minutely cross-examined about what the GLC did and should do.

What seems to emerge from the somewhat contradictory findings of this survey is that there was a solid core of opponents (about one quarter of Londoners) critical of the GLC; a larger group of sympathizers whose support was, however, less committed and consistent and who were, in many cases, critical of the GLC; and an intermediate group of those who were apathetic or in two minds. Thus, despite press attacks, the GLC could turn to what was potentially a large body of support.

The causes of the GLC's resilience 1981–3

London has a strong left-wing tradition, rooted in its traditional working-class areas, ethnic minorities and, particularly since the development of a counter-culture in the 1960s, in a number of radical middle-class milieux. Even before mid-1983, the GLC was beginning to weld these disparate elements into a pro-GLC coalition. It secured very much more air time on regional BBC and ITV television, the three local radio stations and nationally networked TV and radio programmes than the previous Tory GLC administration. Ironically, this was partly a consequence of the press campaign which made the GLC and Ken Livingstone more newsworthy. The GLC also worked hard to secure this publicity, giving radio and TV publicity high priority over other competing demands.[75]

This exposure created opportunities for Ken Livingstone and his colleagues to put their case and answer their press critics. In this they were helped by the way in which the broadcasters' agenda began to deviate from that of the press. In the early days, the focus of broadcast programmes (including regional TV and local radio) was similar to that of the national press.[76] But from October 1981 onwards, regional television and local radio devoted less attention to Livingstone's views on non-London issues, rates and controversial grants, and more to the GLC's transport policies, services for London, and new initiatives, particularly in the field of leisure and recreation, than was the case in either the *New Standard* or the national popular press.

Ken Livingstone also proved to be an adept performer on both radio and television – funny, relaxed, self-deprecating and direct. A conscious attempt was made to exploit this talent by placing him on chat shows and programmes without an overly serious political format in order to counteract his press image as the extremist commissar of County Hall. 'We set out', recalls his skilled press officer, Nita Clarke, 'to make him the Terry Wogan of British politics.'[77] In 1982, Ken Livingstone came second, after the Pope, in the poll for Radio Four's Personality of the Year.

The GLC also sought to circumvent the press through direct promotion. It introduced a quarterly freesheet newspaper, the *Londoner*, distributed direct to people's homes, although the available evidence suggests the paper had only a limited impact.[78] Between 1981 and mid-1983, it also commissioned a number of advertising campaigns, attacking the Law Lords' judgement against Fares Fair (£300,000), the withdrawal of the rate support grant for London (£200,000) and the proposed withdrawal of the GLC's control over London Transport (£150,000). In addition, it mounted campaigns proclaiming GLC's Peace Year (£200,000), London as a nuclear-free zone (£80,000) and the medical effects of a nuclear holocaust (£100,000). However, the GLC probably reduced the effectiveness of its promotion by trying to say too many things at the same time, given the relatively modest budgets it allocated at this stage to advertising.

More important was the way in which the GLC connected with different sections of the community. The GLC funded voluntary groups on an unprecedented scale, rising from little over £2 million in 1981–2 to £10 million in 1982–3, and £47 million in 1983–4. By December 1983, the GLC was financing over 1000 voluntary organizations, with a heavy emphasis on ethnic, women's, gay, youth and disabled organizations. It also co-opted people from these different groups in the GLC's decision-making process over the allocation of grants. Thus, when the GLC was faced with abolition, it was already constructing a powerful network of support. This reached more widely into the community than the shrunken and, in terms of social composition, increasingly unrepresentative activist organization of the London Labour Party which had been the Labour administration's original power base.

The GLC's resilience is also partly to be explained by sheer good fortune. In 1981, it was heading towards the kind of internal bickering and splits that weakened a number of other left-wing councils in the early 1980s. The GLC's root problem was that its subsidized fares policy had become exorbitantly expensive because of the way in which the government had reduced central funding. To have maintained this policy unchanged would have required *both* cuts in other areas unacceptable to left-wing councillors and very high rate increases unacceptable to right-wing Labour councillors.

The Law Lords came to the rescue by declaring the GLC's cheap fares policy illegal. This restored the unity of the Labour group; provided a perfect issue on which to rally support and rehabilitate the GLC's public image; and, above all, transformed the GLC's finances. The GLC increased its rate precept by 120 per cent in 1982–3 in order to pay off the deficit incurred by its outlawed cheap fares policy. This left it free in subsequent years to improve services and adopt new initiatives, without a large increase in the rates. No other council in Britain was in such a fortunate position.

Public opinion rallies to the GLC

A consensus has developed that the GLC's expensive advertising campaign, skilfully masterminded by the agency Boase, Massimi & Pollitt (BMP), was crucial in mobilizing public opinion against the GLC's abolition. It is a view expressed by newspaper commentators, GLC councillors and Labour movement activists alike.[79]

In fact, public opinion was against the GLC's abolition well before March 1984, when BMP's advertising campaign got off the ground. As early as October 1983, 54 per cent of Londoners opposed the abolition of the GLC and only 23 per cent were in favour.[80] In January 1984, 50 per cent were against abolition, while only 19 per cent were for it.[81]

One key reason why so many people rallied to the support of the GLC was the belief encouraged by two and a half years of press campaigning that the proposal to close it down was prompted by political prejudice rather than an impartial desire to improve local government. In vain, Patrick Jenkin, the Environment Minister, protested that the case for abolishing the GLC 'has nothing to do with black babies against the bomb'.[82] Yet, the pro-government press insisted that, on the contrary, the excesses of the GLC were the cause of its undoing. Moreover, it continued to present the case for abolition in crudely partisan terms. 'The government does not need to produce arguments for killing off the GLC', the *Sun* declared. 'Red Ken's antics say it all.'[83] The case against the GLC, echoed the *Daily Express*, amounted to 'jettisoning the extremist rubbish'.[84]

This style of press campaigning influenced public perceptions of the GLC issue. In January 1984, 54 per cent of Londoners agreed that 'the government is really trying to abolish the GLC in order to silence a political opponent'. In contrast, only 21 per cent agreed 'that the government is trying to abolish the GLC in the interests of Londoners'.[85] In the technical language of media sociology, many people decoded the preferred meaning of press propaganda but adapted it selectively in a way that frustrated its intention.[86]

The government must also carry some of the responsibility for failing to get across its message. The polling evidence suggests that some of the GLC's support was negative, based not on enthusiasm for County Hall but the belief that what would replace it would be worse. In January 1984, 52 per cent thought that rates would go up if the GLC was abolished whereas only 8 per cent thought that they would go down.[87] In April 1984, 62 per cent thought services would get worse after abolition; 75 per cent thought fares would go up; and 55 per cent believed that the administration of London would be less efficient.[88] The government thus lost the battle for public opinion partly because it failed to project an attractive alternative to the GLC.

The government did little to help its case. It took four months of preparation before it unveiled its plans for replacing the GLC. During this period, the GLC had almost a clear field in which to campaign against abolition. Damaging reports also leaked out during the summer of 1983 that experts had reservations about the wisdom of going ahead with abolition, and even that the government was having second thoughts. 'Anxiety is spreading among Whitehall civil servants and many prominent Tory councillors', reported the *Sunday Times*, 'over the consequences' of abolition. 'Subsequent costs could rise, not fall.'[89] Similar leaks were published in the popular press during this period, prompting editorials calling on the government to 'axe now' or at least say what it was going to do, when and how.[90]

The government's White Paper, *Streamlining the Cities*, published on 7 October, was a missed opportunity. It did not spell out clearly where all the GLC's powers would be transferred to. It failed also to confront head-on the GLC's propaganda by estimating the savings that might be achieved through abolition. The White Paper, concluded *The Times*, was 'half-baked' – a judgement echoed by a number of other pro-government supporters.[91] Although the government subsequently refined its case for abolition, its arguments were never fully presented in the popular press which continued to focus its attention on the alleged excesses of the GLC.[92]

The government also made a serious blunder by announcing that it would cancel the GLC elections scheduled for 1985 and transfer control of the GLC in its last year to nominees from the London boroughs. Since this was likely to produce a Tory majority, the government immediately exposed itself to the accusation that it was imposing a political change of administration through central government diktat. As Edward Heath succinctly put it, this laid 'the Conservative Party open to the charge of the greatest gerrymandering of the last 150 years of British history'.[93] The government's maladroit move thus reinforced the suspicion that it was seeking to silence a political opponent.

The row over the cancelled GLC elections also deflected attention from the government's presentation of the benefits of local government reform. And it further helped the GLC by shifting the focus of political debate. The GLC's basic case against abolition was that it would move control of local government more towards the centre; it would increase costs since it would lead to a duplication of functions; it would leave London without a voice and make local government less responsive to local wishes; and it was a way of changing the GLC's policies by subterfuge without consulting Londoners. The proposed cancelling of the GLC's elections thus helped the GLC to dramatize and make more convincing its claim that the government was overriding local democracy.

The GLC was helped by both the quality press and the broadcasting media in its bid to shift the focus of public debate. Between mid-October 1983 and mid-March 1984, the popular press maintained a steady barrage of attacks on Red Ken and the GLC's 'loony' policies. It also imposed what amounted almost to a blackout of criticism of the government's plans for abolition –

including highly newsworthy criticism from within the Conservative Party's own ranks. In contrast, the quality press gave prominence to criticism of the government's plans: indeed, four quality newspapers published leaders opposing abolition.[94] While their circulations were not large, they encouraged the broadcasting media to give prominence to the democracy–centralization issues raised by the GLC's abolition rather than the loony left themes promoted by the popular press. Thus to give just one example, radio, television and every quality national daily all reported on 19 January 1984 that the GLC Tory leader, Alan Greengross, had supported Ken Livingstone in demanding a directly elected London council in a press conference unveiling the GLC's response to the government's White Paper. The only GLC stories reported that day in the national popular press were a report of 'the latest daftness from Ken Livingstone's apparatchniks' at the Old Vic Theatre and an editorial denouncing the GLC's latest grant to resettle black female prisoners in the community as an example of 'its search for ever more imaginative and offensive ways of wasting the ratepayers' money'.[95]

The GLC was also highly adept in the way in which it mobilized support. After the general election, the resources and energies of County Hall were directed primarily towards campaigning for survival. Civil servants were dispatched to speak to the professional associations and organizations to which they belonged; the GLC's leaders spoke at every available forum including a fringe meeting at the Conservative Party Conference; GLC workers called on the organizations funded by County Hall to rally to its defence (and sometimes advised them how to campaign – which, for many of these organizations, was a new experience). A stream of press releases was issued attacking abolition, in marked contrast to the infrequent statements coming from the Department of the Environment. A 'democracy day' in London, consisting of large demonstrations, strikes and meetings, was also organized.

The GLC further consolidated its support by taking full advantage of the additional funds it possessed in the financial year 1983–4. In addition to advertising its services, it reintroduced a cheap fares policy (on a more modest scale than before), established a Forum for the Elderly, inaugurated the Greater London Enterprise Board to save jobs under threat and create new ones, established a 'lorry ban' policy to reduce heavy traffic in the city, and increased its support for minority groups. Its financial freedom, in marked contrast to other local authorities, thus enabled it to appeal to a broad cross-section of the community from executives travelling to work by London Transport to Afro-Caribbean minority groups supported by the council.

That the GLC succeeded early on in generating community support is borne out by the survey evidence. In October 1983, many more Londoners (54 per cent) opposed the abolition of the GLC than did the population as a whole (32 per cent). This difference was only partly to be explained by the higher level of support for Labour in London compared with the rest of the country: this only amounted to a difference of 8 percentage points in late October 1983.[96] The difference was mainly due to the higher level of awareness of the plan to abolish the GLC that local campaigning had created, and the increasing local support that the GLC had begun to harvest.

The consolidation of support

By March 1984, the GLC had won the battle for public opinion. In the subsequent period, support for the GLC was merely strengthened and extended.

The GLC spent £5 million on a major advertising campaign mounted by BMP.[97] The first phase of this campaign, crystallizing around the slogan 'Say No to No Say', attacked the cancelling of the GLC elections. This strategy was adopted, after initial qualitative research, because it focused on an aspect of the GLC's abolition that aroused most opposition; it chimed with many people's fears about increasing government centralization and high-handedness; it was intended to enable Tories to adopt dissident views about the GLC without challenging their basic beliefs; and its overriding aim was to overwhelm the popular press arguments against the GLC by making the democracy issue more salient. The campaign was initially targeted towards the 37 per cent of Londoners who, unprompted, were not aware of the government's plans to abolish the GLC.[98] It was a skilfully conceived campaign aimed at people with lightly held views, emphasizing a message to which many people were already predisposed to respond, designed to persuade by shifting the agenda to the advantage of the GLC. It thus conformed to the specifications of what social scientific research suggests would be an effective communications strategy.[99]

The second phase of the campaign was a pre-emptive strike designed to blunt the government's arguments that abolition would lead to more decentralized and less bureaucratic local government. It sought to overwhelm negative images of County Hall with still more negative images of Whitehall such as a bowler-hatted snail, a bowler-topped brick wall, and poster boards bound with red tape with the slogan 'Imagine what London would be like run by Whitehall'. By thus projecting a simple (and partly misleading) message that the GLC would be replaced by central state control, the campaign sought to convince people that the alternative to the GLC would be less responsive to local views, more impersonal and, by implication, more expensive. The final phase of the campaign, extending through to 1985, was designed to raise the political temperature by emphasizing the government's insensitivity to majority opinion and the political price it would pay if it pressed ahead with abolition. It was summed up in the slogan '74% Say No'.

The GLC also fully developed during this period what was, in a British context, an innovatory style of campaigning based on a massive programme of public meetings, festivals, rallies and events. These ranged from family jamborees like Thamesday, which promoted the council by fostering people's collective identification as Londoners, to pop concerts and festivals which skilfully associated the GLC with the life-style of subgroups who traditionally display little interest in municipal politics, to locally based agitation such as hiring the main Brixton disco to promote union membership among low-paid workers in fast food chains.[100] The scale of this programme is best indicated by summarizing what happened in one month, selected at random: in March 1985, the GLC's 'link team' organized or intervened in thirty-four local meetings, events and festivals as well as nine general, London-wide events.[101] During 1984, the GLC also organized a petition which 27 per cent of Londoners were asked to sign.[102] As a symbolic protest, it caused a number of by-elections to occur in a mini-referendum which Labour candidates all won but with very low polls. It 'branded' its buildings and services with the GLC label in order to project more effectively the work it did for the community. And it also expanded its social network of support by increasing the number of organizations it funded to over 2500 by 1985–6.

The GLC also secured more favourable media coverage than before. TV and radio continued to give prominence to the democracy and centralization aspects of the GLC's case, while the popular press campaign against County Hall began to buckle. All three national newspapers in the Mirror Group were converted to the GLC's cause, beginning with the *Sunday Mirror*'s dramatic conversion in January 1984 – only a few months after it had been pressing the government to speed up the GLC's abolition.[103] The *New/London Standard*, long the leading prosecutor of the GLC, also came round to supporting a directly elected authority for London.[104] And a large section of the press, including such pro-government papers as the *Mail on Sunday* and the *Daily Express*, broke ranks and opposed the cancelling of the GLC elections.[105] While most of the popular press continued to be critical of the GLC, its criticism became less shrill and vehement.

The change in the general tenor of the popular press was mainly due to the GLC's successful campaign. Headlines like 'Goodbye to the Clowns'[106] could no longer be run without seeming to dismiss the views of the substantial majority who opposed the GLC's abolition. The growing number of Tory dissidents who spoke out against abolition further complicated the issue, dissolving the simple equation between opposing extremism and closing down County Hall. The GLC's leaders also became more diplomatic, which helped to placate press opposition. Whereas Ken Livingstone had boycotted the royal wedding in 1981, he was happy three years later to invite the Queen to open the Thames Barrier and claim that she was on the GLC's side.[107] The fears that fuelled the initial press attacks on 'Red Ken' had also subsided. Bennism had been defeated in the Labour Party, and Britain's inner city ghettoes had not been put to flames by disaffected youths. Indeed Livingstone came to be identified in 1985 as part of the 'cuddly left' – a phrase which his astute press officer claims to have coined[108] – whose emergence further marginalized Tony Benn as a political force.

The GLC was also helped by changes in the wider political context. It benefited from the revival of support in London for the Labour Party from mid-1983 (as well as contributing to this revival).[109] The fragmentary evidence of opinion polls suggests that there developed a growing public perception that the government was too high-handed. Those predicting that the Conservative government's term of office would result in less personal freedom increased significantly between 1983 and 1985, while substantial majorities expressed disapproval of the government's rate-capping policy, the Home Secretary's attempt to persuade the BBC not to screen its *Real Lives* documentary on Northern Ireland, and the government's ban on trade unions at the secret communications headquarters, GCHQ, at Cheltenham.[110] People also adopted during the early 1980s much more favourable attitudes towards maintaining public services even if this required higher taxation.[111]

The GLC also appears to have rallied support as a direct consequence of what it did as a council. A new Harris survey commissioned by the GLC in 1985 revealed majority support for all the GLC's main policies including cheap fares subsidized by the rates, its lorry ban, job creation measures, grants to minorities, and police accountability campaign – with only one exception, its stance on gays and lesbians. But the extent to which the GLC's policies helped it to win additional support is not clear. Part of the apparent growth of support for its policies, compared with earlier surveys, was due to the way in which questions were asked in the Harris survey which bears all the marks of enthusiastic client participation.[112]

In short, the GLC mounted an effective advertising and grassroots campaign. It also obtained better media coverage, earned additional support from its performance as a council, and benefited from a general, nation-wide shift in political orientations.

The cumulative effect of these different influences can be discerned in the broad trend of the opinion polls.[113] Opposition to abolition of the GLC rose from 50 per cent of Londoners in January 1984 to 62 per cent in April 1984. According to the MORI series, it fluctuated between 62 per cent and 66 per cent from then until April 1985. However, the Harris series, which formulated the question about abolition in a slightly different way, registered a greater fluctuation from 61 per cent to 74 per cent during roughly the same period. The peak of 74 per cent, which it registered in September 1984, was not consistent with the MORI finding for the same month and may have been a rogue (though much publicized) result. Both poll series are consistent in showing that support for abolition remained very low, never rising above 21 per cent between April 1984 and April 1985.

The rapid growth of opposition to the GLC's abolition in early 1984 was largely a consequence of increased public awareness. The proportion of Londoners who knew that the GLC was due to be abolished rose from 56 per cent in January 1984 to 77 per cent in April 1984. This shift was accompanied by a reduction in the number of people who were undecided – many of whom decided in favour of the GLC.[114]

A higher level of public awareness would also seem partly to explain why the GLC mobilized relatively early in its campaign more opposition to abolition than the metropolitan county councils (MCCs). In July 1984, 66 per cent of Londoners opposed the abolition of the GLC – 14 per cent more than opposed the abolition of MCCs in their areas. This was partly because the London orientation of the national media and the GLC's more vigorous campaign made abolition a more salient issue in London. In July 1984, 80 per cent of Londoners knew without prompting that the GLC was due to be abolished, whereas only 47 per cent were similarly aware of abolition plans in MCC areas.

The success of the GLC also stemmed from the continued failure of the government to project an attractive alternative to the GLC. Only 14 per cent said in July 1985 that they thought that Londoners would be better off after abolition compared with 57 per cent who thought the opposite. The biggest single reason people gave for thinking London would be worse off – mentioned by 34 per cent – was that London would lose GLC services.[115] There was little justification for this view since most of the GLC's services were transferred not abolished: support for the GLC was thus partly rooted in a myth.

But the GLC did not have it all its own way. Its centralization campaign failed to convince the majority that its functions would come directly under the control of central government,[116] which perhaps explains why the GLC did not make more headway than it did after April 1984.

Government's limited victory

It was a tribute to the effectiveness of the GLC's campaign, nevertheless, that the government had difficulty in getting abolition legislation through Parliament. Support for abolition declined among Conservative MPs and peers as well as among Conservative voters. A significant section of the Parliamentary Conservative Party – 43 per cent according to one poll[117] – also became convinced that abolition would be a vote-loser.

The government was forced to abandon the first part of its legislation. Nineteen Conservative MPs, including both a former Conservative Prime Minister and a former Foreign Secretary, voted against the government's 'Paving' Bill which would have cancelled the GLC 1985 elections. A second reading of the Bill was passed by only twenty votes in the Lords, despite its large Conservative majority. This prompted the government to climb down and allow the GLC and metropolitan county councillors to stay in office for a further eleven months until the day of abolition.

The government's main Bill also ran into heavy political flak. A wrecking amendment was defeated by a majority of only twenty-three in the Commons on 14 December 1984. The government was forced to guillotine the committee stage of the Bill after 220 hours of debate – exceeding in length any previous debate since the Conservative government's controversial housing legislation in 1971. In a tense Lords debate, the Bill then passed through its second reading with a slim majority of only four on 30 April 1985. The abolition of the GLC finally passed on to the statute book on 16 July 1985.

A number of people at the GLC were convinced that only the demoralization produced by a major split within the Labour group over rate-capping had enabled the government to scrape through. A full muster of

Labour and rebel peers was not present at the crucial vote on 30 April 1985, they argue, because insufficient pressure had been exerted on them during the previous month.[118] This is contested by Stephen Benn, the councillor responsible for the parliamentary lobby.[119]

However, the government's victory over the GLC was only a limited one since it was forced to make a further concession. Originally, it had intended to abolish ILEA along with the GLC. Under pressure, it reluctantly agreed to resurrect ILEA as a directly elected authority but retained the option to close it down by administrative order after five years. This reserve power was removed by the Lords on 15 May 1985.

The government backed down over ILEA mainly because the ILEA campaign made greater inroads into the Conservative Party than the GLC campaign. Unlike the GLC, ILEA representatives formed from the start a common front and fought for survival as a bi-partisan team. They also mobilized a formidable lobby of both teachers and parents in a successful grassroots campaign. In the end, the government became convinced that a tactical concession over ILEA would help to get its abolition legislation through Parliament since it would add weight to its argument that it was intent on promoting 'better democracy'.

But there was another dimension to the government's decision. The press campaign against 'Red Ken' , and the GLC's subsequent counter-offensive, had raised the political temperature in a way that would have made failure to abolish the GLC a serious political defeat for the government. But backing down over ILEA, even though it had a budget approaching that of the GLC, did not involve a comparable loss of face, partly because ILEA's style of campaigning had been consensual and discreet rather than confrontational.

But even though the GLC was defeated, it left an enduring legacy. Its style of campaigning has become an influential model for activists in the Labour Party,[121] and has prompted the government to introduce new curbs on local government advertising. The GLC's massive funding of minority groups also broke with two powerful local government traditions – a suspicion on the left that some voluntary organizations outside the political arena take away people's jobs and are a skinflint substitute for the public service functions of the state, and a feeling widely diffused on the right that voluntary organizations should be funded voluntarily and not become a charge on the rates. The GLC's funding of minority groups and associations on an unprecedented scale will have a powerful long-term influence affecting the policies of local authorities on the right as well as the left.[122]

The manner in which the GLC went is also likely to have a bearing on what happens in the future. By winning the support of the substantial majority of Londoners, the GLC established a clear consensus for its return in a way that the metropolitan county councils never quite succeeded in doing. It is perhaps no coincidence that the Labour Party is currently committed to restoring the GLC but not necessarily the metropolitan counties.

Finally, the ending of the GLC saga had an unexpected personal twist.

Patrick Jenkin, the luckless Environment Secretary, replaced 'Red Ken' for a time as the favourite target for press attacks. He became 'Pitiful Patrick' who 'turned the loopy leftie Ken Livingstone into a Cockney folk hero' in a sorry exercise in 'fumble, bumble and botch'.[123] He has since been banished to the back-benches after a long and hitherto unchequered career as a senior cabinet minister in both the Heath and Thatcher administrations. In contrast, Ken Livingstone has been propelled into national prominence by the press attacks on him and is now a leading figure in the Labour Party despite holding, at present, no senior public or political office (1986).

Retrospective

The popular press played an important role in supporting – though not in initiating – the campaign against the GLC and in persuading senior Conservative politicians to include a pledge to abolish the GLC in the Conservatives' 1983 general election manifesto.

But the re-elected Thatcher administration found itself committed to a policy for which there was no élite or popular consensus. Significant differences of opinion over the GLC's abolition within the Conservative Party and within the professional–administrative milieu in which many current affairs broadcasters moved helped to ensure that TV's and radio's coverage was much more sympathetic to the GLC than that of the popular press.[124] The opening this provided was widened by the GLC in a skilful campaign which combined advertising, grassroots agitation, and popular new policy initiatives. The GLC's counter-offensive was further aided by a growing belief that the government was becoming high-handed and by a more positive valorization of public services. As a result, the GLC consolidated its support. In the last week of the GLC's existence, 62 per cent of Londoners disapproved of its abolition compared with only 22 per cent who approved.[125]

The press's attempt to engineer a moral panic around 'Red Ken' and the GLC 'loons' was thus defeated in marked contrast to other well-documented press crusades. This was largely because Ken Livingstone and his colleagues had more resources, greater legitimacy and a better organized network of support than the various 'outsider' groups that have been studied. Indeed the GLC deployed more resources in the battle for public opinion than even the central state.[126] It funded an expensive advertising campaign unlike the government; it devoted more energy and time than the government to influencing media coverage of the GLC; it involved many more people in grassroots campaigning; and its leaders outgunned ministers in political debate partly because County Hall commanded more information about the problems of administering London than the Department of the Environment.

Because the GLC campaign is so untypical, caution needs to be exercised in deriving generalizations from it. Even so, it highlights two significant limitations on press power which are present, to a lesser or greater extent, in other contexts. First, the predominantly right-wing views expressed by the popular press are offset by alternative views mediated by other agencies – in this instance, by advertising, a house newspaper, broadcast media and word of mouth communication in an organized grassroots campaign. Second, individuals bring to their newspaper reading ideas, values and experiences which enable them to adapt, negotiate or even subvert what they read. In this case, a very large number of newspaper readers clearly adapted in an aberrant way or rejected what they read about the GLC over a number of years.

Indeed, it is probable that press attacks boomeranged to the advantage of the GLC in seven different ways. The press created support for the GLC by undermining its image as an impersonal bureaucracy and by creating interest in what it was doing;[127] it generated additional airtime for GLC leaders to put their case by making the GLC more newsworthy; it increased public awareness of the government's plan to abolish the GLC and consequently made it easier to mobilize resistance; it probably galvanized Labour supporters to rally behind the GLC;[128] it deflected attention from the government's attempts to win support for its alternative to the GLC by concentrating on the GLC's 'antics' to the very end; above all, it encouraged the widespread belief that the government was seeking to suppress a political opponent rather than improve local administration. In this last crucial way, the main impetus of the press attack was adapted and harnessed to the GLC's defence. In short, one reason why Ken Livingstone was justified in claiming in 1986 that 'we've lost the vote but we've won the hearts and minds of Londoners'[129] was paradoxically that he had the good fortune to be attacked in the press.

Notes

My thanks to Jane Fountain who, on placement from her social science undergraduate course at Middlesex Polytechnic, gave me very valuable help on this project; and to Goldsmiths' College, University of London, for a small research grant.

1 S. Cohen, *Folk Devils and Moral Panics*, Oxford, Martin Robertson, new edn, 1980; J. Young, 'Mass media, drugs and deviances', in P. Rock and M. McIntosh (eds), *Deviance and Social Control*, London, Tavistock, 1974; P. Golding and S. Middleton, *Images of Welfare*, Oxford, Martin Robertson, 1982; S. Hall, C. Critcher, T. Jefferson, J. Clarke and B. Roberts, *Policing the Crisis: Mugging, the State and Law and Order*, London, Macmillan, 1978; Garry Whannel, 'Football crowd behaviour and the press', *Media, Culture and Society*, 2, 4, 1979, pp. 327–43; John Muncie, *The Trouble with Kids Today*, London, Hutchinson, 1984.

2 S. Hall *et al.*, op. cit.

3 See, for example, Melvin L. De Fleur and Sandra Ball-Rokeach, *Theories of Mass Communication*, New York, Longman, 4th edn, 1982; Elizabeth Noelle-Neumann, 'Mass media and social change in developed societies', in E. Katz and T. Szecsko (eds), *Mass Media and Social Change*, Beverly Hills, Sage, 1981; M. Gurevitch, T. Bennett, J. Curran and J. Woolacott (eds), *Culture, Society and the Media*, London, Methuen, 1982.

4 *Survey of Public Opinion in London*, Harris Research, London, June 1983.

Although these data relate to 1983, it is unlikely that such widespread attitudes did not exist earlier.

5 Sir Frank Marshall, *The Marshall Inquiry on Greater London*, London, Greater London Council, 1978; K. Young and J. Kramer, *Strategy and Conflict in Metropolitan Housing: The Suburbs versus the Greater London Council, 1865–1975*, London, Arnold, 1978; K. Young and P. Garside, *Metropolitan London, Politics and Urban Change, 1831–1981*, London, Arnold, 1982; *Governing London* (Conference Proceedings), London, University College and London School of Economics, 1984; K. Young, 'The background to GLC abolition', *Political Quarterly*, July/September 1984; A. Forrester, S. Lansley and R. Pauley, *Beyond Our Ken: A Guide to the Battle for London*, London, Fourth Estate, 1985; K. Young, 'Metropolis, RIP', *Political Quarterly*, January/March 1986, pp. 36–46.

6 Cited in A. Forrester *et al.*, op. cit., p. 43 and p. 103.

7 Ironically, the two men principally responsible for pushing through the GLC's abolition – Kenneth Baker and Patrick Jenkin – both argued at about this time that the GLC should be strengthened.

8 This was a central theme of GLC propaganda, often echoed by those I interviewed.

9 *Guardian*, 29 April 1981.

10 *Sunday Times*, 10 May 1981.

11 *Observer*, 10 May 1981.

12 *Daily Telegraph*, 15 June 1981; *Sunday Telegraph*, 12 December 1982.

13 For examples of not unflattering assessments of Ken Livingstone in the quality press see, for instance, *Guardian*, 15 October 1981; *Observer*, 11 November 1981; *The Times*, 13 May 1982.

14 The circulation of the *Guardian*, the most pro-GLC paper, was particularly high in London where it was read by an estimated 11 per cent of Londoners. See *Survey of Public Opinion in London*, op. cit., pp. 121–5.

15 *Guardian*, 29 April 1981, cf. *Daily Telegraph*, 30 April 1981.

16 When Livingstone said on 5 July 1981 that the fifteen Asians arrested in the Southall riots should be freed because they had been 'fighting for their liberty', it was not reported in a single national paper at the time. Similarly, when he declared his support for the protests of IRA prisoners in the H-blocks of the Maze Prison, it was only reported in the *News of the World* (14 June 1981) and *Daily Mail* (15 June 1981).

17 *Daily Express*, 22 May 1981.

18 John Carvel, *Citizen Ken*, London, Chatto & Windus and the Hogarth Press, 1984, p. 13.

19 ibid., p. 90.

20 *The Brixton Disorders, 10–12 April 1981; Report of an Inquiry by the Rt Hon. Lord Scarman*, Cmnd 8427, London, HMSO, 1981.

21 *News of the World*, 12 July 1981.

22 *Daily Express*, 16 July 1981.

23 *Sunday Express*, 19 July 1981.

24 For example, *Daily Mail*, 14 July 1981, *The Times*, 13 July 1981, *Daily Mirror*, 14 July 1981.

25 *Sun*, 12 July 1981. According to the *Daily Telegraph* (12 July 1981), the Tower Hamlets group included people from the local churches, the Commission for Racial Equality and other important local groups.

26 *New Standard*, 20 July 1981.

27 The best and most unselfconscious sources for his views are *London Labour Briefing* from 1980 and *Labour Herald* from 1981 onwards. For more accessible sources, see Carvel, op. cit., and *Who's Afraid of Margaret Thatcher? Tariq Ali in Conversation with Ken Livingstone*, London, Verso, 1984.

28 *Daily Mail*, 24 July 1981.

29 *Daily Mirror*, 11 May 1981.

30 *Daily Express*, 9 May 1981; *Daily Star*, 4 April 1984; *Daily Express*, 30 April 1984. The popular press was perhaps right to question whether Labour would have won so many votes in May 1981, if Livingstone rather than McIntosh had been the leader.

31 *New Standard*, 11 May 1981.

32 *Daily Mail*, 20 August 1981; *Sun*, 27 July 1983; *Mail on Sunday*, 8 July 1984; *Daily Star*, 24 July 1984; *Daily Express*, 7 September 1984.

33 *Sunday Express*, 6 June 1982; *Daily Express*, 8 December 1982; *Sun*, 10 June 1983.

34 *Daily Mail*, 20 August 1981.

35 *The Press and People 1982–83* (29th/30th Annual Report of the Press Council), London, 1985.

36 *Daily Star*, 24 July 1984.

37 *Daily Mail*, 16 February 1983; *Daily Mail*, 22 April 1983; *Sun*, 20 September 1984.

38 *Daily Mail*, 19 May 1983; *News of the World*, 15 April 1984.

39 Frank Chapple in the *Daily Mail*, 27 March 1986.

40 The Tammany Hall image was invoked only once in the press – in a report of a speech in the *Daily Telegraph*, 17 February 1983 – although the press did, on occasion, accuse the GLC of buying support through patronage.

41 Computer print-out kindly undertaken by Mr Tim Cook at the GLC.

42 *Daily Mail*, 19 May 1983.

43 *Sun*, 28 June 1983.

44 *Daily Express*, 28 June 1983.

45 *Daily Mail*, 22 October 1983.

46 *Daily Express*, 29 May 1984.

47 For instance, *Daily Mail*, 2 November 1984.

48 *Sun*, 31 March 1982.

49 *Sun*, 10 April 1982.

50 *Daily Star*, 6 December 1982.

51 *Sun*, 10 August 1982.

52 *Sunday Express*, 27 September 1981; *Daily Mail*, 12 October 1981; *Sunday Express*, 6 June 1982.

53 *Sun*, 10 June 1983.

54 *Daily Mail*, 30 March 1984.

55 *Sun*, 8 February 1984.

56 *Sun*, 9 September 1982.

57 Audience Selection, August 1981; cf. Opinion Research, September 1981.

58 MORI, April 1983.

59 Conversation with the author, 22 April 1986.

60 Cited *Daily Telegraph*, 6 July 1982.

61 Cited *Daily Mail*, 9 November 1982.

62 Carvel, op. cit., p. 101.

63 Nine Labour councillors abstained over a censure motion deploring the GLC's invitation to Gerry Adams and Danny Morrison of Sinn Fein to a conference, following a campaign of denunciation in the press. The motion was carried but Livingstone remained, as the *New Standard* put it, 'unmoved'.

64 As reported in the *New Standard*, 23 October 1982.

65 ibid.

66 Carvel, op. cit., p. 165.

67 *New Socialist*, no. 37, 1986, p. 31.

68 *New Standard*, 29 June 1981; *Sunday Mirror*, 18 October 1981.

69 *New Standard*, 23 September 1982; *Daily Telegraph*, 3 January 1982; *Daily Telegraph*, 2 March 1983; *Daily Mail*, 10 May 1983.

70 For example, *Daily Express*, 27 December 1982; *New Standard*, 14 January 1983; *Daily Express*, 21 January 1983; *The Times*, 26 January 1983; *New Standard*, 27 January 1981; *New Standard*, 11 April 1983; *Daily Express*, 6 May 1983; *Daily Telegraph*, 6 May 1983.

71 *Daily Telegraph*, 3 January 1983.

72 *Daily Express*, 19 May 1983.

73 The press was clearly briefed about Margaret Thatcher's personal involvement in having the abolition of the GLC included in the Conservative Party election manifesto.

74 *Survey of Public Opinion in London*, op. cit.

75 'Politics and the Media' Conference, Goldsmiths' College, 22 April 1985.

76 This and other comments on TV and radio coverage of the GLC are based mainly on an analysis of the daily GLC Broadcasting Logs 1981–6.

77 Interview with Nita Clarke, 17 April 1985.

78 *Survey of Public Opinion in London*, op. cit., pp. 129–31.

79 For example, *New Standard*, 27 March 1984; conversation with Frances Morrell, 26 March 1986.

80 MORI, October 1983.

81 MORI, January 1984.

82 Reported in the *Guardian*, 8 October 1983.

83 *Sun*, 5 December 1984.

84 *Daily Express*, 28 September 1983.

85 MORI, January 1984.

86 This was brought out in the qualitative research undertaken by Boase, Massimi & Pollitt which found that a number of people thought that abolition was prompted by a desire for political retribution but thought that this retribution was 'excessive'.

87 MORI, January 1981.

88 MORI, April 1984.

89 *Sunday Times*, 25 September 1983.

90 *Daily Express*, 17 June 1983; *Sunday Mirror*, 19 June 1983; *Daily Mail*, 23 June 1983; *New Standard*, 21 September 1983.

91 *The Times*, 10 October 1983.

92 This editorial policy was influenced more by what journalists thought made 'good copy' than by careful calculations about what would be politically effective. This was the main reason why the pro-government press unwittingly weakened the government's campaign against the GLC.

93 Cited in Forrester, Lansley and Pauley, op. cit., p. 67.

94 *The Times*, 8 October 1983; *Guardian*, 8 October 1983; *Observer*, 15 April 1984; *Financial Times*, 12 December 1984.

95 GLC Broadcasting Logs, 19 January 1984; *The Times, Guardian, Daily Telegraph, Financial Times* and *Daily Express*, 19 January 1984.

96 *London Attitude Survey* (July 1985), Harris Research Centre, September 1985, p. 25.

97 Information on the BMP campaign comes mainly from 'Outline of the GLC anti-advertising campaign', BMP, 18 February 1985; 'Issue and public service advertising experience', BMP (no date); and an interview with Chris Powell of BMP in the summer of 1985.

98 MORI, January 1981.

99 D. McQuail, *Mass Communication Theory*, Beverly Hills, Sage, 1983.

100 Interviews with Bill Bush, Ken Hume, Hilary Wainwright and Dick Muscott in March and April 1986.

101 GLC Events Diary (34), Campaign Link Team, 25 February 1985.

102 MORI, June 1985.

103 *Sunday Mirror*, 19 June 1983, 15 January 1984.

104 *New Standard*, 1 March 1984.

105 *Mail on Sunday*, 17 June 1984; *Daily Express*, 13 June 1984; *Financial Times*, 11 June 1984; *Daily Mirror*, 11 June 1984; *The Times*, 11 June 1984.

106 *Daily Express*, 7 October 1983.

107 Livingstone was also at pains to stress the Queen's 'real sense of service to the people' and how he found her 'very nice', while his press officer lined up interviews with Livingstone's mother who had been invited for the occasion.

108 Interview with Nita Clarke, 17 April 1986.

109 During the course of the abolition campaign, the gap between Labour's support in London and the country as a whole increased, rising to a maximum difference of 13 percentage points in September 1984. This would seem to confirm that the GLC's abolition campaign boosted Labour's fortunes in London as well as vice versa.

110 Anthony King, 'Rumours of Revolt in a Land That's Not So Free', *Guardian*, 8 November 1985.

111 R. Rose and I. McAlister, *Voters Begin to Choose*, London, Sage, 1986.

112 *London Attitude Survey* (July 1985), op. cit. For example, the questionnaire included the following question: 'I am going to read out some specific propositions which some people think might improve things in London. Could you tell me how strongly you approve or disapprove of each bearing in mind that any money necessary would have to come from rates and taxes. . . . Make changes so that the Metropolitan Police, like the police in other cities, is controlled by elected representatives of Londoners and not by the Home Secretary?' Similarly, the question on 'grants to ethnic minority groups' in the first Harris survey was modified to 'support ethnic minority self-help groups' in the second survey.

113 The following is based on two poll series – MORI (January, April, May, July, September 1984 and April 1985) and Harris (September 1984, December–January 1984–5, April and July 1985).

114 MORI, April 1984. This rapid increase of awareness was probably due principally to the GLC's advertising campaign.

115 *London Attitude Survey*, op. cit., p. 55.

116 In September 1984, MORI found that 40 per cent thought that abolition would

result in GLC functions coming directly under central government; 31 per cent that they would be devolved to local boroughs; and 12 per cent that they would split equally; 17 per cent didn't know.

117 MORI, June 1984, based on a sample of sixty-seven Conservative MPs.

118 This was forcefully argued with circumstantial detail by Bill Bush, a senior civil servant at the GLC, in an interview with the author on 14 April 1986.

119 Conversation with Stephen Benn, 26 March 1986.

120 This was also true of her predecessor, Bryn Davies.

121 See 'Goodbye GLC', *New Socialist*, 37, April 1986, 28–32; Beatrice Campbell and Martin Jacques, 'Goodbye to the GLC', *Marxism Today*, 30 (April 1986) pp. 6–10; 'The Big Yin versus Carry On Up the Khyber', *Tribune*, 11 April 1986.

122 In this context, it is worth noting that the majority of Londoners accepted that funding of minority groups was a legitimate local government function (even if they were critical in some cases of which groups were supported). See the Harris surveys 1983 and 1985, already cited.

123 *Daily Express*, 30 June 1984; *Sunday People*, 1 July 1984.

124 A fuller account of broadcasting coverage of the GLC, and of the influences which shaped it, will be given in James Curran, *The Impact of the Mass Media*, London, Weidenfeld & Nicolson (forthcoming).

125 Harris Research Centre, March 1986.

126 Tony Wilson, who was in charge of the GLC's public relations, estimates that the GLC spent approaching £30 million on promotion during its anti-abolition campaign.

127 In retrospect, the best way to have removed the GLC would have been to have mounted a low-key media campaign rubbishing the GLC as a bureaucratic irrelevance. This would have exploited the GLC's principal vulnerabilities, as revealed by the attitude research which it commissioned. Instead, the popular press projected the GLC as an institutionalized ogre and gave it a significance and interest which it would have lacked otherwise.

128 The suggestion that partisan press attacks rallied Labour voters to the GLC's defence is consistent with MORI survey evidence showing that a high proportion of Labour supporters opposed abolition of the GLC at an early stage.

129 Quoted in the *Daily Telegraph*, 12 February 1986.

Part 2

Media and social control

Introduction

The mass media have transformed the political process. They have revolutionized political campaigning, changed the nature of political representation, modified the functioning of the political system. But arguably these effects, though important and far-reaching, have been less significant than the media's cumulative influence in maintaining the political system itself and renewing support for the economic and social structures that underlie it.

According to Tony Aldgate, for instance, newsreels operated as a virtual apparatus of the state during the 1930s. He shows how they decontextualized the protests and demonstrations of the ultra left and right, presenting them principally as threats to law and order, while providing relatively favourable coverage of other forms of dissent (such as the Jarrow March) oriented towards the parliamentary system. More generally, newsreels portrayed the economic systems as successful and functioning for the general good. This conservative policing of the consensus, according to Aldgate, was prompted by the personal convictions of newsreel controllers, reinforced by the economic advantage derived from working closely with the state.

David Cardiff and Paddy Scannell also argue that the BBC functioned as an instrument of social control. They show how BBC Radio and, later, TV fostered a feeling of communal identity among their dispersed audiences and linked them to the symbolic heartland of national life by regularly featuring public events, ceremonial occasions and festivals. But in contrast to Tony Aldgate, who sees the role of newsreels as being one of state-linked manipulation by the dominant power group, Cardiff and Scannell argue that the BBC was primarily responding to the deeply felt psychological needs of its audience. By furnishing reassuring symbols of national community, they maintain, the BBC satisfied a desire for stability and coherence, gave viewers and listeners acceptable and recognizable collective identities and compensated for a sense of lost community.

The key role played by television in transforming and transfiguring the meaning of one powerful symbol of national unity, the royal family, is examined in greater detail by Daniel Dayan and Elihu Katz. They show how TV coverage of the wedding of Prince Charles and Lady Diana Spencer expressed and orchestrated the collective values embodied in the event. Television, they suggest, became a phatic channel of communication, involving the audience as communicants in a national ritual. It turned 'observation' into 'observance'; a privileged couple, extracted from their leisure class, into the embodiment of the universal image of youth and the drama of marriage; and an occasion of national celebration into a liminal period in which a feeling of community and mutuality was so overpowering as to temporarily suspend, in some cases, conventional norms of behaviour.

6

The newsreels, public order and the projection of Britain

Tony Aldgate

> Enter the dream-house, brothers and sisters, leaving
> Your debts asleep, your history at the door:
> This is the home for heroes, and this loving
> Darkness a fur you can afford.

The message contained in the opening verse of C. Day Lewis's 1938 poem 'Newsreel' is clear and concise. Like many a critic before and after him, he considered the cinema to be 'a dream factory', where reality was dispelled and fantasy engendered. It was a cheap place of entertainment, which all could afford. But for the large audience of 18 to 20 million people who frequented the British cinema every week during the 1930s, it acted as no more than a soporific.[1]

The rest of C. Day Lewis's poem goes on to chart his misgivings about the newsreels in particular. They formed a part of virtually every cinema programme but, the poet argued, they were basically trivial in content and offered nothing to trouble the conscience. To appreciate them, it was required simply that you leave 'your history at the door' of the cinema. For there was little likelihood that they would deal with the pressing or urgent issues of the day and essentially their purpose, C. Day Lewis concluded, was 'to prove that all is well'.

The newsreel companies, not surprisingly, saw the situation in a different light. For their part, they thought they were doing a good enough job in the presentation of newsfilm to the cinema-going public and they took their role as purveyors of news and current affairs very seriously. On the whole they adhered to the same terms of reference and credence as the news-bearing media in general and they clearly wished to be judged by similar criteria of excellence.

'Naturally *British Movietone News* does not identify itself with the views of any one leader or party', suggested one newsreel during the course of a 1931 pre-general-election release. 'These pictures are presented by *Gaumont British News* as an actual and impartial record of the conflict', commented another in an opening story on the Spanish Civil War. 'In impartially presenting these pictures *British Paramount News* is solely actuated by its obligation to report a news item of surpassing importance to the nation and the Empire', added a third in a story which was prepared late in 1936, though not released finally, relating to the abdication crisis. 'Of course, we remain strictly impartial in this unfortunate dispute', stated the *Pathe Gazette* in its 1937 coverage of an eve-of-coronation bus strike.

The newsreels, then, consciously invoked the neutral ideology of the contemporary news media and openly sought to manifest the professional goals of balance, fairness and objectivity. But to what extent did they exhibit those elements of 'impartiality' and 'actuality' which were invariably claimed for their reportage? What sort of 'reality' did they seek to construct in their coverage of events and to what purpose?

Some work has already been forthcoming in answer to these questions.[2] In large measure, this work has attempted to ascertain how much the newsreel companies were permeated by ways of seeing and thinking which belonged to the dominant structures of power, and how far they succeeded in selecting and interpreting the news within a framework which supported the dominant political consensus of the day. The intention here is to further examine the newsreel coverage of domestic events in the 1930s and to look briefly at the depiction of 'hunger marches' and demonstrations by the fascist movement, in particular, in order to outline the specific ideological framework within which such areas of dissent were reported and presented.[3] Thereafter, the purpose will be to assess the motivating factors which most likely account for the stand that the newsreels adopted generally, as gleaned from a reading of the existing records for the Newsreel Association of Great Britain.[4]

One thing is immediately clear: the arguments which have lately been advanced regarding the incorporation by the current media of 'wildly differing activities' with 'quite distinct causes' into the framework largely of one specific debate, that of 'law and order' news, are borne out once again in the context of the 1930s.[5] When they chose to mention them, the newsreels proved especially prone to present issues like the hunger marches and the fascist demonstrations without adequate contextualization or analysis. They were seen, quite simply, as matters relating primarily to the question of law and order. As a result, the newsreels played their own significant part in helping 'to police the boundaries of legitimate dissent' and in articulating 'the threshold of violence' that was permitted in British society.

The agenda for the media coverage of the hunger marches was very much set by the government response to them. It viewed them with hostility and, as John Stevenson has argued, sought 'to give a lead to public opinion by suggesting that the hunger marches were a major threat to public order'.[6] Subsequently the bulk of the British news media took up the same line, adopted an antagonistic stance, and denounced them accordingly.

In anticipation of the arrival in London in October 1932, for instance, of the first 'Great National Hunger March against the Means Test', as it was called by its organizers – the National Unemployed Workers' Movement (NUWM), the Home Secretary of the day, Sir John Gilmour, remarked in the House of Commons upon two points especially with regard to the nature of the NUWM. First of all, he commented, there was a 'very material connection between those in Moscow and some of this organisation'. And, secondly, there was a strong possibility that the NUWM would use every means at its disposal to compel the authorities to abandon the operation of the means test, not least by the expedient of calling for, in the words of the *Daily Worker*, 'mass struggle in the streets'.[7]

Sir John Gilmour's comments found their mark. Little was said about the marchers en route. But in late October and early November, after the marchers had converged on London, the same themes and dire warnings were taken up and reiterated by much of the press. Newspapers like the *Daily Mail*, the *Manchester Guardian*, the *Daily Telegraph*, and *The Times*, all made some play or other, often sensationally so, upon the idea that the marchers were 'Moscow dupes' or 'pawns in a Communist game', and that they threatened 'incalculable damage' and 'violence'.[8]

Such newsreel coverage as there was of the 1932 hunger march, however, tended to ignore most of the political connotations.[9] At that point, the newsreel reportage settled solely on emphasizing the extent of the threat to public order. Indeed, as is clear from a *British Paramount* story on the welcoming rally which was held in Hyde Park on 27 October 1932, this event provided the occasion, most of all, for a fulsome panegyric to the British police and its attempts to preserve law and order.[10]

The commentary for the story began simply by announcing that 'hunger marchers from all over England converged on London, and the southern contingent crossed Chelsea Bridge on the way to Hyde Park. At the end of their 30-day, 400-mile trek the Scottish section approached the park from Edgware Road.' It added, in passing, that 'all available police, specials and the entire strength of the mounted section are here and every precaution is taken to keep order'.

Then, the commentary immediately got to the major point it wished to make and the contrasts it wished to draw, in stating:

And in Hyde Park, home of free speech, the marchers' leaders rally their followers with extremist speeches. The march is completely disorganized and the police are hard put to keep things moving. But the most humane force in the world has its own methods of keeping order. Mounted reinforcements are quickly on the scene.

Thereafter, *British Paramount* raised some interesting questions about the sources of violence on the day, when stipulating that 'the hooligan element is getting out of hand, and inside the park ruffians unconnected with the marchers give the police a warm time'. However, it concluded on a suitably heartening and reassuring note: 'the mob slings anything they can lay their hands on, but discipline tells and it's long odds on the police. By calmness and great courage the police have averted bloodshed and serious disturbance.'

The debate about law and order provided a ready-made mould in which many such stories were cast. And the newsreel depiction of the marches by the British Union of Fascists (BUF) was permeated by much the same sort of emphasis and reassurances. It showed, if anything, even less inclination to delve into the issues at stake. The events in October 1936, for instance, which culminated in the 'Battle of Cable Street', were reported by the *Universal Talking News* in the following terms:

> All this shemozzle arose because one man in whom a lot of people placed faith said 'We'll take a walk through the East End of London.' Then several other men, in whom a lot of people placed faith, said 'Not on your —— life, you don't.' Then the police said 'Now, now, you children, you can't do that there 'ere', and started sorting them out. It wasn't easy, but they did it because if you want to place faith anywhere safe, put your money on the police.
>
> Batons and truncheons were drawn, exhibited quite a lot, but used comparatively little. A look was usually sufficient. A hundred arrests were made and, while watching, I realized how right film stars don't know they are when they say, 'I think your police are wonderful.'
>
> The way they kept their heads in the middle of a mob which had lost theirs, was an object lesson. Watch how this baton doesn't hit! You've read all about the whys and wherefores of the riot, so I needn't go into that . . . it's been written about enough, or too much, already. But whatever colour of political roulette you back, pink, red or black, every perfervid party punter will, I think, agree that blue is a wonderful saver.[11]

The fact that the clashes on Sunday 4 October proved the final straw before the government set about legislating its Public Order Act, was subsequently acknowledged by *Universal*, albeit briefly and in the same light-hearted, punning vein. Its issue for 28 December 1936 contained a short item looking back on the October events, which stated:

> Disorderly scenes in London's East End, caused by the clashing of political factions, took place, and gave rise to a few new laws regulating or banning the use of uniforms for political bodies . . . Arthur and Ernest didn't want them – it was Oswald Mosley.[12]

Beyond that *Universal* was not prepared to comment.

Yet the newsreels were not above injecting overt political comment into their stories, as and when they thought it necessary. A comparison of their coverage of the 1934 hunger march and the 1936 Jarrow march shows that to be the case.

On the occasion of the former march, which was destined to arrive in London by late February 1934, the Home Secretary repeated the earlier warning that such events were bound to lead to 'grave disorder and public disturbance'.[13] In fact the march turned out to be comparatively disciplined and orderly. But *Paramount*, who covered from the outset the march of a Scottish contingent this time, also feared the worst and let its thoughts on the matter be known a full month before the marchers were scheduled to congregate and demonstrate in the capital. Furthermore the story contained in its issue for 25 January 1934,[14] laid great stress upon the political ramifications of the march. It started: 'As a protest against the government's new Unemployed Bill, the Communists of Great Britain, with the approval of the Moscow Third International, staged another mass march of unemployed on London.'

It noted that 'the first contingent to leave is from Glasgow and the unit of Scottish unemployed start on their 400-mile walk led by the Clydeside MP John McGovern', and then proceeded to allow John McGovern of the Independent Labour Party (ILP) to state 'the men's case', in a brief interview before the camera. He commented that 'this march to London is being undertaken with a view to securing the restoration of unemployment cuts'. Whereupon the newsreel commentator concluded:

The Scottish contingent is only one of many that are converging on London for the mammoth demonstration in Hyde Park on 25 February. The hunger march has been heavily criticized for its exploitation of the unemployed for communist propaganda, the party assuming no responsibility for the marchers after the meeting in London.

By way of contrast, the 1936 Jarrow march was greeted by the newsreels, as indeed it was by much of the news media, in terms of positive approval. It did, after all, unlike the 1932 and 1934 NUWM marches, get some support from the Labour Party and the TUC. Its organizers consciously disavowed any sort of connection with the NUWM or the Communist Party, rejected the former's offer of co-operation and carefully followed the conditions laid down by the police for the march. It was therefore, for the most part, considered to be 'respectable' and conducted by 'responsible' people, not least being one of its leaders, Ellen Wilkinson, who was singled out for especial praise.

The Jarrow march received a particularly sympathetic treatment from the newsreels, it afforded them an admirable opportunity to minimize many of the larger issues at stake by concentrating upon the plight of one town, and to personalize the story by highlighting some of the individuals involved. *Movietone*'s report in its issue of 2 November 1936 was short and succinct though its sympathies were clear and its approbation obvious:

London at last. The Jarrow crusaders must be glad to have reached the end of their 300-mile trek, despite the rain in town. Miss Ellen Wilkinson, their MP, is at their head and marching with them is a dog that has joined the crusade. The demonstration has been most orderly, their object – a petition to aid their town – a worthy one. So, here's the very best of luck to them, every one.[15]

Paramount's report for the same date was considerably longer and sought, as *Paramount* occasionally did, to provide a more comprehensive overview of the situation. Ultimately, though, it differed little in tone or intent. The approving terms of reference remained much the same, the march was sanctioned and both Ellen Wilkinson and the marchers' dog were spotlighted for attention once again.[16] The commentary ran:

The unemployed Jarrow marchers have reached London accompanied by their courageous MP, Miss Ellen Wilkinson. Councillor Riley, wearing the bowler, is in charge of the march. The 200 men bear a petition signed by 12,000 Jarrow people to draw the attention of London and Parliament to the plight of their stricken town. The oldest marcher, George Smith, is 62.

Jarrow's unemployed are all but 1300 in a population of 35,000. Staying the night at a school in Mill Hill each man is given 2s from a fund raised by sympathisers, then blankets. All who set out on the 5th of October have reached London. In its petition Jarrow calls on Parliament to rescue the derelict town from its appalling plight. Once a prosperous shipbuilding centre, its yards are now deserted and its men idle. Without hope of a job these despairing 200 men have trekked 300 miles south.

Miss Wilkinson, who admits she loathes walking, gets help from Pat, the marchers' mascot. Knowing that shipbuilding will not return to Jarrow, the town wishes the Government to establish there a big oil-from-coal plant, and so give productive work to thousands now on relief. On the 4th of November, Parliament will receive the petition. Jarrow prays that good will result.

Inevitably, given the large amount of attention which the Jarrow march had received and the interest it had generated, there were 'follow up' stories as well. The *Gaumont British News* of 5 November, for instance, contained one such report.[17] It noted, yet again, that the Jarrow unemployed had been 'led by the red-haired and indefatigable Miss Ellen Wilkinson, MP', and then confidently announced that they had 'already secured some assistance for their specially distressed area'. It concluded in the same optimistic vein that was symptomatic of the overall newsreel response to the march: 'We rejoice with them, and we hope their prosperity may be on the way.'

In fact, one historian at least has concluded that 'the Jarrow Crusade achieved few tangible results'.[18] It was certainly 'an immense publicity success' and the copious coverage it received, not least from the newsreels, ensured that it would become 'a folk legend'. A good deal of genuine sympathy was evoked for the town's plight though little, if anything, was done on a practical level to revive industry in the town. Yet for a newsreel company like *Gaumont British*, especially, to suggest in November 1936 less than that 'prosperity may be on the way' for Jarrow, would have been quite out of keeping with the picture it sought to project of the country at large. Outside of the 'specially distressed areas', the rest of the country had indeed begun to experience a measure of economic recovery and for some time *Gaumont British*, in particular, had charted this recovery and attempted to foster the image of a Britain well on its way towards 'prosperity'.

This image had already been seen during August 1936 in a *Gaumont British* story which was scripted under the title 'Wonderful Britain' but released with the title 'The World Today':[19]

At this time when the agony of Spain streaks like a jagged scar across the face of Europe, it is well to pause and reflect upon the position of the world today. In the passage of time it is no far cry back to Abyssinia, so recently wracked with the torments of awful war. From Abyssinia our review takes us to Palestine where racial factions clash unhappily day by day, where riot and slaughter crowd an all-too-complete programme of misery and despair.

In a spirit not of boastfulness but rather of gratitude we turn from these fitful scenes to fortunate Britain – still, with its tradition of sanity, the rock of steadying influence amid the eddying streams of world affairs. Britain's industries have shaken off the chains that kept them fettered in the aftermath of the world war. They have risen from the Slough of Despond which clogged the wheels of progress in the depression of the last decade. Trade returns are steadily improving. Weekly and monthly the official statistics form a heartening accompaniment to the efforts alike of the small merchant and the big boss of giant industry to better times. Our railways today stand second to none. Shipbuilding yards, for many years hushed in the inertia of unemployment, have been given a lead by the triumphant completion of the *Queen Mary*, now unquestionably supreme upon the mercantile lanes of the sea.

Frequently overlooked but never to be forgotten is the vital factor of British justice – the fairest in the world – the physician of civil life whose equity and incorruptibility has never been called into question. This honesty in the courts of evil and wrongdoing is a sure fortress against the social hatred that fosters revolution. The army, the navy and the air force of this country have proved a sure protector and deterrent in the unrest that has prevailed abroad. Britain is taking her stand in the belief that a strong defence is a guarantee of peace. Statesmen who may have drawn upon themselves criticism from time to time, have none the less worked unremittingly for peace at home and abroad. As we look back we realize that their efforts have brought this country safely through the innumerable crises that have beset it in the past few years.

And above all we look to the head of this great nation whose example and courage have won the admiration and envious respect of other nations less happy. Every member of the royal family works unselfishly and without stint in the cause of social service -- the aim and the achievement of Queen Mary and the royal dukes and duchesses has been less to rule than to serve the country of which they stand head. The King – already in the short time since his accession, he has proved a worthy successor to his great father and to his grandfather Edward the Peacemaker – long may he continue to lead Britain from the chaos of world affairs closer to the days of lasting peace, prosperity and happiness.

Nor indeed was *Gaumont British* alone among the newsreels in reaching the summary appraisal it did of Britain's situation. 'Wonderful Britain' was, perhaps not surprisingly, a common enough theme. And it was augmented as often as not by coverage of politicians' speeches, such as the one by Stanley Baldwin which all the newsreels carried on 23 November 1936. There Baldwin asked the populace to contrast the conditions abroad 'with the peace and prosperity of our own country'. And emphasized, once again, that 'for five years we have enjoyed a steady industrial recovery which is still continuing', adding that 'in the first nine months of this year, employment increased by well over half a million'.[20]

Subsequently, despite the need for a greatly increased rearmament programme,[21] and a worsening European situation which compelled more attention, nevertheless *Universal* was one newsreel still happily contemplating the vision of 'Wonderful Britain' in August 1938 and predicting, furthermore, the best for the country both at home and abroad. In yet another report entitled 'The World Today',[22] *Universal* saw just one blight on the domestic scene, 'the burden of taxation', which had been made 'well-nigh intolerable by the power politics of other nations'. Abroad, of course, as *Universal* readily admitted, there was 'a dangerous kaleidoscope of ever changing design' which meant that 'the immediate future is undoubtedly critical'. 'Out of a blue sky the bolt may come', the commentator continued, before relaxing, confident and optimistic to the end: 'But I think not . . . . Let us be old-fashioned enough to believe also that right must prevail, as it will.'

Where, though, did the inspiration for such visions spring from and what prompted the newsreels to produce the comforting and comfortable messages that consistently permeated their reportage?

To judge from remarks made in 1938, emanating from the higher echelons of both the Newsreel Association of Great Britain (NRA) and the Conservative Central Office, it is clear that the newsreel companies were motivated, in large measure, by feelings of loyalty towards the National Government. In June of that year, for instance, the NRA executives (with the exception of Paramount) invited Sir Albert Clavering of the Conservative and Unionist Film Association along to one of their council meetings, at which, and not for the first time, they 'emphasized the readiness of all the newsreel companies to assist the government and public departments on all suitable occasions in reproducing items deemed to be of public interest, although not necessarily of great news value'.[23] In that same month, Sir Joseph Ball, director of the Conservative Research Department and deputy director of the National Publicity Bureau, confided to Neville Chamberlain that he had cultivated close personal contacts with the leaders of the British film industry, including the chairmen of the five newsreel companies, and he felt satisfied that he could 'count upon most of them for their full support to any reasonable degree'.[24]

Certainly, Ball's confidence in the newsreels was not misplaced. The direct political help which the newsreels gave in promoting the government and prominent politicians such as Baldwin and Chamberlain, particularly at election times, has been well charted.[25] And the minutes of the NRA council meetings amplify the extent of the newsreels' willingness to be of help in many other directions. When, for example, the NRA secretary reported approaches from the Foreign Office, which was anxious that a visit by the Sultan of Muscat should be 'fully covered', then 'it was agreed that all companies would do so'.[26] Similarly, when in 1939 a formal request was received from the Ministry of Labour and Department of the Lord Privy Seal 'for the assistance of the newsreel companies in making known the objects of National Service during the period of distribution of the National Service Guide', then it was agreed in principle that the newsreels were prepared to be of 'such assistance as they could'.[27]

The point was, of course, that the relationship between the government and the newsreel companies could be a mutually beneficial one. The NRA meetings are littered with references to the fact that 'the propaganda and interest value of newsreels was universally recognised'.[28] The newsreels well knew they could be of immense benefit to the government. And they were not slow in seeking to capitalize upon the support they willingly offered.

The meeting with Clavering, for instance, was called in part to protest that on a recent occasion the newsreels had not been invited to assist in filming a speech by the Prime Minister. Newsreels had often fulfilled that role in the past, yet in this instance the small Ace Studios had been used. The newsreel companies pointed to 'the considerable amount of publicity that the making of the film had secured in the press' and reiterated that they 'would gladly undertake the work at competitive prices even if there were no question of the resultant picture being circulated in the newsreels'. 'It was a question', the NRA indicated, 'of prestige and not of financial profit. If any genuine publicity attached to the making of such films, it would seem only right that it should accrue to the advantage of those who helped the government and government offices rather than to unknown producers of but little account.' It was minuted that Clavering 'recognised the valuable help that they all repeatedly gave and explained that he really had scarcely felt justified in troubling any of them with so trivial a matter'. He undertook, though, to ensure they would not be so overlooked in the future.[29]

It was not a trivial matter to the newsreel companies for in addition to the point about 'prestige' there were, in fact, commercial considerations to be taken into account, as the NRA fully recognized in its many deliberations. One of the objects of the association, after all, was 'to eliminate competition' among themselves (clearly, that was one reason why *Paramount* finally consented to join the NRA having been initially 'somewhat contemptuous as to its utility'[30]), and there can be little doubt that the objective extended to outside competition as well.[31]

Indeed, an acute sense of business regularly permeated all of the NRA's dealings. In considering an application for the supply of free copies of newsreels for showing at borstals, for instance, it decided that 'the newsreel companies did not feel that they should be called upon to act as public benefactors in supplying their newsreels free of charge to any such institutions, and felt that those responsible for organizing the exhibition of films in prisons or places of detention should be prepared to pay a reasonably high price for the films shown'. It concluded, finally, that 'a large number of calls were made upon the newsreel companies who seemed in many quarters to be looked upon as philanthropic organisations, whereas they were in fact engaged in business'.[32]

The newsreels put a price, then, upon their services. Sometimes the price was simple enough. If the Board of Trade wanted British newsreels to be supplied to Brazil in order to offset the considerable amounts of German and Italian reels which were being disseminated in that country, then it 'should be prepared to pay the cost of such national propaganda'.[33] Similarly, if it was thought that 'newsreels depicting life in England would be a very valuable part of any film shows' to be presented at the New York World's Fair, then 'the newsreel companies did not feel that they should be called upon to incur expenses themselves in the furthering of what was in effect national propaganda'. 'The question of expense was of prime importance', the newsreels would be willing to provide appropriate material 'at cost without any profit', but 'beyond this the companies did not feel justified in going'.[34]

Sometimes there was more than expenses at stake and the demands of the newsreels proved complicated to exact. The 1939 budget, for example, contained proposals for increased taxation on films entering the country and, in particular, for the imposition of an excise duty on raw stock manufactured in this country. The NRA concluded that 'unless the excise tax were repealed or the newsreels exempted from it, they could not continue their businesses'.[35] A campaign was mounted against the taxes on films by the film industry generally but the NRA felt this to be of 'little, if any, assistance to the newsreel case'.[36] Consequently it mounted its own campaign which included letters to the Chancellor of the Exchequer, meetings with Customs officials, reply-paid telegrams to every Member of Parliament, and the enlistment of help from parliamentary agents. A satisfactory result was obtained after the NRA had agreed that its members would reduce the length of their newsreels, temporarily, and that they would proceed, in particular, to omit 'official material'.[37]

The newsreels could not be lightly dismissed. It is therefore no surprise that at the same meeting at which the NRA was congratulating itself upon the successful outcome of its budget taxes campaign, members should go on to discuss an invitation from the Home Secretary for the NRA to join in 'the setting up of a skeleton Ministry of Information which would become effective immediately in the event of an outbreak of war'. It was made clear that the minister considered the newsreels to be of 'no little importance'.[38]

Notes

Epigraph: the lines from 'Newsreel' (in C. Day Lewis, *Collected Poems*, 1954) are reproduced by permission of the Executors of the Estate of C. Day Lewis, Jonathan Cape Ltd, the Hogarth Press and A. D. Peters & Co. Ltd.

1 For two contrasting reactions to this argument when applied to the mainstream cinema generally, see Peter Stead, 'Hollywood's message for the world: the British response in the nineteen thirties', *Historical Journal of Film, Radio and Television*, 1, 1 (March 1981); and Tony Aldgate, 'Ideological consensus in British feature films, 1935–1947', in K. R. M. Short (ed.), *Feature Films as History*, London, Croom Helm, 1981.

2 See Nicholas Pronay, 'The newsreels: the illusions of actuality', in Paul Smith (ed.), *The Historian and Film*, Cambridge, Cambridge University Press, 1976; Rachael Low, *Films of Comment and Persuasion of the 1930s*, London, Allen & Unwin, 1979; and Anthony Aldgate, *Cinema and History: British Newsreels and the Spanish Civil War*, London, Scolar, 1979.

3 The hunger marches have been well chronicled in archive film compilations by Arthur Marwick, 'Images of the Working Class in Film of the Thirties', Milton Keynes, Open University, 1974, and 'The Unemployed', London, Macmillan, 1976; and by Peter Stead, 'The Great Depression', Inter-University History Film Consortium, 1976. And I am particularly grateful to both Arthur Marwick and Peter Stead for bringing certain newsreel stories to my attention. The British Union of Fascists (BUF) still awaits a comprehensive film chronicle, though

Antony Polonsky, 'Fascism', Inter-University Film Consortium, 1981, admirably provides the wider context.

4 The existing records of the Newsreel Association of Great Britain and Ireland are to be found at British Movietonews Ltd, Denham. Access to the records is restricted and enquiries should be addressed to Mr E. A. Candy, director and general manager. I am particularly grateful to Ted Candy for allowing me freedom of access, and to Pat Wyand who in 1977 drew my attention to the whereabouts of these records.

5 See Philip Schlesinger, 'Prince's Gate, 1980: the media politics of siege management', *Screen Education*, no. 37 (Winter 1980/81), 36, for a summary account.

6 John Stevenson and Chris Cook, *The Slump: Society and Politics during the Depression*, London, Jonathan Cape, 1977, p. 222. See also John Stevenson, 'The politics of violence', in Gillian Peele and Chris Cook (eds), *The Politics of Reappraisal, 1918–1939*, London, Macmillan, 1975.

7 Quoted in Stevenson and Cook, op. cit., pp. 231 and 222. The Home Secretary's speech was made on 19 October 1932.

8 Stevenson and Cook, op. cit., p. 177. It seems that there was a fair amount of violence attendant upon the 27 October Hyde Park rally and the various demonstrations held on 1 November, with 77 people including 9 policemen being injured on the first occasion and 12 arrests made, and 50 people injured with 40 arrests made on the second occasion. The 30 October Trafalgar Square meeting appears to have proceeded without major incident. The total estimate of damages done throughout amounted to £200.

9 Stevenson comments that officially the 'news cameras were not allowed to film the NUWM demonstrations in Hyde Park on 27 October 1932, though in 1936 the Jarrow marchers were made a significant exception to this ruling' (op. cit., p. 223), and he also mentions that the police 'gave permission for news cameras to position themselves in Hyde Park to film the meeting' which was organized by the TUC, 'sanctioned by the official labour movement', and set to take place in February 1933 (op. cit., p. 180). However, it is clear from the film evidence that the 1932 and 1934 hunger marches were covered and that *Paramount*, for one, did not accept the restrictions placed upon the newsreel companies.

10 'Hunger Trek Ends', *British Paramount News*, issue no. 175, library no. 1451 (31 October 1932) (London, Visnews).

11 'Demonstrations in London', *Universal Talking News*, issue no. 652 (8 October 1936) (London, Visnews). Based upon a reading of the script alone. See also 'Demonstration: Police are kept busy by street clashes in a tale of two cities', *British Movietone News*, vol. 8, no. 383A (8 October 1936) (Denham, *Movietone*); and 'Fascists in East End', *British Paramount News*, issue no. 586, library no. 5464 (8 October 1936) (London, Visnews).

12 'Retrospect, 1936', *Universal Talking News*, issue no. 675 (28 December 1936) (London, Visnews), script alone. See also the comments upon the same in *World Film News*, 1, 11 (February 1937), 43.

13 Stevenson and Cook, op. cit., p. 182.

14 'Hunger Marchers Leave Scotland', *British Paramount News*, issue no. 304, library no. 2413 (25 January 1934) (London, Visnews).

15 'Jarrow Marchers Reach London', *British Movietone News*, vol. 8, no. 387 (2 November 1936) (Denham, *Movietone*).

16 'Jarrow Marchers Arrive at London', *British Paramount News*, issue no. 593,

library no. 5538 (2 November 1936) (London, Visnews).

17 'Jarrow Marchers', *Gaumont British News*, issue no. 298 (5 November 1936) (London, Visnews).

18 Stevenson and Cook, op. cit., p. 188.

19 'The World Today', *Gaumont British News*, issue no. 278 (27 August 1936) (London, Visnews).

20 'Premier Takes Stock, Finds Britain Best', *British Paramount News*, issue no. 599, library no. 5583 (23 November 1936). See also all other newsreel issues for that date.

21 See Aldgate, op. cit., p. 153, and Nicholas Pronay, chapter 3 in this book, for a discussion of the newsreel reaction to rearmament.

22 'The World Today', *Universal Talking News*, issue no. 846 (18 August 1938) (London, Visnews), script alone.

23 Minute 50 of the 8th meeting of the Council of the Newsreel Association of Great Britain and Ireland Ltd, held on Monday 13 June 1938.

24 Quoted in Jill Edwards, *The British Government and the Spanish Civil War, 1936–1939*, London, Macmillan, 1979, p. 198; and T. J. Hollins, 'The Conservative party and film propaganda between the wars', *English Historical Review*, xcvi, 379 (April 1981), 368.

25 See the archive film compilations, and accompanying literature, on 'Neville Chamberlain', by Alan Beattie, David Dilks and Nicholas Pronay, Inter-University History Film Consortium, 1975; and 'Stanley Baldwin', by John Ramsden, Inter-University History Film Consortium, Leeds, 1979.

26 Minute 42, 6th NRA council meeting, 15 March 1938.

27 Minute 124, 14th NRA council meeting, 9 January 1939.

28 See minute 19, 4th NRA council meeting, 24 January 1938; minute 54, 8th NRA council meeting, 13 June 1938; and *passim*.

29 Minute 50, 8th NRA council meeting, 13 June 1938. See also minute 48, 7th NRA council meeting, 19 May 1938.

30 Minute 51, 8th NRA council meeting, 13 June 1938.

31 Minute 128, 14th NRA council meeting, 9 January 1939. See also Aldgate, op. cit., pp. 31–2, for the newsreel reaction to the short-lived National News.

32 Minute 78, 10th NRA council meeting, 11 October 1938.

33 Minute 153, 16th NRA council meeting, 13 March 1939.

34 Minute 77, 10th NRA council meeting, 11 October 1938. See also P. M. Taylor, *The Projection of Britain: British Overseas Publicity and Propaganda, 1919–1939*, Cambridge, Cambridge University Press, 1981, for an extended discussion on the newsreels and the New York World's Fair.

35 Minute of the NRA emergency meeting, 26 April 1939.

36 Minute 206, NRA meeting of principal representatives, 4 July 1939.

37 Minute of NRA special meeting, 14 June 1939.

38 Minute 209, NRA meeting of principal representatives, 4 July 1939.

7

Broadcasting and national unity

David Cardiff and Paddy Scannell

'There is a grumble and a cause of complaining if the crofter in the North of Scotland or the agricultural labourer in the West of England has been unable to hear the King speak on some great national occasion.'[1] These, the opening words of the chapter on the function of broadcasting in John Reith's book, *Broadcast Over Britain*, written in 1924, express a concern, in the earliest years of broadcasting, to employ radio to forge a link between the dispersed and disparate listeners and the symbolic heartland of national life. It is true that in the same sentence Reith went on to mention news, music and scientific ideas as items which wireless should bring to people 'as a matter of course'. But it was those programmes which brought the words of the monarch and the sounds of ceremonies of state or which celebrated national festivals, that came to hold pride of place in the annual cycle of broadcasting in the 1920s and 1930s. Such programmes were often technically ambitious, stretching the resources of the BBC to their limits in order to display the versatility of the microphone in capturing the different stages of a procession or the power of radio to leap continents and unite an empire in the space of a few minutes. Many were remarkable for the very regularity of their appearance in a schedule that otherwise avoided routinization. They were exceptional because, as Reith once put it, they offered the possibility of 'making the nation one man'.[2]

Throughout its history, the BBC has produced a range of programmes designed to promote a sense of communal identity within its audience, whether at a regional, national or imperial level. The relationship between broadcasting and national unity in Britain can be explored in several ways. In recent years research has centred on the theme of political cohesion, analysing the extent to which the output of news and current affairs programmes serves to maintain or construct consensual frames of reference for the interpretation of political events. As Blumler *et al.* pointed out, in their 1971 study of the impact of the televised investiture of the Prince of Wales, while media coverage of the secular part of political activity has received much attention, coverage of events such as royal occasions and ceremonies of state, 'which might be said to symbolise the more "sacred" dimensions of politics', has been neglected.[3] Perhaps the reason for this neglect lies in the belief that whatever impact such broadcasts might have upon public sentiment is to be explained in terms of the structure of the events themselves and a range of traditional and embedded attitudes towards them. On this view, the role of broadcasting is limited to a process of diffusion, allowing a wider public to experience the spectacle in a relatively unmodified form. Yet if we explore the history of this style of broadcasting we find that the forms it has taken and the positions it has occupied within the general pattern of output have varied in a number of significant ways. In the first place it is a type of broadcasting which has not evolved evenly. There are peaks and troughs in its prominence within the schedules which can be explained in terms of the changing relationship between broadcasting institutions and both the state and the public and in terms of wider social changes. Secondly, the form it has taken has not always been the outside broadcast, the relatively unreconstructed image of the event. In the 1930s particularly, the BBC attempted to establish its own ceremonies of the air, employing techniques which were specific to the new medium of radio. Thirdly, changes in both the prominence and style of such broadcasts are closely related to developments in other spheres of programme-making. In some periods new programmes which were thought to be more popular or more socially effective simply displaced the programmes of national identity from their position of dominance. In other periods new styles of coverage came into being which either undermined the rhetoric of the programmes of national identity or began to represent, in a different context, events which had previously fallen within their domain. By examining these historical themes we may succeed in getting a purchase on the part played by broadcasting in promoting national unity at a symbolic level, which would not be achieved if we limited our analysis to contemporary forms.

In order to understand the peculiar position which the programmes of national identity occupied within the pattern of the BBC's output during the early years of the monopoly, we have first to unravel some of the intentions which lay behind the ideal of radio as an instrument of national culture. The original idea of public service broadcasting rested on the intention of democratizing culture and politics by offering a new mass audience access to forms and processes from which it had previously been excluded. It aimed to raise the level of taste, information and understanding and so to make all members of society more actively responsive to, and responsible for, the nation's culture and politics. The policy was democratic not in the sense that it bowed to the popular will or sought to cater for the tastes and expectations of the average citizen, but in the sense that it tried to bring within the reach of all, those cultural goods which had previously been available only to the privileged. This prescriptive attitude, with its roots in late-nineteenth-century liberalism, should not be dismissed as élitist or manipulative. Its major contradiction lay in the fact that it separated culture, knowledge and political attitudes from their basis in the differing economic and social circumstances of the population. It idealized culture and politics and the national community, and required for its sustenance a utopian position of genuine autonomy for broadcasting as a social institution. It was always Reith's contention that only the BBC, armed with 'the brute force of monopoly', could achieve these aims. But in fact, the original concept of public service broadcasting was eroded from the very moment the corporation came into being.

The BBC had serious difficulties in gaining access to the material it wished to distribute. In the fields of entertainment and news it met with resistance from the vested interests of the theatre and newspaper proprietors. Nowhere was its development more stunted than in the sphere of political broadcasting. Here there can be no doubt of the radical bent of Reith's original intentions. He wrote of 'a new and mighty weight of opinion' being formed,[4] and confidently expected that the live coverage of the proceedings of Parliament would be permitted. But at the time when the BBC received its charter, in 1926, he met with what he clearly saw as a betrayal at the hands of the first chairman of the Board of Governors, who capitulated to a government demand for a ban on the broadcasting of controversial matter. Even after the ban was lifted in 1928, the BBC had to face continuing government interference in the broadcasting of political issues while at the same time it failed to gain reasonable access to politicians, because of the inability of the main parties to agree on an equitable means of sharing air time. The ambitious Reith moved increasingly in the establishment and began to absorb its attitudes. Although the BBC continued, sometimes successfully, to further debate on current political and social issues, the bulk of its political output took on the character of an education for citizenship, offering elucidation of issues at an abstract level which transcended current controversy. There was a shift away from the early concept of public service primarily as an instrument of access which would stimulate participation in the democratic process. In later years Reith wrote of broadcasting as 'the integrator of democracy', adding 'integration is a process not of gross summation but of ordering and evaluation'.[5] Underlying this shift of emphasis was a tacit acknowledgement that the BBC did not possess the autonomy to conduct such ordering and evaluation independently. The policy of integration was designed as much to persuade the authorities of the integrity of the BBC as a national institution as to serve the interests of democracy. Largely avoiding current political controversy,[6] broadcasting attempted to provide a stable framework of knowledge and an enduring sense of the moral order. In the secular sphere of politics, radio talks offered a progressive and pragmatic syllabus for the modern citizen. In the sacred sphere, the programmes of national identity tried, through a new and universal means of communication, to restore the currency of older cultural traditions and to re-establish their purchase on the heart and imagination of the public.

If we seek regularity in the early schedules, we find it not so much in the daily or weekly recurrence of individual programmes as in the annual return to a range of key public events, ceremonies of state and national festivals, all presented within a single, unified context. Special anniversary programmes marked the great religious festivals, Christmas and Easter, the national saints' days of Scotland, Wales and Ireland, days of solemn remembrance and national pride such as Armistice Day and Empire Day. But included in the same round were sporting occasions, the FA Cup Final and the Boat Race, civic ceremonies such as the Lord Mayor's Banquet, the annual relay of the Ceremony of the Keys from the Tower of London. To these may be added some events brought to prominence by the BBC itself: the broadcast, each Christmas, of the nativity play from the church of St Hilary in Cornwall and, each spring, of the song of the nightingale from the Surrey woods. Such items slipped easily into the repertoire, even became national institutions, allied as they were to the preordained cycles of church and nature. Most of these programmes took the form of an outside broadcast, a live relay of the event itself. Here radio minimized its own presence as witness, claiming simply to distribute the event beyond its particular location and participants to the whole listening community. For some occasions, special feature programmes were produced. While these involved more artifice and a more self-conscious display of the potentialities of radio, they dealt for the most part in the material of pre-established tradition and sentiment.

The unity in diversity of this programme material is best understood not so much as a cluster of distinct styles or categories of content (outside broadcast or feature; sport, religion or state ceremonial), nor in relation to normal daily or weekly output, but as constituting a stable framework which organized and defined the broadcast year. Not all programmes which symbolized national unity fitted into this annual rhythm. The activities of royalty were covered whenever possible and unique events such as the royal jubilee of 1935 and George VI's coronation received the elaborate attentions of the microphone. But nothing so well illustrates the unobtrusive way in which the BBC came to establish itself as an agent of the national culture as this calendrical role of broadcasting, this cyclical reproduction, year in, year out, of an orderly and regular progression of festivities, rituals and celebrations which marked out the unfolding of the year. Through the wireless, the previously separated idioms of national identity entered into a new relationship both with one another and with a national audience. Innocently and naturally, broadcasting appeared to be holding together the great chain of social being, linking individuals to the centre of national life, town to country, region to region and even nation to nation. The *BBC Yearbook* for 1930 claimed: 'The broadcasting of ceremonials appeals, it would appear, to a very wide circle of listeners. Perhaps it is the only activity of the BBC to attract an audience drawn equally from all grades of the listening public.'[7]

If we are to be more than suggestive in imputing a 'sacred' character to such diverse forms of programme, we must clarify our use of the term. Durkheim's dichotomy between the sacred and the profane and his account of the function of ritual have caused enough problems for anthropologists studying traditional societies to make us wary of adopting them in an analysis of the role of a new technology of communication in a secular and industrial society. Even those anthropologists who have claimed a role for 'secular ritual' in more developed societies have restricted themselves to exploring ceremonial activities which involve the active participation of small and bounded communities.[8] It could be argued that broadcasting was too distant and impersonal a medium, that its audience was too diverse, that the significance of the collective symbols in which it dealt had become too attenuated for it to act upon mass consciousness with the force of sacred ritual. Yet if we restrict ourselves for the moment to the level of strategy, to the intentions which lay behind the programmes rather than to their realization or effects, the analogy is too compelling to be ignored. Like sacred objects and occasions, the programmes were 'set apart' in several ways from normal, daily output.

Broadcasting was received in the home and the normal structure of programming, at least until 1937, was developed by producers who held constantly in mind the image of a family audience, seated round the fireside at home. To see the audience in terms of a vast cluster of families rather than in terms of social classes or different taste publics was to adopt a model which was consonant with the idealized and abstracted nature of the concept of public service broadcasting. Because radio was directed at the home it was the duty of broadcasters to thread their material into the fabric of family life without warping it; to diffuse ideas, information, music and entertainment without being brashly intrusive; to take account of the diversity of taste by providing diversified programmes; above all to avoid standardization. One of the most striking features of the programming of the period is the absence of routinization. A cursory appreciation of listeners' life-style and the exigencies of programme planning might result in a few 'fixed points' during the day when particular types of programme, like news, talks or light music could be heard. But on the whole these were not arranged in series, with a regular presenter and a settled format. Listeners were enjoined to be selective in their choice of programmes, not to use the wireless to provide a continuous background of noise to punctuate the domestic round. The frequently voiced objection to American commercial radio was not simply that it pandered to popular taste but that it treated listeners as a mass market to be exploited rather than as individuals who should themselves be invited to exploit the range of cultural goods on offer. A writer in the *Radio Times* was pained to discover that America 'should be content to use the great new gift of radio as nothing more than a soothing tom-tom for the Tired Business Man'. More significantly, he complained that 'the backbone of broadcast programmes in the United States is not the big occasion – a speech by the President or a visiting Queen – not the news or the talks or anything else, but the jazz band'.[9] For while British broadcasters wished to preserve the individuality of their listeners they recognized that radio had a unique potential for uniting the public to the private sphere of life, and it was for this reason that the programmes of national identity formed the backbone of British broadcasting.

The programmes of national identity were 'set apart' because, appearing with ritualistic regularity, they gave order to a pattern of output that was otherwise diverse and random. Only on special occasions like Christmas Day could one discover a thematic unity within one day's output. That this order and regularity went against the grain is demonstrated by the worry expressed by BBC planners that output was becoming too stereotyped, that items such as the broadcast of the nightingale or the Ceremony of the Keys were tried once and then became regular fixtures. Again, like sacred rituals, the programmes diffused symbols of collective identity. They were designed to be listened to *en masse*. Often no alternative programmes were offered, the principle of selective listening was temporarily abandoned, the taboo against standardization defied. Just on these special occasions, it appeared, each family of listeners was encouraged to desist from the profane pursuit of its individual tastes and habits and to experience a tribal unity as radio paraded the sacred emblems of church or state or empire.

It may seem tempting to regard all this from a narrowly political position – as a form of social manipulation and control, as serving to gloss over the sharp class divisions of inter-war Britain with the bland pabulum of national community. On a cynical interpretation, the BBC's promotion of this sense of community could be seen simply as a means of legitimizing its own status as a national institution. Such an analysis would be superficial for it fails to take into account the wider needs and dilemmas of a society characterized by continual dislocation and change. Raymond Williams, among others,[10] has suggested that the press since the nineteenth century, and broadcasting in the twentieth, have come to fulfil a complex ideological role which older institutions such as the church and school could no longer deliver. Though they were placed in close association with the centres of political, economic and cultural power and authority, the press and broadcasting nevertheless became accepted as 'unofficial' channels which linked private individuals to an increasingly corporate, public and national process. In doing so they became for society, if not for the institutions of power and authority, primary definers of that process. The press by the rapid transmission of news and comment could reorientate private individuals to accelerating political and social change and to the controversy and anxiety to which it gave rise. But while newspapers fuelled controversy and played upon public anxieties, broadcasting, wary of the topical and contentious, attempted to supply its isolated listeners with a sense of the community they had lost, translated from a local to a national and even global level.

It is only when we consider the actual style and content of the programmes that we can detect the difficulties and uncertainties that producers experienced in implementing this strategy. Except in the case of particularly spectacular events which lent themselves to transmission in sound, the novelty value of the simple, unmediated outside broadcast soon wore off. As early as 1929 newspaper critics were arguing that only television, when it came, could do justice to the live portrayal of events. 'So into the Severn Tunnel for more sentimental and patriotic platitudes by an octogenarian, and buzzing sounds which we were told were the noise of a train in the tunnel, not at any time a vastly thrilling sound.'[11] This critic's response to an outside broadcast from Wales is not unrepresentative. The art of live commentary had yet to be perfected. The more elaborate attempts to combine narrative with music and actuality in the mosaic form of the feature could give rise to uneasy transitions between the symbolic and the actual, the poetic and the prosaic, the impersonal and the personal. The problems went deeper than style. How should such entities as empire or nation be represented? If the BBC drew on older cultural traditions, on history or folk music and poetry, the fare might be too archaic, even meaningless to large sections of the audience. If it attempted to construct its own collective images, it was in danger of indulging in an empty and pretentious rhetoric. If it dealt in the contemporary and actual, it might encounter controversy. Empire and nation were in themselves unstable; there was India, there was Ireland. To expose such rifts would be to defeat the purpose of the programmes. Perhaps the idealized and the actual could be combined if the perfect typification could be discovered, an essentially British location, a New Zealand sheep farmer who could serve as the model for colonial virtue and honest loyalty. Producers explored each of these avenues but none guided them out of their difficulties.

These tensions were most evident in the anniversary programmes which marked Christmas, New Year, Empire Day and the regional saints' days. A salient aspect of their development was a transition in style from the symbolic, rhetorical and impersonal to the actual, vernacular and personal. The pervasive symbol was that of the family, connoting Mother Britain and her children in the empire, as well as the royal family and each little family of listeners. In the Empire Day programme for 1935, a mother was heard explaining to her daughter: 'The British Empire, Mary, is made up of one big family.' Mary asks, 'You mean a family like ours, Mummy?' and mother replies, 'Yes, darling. But very much larger.'[12] King George V who, from 1932, broadcast a personal Christmas message to his people, using a special microphone encased in empire walnut, frequently invoked the emblem of the family. He addressed his listeners as 'all the members of our world-wide family', hoping that he could be regarded as 'in some true sense the head of this great and widespread family' and commending them to 'the Father of whom every family in Heaven and on earth is named'. Although his broadcasts were praised for their intimacy, there was a certain formality in this artifice and in his last talk, in 1935, he dropped it in favour of a more direct and spontaneous approach. Addressing his listeners as 'my dear friends' he explicitly distinguished the general respect of the people for the throne from the loyalty and love he had received as an individual. 'It is this personal link between me and my people which I value more than I can say. It binds us together in all our common joys and sorrows.'[13] To his own Christmas greetings he added for the first time those of his wife, children and grandchildren. It was a small but significant shift. For the abstract unity of the imperial family was substituted a concrete and personal link between the actual royal family and the families listening at home. It was the beginning of a process of personalization.

A similar process can be detected in the elaborate international relays which introduced the King's talks. In these, the BBC sought to give concrete expression to the metaphor of the family. For the first one, described as a 'poetic juggling in space and time in terms of broadcasting',[14] the British announcer was transmuted into an 'aerial postman' who surveyed the spinning globe from a great height and intoned his greetings to each dominion and colony to the sound of a striking clock. This pitch of poetic elevation was not sustained when the postman set foot on land with his 'Hullo Brisbane' or 'Are you awake Vancouver?' and handed over to a local announcer who might mingle expressions of loyalty to the crown with accounts of butter and cheese production or descriptions of a new hydroelectric plant.[15] While critics welcomed the programme as a technical triumph, it was evident that a more intimate style would be needed if a sense of the community as family was to be evoked. In succeeding Christmas features, such as *Absent Friends* (1933) and *The Great Family* (1935), poetic narration and the chain of empire greetings played a diminishing part. Instead listeners were offered slices of life, outside broadcasts from a lighthouse, a coal mine, church services, children's parties and family gatherings, talks from individuals representing different regions of Britain. The characters selected were statistically untypical; speakers of pure regional dialect, members of closed communities, practitioners of traditional crafts. A critic of the 1933 programme pointedly preferred characterful episodes from a Welsh home, Rhondda miners and Highland Scots to the less distinctive Glasgow and Lancashire Christmas parties which he found 'noisy and tedious'.[16] Within the BBC the most successful contributor of this type was reckoned to be the 'grand old shepherd of Ilmington' who introduced the King's talk in 1934. Similar tendencies could be found in the saint's day programmes produced by the BBC's regional stations and intended to give new expression to waning national cultures. For St Patrick's Day in 1933, Belfast put out *Ireland*, a programme 'of the dear familiar things that memory loves' in which folk music and poetry were melded with disembodied voices evoking Irish landscape and custom in the lush verbiage of the tourist brochure. But in 1937 we find the station director planning an outside broadcast from Rathlin Island where 'the people are very timid and live in circumstances that are almost unbelievable'.[17] When this proved impossible, a producer drove up the Sperrin mountains in a blizzard to fetch to the studio a shepherd, a gamekeeper, an embroideress and a country fiddler.

In a fragmented industrial society, such primitive characters and locations are treasured as exemplars of a lost communal identity. They belong not so much to the realm of the sacred as to what Raymond Williams has called 'residual culture',[18] an element of culture that has been formed in the past but is still effective because, however sentimentalized or idealized it may have become, it supplies a lack in and even offers an alternative to the dominant contemporary order. Radio was still regarded as a medium of reproduction; it could diffuse pre-established ceremonies but could not create its own. Instead it presented the nation with an almost arcadian image of itself. Actuality was used to authenticate this myth of the nation as a *settled* community with traditional roots, a diverse but atavistic family, rather than as a means of reflecting actual social reality. The production files for all the anniversary programmes reveal the problems producers experienced in trying to square myth with reality. Empire Day was a constant source of embarrassment to producers who were aware that its traditional celebration involved aggressive and ultra-patriotic sentiments which were becoming obsolete and might offend supporters of internationalism and the League of Nations. Yet attempts to devote the programme to current imperial themes, such as constitutional change in India, were abandoned for fear of controversy. Similar difficulties afflicted the producers of the St Patrick's Day programme. The BBC's station was in Belfast and served the people of Ulster, but as long as the Irish Free State retained its nominal status as a dominion, the programme was supposed to reflect Irish culture in general. In this case, producers' suggestions were scrutinized so severely that the feature format was sometimes dropped, an entertainment being provided in its place. The New Year's Eve programme for 1932 caused a diplomatic incident by mentioning Polish rearmament. Even the Christmas features were not free from controversy. In 1935 it was reported that there were too many difficulties in the way of including a representative of the unemployed in *The Great Family*. This programme was criticized internally as being too pompous and formal for a family audience. Significantly, the objections came from producers in BBC North Region where more honest styles of social documentary and more populist styles of presentation were being developed.[19]

By the late 1930s, the regular, calendrical function of the programmes of national identity was being displaced by a different kind of regularity in the pattern of output. BBC programmes were undergoing a process of popularization. This was initiated partly from fear of the competing attraction of commercial broadcasts from the continent, but more importantly because listener research was beginning to reveal that the policy of mixed programming had not achieved its object of cultural amelioration and that the bulk of audience demand was for entertainment. For reasons of economy and ease of production, entertainment was increasingly organized into weekly series and serials which were found to be particularly popular with the working-class public. The attention of listeners was diverted away from the seasonal round of national occasions towards the weekly date with Arthur Askey in *Band Waggon* or with Paul Temple in the thriller serial. Broadcasting began to look less like an arbiter of national culture, offering a selection of existing cultural forms to a public differentiated only at the level of individual taste. Rather it began to cater more proportionately to different taste publics, producing forms which were more specific to the medium and in this sense taking its place alongside other, more market-orientated producers of culture and entertainment. One symptom of this change was the increase in the number of magazine programmes directed at specific sections of the audience, such as women and youth, and covering specific interests such as sport. These took items which would have been scattered among individual programmes and packaged them in a style appropriate to a target audience. This was a new type of public service, with undertones of consumerism, but still intended to serve rather than to exploit identifiable markets. There was a heightened contrast between the two BBC channels, the National and Regional programmes. Whereas in the early years the Regional had drawn on relatively thin provincial resources to provide the same kind of mix of programmes as the National, the stronger regions, like North and Midland, now began to reflect more wholeheartedly local character and interest. The popularization of content and the compartmentalization of listeners were at odds with the spirit of the programmes of national identity. It is notable that in the late 1930s the Christmas Day features were sometimes dropped and that the highlight of the day's broadcasting, at least as far as the press was concerned, was the radio stars' Christmas party. The folksiness of the old Christmas features was lampooned in a stage review, *Nine Sharp* by Herbert Farjeon, which had Captain Snaggers of the North Sea Bloater Fishing Fleet quoting poetry and a BBC commentator bidding him farewell with 'Goodbye and good bloating'.[20]

It might be thought that the coming of war would have stimulated a resurgence in the programmes of national identity. In fact, during the phoney war period, the BBC's reflex was to put out several programmes of this type. *For Ever England*, a tapestry of famous passages from literature, began, inevitably, with King Hal at Agincourt; there were similar series such as *The Land We Defend* and *The English Heritage*. But this was a transient phase. In a period of anxiety and accelerating social change, the imperatives of the moment were uppermost in people's minds and it was in vain to summon ancestral voices at a time when war had not only been prophesied but had been declared. As the Ministry of Information got into its stride, the BBC began to address itself to more specific aims in relation to specific social groups. The fighting forces required entertainment and diversion. All aspects of war work, on both industrial and military fronts, were to be recognized in special documentary features. Factory production was to be stimulated with programmes such as *Music While You Work*, *Works Wonders* and *Workers' Playtime*. As the war progressed, listener research revealed that such propaganda was often regarded cynically by those at whom it was aimed. It was slowly realized that the communal experience of the British at war was by itself generating a sense of social cohesion which made such exhortation seem not only redundant but even insulting. By the end of the war, the BBC was concentrating on the supply of information and entertainment. This is necessarily a synoptic account,[21] but one aspect of wartime broadcasting may be selected as germane to our theme. This was the tendency to glorify 'ordinary people' as the heroes and heroines of the national drama. The BBC drew on its pre-war experience in regional broadcasting, producing a range of programmes in which 'ordinary folk' were brought to the microphone, whether from factories, military camps or the bombed city streets. A drama series, *At The Armstrongs*, portrayed a typical working-class family facing up to the problems of war. It was the very ordinariness, the girl-next-door qualities, of Vera Lynn that made her a suitable candidate for the title of 'Forces' Sweetheart'. In the 1930s the BBC had thought it necessary to try to attach what it saw as an increasingly fragmented public to the symbolic centres of national life. The aim was not abandoned in war and there is no doubt that Churchill's broadcasts provided, for many people, a focus for national aspirations. But at the same time, the BBC recognized that a genuine, if transient, sense of communal identity was developing in society at large and it learnt to reflect this, albeit in partial and instrumental ways.

The cheerful populism of wartime programmes continued into the late 1940s. *Workers' Playtime* was joined by *Have A Go!* with Wilfred Pickles. The cult of the ordinary reached its peak in a 1948 series, *Meet The People*, in which the lives of actual, representative families were dramatized for broadcasting. The end of this tradition was signalled in a series of outraged letters to the *Radio Times*. 'For our health's sake, let us stop painting a false and dreary picture of our nation as if it were entirely composed of industrial workers, salesmen and "clippies"',[22] wrote one correspondent, begging the BBC to portray heroic figures from British History such as Drake and Florence Nightingale. The reaction was symptomatic of the demise of the wartime spirit of collective endeavour which had seemed, temporarily, to transcend class divisions. If there was once again a need to return to pre-war methods of projecting national identity, radio was now less suited to meet it. With the division of its channels into Light, Home and Third, the BBC had finally recognized the stratified nature of its audience and no longer provided a unified national service. Although the Christmas Day features were revived and were broadcast simultaneously on all channels, they were less nationalistic in content and reflected social divisions. The 1946 programme included relays from Europe and the USA and national contributions were divided into sections covering the armed forces or 'Christmas with the workers'.

It was now television which, like the old National programme, broadcast a mixed diet of items on a single channel. To a remarkable extent, the early development of British television echoed that of radio. There was a similar restraint on television news and current affairs, imposed not by the press this time but by the suspicious senior service of radio, whose hierarchy still dominated the BBC. There was the same inability, for technical and financial reasons, to offer genuinely popular entertainment. In programming, there was the same absence of continuity between items and an almost equally determined avoidance of serial forms, accompanied by a return to the old pleas to the audience to use the service selectively. Once again the outside broadcast became, as Jonathan Dimbleby has expressed it, 'the most valued jewel of the BBC television crown'.[23] Television could portray the spectacle of ceremonies like Trooping the Colour in a way that radio had never been able to but, like radio, it could bind together a range of national events within a unified context; sacred occasions like the Coronation, along with secular events like the Cup Final or visits to national exhibitions. Through such broadcasts it overcame the resistance of the establishment to what was often regarded as an inherently trivializing or sensationalist medium. In this it was aided by the monumental presence of Richard Dimbleby whose dignified and meticulous commentaries defied disapproval. But the charm was again broken – this time by the arrival of independent broadcasting. Not only did commercial television deprive the BBC of its national audience by providing more popular entertainment but it introduced a brash, journalistic approach to the coverage of national events in its news and current affairs programmes. Jonathan Dimbleby has epitomized this change of style in a penetrating comparison between his father's commentary and that of his then commercial rival, Robin Day, at the state opening of Parliament in 1958. While Dimbleby 'heightened and romanticised the occasion, concentrating on its symbolic and historical significance', Day played down the ceremonial content, 'dryly treating the occasion in the same terms as one might a school "open day", when teachers and pupils are on show to curious outsiders'. Underlying Day's commentary was 'the recognition (now a commonplace) that it is what happens within the institutions of state, rather than the institutions themselves, which is significant'.[24]

The one institution which escaped this process of demystification was the royal family. Certainly the veil of royal formality has been lifted fractionally in programmes such as Richard Cawston's 1969 documentary, *Royal Family*, which showed off-duty moments like a family barbecue in Windsor Great Park. (The young Prince Edward asks his eldest brother what he's cooking. 'Er . . . sausages', replies the Prince of Wales.) But in general television has enhanced rather than undermined the symbolic power of the monarchy. While Blumler *et al.*, in their study of attitudes to the monarchy, found that the feelings of the public were ambivalent and even incompatible ('They would like the Queen to be at one and the same time grand and common, extraordinary and ordinary, grave and informal, mysterious and accessible, royal and democratic'),[25] their research suggested that at least in some cases, television could help to resolve the conflict. For the older section of the audience, the effect of the televised investiture of the Prince of Wales was to make Prince Charles appear more formal and distant but at the same time to lead to a revaluation of those very attributes in a positive direction; an altogether appropriate reaction to what was, for the prince, a rite of passage on the road to kingship. Indeed Blumler *et al.* were a little ingenuous in regarding the ambivalence of public attitudes as signifying a potential conflict, for the effectiveness of symbols rests on their ambiguity. Symbols attract and condense a cluster of diverse and sometimes mutually antagonistic associations. They possess a mysterious duality, being simultaneously mundane material things and sacred emblems. It seems reasonable to argue that broadcasting, with its tendency, detectable in the earliest royal broadcasts, to personalize the monarchy, coupled with its ability to diffuse the image of royalty in its ceremonial guise, has accentuated the necessary ambiguity of this symbol both of nationhood and of the family. It would probably be impossible to test such a hypothesis empirically but, by way of illustration, one might ask whether the sacred ceremony of the wedding of the Prince and Princess of Wales in 1981 would have been as effective as a spectacle if it had not been preceded by the purely journalistic and personalized coverage of the secular romance between Charles and Di. Ritual always works to transform and, if it is to be effective, the spectator must have the opportunity to witness the object of ritual in its earlier, untransformed state. By purveying images of royalty in both its secular and sacred state, television enables this chemistry to work at a national level. Allowing for both personal identification and collective awe, it binds together the private and the public spheres, thus fulfilling what has always been an underlying aim of public service broadcasting.

We have traced a single thread in the tapestry of broadcasting – those programmes which offered audiences symbolic images of national unity and identity. The most obvious point to make about them is that their heyday, first in radio, then in television, corresponded with the establishment of the social presence of the medium itself. For their newly constituted audiences they were proof of the wonders of broadcasting. In its very early days the wireless was sometimes described as a 'magic carpet' that gave access to a wider public world beyond the daily routines of a narrow existence. That sense was quite quickly dissipated as radio and television in turn adapted themselves to the rhythms of everyday life. What at first had seemed strange and wondrous became familiar and taken for granted, and has been so ever since.

For the broadcasters these programmes had a more ambiguous purpose. They were peculiar to the BBC in the era of its monopoly and it is significant that commercial television, even in the early years of competition, never sought to emulate them. For the corporation they fulfilled, at one and the same time, instrumental and idealistic intentions. They were idealistic in that they sought to provide a fragmented audience with a common culture, an image of the nation as a *knowable* community. They were instrumental in that they were one means by which the BBC sought recognition for itself as a member of the establishment. Invoking the rhetoric of British pomp and circumstance was a way of winning for broadcasting its own institutional niche within the existing order of things. By the end of the 1930s the BBC had acquired the patina of tradition. It seemed as entwined with immemorial ivy as Oxbridge, the public school system (itself a recent but remarkably successful case of new wine in old bottles) or the Bank of England.

We have commented on the difficulties of the broadcasters, before the war, in finding an appropriate voice, mode of address and style of presentation for royal broadcasts, anniversary programmes and the like. But it remained largely a matter of striking the right note. The symbolic content was seldom questioned. The problems lay elsewhere. People in the BBC were becoming increasingly aware of the difficulties in arbitrating between the demands of different taste publics in a single national channel and in meeting the growing pressure for more programmes that were popular and entertaining in their appeal. We have discussed elsewhere in some detail how, before and during the war, the BBC adjusted its service to correspond more closely with audience demand.[26] The result was, in the aftermath of the war, a stratified programme service – the Light, the Home and the Third – styled to suit three broadly identifiable publics for lowbrow, middlebrow and highbrow fare. With this compartmentalization of the audience, the unifying context for the presentation on radio of 'the nation as community' was lost.

But that did not mean that the aura with which the idols of the tribe were invested had itself been dissipated. Deference to the monarchy, church and parliament remained deeply embedded in the BBC's programmes for a decade after the war. Television outside broadcasts continued to provide the slowly growing audience with the visible ritual displays of corporate national life. These displays were never criticized. They remained expressions of national self-esteem that were offered to viewers as their own social heritage. This national smugness, though endorsed by the BBC, was not created by broadcasting. It was finally shattered in 1956 by the Suez débâcle, which triggered off an immediate and distressing crisis of identity for the British. It compelled them at last to begin the painful task of reassessing their sense of themselves and of their position in the world. In April 1956, several months before the political crisis, the BBC launched a television series called *We The British* to examine the following questions.

> Can a people be in decline? Can a nation be in decline? Is, in fact, Britain in decline? And if you say 'Why ask such questions?' just listen to the talk you hear around you – to the people who say 'We can't win at anything nowadays – not even at football' or 'We get pushed out of Egypt, we leave the Sudan, They've dismissed Glubb Pasha, everyone thinks today that the British can be pushed around. Why don't we stand up for ourselves?'; to the foreigners, Americans, Germans and Swiss, who complain that British workmanship isn't what it was, that the English have forgotten how to do an honest day's work; to the voices at home that declare that delinquency is going up and morals going down; that family respect is dying; that religious faith is moribund.[27]

The next few years saw a sharp challenge, from many directions, to traditional political and religious authority. Here the advent of commercial television was of crucial importance, for it was ITN that pioneered new styles of interviewing, posing aggressive and critical questions, and a more popular, less detached manner of presentation. The BBC responded quickly. *Tonight* (1957) and its spin-off, *That Was The Week That Was* (1962), were new departures for the corporation. Both defined themselves as on the side of the audience and against the powers that be. They were cheerfully irreverent. Satire had become fashionable and its target was the establishment. A *TW3* sketch that looked back over 1962 summed it up as 'a year in which principles went by the board. A year of incompetence. A year of mendacity. A year of lying.' The moral bankruptcy of the British ruling class, the hollow fraud of their claim to govern the nation, as of right, had been exposed by the hypocrisy of the Vassal case and the shabby sensationalism of the Profumo affair.

Since then the unquestioned authority of the state, in its guidance of the nation's destiny, has never been recovered. The one institution within it to weather those storms with complete success has been the monarchy. Where other national idols have been found wanting, the affection and esteem bestowed upon most members of the House of Windsor by the public has remained undimmed. One reason for this has been the discreet but highly effective way in which the royal household and its advisers have managed the self-presentation of the royal family, through television, to the British people. This continuing success points to some teasingly difficult questions about the role of ideology, the effectiveness of symbols and the management and presentation of acceptable images of individual and collective identity, all of which underlie the material we have presented here.

We have paid attention, for the most part, to what Bagehot called the '*dignified* parts of the constitution' as distinct from its *efficient* parts. He thus distinguished those corporate emblems, rituals and ceremonies 'which excite and preserve the reverence of the population' from the means by which government 'in fact, works and rules'.[28] Bagehot was quite explicit about the 'incalculable value' of the dignified parts, especially the monarchy. They were also the *theatrical* parts – a form of theatre which, by arousing admiration and awe, kept the lower orders distracted and allowed the ruling class to manage the state without let or hindrance. He wrote, in 1967, that by far the greatest value of the monarchy was that 'it acts as a *disguise*. It enables our real rulers to change without heedless people knowing it.'[29] The trouble with such an analysis, which has much in common with contemporary critiques of ideology, is that it presents symbols and rituals as a masquerade, or a kind of thimble-rigging, to beguile the innocent or gullible. It does nothing to explain the necessity of ideologies, or the ways in which they provide a stability and coherence that gives individuals acceptable and recognizable collective identities.

Television's natural domain is now the familiar and everyday rather than the ritualistic and sacred, and it is here that we can still find older patterns of community and identity renewed in current popular formats. *Coronation Street*, 21 years old at the time of writing and still going strong, is a notable instance, but in terms of the images of nationhood which we have described above, the BBC's *Nationwide* is probably the best example from recent television. As Brunsdon and Morley[30] have shown, *Nationwide* both addressed the audience as a nation of families and invoked the nation as a family composed of different regions rather than different classes. Like the pre-war features it tended to draw its imagery from rural rather than urban Britain, and to seek out eccentrics whom it presented as typically British 'characters'. Morley's later research[31] suggests that a surprisingly large section of the audience was prepared to accept the self-image offered by *Nationwide*, in which such enduring emblems of nationhood were juxtaposed with coverage of current affairs and of a range of family leisure pursuits. The programme's team worked hard to encourage public participation in symbolic national occasions, like the royal jubilee of 1977 or the royal wedding of 1981, by promoting local activities and competitions linked to the events. This is probably as close as television can come to engaging its audience in a corporate ritual.

But the BBC has by no means abandoned its pursuit of national unity. As

Sir Michael Swann, then chairman of the BBC, commented to the Annan Committee in 1976, 'an enormous amount of the BBC's work [is] in fact social cement of one sort or another. Royal occasions, religious services, sports coverage, and police series, all reinforce the sense of belonging to our country, being involved in its celebrations, and accepting what it stands for.'[32] Ten years later the work continues.

Notes

A major source for material in this article is the BBC Written Archives Centre at Caversham.

1 J. C. W. Reith, *Broadcast Over Britain*, London, Hodder & Stoughton, 1924, p. 15.

2 J. C. W. Reith, 'memorandum of information', presented to the Crawford Committee, 1925.

3 J. G. Blumler *et al.*, 'Attitudes to the monarchy: their structure and development during a ceremonial occasion', *Political Studies*, XIX, 2 (1971), 150.

4 Reith, op. cit., p. 19.

5 J. C. W. Reith, *Into the Wind*, London, Hodder & Stoughton, 1949, p. 136.

6 For discussions of some pre-war controversial programmes which the BBC either broadcast or was prevented from broadcasting, see Asa Briggs, *Governing the BBC*, London, BBC Publications, 1979, chapter IV, sections 1, 2 and 3. See also Paddy Scannell, 'Broadcasting and the politics of unemployment 1930–1935', and David Cardiff, 'The serious and the popular: aspects of the evolution of style in the radio talk 1928–1939', both in *Media, Culture and Society*, 2, 1 (January 1980), 15–49.

7 *BBC Yearbook*, London, BBC, 1930, p. 82.

8 See Sally F. Moore and Barbara G. Myerhoff (eds), *Secular Ritual*, Van Gorcum, The Netherlands, 1977. Jack Goody, chapter 2, is particularly sceptical about the usefulness of the term 'ritual' when applied outside traditional societies.

9 Book review in *Radio Times*, 23 November 1928, p. 506.

10 Raymond Williams, *Television, Technology and Cultural Form*, London, Fontana/ Collins, 1974, p. 21.

11 Critic in the *London Star*, quoted in *Bristol Evening News*, 10 September 1930.

12 Script, Empire Day (1935). Quoted in Monica Delaney, 'An examination of the BBC empire service, its establishment and function, 1932–39', undergraduate dissertation, School of Communication, Polytechnic of Central London, 1979, p. 21.

13 Broadcast Christmas messages of George V for 1933, 1934 and 1935, *BBC Annuals*, 1935, 1937.

14 *Radio Times*, 21 December 1934, p. 974.

15 Script, *All The World Over*, 1932.

16 Review in *Manchester Guardian*, 27 December 1933.

17 BBC memorandum from Northern Ireland Region Director to Director of Features and Drama, February 1937.

18 Raymond Williams, *Marxism and Literature*, Oxford, Oxford University Press, 1977, p. 122.

19 For a useful account of the work of BBC North Region in pioneering techniques of

social documentary, see D. G. Bridson, *Prospero and Ariel*, London, Gollancz, 1971; also G. P. Scannell, ' "The stuff of radio": developments in radio features and documentaries before the war', in John Corner (ed.), *Documentary and the Mass Media*, London, Edward Arnold, 1986.

20 Quoted in Ernest Short, *Fifty Years of Vaudeville*, London, Eyre & Spottiswoode, 1946, p. 169.

21 For a fuller account see David Cardiff and Paddy Scannell, 'Radio in World War II', in Open University course U203, Popular Culture, block 2, unit 8, Milton Keynes, Open University Press, 1981.

22 *Radio Times*, 15 April 1949.

23 Jonathan Dimbleby, *Richard Dimbleby*, London, Coronet Books, Hodder & Stoughton, 1977, p. 238.

24 Dimbleby, op. cit., pp. 326–30.

25 Blumler *et al.*, op. cit., p. 158.

26 See Cardiff and Scannell, op. cit., and Paddy Scannell and David Cardiff, 'Serving the nation: public service broadcasting before the war', in Bernard Waites, Tony Bennett and Graham Martin (eds), *Popular Culture: Past and Present*, London, Croom Helm, 1982.

27 *Radio Times*, 20 April 1956, p. 5.

28 Walter Bagehot, *The English Constitution*, London, Collins/Fontana, 1963, p. 61.

29 Bagehot, op. cit.

30 Charlotte Brunsdon and David Morley, *Everyday Television: 'Nationwide'*, BFI Television Monograph no. 10, London, British Film Institute, 1978.

31 David Morley, *The 'Nationwide' Audience*, BFI Television Monograph no. 11, London, British Film Institute, 1980.

32 *Report of the Committee on the Future of Broadcasting*, Cmnd 6753, London, HMSO, 1977, p. 263.

8

Performing media events

Daniel Dayan and Elihu Katz

The televising of public occasions must meet the challenge not only of representing the event, but of offering the viewer a functional equivalent of the festive experience. By superimposing its own performance on the performance of the organizers, by displaying its reaction to the reaction of the spectators, by proposing vicarious forms of participation to compensate viewers for the participation of which they are deprived, television becomes the primary performer in the enactment of public ceremonies.

Television not only treats the event in narrative fashion, it treats it as a *single narrative spectacle*. This unifies the disparate elements of an event for an audience which is in attendance for all segments, from beginning to end. Indeed, it constrains even the organizers to think of the event as a whole and organize its flow thus endowing it with an original coherence and unexpected 'beat', a new 'figure'.

An anthropological artefact, a ritual hybrid, is thus born, about which it might be legitimate to ask: is the broadcast a representation of a ceremony or is the ceremony nothing more than a live prop for the media event? And if what we call 'ceremony' for the sake of simplicity has traditionally been a string of distinct ceremonies, a series of ritualized encounters with various groups within the public, what is the consequence of having the whole public attending all ceremonies? What becomes of the very notion of participation?

Our study of the many roles imparted to television in the performance of such events relies on a fundamental assumption. The transformations wrought in the original event must not be considered as mere 'alterations' or 'additions' on the part of television. Rather, they should be perceived as elements in a qualitative transformation in the nature of public events. Thus, we believe it is conceptually distracting to ask if a broadcast offers a 'true' rendition of the corresponding event. Given the openly 'performative'[1] nature of television's role, the problematics of 'truth' and 'falsehood' become almost irrelevant. The issue is less one of 'truth' than one of loyalty. Television discourse offers less a reproduction of, than a commitment to, the event. It bets on the event's importance, ties itself to its fate, repudiating journalistic criteria and paradigms. A first question is then: what does it mean to say that a broadcast is 'faithful' to the ceremony as organized?

This commitment is not only a moral or an ideological one, it is also a commitment to the form of the event. The original event is clearly a ceremony. Its retextualization by television unavoidably flattens it into a spectacle. The rhetoric of television consists then largely in trying to reinject the lost ceremonial dimension, in offering substitutes for 'being there', in developing an aesthetics of compensation. How creative is the medium in overcoming its own limitations?

But there is much more to the aesthetics of a 'media event' than the impoverishment and reconstruction of the ceremonial domain.

Three aspects of television's performance are implicit here, and this chapter will take up each in turn. First, we examine television's loyalty to the event, what we call the aesthetics of upholding definition. Then, in a second section, we explore television's vain attempt to provide a 'phatic' channel through which viewers and celebrants can actually reach out to each other in interaction, and to multiply in some miraculous way the reality of ceremonies as if they were loaves and fishes. From this more nostalgic use of the medium, we turn, finally, to television's ability to provide not reproduction nor access but its own original event.

Loyalty to the event: television as wedding photographer

Television commitment to the event is, first of all, definitional. It recognizes the event, conveys its distinctive features, exposes what Searle[2] would call its 'constitutive rules', what Barthes[3] would recognize as its 'denotative' level. A second aspect of definition is 'hermeneutic'. Beyond identifying the event, television explores what the event is about and proposes what Pierre Nora[4] described as an 'instant interpretation' of it. To expropriate a famous sociological distinction one might say that television proposes the event's 'ascribed' meaning, as opposed to the meaning the event will eventually 'achieve', the meaning which historians will retrospectively confer upon it. Television, moreover, is overtly protective of the event. It makes clear the event's absolute priority, and, in particular, its precedence over news of all sorts. It gives resonance to the event's specific mood. An aesthetic watchdog of sorts, television makes sure that the event's unity of tone and action are preserved from interference.

Upholding definition

Unlike physical objects, ceremonies are self-defining; their performance consists in the proclamation of their identity. Television serves to relay the pertinent features through which this identity is proclaimed, allows viewers to identify the nature of the event. Given the contractual character of most public events, the equally important role of principals and public, these features are to be found both in the realm of performance and in the realm of reaction. Let us first address ourselves to the latter.

The very nature of a ceremony implies the existence of a response dimension. Television underlines this dimension in many ways. It first highlights the reactions of the primary audience of spectators who are present at the event. Among the multiple behaviours recorded in close-ups by the cameras, directors select the 'relevant' ones for transmission and emulation. Besides these behavioural cues to home audiences, television stresses the communal nature of the depicted experience, the unanimous adhesion of the crowd to the celebrated values or symbols. What is stressed here is not only unanimity, but unanimity within diversity. Consensus is portrayed as a process, as an overcoming of differences. The event requires that rivals suspend their feuds and strangers their particularisms to join in the effusive, contagious mood of the moment. Close-ups offer not only normative suggestions, but a qualitative sampling as well. As in the Roman *adventus* – the ceremonial welcome of a distinguished visitor at the town gate – the absence of a given group might imply rejection or defiance.[5] The event must therefore be shown to be adequately representative of the entire community.

Television also provides means for identifying the event through such things as the tone and cadence of the narrator's voice. Some presenters have become famous – indeed, some have become indispensable – for their specialization in the narration of public events. Their reverent tone, frequent silences, strangled or contained voices can be identified as consubstantial to the nature of the event. Like the cheering crowd, they have become, over the years, part of the event's prerequisites. In fact, narration and cheer are so similar in function that one can be substituted for the other. In the coverage of the royal wedding in 1981 by both the BBC and ITV, the roaring of the crowds was permitted virtually to drown out the voice of the presenter, as if the narration was but a slightly more verbalized form of cheering.

The absence of a responding crowd, and, in some extreme cases, the unavailability of a narration may leave home spectators in wonder as to what type of reaction is called for, and ultimately, as to what is going on. For example, the decision by Polish television to focus on the Pope's ritual functions when Pope John Paul revisited his homeland and to (deliberately) play down public reactions resulted in a blurring of the event's definition as a reunion between a people and the representative of the spiritual heritage from which it was forcefully separated. Illustrating the nature of Catholic liturgy is not what the whole thing was about. In similar fashion, the funeral of President Sadat caused obvious embarrassment (and hardly disguised irritation) to the narrator of the event's French broadcast (TFI's Leon Zitrone). Ambiguity concerning the type of response expected, and uncertainty about the fact that any response was expected at all, ultimately backfired on the performance itself, casting doubts on the nature of what was taking place. In this particular case the event remained 'mute'. While lending a helping hand in the technical tasks of burying his president, Mr Mubarak abstained from making any decisive statement, thus further preventing the burial from becoming a 'full' public event, and as such, a funeral. Television was unable to uphold a definition which the event itself was reluctant to provide.

When events are less ambiguous, television comes to the rescue of their self-definition, reiterating the features by which their organizers wish them to be identified. Emotional displays, for example, are not supposed to be part of a hero's funeral. Emotion, however, is quite compatible with the ethos of a wedding. Thus, in the case of Lord Mountbatten's funeral, British television resists the temptation of displaying 'private' emotions: the fact that Prince Charles is apparently fighting back a tear during his reading of the scriptures is not shown in close-up. When the expression of emotion takes the form of a newly wed couple kissing on the Buckingham Palace balcony, it is perceived as a public gesture and therefore meant to be filmed.

In respect to the definition of the wedding event, television deliberately overlooked not only the deviations of the performers from their scenarios, but also the antics of the would-be performers among the spectators. The carnival ambience which could be observed along the procession route of the royal wedding led many observers (including novelist John Fowles) to comment on the contrast between what they perceived as 'English' playfulness (that of the crowd) vs 'British' arrogance (the procession), or as Elizabethan jocularity (street behaviour) vs Victorian etiquette (behaviour of the principals). Only the 'Victorian' or 'British' in tone survived the broadcast which left little place for the ironic dimension of many a patriotic gesture. Tact, good taste, and restraint were here but attributes of the performing role imparted to the broadcasters as custodians of the event's definition.[6]

Loyalty to definition is probably the essence of that which makes broadcasters performers rather than observers. As loyalty often does, it may render the loyal broadcasters blind to the non-scripted aspects of the very spectacles they are transmitting. This was strikingly illustrated by the episodes which took place during the Queen's silver jubilee, when the mock attempt on the life of the Queen was perceived by everyone except by the television team which was unwittingly recording it. Of course, the dilemma of whether to transmit an aberration or 'hijacking' of an event such as Sadat's review of troops turned assassination, or the Munich Olympics turned massacre, involves an uneasy editorial choice. It requires a decision to violate the integrity of the event by introducing journalistic considerations which are beyond the authority, and sometimes alien to the competence, of the special teams charged with the broadcasting of ceremonial events. However, in this case, there was no decision to ignore, but rather inability to see.

Providing interpretation

Television serves as a guide in identifying the meanings for which the event is a carrier. It first does so abruptly or, as Austin would put it, 'exercitively', by imposing on the event a narrative coherence, by endowing it with a story-line, by investing its participants with roles and attributes the range of which obviously constitutes an interpretation. Thus it carves a denotative identity out of the event.

But television also relies on connotation by highlighting those generally non-verbal elements which illuminate the 'why' of an event, and by adopting, in so doing, the perspective of its organizers. Camera discovery of an inlaid message tends to mask the fact that the message was made available by a deliberate decision. Television's reading of such a message is, thus, less interpretative than 'elucidative', in Austin's sense of the word. It is an exercise in authority.

These two processes take place simultaneously, reinforce each other and are often indistinguishable. Let us illustrate them through a case study.

The royal wedding was an outspoken event. Its messages were organized in eloquent dramaturgies and spelled out by an articulate voice, that of the Archbishop of Canterbury. Television's performance joined that of the archbishop and that of the other organizers in a way so strikingly complementary that while the three performances were organized independently – so we were told – we experienced the insistent feeling of team work, of a division of labour whose roles were almost interchangeable.

The archbishop's speech fulfilled an editorial function. Constituting an event within the event, it made reference to the main themes running through the occasion and, in the process, imposed additional meanings which, while persuasive, existed primarily by virtue of his speech. Reciprocally, television abandoned its role as journalistic observer and reverently assumed an 'observant' role. Organizers, finally, acted as directors, multiplied visual clues, offered a choreographed ceremony, anticipating the transformation of the heroes of the day into images. In short, the organizers were putting on a show; the priest was commenting upon it; television was leading the 'amens'.

We perceive television's role as an answer to that of the archbishop. It consists, we think, in underlining, on the spectacular surface of the event, the messages the archbishop spoke from its depths. While the meanings proposed by the archbishop were those of the event, by simple virtue of his authority (they were such, because, in a 'performative' act, he said so), the meanings proposed by television were not openly ascribed to the event but rather 'perceived' during its unravelling. What strikes us, though, is that with the exception of one message, these meanings were identical. The nature of the relationship between organizers, archbishop and television requires further analysis.

The archbishop's speech explicitly stressed the themes which the organizers tried to communicate in their handling of protocol and ceremony. The 'what' of the performance (its definition) imposed many constraints and could not allow much creativity, given the exigencies of ritual and tradition. The 'how' of the performance, however, did allow options and, therefore, significant choices. The organizers had to exploit this 'how' in order to load the performance of the event with connotative meanings. Within the continuity of the ceremony, they introduced a number of discontinuous messages, each of which consisted in a given 'manner of performing'. Thus, the messages, later made articulate in the archbishop's speech, were also visually or gesturally offered to the spectators throughout the occasion, in flickering, discontinuous cueings within the performance.

To take an example from another event, consider President Sadat's visit to

Israel. On arrival at Ben Gurion airport, obviously he had to come out of his plane in some way. The particular way in which this exit took place was hailed by almost every narrator as 'symbolic' of the trip as a whole. While crew members opened the door of the Boeing, impressively decorated with the emblems of the Arab Republic of Egypt, an El Al gangway was pushed alongside. This juxtaposition, unthinkable until that very minute, was the paradigmatic example of what television teams were there to film. Missing that image would have been a minor catastrophe for any network (in the same way it was a minor catastrophe for ITV to have missed the royal kiss on Buckingham Palace balcony, and for BBC to have failed to show it in close-up). This example allows us to delineate the role of television.

Television directors have to be constantly on the look-out for such situations which express in a *condensed way* the whole purpose of the event (or, at least, one of its main purposes). Television narrators have to make sure that the significance of such images will not pass unnoticed and will be correctly assessed. In other terms, television's interpretative function consists (a) in making sure, at the image level, that the significant features of the event, its visual messages, are properly highlighted; and (b) at the narration level, that these features, once noticed, are correctly interpreted, that is, within a frame of reference consonant with that of the organizers.

Let us now consider what took place in the royal wedding. The archbishop firmly established the first theme in the very act of brushing it aside. 'Here is the stuff of which fairy-tales are made', he began. Having thus ushered in *Cinderella*, the archbishop continued by rejecting the sufficiency of the metaphor. This metaphor, however, was obviously on the minds of the organizers of the event who made sure that Lady Diana would be accompanied to St Paul's by ordinary policemen, but escorted back to Buckingham Palace by the Household Cavalry. The same organizers dutifully displayed the room-mates of her working day now seated in the front pews, where television cameras could easily underline their presence. The narrators took on from that point, announcing that the bride's dress was a 'fairy-tale' dress, that the state carriage in which she rode was a 'glass carriage' (indeed, there were windows), and thus submitting her to a narrative metamorphosis which, for a moment, demoted the granddaughter of Lady Fermoy to a fairy-tale 'commoner', kindergarten teacher, and Earl's Court boarder, the better to celebrate her promotion.

The archbishop's second theme redirected attention from the institution of royalty to the institution of family. Extracting an aristocratic, wealthy and outrageously privileged couple from its leisure class, the orator proposed it as an embodiment of the universal image of youth and of the drama of everyman's marriage. 'There is an ancient Christian tradition', said the archbishop, 'that every bride and groom, on their wedding day, are regarded as a royal couple.' The archbishop thus allowed himself to translate the extraordinary status of this particular couple into something equally extraordinary, but no longer 'above' ordinary: the universally shared, but once-in-a-lifetime ceremony of marriage. In Turnerian terms, the archbishop expertly transposed the originality of the event from the realm of 'structure' into that of 'anti-structure'.[7] What brought the change from particular to universal, in the present instance, was his insistence on recognizing the ceremony of marriage as part of the institution of family. 'Our faith sees a wedding day, not as a place of arrival, but as the place where the adventure really begins.'

Little effort was required from the organizers to put this particular message across. Obviously, there is a difference between the progression of royal family events and soap operas, in that the former have only a public face offered intermittently and in ceremonial settings, while the latter expose private life as a continuous performance. Both, however, deal with the interaction between individuals and norms; both are concerned with the *fate of families* and the transmission of values from generation to generation. While this analogy deserves further analysis it explains that the event's organizers did not need to emphasize its family dimension. It was explicitly inscribed in the situation. Television's performance echoed their attitude, while making room for the archbishop's concern. The strategy of close-ups during the ceremony consisted (BBC) in stressing the theme without spelling it out, by rapidly pointing to a worried mother, a proud father, an emotional grandmother. These domestic figures provided a parallel story to that of the royal personae, a connotative frame which, at least superficially, competed with the Cinderella story.

The archbishop's third theme stressed the power of marriage to improve society in accordance with God's will. 'We, like them, are agents of creation' is a complex message, a large part of which came into existence by virtue of the speech. This particular statement consisted in stressing the similarity between a 'we' (the people) and a 'them' (the princely couple). The archbishop's statement that 'we are like them', or more exactly, that 'we, like them' are 'agents of creation', invites the overcoming of distance. But, while overcoming it, it subtly maintains it. The royals become closer, but only if you imitate them. Their approachability is not physical but moral. They are 'approachable' in as much as they are embodiments of norms to which you may subscribe. From approachable individuals, they are put out of reach, by being translated into attainable ideals. The archbishop's rhetorical gesture was particularly interesting in that it offered a superb solution to the paradox highlighted by Jay Blumler in his analysis of the contradictory attitude of the British public *vis-à-vis* the royal family. The royal family, revealed Blumler's study, was expected to meet the impossible requirements of both dropping and maintaining decorum; of abolishing protocol and perpetuating it; of keeping its distinctiveness, while renouncing the thought of being different.[8]

The event's organizers also catered to this ambivalence of the British public *vis-à-vis* the desirability of monarchical distance, but less subtly, somehow, than the archbishop. The rhetorical core of the event consisted in a series of back and forth motions stressing alternately two antithetic themes: 'now they are like us . . . now they are not . . . ' Relayed by television, the pomp and pageantry served of course to establish distance, but they were used as a continuous background for many discrete signs of approachability, such as the lipsticked 'Just Married' sign stuck to the back of a state carriage, together with a flock of balloons echoing those in the hands of the myriads of well-wishers, or the honeymoon departure at Waterloo Station, where cameras showed the honeymooners delivered into the realm of public transportation from a six-horse carriage via a red carpet.

Television was faithful to the organizers' view of the problem of monarchical distance. Humanizing devices were stressed as often as possible against the background of the event's definitional grandeur. The 'Just Married' sign received full attention. Royal children were celebrated as childlike, the princely couple as young, and biology was generally allowed to obliterate caste. Such details may seem pedestrian, compared to the archbishop's elevated message. They provide, however, a translation of its gist. A reliable wedding photographer, but under the guise of 'connotations', television highlights messages which are in fact the wedding's *raison d'être*.

This translation process has an importance which goes far beyond its technical achievement. It provokes a metamorphosis in the access to the event's meaning, it does so by diminishing the role of exhortations and announcements emanating from the organizers of the event or its principals while simultaneously exalting the event's visual or gestural aspects.

By displacing audience focus from explicit statements to visual clues, television 'naturalizes', authenticates the inlaid messages, transforms the performative aspects of ceremonies (utterances emanating from figures of power) into visual anecdotes which television cameras record. It also makes audiences active partners in the significative nature of the event, invites interpretation, encourages hermeneutic pleasure at deciphering indexes, at looking for 'symbols'. Television converts pronouncement of authority into exercises in seduction.

Protecting tone and prerogative

Let us compare the glance of television broadcasters with two neighbouring types of glance that are equally concerned with events of this style. We refer to the glance of journalists (including those television journalists who do not treat the occasion as a 'media event') and the glance of security people.

The glance of journalists may be characterized by distance and, within distance, by mobility. It is typically involved in recontextualizing the event by situating it in larger frames. It is always alert to possible departures from the announced script: such departures constitute information.

Now a familiar feature of media events, the perpetually shifting eyes of unidentified characters surrounding the principals reveal security people constantly scanning the event for possible sources of disruption. For them, the event is not an activity whose definition has to be upheld, but a surface which their eyes have to keep sweeping.

Unlike the journalist's glance, the broadcaster's is stubbornly focused. Unlike the security glance, it is participatory, actively involved in the official meaning of the event, busy endorsing and conveying its definition. The security glance is blind to meanings. The journalistic glance is cynically receptive to all meanings. The broadcaster's glance performs a given meaning, faithfully helps the event spell its name. Yet, television's role goes much beyond this helping with the event. The event is given absolute priority over all other programmes, it is placed above all competing concerns, and tightly protected from any interference with its political content, its temporal sequence, its tone, its mood.

Television's power lies not only with the way in which it structures the flow of daily life, but with its consequent ability of deciding to interrupt this flow. Media events are an example of this interruptive dimension. They cancel all other programmes, bringing television's clock to a stop, and, while they are on the air, they cannot themselves be interrupted. Their performance belongs to 'sacred time'. It brings social activity to a standstill. For a while, the event occupies society's 'centre'. No matter what happens, the event has to go on. Thus, the riots at Toxteth during the royal wedding ceremonies are not mentioned until the ceremonial occasion is over. This protectiveness towards the event goes to such extremes as to inspire plans for the continuation of the broadcast in the eventuality of a terrorist incident affecting some of the principals. The BBC preparation for the royal wedding includes contingency plans and alternative editing routes. The occasion may go on while the crisis is being dealt with. Somehow the only reality which can compete with a media event is that of another media event. Thus one major American channel, ABC, chose to commute between the Superbowl and Sadat's arrival in Jerusalem. Yet this compromise might have ended up frustrating both potential audiences, damaging both events. Both were robbed of their symbolic resonance, of their mood. The Jerusalem event looked unbearably slow and pompous; the American event looked gratuitously hysterical.

Television's double commitment failed in this case to protect an essential dimension of the event: its tone. While anthropologists keep stressing the messy and often chaotic dimension of rituals they have attended, media events are characterized by an almost pedantic concern with unity. Unity of time (related to the duration of the live broadcast), unity of space (circumscribed in advance by the distribution of cameras around the 'stage' of the event) and unity of action. Only in news broadcasts and never in media events does one mention side by side and give equal importance to, say, the peace moves of President Sadat and the bellicose declarations of rejection-front leaders. Media events thus evoke some of the characteristics of the French classical theatre, a theatre often concerned with majestic, or sublime, political gestures.

Of course, the Dallas assassination of President Kennedy was a 'tragedy', and as such, an occasion to invoke fate and to turn the youngish president into an effigy of human suffering, the central figure of a 'tableau' which might have tempted Warhol: *pietà* in a convertible. But 'tragedy' was also a stylistic concern. Television homage to the departed president stressed the dignified stoicism of the principals, the Hecuba-like composure adopted by Jackie

Kennedy after a few seconds of petit-bourgeois dismay. Once this tone was established, the point was to keep it, to maintain it through the event. Hence the uneasiness felt by television teams and expressed by the commentator of the programme concluding the CBS tribute to Kennedy (*Four Dark Days*) over the assassination of Lee Harvey Oswald. One had to deal with two assassinations, two corpses, two funerals, and the second corpse could not be dismissed, kept in the closet, brushed aside for the duration of television's 'requiem'. The problem – a largely stylistic one – received a rhetorical solution. The first assassination was a 'tragedy'. The second was a 'farce', a caricature, a travesty. Notwithstanding illustrious examples, Kennedy's crucifixion could not take place in bad company. Genres are not to be mixed.

Television's protective role stems from the fact that it is not reporting on an event, but actively involved in performing it. In view of this fact, one can hardly expect the journalists to display a penelopean abnegation and to coldly dissect what is largely their own creation. They are not simply transmitting an event or commenting upon it; they are bringing it into existence. Thus, broadcasters double as monument makers or priests. For this reason, in part, media events are then made the responsibility of sports units, or 'special events' units. But still, how can one avoid bringing in journalists, when the event has news value, political or diplomatic implications? Why should a network deprive itself of its experts, precisely when they are most needed?

And yet, this is not journalism. Unlike news, media events are not descriptive of a state of affairs, but symbolically instrumental in bringing that state of affairs about. They do have some of the qualities inherent in 'primitive' rituals with which they share, in particular, a pragmatically oriented reliance on 'magical' evocation: media events symbolically display what they wish to achieve.

Agreeing to promote a political occasion to 'media event status' implies a willingness on the part of television organizations to become part of the magical process. It implies on their part an endorsement of the event's goals and an assessment of the event's efficacy; of its power to achieve these goals. This power depends on their co-operation, since it is tied to the very nature of ceremony, to its appeal, to its evocative character. But it does not rely on this co-operation only. Assessing the event, in other words, is like placing a bet.

There is another aspect of television's commitment. Something takes place in the symbolic realm which might affect reality. This something is akin to the medieval dramaturgy of 'mysteries'. Giving 'media event status' to a proposed event implies a belief in this 'mystery'. As in all religious rites, attendance cannot be neutral, uncommitted. Television here is not an observer. It reactivates an ancient function: the act of attending, of being present, of being an eventual propagator, a subsequent medium. Those present at early Christian events were used as such 'media'. They were called 'witnesses', or, in Greek, 'martyrs'.

In the face of media events the journalistic paradigm of objectivity and neutrality is simply irrelevant. Either you maintain your agnostic role, treat the event as 'news', and address it within the news broadcasts, or you enter the media event ceremonial and become the event's 'witness'. A journalist assigned to a media event undergoes a conversion, one which is not always to his or her liking.

That is why broadcasters are so uneasy about switching back again in the case of the 'hijacking' of an event. The journalist-turned-priest must agonize over a difficult choice. Should one cover a political event such as Chicago's '68 Democratic convention and ignore the riots taking place outside the convention hall? Isn't the fact of filming the protest a negative comment on the convention? What should one do when two heads of state and a prime minister are signing a peace treaty – the Camp David accords, ceremonially ratified in the gardens of the White House – while a small crowd of protesters within earshot are challenging this treaty and railing at its authors? Should one cut the sound and thus miss the distinctive – and conflictual – atmosphere? Should one include the protesters and thus expose the fragility of the organizers' claim to having achieved any peace at all? The networks have improvised different answers to these questions on different occasions.

Longing for ceremonial aura: an aesthetics of compensation

Television, however, wants to go beyond the role of witness, beyond upholding definition. It wants nothing less than to give the viewer the feeling that he or she is 'there'. It does so by simulating ceremonial participation, by refusing to be reconciled to its essential inability to serve as a 'phatic' channel for the actual interaction between celebrants and home audiences. It insists at least on trying.

This second aspect of television's performance brings Walter Benjamin to mind. Benjamin asks what becomes of the public's relationship to works of art, when works of art become copies diffused through mechanical reproduction.[9] As students of mass communications, we wish to raise a similar question: what happens to ceremonies when, instead of being attended in person, they are delivered to each of us at home? Is it possible, we are asking, for television to do more than make a spectacle of a ceremony, a show of a performance? How does television attempt to give a sense of ceremonial participation? How can it compensate viewers for the absence of interactivity?

Anthropology will help here.[10] Consider the distinctions among the modes of interaction between performers and audience which characterize different kinds of occasion. Consider *spectacle*, with cinema as its extreme form. *Festival* would be the other polar extreme, almost entirely free of spectacle. *Ceremony* would stand on a middle ground between the two. We suggest that these forms differ along dimensions of (1) specificity of focus; (2) specificity of response; and (3) interaction between audience and performers.

Spectacles – such as sports and theatre – share a narrowness of focus, a limited set of appropriate responses and (excepting such modern rediscoveries as 'theatre total') a minimal level of interaction. What there is to see is very clearly exhibited. Spectacle implies a distinction between the roles of performers and audience. Performers are set apart and audiences are asked to respond cognitively and emotionally in predefined categories of approval, disapproval, arousal or passivity. Audience interaction with the performance may enhance it, but it is not meant to be part of its definition. (In the case of cinema, such an interaction becomes so irrelevant that audience response is almost entirely internalized.)

Festival, on the contrary, is diffuse in focus. No simple picture or pageant imposes itself monopolistically on participants. The occasion offers many different foci, and much room for *ad hoc* activity. Appropriate responses may be many and varied. Indeed, creative responses are quite often welcome. Interaction is obviously called for since the roles of performers and spectators are neither fixed nor irreversible. Equally obvious is the observation that the nature of the resultant 'performance' is altogether dependent on audience 'response'.

Ceremony shares features with both spectacle and festival in that, on the one hand, it offers a clear focus, a definite distinction between performers and respondents – the latter being expected to respond in specific (and usually traditional) ways – while, on the other hand, its existence consists in an interaction between audience and performers. Audience response is one of the constitutive features of ceremony. Without it, a ceremony might become empty.

If an event as organized contains elements of both ceremony and festival, it is reasonable to assume that the event as televised would only be spectacle, since its focus is irremediably narrowed, since reactions are highly limited and can in no way affect the performance. But is this really so? Television says no; at least it tries to. The media events viewer, claims television, has better access; the event is 'three-dimensional'; the audience *can* respond. Let us see how.

Equalizing access

First and most obvious, television equalizes access to the occasion. Nobody need (or can) pay more for a better seat; nobody need spend the night in a queue hoping to secure a better vantage point. There is some loss in this, of course. Ostensibly, the 'festival' aspect of the experience is lacking. Being jostled by a crowd, and rising as one man to cheer, has its attractions. But television offers compensation by removing invidiousness; neither power, nor money, nor dexterity gives advantage. As far as access is concerned, the structure of the broadcast audience is altogether different from the socially stratified audience on the spot. Moreover, the event is in better focus at home. The home audience 'sees' more not only because the view is not blocked, but because television, as we have shown, underlines the definition proposed for the event by its organizers and adds interpretation. The television viewer knows far more of the symbolic meaning of the event than the primary audience on the spot.

Reinjecting unequal access

Not satisfied with the magic of equalizing access, television also attempts to reintroduce differentiation of participation – not in the audience but among its own personnel.

The experience of anybody who tries to attend a public event or ceremony reveals that 'attending' means attending *part* of the event. One cannot view a procession from all vantage points unless one moves along with the procession (and therefore one loses one's place), or unless one is part of the procession (and therefore totally unable to focus on it as a spectacle). You see an event from a given place, from a given distance and this place and distance tell you (and tell the others) who you are. In the case of the royal wedding, either you are in the church (that is, a guest of the royal family), or you are outside the church, and the conquest of a place with good visibility has to be paid for, in terms of waking up before dawn or sleeping on the pavement. As in the theatre, your distance from stage, your placement in regard to the centre of the event, is a very clear reminder of your place in society. (To use Benjamin's notion, distance from the event constitutes its 'aura'.)[11]

What happens with the introduction of television is that, in accordance with narrative structures and their need for continuity, everybody attends the whole of the event; at least it is called 'the whole of the event'. What seems new to us is this very notion of a totality of the event; a notion which seems inherited from the domain of spectacle.

Traditionally, an event such as a royal wedding was a string of smaller ceremonial units, featuring the same actors (the royal family, the newly weds) but different audiences, and the dramaturgy of each of these units was oriented to the nature of the several audiences. With television, the distinctive self-presentations of royalty to the different constituents of the British public are no longer exclusive of each other. The different groups now form one audience. The different sub-events now form one narrative (and one of the tasks of the broadcaster is to organize the rhythmic continuity of the performance). By turning the event into a single spectacle, TV acts as an enfranchiser; only the primary audience maintains the privilege of seeing part of the event, thus experiencing their deprivation as its aura. However, the equidistance introduced between the various segments of the public is compensated for by a television-performed reintroduction of distance.

This new distance is that which separates members of the broadcasting organizations involved in the event. A clear distinction is made between those television people who are part of the event (for example, Tom Fleming for the BBC) and those television people who are in the studio and out of the event (for example, Angela Rippon, also for the BBC). To be 'in' and not 'out' in the desolate limbo of television studios, is a mark of added prestige, of seniority, of participation in the event's 'mana' as evidenced by Rippon's interview of Fleming. Similarly when President Sadat leaves on his historic journey from Cairo to Jerusalem, the stars of American TV are with him on the plane: Walters, Cronkite, Chancellor. From the tarmac they are observed by the special correspondents of their respective networks. The less elevated status of these envoys means not only that they are out with the crowds, while their prestigious colleagues are 'in' with the actors, but also that they see less of what is taking place than either the telespectators or the studio-anchors at home.[12]

Being pressed in the crowd, with no monitors at their disposal, they have to guess a large part of what is happening from visual deductions or audio clues, and their commentaries seem to corroborate the images on screen by a constantly renewed miracle. In such an extreme case, one wonders why these special or local correspondents are used at all, since they know less than the stars accompanying the President and see less than their studio counterparts who monitor the output from the many cameras. One might answer that their function, perhaps, *is* to know less, to be pressed in the crowd, elbowed, pushed around, frantically trying to perceive, see or guess. Their function is an aesthetic one (even though it is probably not planned that way). They are there to compensate, as in festival, for the spectacular display of the whole of the event, to restore the sense of distance, of specific involvement in this or that partial aspect. They are in charge of reinjecting the lost aura of the event, by their frantic and futile attempts to see and know. They are performing that archaic dimension of events which is specific to audience participation and which disappears when a ceremony is flattened, ironed out, indifferently offered to equidistant glances, evenly soaked in a banalized knowledge. It is within this framework that one can understand the reference made to 'rumours' in so many media events. Rumours reinject depth into a televised event, differentiating those who know from those who do not know yet. They suggest the existence of physical volume in the event, counterbalance its pedagogic efficiency, its ironed-out flatness.

The model of contagion

Television simulates what its presence has abolished: status difference among spectators. Simultaneously, it tries to erase the actual distance which separates them from the physical celebration. Thus, in the carefully planned royal wedding, the point was to deny any discontinuity between the celebration in London and the audiences who were receiving the broadcast, to ignore the transformation of celebration into spectacle. In order to achieve this, an image was proposed: that of an epidemic, of a contagion of celebrations which progressively merged into each other until one was plunged into a vast party involving the whole of Britain.

Such tactics threaten to become permanent features of media events. On the day of the investiture of President Mitterand, French television's second channel (Antenne 2) chose to transport its studio to a village, away from the Paris-based ceremonies. Within this bucolic setting (possibly chosen for its affinity with the Rousseauist ethos of the festivals that followed the French Revolution),[13] local ceremonies and celebrations transformed the reception of the broadcast into an event in its own right. The spectacle of a celebration was immediately converted into a focus for another celebration. The result was not very convincing: differences in celebrating styles tend to act as cruel reminders of the importance of props and pageantry. The royal wedding used a slightly different *mise-en-scène*. Instead of two celebrations, three were offered. The original celebration (wedding) was viewed from a studio where it became the occasion for a party-like talk show which, in turn, included a feature on a village celebration during which children stuffed with ice-cream waved little flags in the direction of majestically displayed TV sets. Despite the ice-cream and flag-waving, TV sets, however, remained TV sets, and the model of contagion remained a wish.

This model was more explicit the night before in the broadcast devoted to the wedding fireworks in Hyde Park. The broadcast began as a sequence showing fire-signals travelling over countryside, from hilltop to hilltop, from beacon to beacon, until the last of them came into actual view of the royal party, signalling Prince Charles to start the fireworks. The use of beacons suggested a progressive unification of Britain, a string of parties situated in a line of sight, a physical contagion of the party mood modelled on that of a forest fire. It is, of course, ironic that the progression of the beacons had to be conveyed by television, but the beacon's metaphor was precisely that by means of which television tried to absolve itself from the sin of 'representing' a celebration rather than diffusing it. Again television displayed itself as a 'phatic'[14] channel, the instrument of a spatial continuity rather than the locus of a semiotic exercise. This was particularly manifest in other, ostensibly secondary, features of the event, such as the menu, or the dress of Lady Diana. Not only was the British public informed that the Queen would offer her guests a party, but the menu was widely advertised, and advertised as one which included no specially 'fancy' item. Anyone who wished could, in other words, buy the food and enjoy a meal similar in composition (if not in culinary expertise) to that served in the dining-rooms of Buckingham Palace. The suggestion, however, was only implicit. It became explicit with the huge publicity given to the copying of Lady Diana's dress. Organized as a suspense story, the reproduction of the dress became one of the threads which helped unify the wedding day as a continuous event. By the end of the day, the copy was to be displayed in a London window. A few days later, it would be mass-produced and on sale. Before the end of the day, a number of young ladies were interviewed saying they would buy copies for their own weddings. Thus the projects provided both by the wedding breakfast menu and the dress served as unifiers of dispersed celebrations. Symbolically, television served as a continuer of the tradition which requires a young bride on her wedding day to distribute fragments of what she is wearing to the brides-to-be around her in order to associate them, by some sort of magical contagion, with the 'mana' which inhabits her on that day. Instead of (metonymic) fragments of veil, Lady Di circulated via television (metaphoric) images of her dress, thus offering to share her good luck with every maiden in the country. Television performs thereby as a means of physical contiguity. Television is that which abolishes distance.

Television also reinstates distance in the very process of abolishing it. The wedding breakfast menu was publicized, but the recipe of the wedding cake emphatically kept secret. So was the wedding dress kept hidden until the last minute, and all sorts of stratagems were used to maintain this secrecy, including that of announcing that many dresses had been prepared and that any leak would lead to the choice of a new dress. Characteristically, the lady who busied herself with copying the dress for the television audience had no access to it, except by television. All her decisions were professional guesses based only on what she could see on screen (with the help of an instant-replay videotape). Linked by television performance were two dresses, presented as – almost – identical. But one was 'original' and destined to remain that, and that only. The other was the matrix for mass reproduction. Copies were *almost* those of the original dress, but they were so in an emphatically *mediated* way.

The activity of copying was both allowed, encouraged, publicized, and submitted to an intricate *mise-en-scène*, the point of which was to assert the 'aura' of Lady Diana's dress, as opposed to the availability of its master copy. Thus television was reasserted as an instrument of distance, dismissed as a means of participation. Participation was a simulation looked upon benevolently as long as it did not infringe on what distinguishes originals from reproductions, or royalty from movie stars: their 'aura'. As soon as it did, television was sent back to its true realm: that of copies, of images; that of 'lesser realities'. Less lucky than Cinderella, the would-be 'diasporic celebration' reverted to its true status: that of a spectacle.

The strategies analysed here are thus revealed as elements in the spectacle rather than means of transforming its nature. An electronically connected agora is what television tries to achieve, even if it cannot succeed. Television's effort to be a phatic channel and to transform viewers into ceremonial participants is defensive and almost nostalgic. By trying to simulate an interactive dimension, television is paying homage to the realm of traditional ceremony. But this is perhaps a secondary aspect in the aesthetics of media events. Television also heralds, sometimes aggressively, its commitment to the new and cinematographically structured rhetorical order. Making full use of the powers of spectacle, it presents its spectators with original modes of participation.

Retextualizing the event: on the experience of not being there

Even if television cannot be truly phatic – even if it cannot convince the viewer that he or she is 'there' – there is something more intrinsic that it has to offer. Instead of offering the viewer equivalents of the ceremonial experience, it offers the 'experience of *not* being there'.

Nobody ever saw a royal wedding or an Easter mass from a blimp or from a fish-eye hanging from the ceiling of a cathedral. These images do not correspond to any previous experience except, perhaps, that conjured by visionary writers like Victor Hugo. Modern television spectators are offered new and unexpected ways of participating in the ritual experience, new aesthetic avenues which no longer stem from the need of exorcising spectacle, but from the decision to use its powers to the fullest extent. Television provides its events with a narration, with a perspective and with a context. It displays in each case an inventiveness which explains why spectators with direct access to the event so often opt for watching it on their screens.

Tracing the boundaries of the event: cumulative editing and textual package

Television's essential gesture consists in separating the event as a figure from a ground, and in dissociating, within the background, what will remain the event's frame from what will be dropped as irrelevant. It is in the periphery of the event that television's role is most inventive since it literally consists in recreating the event's environment. This creation serves three main purposes: mastery over meaning; network differentiation; liturgical inter-ruption of the world's daily business.

Producers highlight the meanings of an event by surrounding it with human interest stories, small features originated by the networks and not the organizers. Forming the event's textual suburbs, these side-shows – interviews, documentaries – allow the networks independence in proposing and reinforcing their readings. Such side-shows seem secondary, anticlimactic. They can be attended in impatience, semi-indifference or mild amusement. Yet they play an important semantic role and do so by being parables cut to the size of the crucial messages; they are little constructions which allow producers, in a process reminiscent of Freudian displacement, to say all they wish to say about the event, without *visibly* altering it or remodelling it. Thus is solved a problem which is specific to the televising of live events, and which stems from the network's obligation to renounce the mastery over meaning that normal editing provides.

The event, being filmed live, has to be filmed in a continuum (which means no temporal cuts). On the other hand, one cannot pre-edit the event at the level of scripting, since television has theoretically no access to the event's dramaturgy (which falls in such cases under the organizers' responsibility). Television's editing thus assumes an original form. It is *cumulative* rather than *subtractive*. It consists in providing extensions to the event, rather than taking off parts of it.

This 'cumulative editing' ('authorship', in one of the original senses of the word), gains in importance when one moves from the centre and towards the periphery of the event. When one moves from the event itself towards its background, television regains the control it could not exert over the main figure. Peripheral stories are thus generated, surrounding the live centre of the event with a vast textual package, typically consuming much more time than the event itself, giving the impression that the event serves to promote the rest of the package and functions as a 'bait'. In view of the competition existing between networks, the rest of the package is certainly far from secondary. 'Live' broadcasts of a given event are electrifying, but they tend to resemble each other. The rest of the package permits some distinctiveness and may consequently enhance the ulterior image of the channel or network which puts it together. Each competitor makes a point of being more exhaustive in its treatment of the event than its rivals, an ambition which often leads to the sisyphean task of 'exhausting' the event by taking each element in it and transforming it into an independent story. Starting from a live centre, the event thus spreads in all directions, is submitted to an endless process of fragmentation and 'cloning' which reminds one of the fate of medieval relics. Finally, if the event itself may still be described in Boorstin's terms as 'genuine', it is nevertheless framed in a consistent background of 'pseudo-events'.[15] Through metonomic contagion, these pseudo-events usually acquire a look of authenticity. Unfortunately, metonomic contagion works both ways.

Building the event's liturgical context

Television is not content with constructing the semantic background of the events it transmits. It also organizes the circumstances of viewing by submitting spectators to a complex *rite de passage*, subverting their usual definition of what is 'important', 'real', or 'serious'. Television offers much more than a stimulus to public reaction. It builds this reaction by surrounding the event with features which make it appear as the only important reality.

Building the event's liturgical context is a two-step process. The first step is one of decontextualization. Television reproduces within its own programming the state-endorsed disruption of social rhythms which characterizes public events and consists in superseding the distinction between work as public and leisure as private: leisure becomes public, and work a business to be conducted in private. Within this new framework, the seriousness and importance of the news as the main definition of social reality (as opposed to the 'futile' world of entertainment) disappears in favour of a new reality, which is neither news in the usual sense of the word, nor entertainment, and makes both look distant, unreal or shabby.

The second step is one of recontextualization. Time is now structured as a vector of expectation and rehearsal, in order to allow full ritual involvement in an exceptional, and therefore unfamiliar, ceremony. Let us illustrate this process by showing it at work in the case of the royal wedding.

Silenced for only a few hours, the world of news lost its immediacy; the everyday became unreal, anachronistic, echoes from another planet. When news bulletins were reinstated at the end of the wedding day, they showed, among other things, riots in Toxteth following the accidental death of a young man run over by a police van. But the horror and absurdity of the incident seemed far removed as if the death of a young man had become less important than the form of a lackey's bicorne. This perception went so far as to create in many viewers sentiments of rejection when a character belonging to the realm of the everyday was filmed and interviewed within the frame of the event. Despite her deliberate self-effacement, and the perfectly proper wedding-guest answers she gave to her interviewer, Mrs Thatcher thus was deemed 'out-of-place'.

Somehow, the reality of the everyday had been replaced by another, stronger, more convincing one. Futilizing – and superseding – the news, the event was something other than entertainment in that it was perceived as essentially serious. Anthropologists, such as Victor Turner,[16] have forged a name for this compelling, if ephemeral shift in the definition of reality. The royal wedding gave Britain an opportunity to enter 'a *liminal* period', one during which social life is characterized by the suspension of usual norms and structures, irrigated by the overflowing of *communitas*. In Turnerian terms, such periods are characterized by a shift from an 'indicative' definition of reality (reality as what *is*) to a 'subjunctive' one (reality as what *could* or *should* be). As it happens, such a shift was perfectly perceptible. Skinheads addressed the coloured celebrants in the streets, convivially sharing the joyful spirit of the moment, while warning that hostilities would resume once the event terminated. Interviewed by television about their opinions on Charles and Diana, spectators in the street tended to suspend doubts and negative judgements, preferring to reiterate platitudinous 'certainties' that the young couple was conforming or would conform to traditional norms. Deliberately, people decided to see in the occasion only what they ought to see. The Emperor's new clothes, they had no doubt, had to be real, and Lady Diana, they were 'certain' of it, would in due time be a good cook.

Not only was the event securely separated from the unwelcome intrusion of everyday concerns (by being, through a significant organizational decision, put under the responsibility of non-news teams, both in the case of BBC and ITV), but television built up the event's predominance over any other reality during the days that preceded the wedding through a pyramidal growth of wedding-related features. This was done in such a way that, when Wednesday morning arrived, switching to the event appeared not as an interruption, but as a culmination. 'At last', titled some of the Tuesday evening newspapers, thus expressing the tension which had been built up and defining the wedding itself as a release from such a tension. The media, especially television, had organized a world hypnosis focused on what *Broadcast* review called 'Wednesday morning fever'. They had acted as ceremonial leaders, taking us away from all worldly concerns and performing the entrance – the *rite de passage* – into the sacred domain.

Once the event was launched and on its way, television faced another problem, one of performing for its audiences what the crowds massed in the parade grounds had to improvise for themselves, namely, how to negotiate the exit from the event; the return to ordinary reality; the departure from the enchanted realm of the possible, of the 'ought-to-be', of the subjunctive. Television again played the part of a ritual limbo, of a threshold between worlds, offering progressive reinsertion into ordinary patterns, ordinary norms, ordinary rhythms. This return trip started immediately after the appearance of the royal family on the balcony of Buckingham Palace.

The time had come to disinvolve oneself from the event and to adopt a retrospective stance. Television guided spectators through the anticlimax of the after-event by proposing a new range of attitudes to them. Crowd members were deliberately provoked into a reflexive attitude by interviewers who asked them which images they thought especially worth remembering. Fragments of the event were played back, recalling its flamboyant pageantry, while withdrawing it from the viewer's experience. It was already an archive record, a spectacle no longer imbued with the magnetism of live broadcast, an ensemble of signs inhabited by intentions, but deserted by life. The event was then discussed by studio panels, made the object of talk shows (thus removing us a step further from it). It was then decomposed into its constituent elements, and despite a convivial party mood, we were introduced to the melancholy knowledge of the machinery, asked backstage, introduced to the wedding cake baker, to the parents of the dress designers, to the man whose disembodied voice had been, for a while, the instrument through which the event spoke. Together with an increasingly peripheral point of view on the event, the event itself was also split into parts (with the Queen's guests having the wedding breakfast at Buckingham Palace while the newly weds rode to Waterloo Station), and retrospectively submitted to a cheerful, but nevertheless anticlimactic, anatomy. The magic that had added parts into a whole was now decomposed into a series of ordinary talents, tricks or expertises.

This anatomy served as a prelude to a series of fluctuations between what remained of the event (the newly wed couple riding to Waterloo) and the outskirts of it, the outside of the event, the real world of the everyday, whose unwelcome presence constantly increased until the event was reinserted, after the final evening wrap-up, in the news broadcast.

Everyday life was claiming its rights, and we were introduced to some of the manifestations organized to protest, reject, deride or 'ignore' the wedding such as the champagne trip to Boulogne of a boatload of anti-royalists. However, the counter-celebrations on display were yet another way of highlighting the event's mood. Thus, the celebration was protected – at least for a while longer – from an intrusive reality. In the very criticism of the event, its liminality was reaffirmed. Criticism indeed, but ritualized and expressed with champagne. We had almost re-entered the ordinary.

Television again acted as a threshold, as a limen, helping the audience to the task of readjusting to a world no longer characterized by the alternative reality of 'antistructure'. Typically, this 'helping us out' took the form of a play between live images of the post-event and recorded images of the event itself, thus allowing a tapering off of its intensity.

Having performed the end of the event, having ritually declared it over, having organized the fall of the curtain, television assumed a new task. After stressing what was worth remembering, it organized forgetting. The event was evoked in shorter and shorter wrap-ups, reduced to images which functioned in almost ideogrammic patterns, seen through the reactions of increasingly distant observers (Argentinian, Russian, Chinese), became a small dot on the horizon, and disappeared from perception. Time was now ripe for abstraction and, a week after the wedding, this object of pleasure or fascination had officially become an object of knowledge: in a BBC programme directed by Michael Lumley (who directed and produced the wedding coverage), Alastair Cooke proposed his interpretations.

We have tried to show here how television served not only as a model-provider for the reactions expected from the spectators, but as a performer of their progressive involvement in and disinvolvement from the 'other' reality constituted by the event; how television superimposed its own *rites de passage* upon the ritual contained in the event; how, within the construct of liminality, it had the essential responsibility of *being* the limen.[17]

Diasporic ceremonies

While far from being exhaustive, our description of 'the experience of not being there' shows that a media event is not an impoverished experience, but, altogether, another experience.

In order to be fully understood, this new experience must be resituated in a larger context. Public events are not fixed in a given form once and forever. Throughout history they have tended to adapt themselves to the prevailing modes of making an event public: 'publicness' is our own neologism. The dominant mode of publicness is now changing. We are witnessing the gradual replacement of what could be called a 'theatrical' model of publicness – an actual meeting of performers and public in such places as parliament houses, churches, convention floors – by a new mode of publicness based on the separation of performers and audiences, and on the rhetoric of narrative rather than the virtue of contact. Born with cinema and first described in aesthetic terms by Walter Benjamin, this new mode of publicness culminates with television which transfers it to all areas of public life including the most traditionally sacred – the political and the religious – profoundly affecting the nature of public ceremonies and occasions. Separated from the large majority of their public, ceremonies now display the texture, internal coherence, narrative beat and visual gloss which used to characterize Hollywood spectaculars. Public occasions acquire most of the formal characteristics of fiction texts.

Distanced from the ceremonial focus, but also isolated from each other, the television audiences no longer form masses or crowds except in an abstract, statistical way.[18] Television celebrants cannot react directly to the ritual performance or to the reactions of the other members of the participating public. They seem to have been turned into mere spectators. And yet, we think they are more than spectators. The very hugeness of the audience has paradoxically transposed the celebration into an intimate register. Ceremonial space has been reconstituted, but in the home. Attendance takes place in small groups congregated around the television set, concentrating on the symbolic centre, keenly aware that myriads of other groups are doing likewise in similar manner, and at the same time.

Can we still speak of a public event when it is celebrated at home? Is there a collective celebration when the collectivity is scattered?

To say 'no' would amount to denying the quality of celebration to many similarly scattered and home-based rituals, often including essential tenets of religious traditions, such as the Jewish celebration of the Biblical exodus: the passover *seder*. This specific example is illuminating because the occasion it constitutes is not only religious, but political as well, and might serve as an archetypal example of Durkheim's symmetrical theses on the social dimension of religion and on the religious dimension of sociality. Characteristically the *seder* has served through the ages as a powerful means of unifying a scattered people, offering a ceremonial structure despite geographic dispersion by translating a monumental occasion into a multiplicity of simultaneous, similarly programmed, home-bound micro events. By proposing a collective ceremony 'without a central cultic temple',[19] by transferring public celebration to the home, the model of the *seder* seems to have solved a problem very similar to that now experienced by the dispersed mass of television viewers. It is almost as if the new public space and the quantitative leap it represents in transforming the vast audience of mass ceremonies into the huge audience of media events has led to the reinvention, in a totally new context, of this ancient and intimate celebratory form. To dispersed communities, 'diasporic ceremonies'?

Notes

This chapter incorporates some of the conclusions of our study on the wedding of the Prince of Wales and Lady Diana Spencer (London, 1981), a study made possible by a grant from the John and Mary R. Markle foundation, and published in French under the title 'Rituels publics à usage privé: metamorphose televisée d'un mariage royal', in *Les Annales: Economie, Société, Civilisation*, Paris, Armand Colin, 1983, no. 1; and in English, 'Electronic ceremonies: television performs a royal wedding', in Marshall Blonsky (ed.), *On Signs*, Baltimore, Johns Hopkins University Press, 1985.

Our thanks to all those who helped or advised us with the various case studies mentioned in our text, and, in particular, with the study on the royal wedding. We are specially grateful to Michael Lumley (producer–director of the BBC programme on the royal wedding); Stephen Hearst, Ian Gilham, Peter Saynor (BBC); Hugh Whitcomb (ITV); Kenneth Lamb (Church of England); John Grist (Radio and Television Service for the Armed Forces); Jay G. Blumler (Centre for Television Research, University of Leeds).

We must thank also for their energetic guidance in the fieldwork and comments afterwards: Anthony Smith (British Film Institute); Don Handelman (Hebrew University, Jerusalem); Pierre Nora (Ecole des Hautes Etudes en Sciences Sociales, Paris).

 1 The opposition between 'performative' and 'constative' statements can be found in Austin's theory of 'speech-acts'. J. Austin, *How to do Things with Words*, London, Oxford University Press, 1976.
 2 R. Searle, see the chapter 'What is a speech act?', in his *Philosophy of Language*, Oxford, Oxford University Press, 1971.

3 R. Barthes, see the chapter 'Rhetorics of the image', in his *Image, Music, Text*, New York, Hill & Wang, 1977.

4 Pierre Nora, 'L'événement monstre', *Communications*, 18, Paris, Seuil, 1972.

5 D. Dayan, E. Katz, and P. Kerns, 'Armchair pilgrimages: the trips of Pope John Paul II and their television public', in M. Gurevitch and M. Levy (eds), *Mass Communication Research Yearbook*, Beverly Hills, Sage, 1985.

6 David Chaney elaborates on the tension between definitions by organizers and broadcasters in 'A symbolic mirror of ourselves: civic ritual in mass society', *Media, Culture and Society*, 5, 2, 1983.

7 V. Turner, *The Ritual Process: Structure and Antistructure*, Chicago, Aldine, 1969.

8 J. G. Blumler *et al.*, 'Attitudes to the monarchy: their structure and development during a ceremonial occasion', *Political Studies*, XIX, 2 (1971).

9 Walter Benjamin, see the chapter 'The work of art in the age of mechanical reproduction', in his *Illuminations*, New York, Schocken Books, 1969.

10 See in particular the converging attempts at constituting an anthropology of spectacles and occasions made by such members of the Turner group as John MacAloon (University of Chicago) and Don Handelman (Hebrew University of Jerusalem). Cf. J. MacAloon (ed.), *Rite, Festival, Spectacle, Game*, Chicago, University of Chicago Press, 1984.

11 Benjamin, op. cit.

12 This is the case for Peter Jennings, covering the event from Ben Gurion Airport's tarmac for ABC. The situation is similar for the CBS team. Bob Simon: 'Of course I cannot see from here, but President Katzir will be greeting President Sadat.' And, from CBS's studio: 'And here is the handshake! If only we had a microphone in that small gathering.'

13 Mona Ozouf, *La Fête revolutionnaire*, Paris, Gallimard, Bibliothèque des Histoires, 1980.

14 Roman Jakobson, 'Linguistics and poetics', in K. and F. De George (eds), *The Structuralists, from Marx to Lévi-Strauss*, New York, Anchor Books, 1980.

15 Daniel Boorstin, *The Image: A Guide to Pseudo Events in America*, New York, Harper & Row, 1964, may grant that promotional events transmitted by the media but originating outside are less 'pseudo' than those initiated by the media themselves. Technically, however, both types of events qualify for Boorstin's derision.

16 Turner, op. cit.

17 Victor and Edith Turner, *Image and Pilgrimage in Christian Culture*, New York, Columbia University Press, 1978.

18 Compare Rothenbuhler's attempt to come to grips with some of the same problems: 'Durkheim's notion of a public festival or solidarity was dependent on a crowd, on the tactile presence of a collectivity. Canetti . . . makes a more explicit and literal use of the sense of touch [it is implicit in Durkheim], claiming that it is the base of all social existence. . . . But Canetti . . . has abandoned this literal logic for a symbolic one; the development of society was the development of symbols of crowd and symbols of touch . . . . I would propose to distinguish between a *crowd* – which is a group of people mutually present, mutually influencing and mutually oriented – a *public* – which is a group of people mutually influencing and commonly oriented – and a *mass* – which is a group of people commonly oriented. . . . The crowd, the public and the mass have existed side by side for as long as touch could be expressed symbolically. The media event works on this symbolic expression to transform mass into public, and achieve the functions Durkheim expected of crowds.' See Eric Rothenbuhler, 'Media events, civil religion and social solidarity: the living room celebration of the Olympic Games', Ph.D. dissertation, Annenberg School of Communications, University of Southern California, 1985.

See also Don Handelman's distinction between the size of a mass audience and its molecular character, particularly in the case of media events, as set out in his paper, 'Presenting, representing and modelling: a theory of public and media events', Hebrew University of Jerusalem, unpublished.

19 Baruch Bokser, *The Origins of the Seder*, Berkeley, University of California Press, 1984.

Part 3

Media and gender

Introduction

The contents of the media pass into the lives of audiences and are absorbed, rejected, reacted against, in a variety of ways. One area of central importance that has not yet received the attention that it deserves in British media research is the influence of the media on the interrelationships between women and men.

Gill Murphy raises the question of how media influence teenagers and suggests that this is not so much through the provision of models for imitation, based on a simple conception of the media–audience relationship as being one of stimulus and response, as through the systematic production of gender representations that mirror, reaffirm, and reconstitute accepted patterns of prescription. In her quantitative content analysis of stories and strip cartoons she shows how little alteration took place during a 60-year period in girls' magazines' portrayals of the 'realities' of femininity. The narrative material on offer to teenage girls in magazines appeared to have responded little to the growth of the feminist movement and changes in the legal status and economic roles of women: the finding of a male partner remained the heroine's almost exclusive ambition.

In contrast, Richard Paterson considers the TV series, *Boys from the Blackstuff*, which seemingly challenged traditional male gender norms. The viewer's experience of television material, Paterson suggests, is criss-crossed with argument, concealed discussion, a constant rehearsal of old conventions and new meanings. The impact of the series lay not so much in what it said as in its relationship with the viewer deemed to be already subject to conflicting views of gender or influenced by certain conventions by reason of his/her own sex, class, ethnic group and ideological disposition. The viewer is thus assessing self while gazing at the programme. *Boys from the Blackstuff* incorporated a particular range of contemporary public discourses, which favoured a shift away from the issues of feminism to a reworking of masculine styles.

9

Media influence on the socialization of teenage girls

Gillian Murphy

A wealth of anthropological evidence suggests that psychological differences between men and women are culturally rather than biologically defined.[1]

> Hormonal differences between the sexes may precipitate differences in aggression or nurturance behaviour and these provide the building blocks for evolutionary development . . . [but] as we move toward modern industrial societies, the impact of human values begins to overshadow differences in innate predispositions or the ability to perform social functions. However while all societies prescribe different attitudes and activities to men and women, they try to rationalise these prescriptions in terms of the physiological differences between the sexes or their different roles in reproduction. While such factors may have served as the starting point for the development of a division, the actual ascriptions are almost entirely determined by culture.[2]

These findings are also endorsed by sociologists who have discovered that sex differences in personality can be traced back to childhood and if not moulded in biology must emerge very early in the process of socialization.[3] The increase that occurs with age in sex differentiation points to a strong cultural influence.[4]

According to Linton, girls actually learn how to behave in a culturally defined 'feminine' way through both direct tuition (a child is taught to call and perceive herself as female) and indirect tuition (a child is responded to and taught how to behave in sex-specific ways and so comes to respond to herself as others respond to her).[5] The finding that girls are educated into a particular sex-role is backed up by a cross-cultural survey based on ethnographic reports for 110 societies, which found very consistent sex differences in the socialization of children aged 4 plus. It found that while boys are trained by parents to be self-reliant and achieve, girls are trained to be nurturant, responsible and obedient.[6]

It is particularly at the ages of 11 and 12 that teenagers are susceptible to being influenced by media definitions of roles and behaviour since for the first time they are unsure of their own point of view. As teenagers break away from primary sources of authority – families and schools – they look more to peer groups to establish norms of behaviour, leisure interests and dress.[7]

These peer groups also provide them with 'mirror' images of themselves and the way others see them is then integrated into their own personality.

However if in real life the peer group does not provide these 'mirror' images, teenagers may look to other sources instead – particularly to the media.[8]

Implicit in teenage media portrayals of 'reality' are cognitions of the way things are, in this case the way teenage girls and boys differ in personality traits, aspirations and roles. This reality is persuasive because it provides clear definitions and concurs with ascriptive beliefs about sex differentiation. 'The media is persuasive not because it provides models to imitate nor explicit directives to follow, but systems of representations that reflect, reaffirm and reproduce normative attitudes towards sex-role differentiation.[9]

This chapter examines the stereotyped image of male and female in the role of hero/anti-hero and heroine/anti-heroine in stories appearing in popular girls' magazines of the period 1920 to 1980 which were read by girls on the point of maturing from childhood to adolescence (the age of maturity being 14 in the 1920s and 1930s, dropping to 11 by the 1980s).

The purpose of my study was to determine the extent to which media portrayals of 'reality' as seen in the images of men and women depicted in stories, were maintained or modified during this period.

The first part of my study was a quantitative content analysis of stories appearing in a random selection of six issues (January, March, July, September, November and December) of *Peg's Paper* in the years 1922, 1928, 1931, 1936 and 1939; and a random selection of six issues (January, March, July, September, November and December) of *Glamour*, which incorporated *Peg's Paper*, in the years 1943, 1946, 1949, 1951 and 1955; a total of 110 stories, 55 in the pre-war and 55 in the post-war period.

I chose these magazines because they are representative of working-class romance weeklies of the period, which reached a wide audience of women from 15-year-old working girls to young married women and older mothers too.

I examined which characteristics (adjectives), from a selection of thirty, story writers deemed masculine or feminine, and further, whether such adjectives were then attributed to the hero or heroine (positive characteristics) or to the anti-hero or anti-heroine (negative undesirable attributes). See Table 9.1.

In most of the stories in the pre- and post-war periods, both the heroines and anti-heroines (to a lesser extent) were described as 'beautiful' or 'lovely'. Anti-heroines were sometimes called 'sirens' or 'alluring women', suggesting that they used their beauty to persuade men to take steps the men would later regret. However it was acceptable for heroines to use their looks to 'catch men' for marriage, indeed this was encouraged. For example, an advertisement for Eve Soap (*Peg's Paper*, 5 December 1936) read 'Come to think of it, life is one long beauty contest of us girls, isn't it? We've got to look our best all the time.'

Anti-heroines were depicted in both periods as 'cruel' and 'mocking'

Table 9.1 Male/female characteristic attribution in *Peg's Paper* (to 1939) and *Glamour* (to 1955)

| Characteristic | 1922, 1928, 1931, 1936, 1939 6 issues per year = 55 stories | | | | | | | | 1943, 1946, 1949, 1951, 1955 6 issues per year = 55 stories | | | | | | | |
	heroine	%	anti-heroine	%	hero	%	anti-hero	%	heroine	%	anti-heroine	%	hero	%	anti-hero	%
bitter/jealous	7	12.7	17	30.9	4	7.3	2	3.6	2	3.6	4	7.3	8	14.5	5	9.1
cruel/mocking	1	1.8	10	18.2	3	5.5	2	3.6	0	0.0	4	7.3	4	7.3	3	5.5
beautiful/lovely	34	61.8	19	34.5	0	0.0	0	0.0	31	54.5	14	25.5	0	0.0	1	1.8
rich	2	3.6	5	9.1	14	25.5	5	9.1	1	1.8	0	0.0	7	12.7	2	3.6
scheming	1	1.8	7	12.7	0	0.0	1	1.8	0	0.0	5	9.1	1	1.8	3	5.5
hard	2	3.6	7	12.7	9	16.4	1	1.8	1	1.8	3	5.5	11	20.6	6	10.9
passionate	6	10.9	4	7.3	12	21.8	6	10.9	2	3.6	2	3.6	4	7.3	3	5.5
vain/arrogant	0	0.0	2	3.6	0	0.0	0	0.0	0	0.0	2	3.6	2	3.6	2	3.6
brave	11	20.0	0	0.0	1	1.8	0	0.0	6	10.9	1	1.8	1	1.8	0	0.0
fainting/weak/frail	20	36.4	0	0.0	1	1.8	0	0.0	11	20.0	1	1.8	1	1.8	0	0.0
childlike, boyish	19	34.5	0	0.0	0	0.0	0	0.0	13	23.6	1	1.8	7	12.7	1	1.8
delicate/dainty/fragile	5	9.1	0	0.0	0	0.0	0	0.0	3	5.5	3	5.5	0	0.0	0	0.0
sincere	1	1.8	0	0.0	0	0.0	1	1.8	1	1.8	0	0.0	1	1.8	0	0.0
obedient	8	14.5	0	0.0	0	0.0	0	0.0	5	9.1	1	1.8	2	3.6	0	0.0

	Freq	%	Freq	%	Freq	%	Freq	%	Freq	%	Freq	%	Freq	%
foolish	2	3.6	0	0.0	0	0.0	0	0.0	4	7.3	0	0.0	1	1.8
dependent	1	1.8	0	0.0	1	1.8	0	0.0	3	5.5	0	0.0	0	0.0
easily led astray	2	3.6	0	0.0	0	0.0	0	0.0	1	1.8	0	0.0	0	0.0
indecisive	1	1.8	0	0.0	0	0.0	0	0.0	0	0.0	0	0.0	0	0.0
submissive/yielding	13	23.6	0	0.0	1	1.8	0	0.0	7	12.7	1	1.8	0	0.0
masterful/dominating/domineering	2	3.6	1	1.8	8	14.5	4	7.3	0	0.0	9	16.4	3	7.3
industrious/efficient	5	9.1	0	0.0	1	1.8	1	1.8	6	10.9	2	3.6	0	0.0
ambitious	1	1.8	3	5.5	0	0.0	0	0.0	0	0.0	0	0.0	0	0.0
gentle	2	3.6	0	0.0	3	5.5	1	1.8	2	3.6	15	27.3	0	0.0
timid/shy	9	16.4	0	0.0	0	0.0	0	0.0	4	7.3	5	9.1	0	0.0
stern	0	0.0	0	0.0	10	18.2	0	0.0	0	0.0	4	7.3	1	1.8
strong	1	1.8	0	0.0	10	18.2	1	1.8	1	1.8	15	27.3	1	1.8
restrained	0	0.0	0	0.0	2	3.6	0	0.0	0	0.0	3	5.5	0	0.0
quiet	3	5.5	0	0.0	4	7.3	1	1.8	9	16.4	5	9.1	0	0.0
handsome/good-looking	0	0.0	3	5.5	25	45.5	3	5.5	0	0.0	24	43.6	5	9.1
pure/innocent	3	5.5	0	0.0	0	0.0	0	0.0	11	20.0	1	1.8	0	0.0

Source: my own calculations.
Note: frequency – % refers to percentage of each group of 55 stories.

although this description was used two and a half times more often before the war than after it. Moreover, anti-heroines were continuously described as 'bitter and jealous' twice as often as heroines and far more often than men in both periods. Much female bitterness was attributed to the fact that 'Hell hath no fury like a woman scorned', a saying which appeared in several stories in *Peg's Paper*. It is interesting to note that women were described as 'bitter' four times more often before the war than after it.

'Hard' was another adjective employed to describe both men and women in stories, though in women it was a negative quality in both periods. Like 'bitter' this adjective was also applied to anti-heroines far less often after the war – the frequency dropping from 13 per cent to 5 per cent. However, in men 'hardness' was seen both as a positive attribute and a negative one; but it was definitely a male characteristic. (Before the war 16 per cent of heroes and 2 per cent of anti-heroes were thus described while after the war 20 per cent of heroes and 11 per cent of anti-heroes were called 'hard' men.)

Although the characteristic 'beautiful/lovely' was attributed to women with the same regularity before and after the war, this regularity was not sustained for many other characteristics; in other words, the media image of women was modified in the post-war stories of romance magazines.

It has been noted that women were apparently less bitter, jealous, hard and cruel after the war – they were also poorer. Anti-heroines were described as 'rich' in 9 per cent of pre-war stories and no post-war stories. (It is interesting here to note that in pre- and post-war stories heroes were described as 'rich' seven times more often than heroines.) But a change also occurred in the idea of the 'obedient' and 'submissive' woman. For though both characteristics were attributed almost always to heroines these qualities were mentioned twice as often before the war. (No men were described as 'obedient' and only one man as 'submissive' before the war and only two stories described men as 'obedient' after the war.)

By the end of the Second World War, the Victorian image of the delicate, childlike wife, submissive to her stern and masterful husband who caught her as she fainted into his arms, an image which persisted in *Peg's Paper* and other romance papers until 1939, was beginning to change. Where the heroine was previously described as 'weak/fainting/frail' in 36 per cent and 'childlike' in 35 per cent of pre-war stories, she was described as 'weak' in only 20 per cent and 'childlike' in 24 per cent of post-war stories. These qualities were rarely attributed at any time to the anti-heroine.

'Childlike' was an interesting adjective to use since it conveys a wealth of images: trust, simplicity, freedom, freshness, brightness, helplessness, impulsiveness and curiosity. Curiosity was seen as an undesirable trait and one peculiar to women: 'You're that wonderful and rare thing – an uncurious woman' (*Peg's Paper*, 7 November 1936).

Women were also more often described as 'timid and shy' before the war (while no men were) but after the war this quality was attributed to both heroes and heroines. Despite the heroine being described as 'shy' and 'fragile' she was also described as 'brave' in 20 per cent of the pre-war stories but in only 11 per cent of the post-war stories. On the other hand 'positive' qualities of 'quietness' and 'purity/innocence' were mentioned as desirable female attributes far more often in post-war than pre-war stories.

The Second World War became a dividing post not only for female stereotypes but also for male stereotypes. However, certain characteristics were attributed to men with the same regularity in both periods, for example the adjectives 'good-looking', 'masterful', and 'strong'. None the less, the ratio of good-looking heroes to anti-heroes was 6:1 while the ratio of 'beautiful' heroines to anti-heroines was only 2:1.

The hero as hunter/initiator appeared constantly over the two periods. For instance, Peg's Man Pal (*Peg's Paper*, 5 September 1936) said:

A man does not like being chased. He likes to feel popular but does not want a girl to run after him. He likes to run that part of the business himself. And he hates feeling he is being hunted into a corner. His own instinct as a hunter rebels against it. No real man likes the girl who makes men her one aim and object in life. Remember he wants a mate and companion.

(This piece of advice ran counter to the message of nearly every story in the romance magazines I studied from 1920–80!)

As well as not 'chasing men', girls were advised not to make the first move, at any stage. 'I've often been asked what I think of pick-ups. For Heaven's sake don't. Let him do it' (advice page, *Peg's Paper*, 18 January 1936). Nor was the girl to propose marriage, in fact one heroine asked the hero anxiously, 'Oliver, you won't despise me because I proposed to you?' (*Peg's Paper*, 6 March 1928). The girl was on the other hand told to bolster the man's own self-importance: 'The Secretary can show the men in the office that she is capable and clever, and she can do it in a way that makes them think they are making their own great discovery' (advice page, *Peg's Paper*, 18 January 1936).

In only one article in the entire period examined was the girl told to take the initiative and then in a rather limited way: 'The modern girl has to take on herself the duties that grandma's father and big brother used to perform for her. Putting a man in his place is one of them. Putting an end to the 6-year courter is another' (advice page, *Peg's Paper*, 18 January 1936). But while lack of initiative and helplessness was acceptable – even expected – in women, it was scorned in men: 'He's the sort some woman will always have to prop up with sympathy and sacrifice – he needs admiration to prop up his vanity' (*Glamour*, 20 September 1949).

Man as woman's protector against unscrupulous bosses, rivals and unwanted suitors often appeared throughout the period I examined. In the pre-war stories the heroines were often rescued by heroes or fainted into their arms. The image of a woman with her arms round her children and her husband's arms round her appeared in several stories. In the following examples, men were seen as naturally protective, and as protectors in their role as husband: 'A girl must be careful to give the impression always that she holds herself so dearly that the man she gives her love to, is the man who will protect and care for her for the rest of his life' (*Peg's Paper*, 18 January 1936). Or in a story in *Glamour* (12 July 1949) the hero says: 'A wife is supposed to preside over a home and have babies. A husband is supposed to protect her and his children and make them all comfortable and happy.' And two years later the story read: 'She was human, she wanted a man's arms around her, she wanted to be cherished and cared for, she wanted a home and children of her own' (*Glamour*, 3 July 1951).

Men were seen as protective in the financial sense as well; for instance, a story in *Peg's Paper* (6 March 1928) described a couple who couldn't get married because the man couldn't support a wife although the girl herself was earning. In many of the stories in the pre-war period, particularly during the depression years of the 1920s and early 1930s, the hero was described as rich and a good catch for the poor, struggling but beautiful heroine who then married and became dependent on her husband's income. In the pre-war period 26 per cent of the heroes were described as 'rich', compared with 13 per cent in the post-war period.

Men were described as 'passionate' three times more often for both heroes and anti-heroes in the pre- compared with the post-war period while the number of heroes described as 'stern' fell from 18 per cent pre-war to 7 per cent post-war. However, other characteristics attributed to males were taking their place. More men were described as 'strong' after the war yet at the same time five times more heroes were described as 'gentle' after the war than before it. And unlike the heroines, heroes after the war also became more shy with an increase from none to 9 per cent over the two periods.

Heroes also became more 'boyish' (carefree, eager, trusting) during the post-war period (unlike the heroines who became less 'childlike'), the number of heroes thus described rising from none (pre-war) to 13 per cent (post-war). However they were also described as bitter and jealous in the post-war period as were anti-heroes, though this again was a reversal of the female trend. (The number of bitter/jealous heroes doubled after the war while the number of bitter anti-heroes increased by two and a half times.)

Thus from a study of the characteristics of male and female characters in romance stories of the period 1922 to 1955 the desirable female image which emerged was a beautiful, passionate, brave, childlike, delicate and shy woman, yielding and submissive to men (also pure and quiet in the post-war period) while the ideal male image was of a masterful, stern, passionate, hard and wealthy nature modified to a strong, boyish, gentle and shy nature in the post-war period. Traits considered undesirable in females in both periods were ambition, jealousy, cruelty and bitterness, and in males the undesirable traits were dependency, indecisiveness, submission, helplessness and frailty.[10]

The second part of my study was a quantitative content analysis of forty-three comic strip stories appearing in a random sample of *Jackie* magazines in the years 1964, 1971 and 1978. In each of these years, I examined one issue in six different months: January, May, July, September, November and December.

Comic strips although not containing all the ideas included in the magazine synthesize the values, aspirations and roles that the magazine presents to its readers. They are similar in structure to the stories in *Peg's Paper* and *Glamour* though they lack detailed description of the main story characters since the story is always outlined in a series of pictures with captions. I therefore broadened my research of stories in *Jackie* to examine the roles and behaviour of the heroes and heroines rather than merely considering their characteristics.

I chose *Jackie* as being representative of the genre of romance magazines aimed specifically at girls on the point of maturing to adolescence at around 10–14 years, and thus it corresponds with the two magazines examined in the first part of this chapter, which were also representative of romance magazines for teenage girls in the first half of this century.

The comic strips I studied are a staple diet of *Jackie* – there were an average of two per issue in the 1964 and 1978 copies and four per issue in the 1971 copies. The strips usually feature both a hero and a heroine, in a predictable story involving their meeting, dating, a misunderstanding, tragedy or reconciliation.

> The characters and plots seldom differ in outline, the stereotype and the formula being part of the attraction for female readers. In much the same way as children are happy with the familiar, so many teenage girls seem to need the security of the familiar style and formula which are found also in the short textual stories.[11]

The comic strip tells young teenagers about the world before they experience the situations portrayed. And these preconceptions, unless education has made them aware, govern their whole process of perception.[12] Relationships with boys are conceived in the terms given by the comic strip and teenagers find it hard to imagine them in other terms because none have been given.

The hero and heroine of the comic strip express the social behaviour and attitudes which the reader may already have acquired through family and school. The hero's and heroine's stereotyped reactions to situations and to each other protect and support traditional roles allotted to male and female and these stereotypes are highly resistant to modification even when there is a total contradiction in the social environment.

> In such a case, they take on the character of delusions and become highly maladaptive. While stereotyping is potentially dangerous since it prevents the individual from freely structuring each situation he confronts, it may, within definite limits, serve a useful function in providing the individual with a kind of psychological shorthand for quick appraisals of situations. Stereotypes are only a special case of cognitive structuring.[13]

In the pre-teen comics, the heroine stereotypes are girls of initiative and courage who confront difficult situations on equal terms with boys. The stories are full of adventure – the heroine rescues, pursues hobbies, investigates action and is self-confident and happy with boys and girls.[14]

But there is a change from this portrayal of girls to a rather different one in the early teen magazines.

> Here, over and over again, on both the serious and the humorous levels, the feminine role is in itself sufficiently problematic to provide the basis for most of the material in this range of comics. In this respect, girls' comics differ fundamentally from boys' or pre-teen comics for they are more than just feminine versions of adventure stories, they are basically concerned with femininity itself.[15]

Particular definitions of 'masculinity' and 'femininity' appear constantly in the comic strip stereotypes and these reinforce girls' self-images already gained through primary sources and other media.

In the comic strips I examined, all but five feature the hero and heroine in a dating situation. And in all but five ambiguous cases, and another where the girl 'rebels', it is always the male who takes the initiative in inviting the girl to go somewhere on a date which she always accepts. Moreover in almost every strip, the hero and heroine are looking for or trying to keep a girl/boyfriend. Only rarely are they seen enjoying the company of friends of their own sex. Nowhere is there any suggestion that the relationship could be platonic or that a crowd of boys and girls could go somewhere together.

Over the twenty years since *Jackie* began, its definition of 'femininity' has not changed.[16] The hero still initiates, the heroine follows, he dominates and she submits. It is the heroine who tries to please the hero, to adapt to him and agree with his ideas. While the hero may have an active interest in hobbies the heroine is *passive*.

Often the comic strip hero owns a motor bike or car – and while the heroine *accepts rides she can never offer them*. The hero's world seems to focus on other *things* besides girls, whereas the heroine's world revolves round *boys*. If the heroines do mix with other girls, it's to discuss how to get a boyfriend, or (occasionally) to make catty comments about other girls (only one hero did the same).

Jackie not only portrays girls with particular characteristics, but also in stereotyped roles. *In over a third of the comic strips, the heroine is depicted in 'nurturing' roles – looking after small children, the sick and elderly, shopping for her mother or washing/shopping for the hero.* Only once is the boy seen in a caring role (and then alongside his girlfriend) looking after a boy who had fallen off his motor bike.

Only one of the forty-three comic strips considered (16 January 1971) depicts the heroine in an independent, self-confident and initiating role. This comic strip stands out for several reasons. First, the heroine is allowed to hold opinions about society and not just about her boyfriend. The story is related largely in terms of a developed conversation and not just in reactions to changing situations. The heroine is adventurous and does not want a boyfriend. She is intelligent and treats the hero as an equal. The story is reminiscent of the pre-teen comics and does not fit into the narrow confines of 'romance'. Perhaps it is included because the heroine's independence is seen as pure fantasy by *Jackie* readers. It certainly challenges the stereotypes in the vast majority of other comic strips.

But it is not just in comic strips that sexist ideas flourish. Throughout the magazine, girls are presented in ways which are consistent with these stereotyped images and are as unrealistic as unsatisfactory. The chance is seldom given to girls to see other girls and women doing things which require *strength of character and initiative.* 'Finding a man and looking after him, helping others and solving personal problems are the only activities women are allowed to undertake.'[17]

Despite the Women's Movement and the anti-discrimination Acts, which have attempted to equalize the position of women and men in society, *Jackie*'s ideas are firmly rooted in the 1950s where women are seen as home-makers. *Jackie*'s comic strips, which show girls as having an overwhelming need to find a man, obviously run counter to all notions of Women's Liberation. They obliterate any idea of girls as independent individuals having their own interests.

There is ample evidence that teenagers still see themselves in the traditional roles of provider (male) and nurturer (female) and adjust their aspirations accordingly.[18] Despite changes in the law to encourage women to enter fields previously only open to men, girls still have lower expectations of their intellectual and academic achievement than boys and so automatically limit themselves.[19]

Besides examining the rarely modified images of male and female in romance stories from the 1920s to the present day, I was also interested in studying the depoliticization of stories appearing in magazines published in years of rapid social, economic and political change from the mid-1930s to the 1950s.

George Orwell wrote of Britain in 1936:

> In a decade of unparalleled depression, the consumption of all cheap luxuries had increased. The two things that have probably made the greatest difference of all are the movies and the mass production of cheap smart clothes . . . you may have three-halfpence in your pocket and not a prospect in the world and only the corner of a leaky bedroom to go home to, but in your new clothes you can stand on the street corner indulging in a private daydream of yourself as Clark Gable or Greta Garbo which compensates for a great deal.[20]

And for adolescent working-class girls, romance magazines could be added to movies and clothes as 'compensation', fostering complacency by providing temporary respite from reality in the success stories of fictional heroines. It seemed from the stories that if all was well in love, the rest of the world could fall to pieces and it would not matter.

In none of the pre-war stories in *Peg's Paper* was there any attempt to make the readers feel indignant or angry at their situation, in fact many of the pre-war issues concerning readers were not mentioned at all in stories. Unjust management, fair pay for women workers, the power of unions, political parties and leaders, suffragettes, hunger and unemployment marches: all were ignored.

For example, there were only two mentions of unemployment facing girls in 1922 *Peg's Paper* stories, and in 1928 in the same magazine unemployment was mentioned once and poverty three times in the nine stories examined. In January 1928 the heroine of one story sought work through an employment agency since few jobs were advertised openly and she faced starvation otherwise. The heroine in this story was employed to act the part of an heir's fiancée and she then became his real fiancée.

Two months later the heroine in another rags to riches story (6 March 1928) felt life was 'just one long endless grind and toil'. This story was the only one of the whole pre-war period to mention Britain's economic position: 'Of course the depreciation in the value of the export trade has hit us pretty hard.' A similar story also appeared in the issue of 1 May 1928 where the 'poor heroine' was described as 'one of a busy swarm of toilers for whom work was the chief thing in life'. In another rags to riches story two months later (3 July 1928) the heroine married a rich man.

Three years later in the middle of the period of starvation for many, hunger marches and severe unemployment, only two stories in *Peg's Paper* mentioned unemployment specifically, and one mentioned poverty. In the issue of 3 March 1931 the author wrote: 'All her life [the heroine] had known poverty, her father had died when she was a baby and her mother, worn out by hard work and worry, had followed when Jill was 16.' Four months later, (7 July 1931) in another story, the hero, a mill manager, tries to keep the mill open because 'there are enough people unemployed in this district already'. And in the 3 November issue of *Peg's Paper* in the same year, another heroine went to an employment agency 'since being penniless and an orphan she was getting desperate for she could not find employment'. By 1936 when the employment situation was beginning to improve, only one *Peg's Paper* story (4 July) was about an unemployed heroine.

Only one story in the 110 I examined mentioned a militant workforce. In the 7 July 1931 issue of *Peg's Paper*, the heroine Polly worked at a mill which was to be closed by the mill owner who had decided it was unprofitable. The workers (all women) protested but the mill's manager told Polly, who represented the workers, 'If you people would stick to your own job and do it well, and leave us to ours we should get on a lot better. If you have a taste of the difficulties of running a mill you'll be able to persuade your fellow firebrands to behave decently.' Polly persuades the workforce not to strike, then gets a loan to buy new equipment for the mill and talks the workers into agreeing to work at half wages till the loan is repaid. Her motive for helping the manager is that she has fallen in love with him. He asks her to marry him as a business partner. Thus there is no manager–worker confrontation, no hint of exploitation, no class conflict, yet there is a class gap: Polly says, 'Dennis was talking to her as though she were one of his equals instead of merely an employee.'

In another story the same year (15 December 1931) the class gap is again apparent: the heroine this time is a despised orphan described by the rich hero as 'just a charity girl, and a boarding house drudge. Cheap and shabby and terribly conscious of her own inferiority.' In 1936, *Peg's Paper* had two stories reflecting class division. In 'Gypsy Bride' (4 July) the heroine's mother had married a gypsy. 'That was wrong. The gypsies are not like other people and it seems that we're all intended to marry amongst our own kind. There's always trouble when anybody breaks that unwritten law.' And in a second story (5 September) the hero was persuaded by an ex-girlfriend not to marry the heroine 'because they belonged to different worlds. She was poor, he was rich . . . she was only an ignorant country girl . . . not the girl to marry.'

Fourteen years earlier class differences were no less apparent. In a story in *Betty's Paper* (3 June 1922) one author wrote: 'Elsie had been clever at school and her father had given her a much better education than is usual with girls in their class. So Elsie grew up with a tendency to "fancy herself" though she was a nice girl at heart.' And in a similar story in *Peg's Paper* (11 July 1922), 'Married above her Station', a poor dancing girl married a rich man who berated her for lacking good taste.

In all these stories the authors regarded such class differences as natural and inevitable – there was no discussion of the distribution of wealth, political power, education and job opportunities which meant that it was difficult to move from one class to another. In fact, stories were often decontextualized and depoliticized providing readers with the vicarious experience of living without want, wearing clothes and jewels, not needing to work, having servants: their image of middle/upper-class life.

From 1928 to 1955 if stories had some particular background apart from the office or a dance, they were usually set abroad in places with which the reader would not be familiar. Therefore the description of the life of those living in these far-off lands might have been the only such information the reader could acquire. Yet the descriptions offered could only promote prejudice as the following examples taken from stories in pre-war issues of *Peg's Paper* illustrate.

In 'Had She but Known' (6 March 1928) the heroine found herself in the middle of the Sahara desert where she was pursued by the 'ruthless half-Arab half-Spanish' anti-hero, 'a savage at heart', who said, 'I wished to win the girl but was wise enough not to attempt it openly because I knew I should have frightened her, for like so many English people she had racial prejudices'. This prejudice, which many Britons had, was revealed by the narrator of 'A Man's Confessions' (1 September 1931) who said, 'I couldn't marry Dallas because she was a half-caste'.

As the effect of the depression reached its climax in England, so stories became less removed from reality – though keeping to the familiar theme of finding true love, or at least romance. The year 1936 saw one story, 'Desert Tropical Island Honeymoon', and four serials set against a foreign background: 'Desert Nights' (in the Sahara), 'The White Rajah' (India), 'Passion's Prison' (India) and 'When a Man Sins' (Canada). The last serial began: 'Lawless love, unfettered hate, primitive passion, all awaited June when she went to the Backwoods of Canada to become a bride . . . she preferred the hero to most of the others – he was white.'

In 1939 the number of stories with a foreign background remained the same – in the issues examined, three serials appeared – 'Pagan Love', 'Call of the East' and 'Love Knows No Frontiers' (in Central Europe 'where there is no law and order') – and two stories, 'Bartered Bride' and 'Island Honeymoon'. In 'Bartered Bride' (4 March 1939) the hero 'has Solomon Islanders as labourers – the fiercest and most savage tribes in the Pacific. Even today many of them are cannibals and must be dealt with firmly and given punishments they understand. A fine or imprisonment means nothing to wild people like that – but a flogging does.'

'Island Honeymoon' (6 May 1939), set on an unnamed Pacific island, began with a description of the island's ruler; a 'half-savage island girl', 'an ignorant pagan', an 'ignorant little savage', 'primitive and passionate, governed by her impulses and emotions [which were] natural and uncurbed, she knew nothing of the ways of the civilised world [but was] wild, and barbaric . . . with as little restraint as a panther would have', who asks to be 'mastered', and is eventually 'civilised'.

Not only were stories in the pre-war period escapist but in a time of uncertainty economically and politically there was a search for some sort of day to day guidance and reassurance. Articles began to focus more on Hollywood, a world totally removed from reality, and on the occult (in the form of superstitions, horoscopes, star prediction, lucky stones etc.). By 7 January 1939 there were six such articles in *Peg's Paper* – the regular 'Gossip from Filmland' and the horoscope, plus 'the Society Clairvoyante's Predictions for 1939', 'Problems solved with the aid of Stars', Peg's Man Pal on 'Superstitions', and 'the Truth about Dorothy Lamour' comprising about a fifth of the total magazine content. At the end of the year, the articles were similar but these topics became less popular during the war though the horoscope continued.

Although *Peg's Paper/Glamour* stories from 1939–45 recognized that a war was being fought, war was often used as the backdrop against which stories with the familiar theme of love, misunderstanding and reconciliation were set.

In each of the November and December 1939 issues of *Peg's Paper*, three stories mentioning war appeared; one about German refugees, two about families receiving a billeted soldier/children, and one about a soldier on leave. There was also one about a pregnant woman deserted by a soldier who joined up and one about a girl's wartime job. The usual plot was that the heroine would fall in love with a war hero; only once was the heroine more than just a victim of injustice, hardship or ill-fated love, in a story where she caught a German spy.

But in other stories, particularly those in the 5 January 1943 issue of *Glamour*, the hero was the instigator of any action. For instance in 'Keep your Heart for Me', the hero exposed a girl member of the Hitler Youth Movement by pretending to love her. In 'Girl in the Munitions Factory', the heroine fell in love with an army commander, while in 'Girl on the U Boat', the heroine was rescued by the hero from the hands of the Germans.

The reality of the role of women in the war years, as efficient, quick and diligent workers on an equal footing with male colleagues, contrasts sharply with the depiction by romantic story writers of a woman as alluring and tender, depending on a man to give her protection, status and financial support while she gave him respite from the harsh world outside by focusing on his feelings of tenderness, cheerfulness, warmth. The stories seem to say to the reader: as long as you're in love and are secure in your immediate world of home and family, the 'outer' world will not really affect you.

Advertisers tried to tie the real and imagined roles of women together and suggested that by using their products the consumer could be efficient and yet remain attractive. For instance (*Peg's Paper*, 18 November 1939), 'White teeth are a true beauty asset and just because there's a war on, there's no reason to neglect your looks.' Or (*Peg's Paper*, 16 December 1939), 'Beauty is your duty. Beauty inspires happiness and cheerfulness both for yourself and others too.'

The conflict between the two roles of women as independent provider and worker versus the dependent home-maker are highlighted in an article by *Glamour*'s editor which appeared on 2 March 1940.

Many of you, I am sure, are thrilled to be in uniform, thrilled to know that you, too, are helping to win the war. It's a grand feeling to know that you are sharing the hardships and sometimes the discomforts that your boyfriend or husband must bear. But are you letting the excitement of taking a man's place go to your head? Are you forgetting that beneath that efficient exterior you are still a girl – sweet, feminine, enticing? Ask yourself honestly – do you tend to swagger about in your slacks, to talk in brief curt sentences, to take on a masculine veneer that is hard and unattractive? Please don't forget that when your sweetheart comes home on leave, he expects to find the 'girl he left behind', not a poor imitation of himself. Particularly in wartime a man longs for tenderness, charm, and that appealing something that calls forth his protective instincts. Don't disappoint him. Be as efficient and hardworking as you can while you're on your job but remember to be a woman when you're off-duty.'

It is evident that the editress equates efficiency and hard work with masculinity and that these qualities are put on, implying that women are normally scatty, disorganized and inefficient. If the editress were correct in assuming women were only superficially 'efficient and hardworking', the stories could be said to provide an idealized image of women as they desired to be. Romance also provided an escape from the grim reality of war for even in war stories heroines were never concerned about bombing, rationing or evacuation.

Fictional stories contained much anti-Nazi propaganda, describing all Nazis in the terms previously used for the anti-hero: cruel, arrogant, cowardly, uncivilized and without honour. For instance here are two excerpts from stories appearing in *Peg's Paper* in the December 1939 and January 1940 issues respectively:

Her husband was a Nazi. Nazi – that word that meant brutality, treachery and everything that revolted civilization. He was so cruel, arrogant, vicious and a coward too!

Hans Heimler like most of the other Nazi rulers was half-insane. They were criminal lunatics turned loose on an innocent world . . . it gave him a sinister half-uncivilised look . . . . A typical Nazi, corrupt and debased . . . [sexual] desire was only too plainly shown in his thin dissolute features . . . there was a streak of cowardice in Heimler's brutality . . . . They were the ravings of a madman.

By the end of the war, *Glamour's* articles still depicted courtship, marriage and motherhood as a girl's main aim in life and ignored topics arising from the increased part women had played in the war; topics such as equal job opportunities, equal pay for equal work, careers open to women, the provision of nurseries at work and whether a woman's place was (as it had been assumed) in the home.

After the war, there were permanent changes in the political, social and economic climate in Britain. More women were working full-time, and unemployment dropped. Between 1945 and 1959 the Welfare State was built up with the institution of National Insurance for workers and a National Health Service. New towns were built and after the 1944 Education Act new secondary schools were built too. People began to watch TV and listen to pop music and, as record players became cheaper, new pop stars arose, whose music was readily available to working-class teenagers.

Yet only gradually did *Glamour* reflect these changes and then only in superficial details like the transatlantic slang used in articles, in cartoon stories, in photo-journalism features on movie and pop stars, in pop star pin-ups, and articles on pop, films and job opportunities. Usually the stories continued to be decontextualized and if they were set against foreign backdrops, they had the same racist overtones as those a decade before.

Of the forty-three stories I examined in *Jackie* covering the period from the 1960s to 1978, only four were put in any kind of social context. Three of these stories appeared in the 1971 January and May issues of *Jackie*, the fourth appeared in 1973. Only one of all forty-three stories ever mentioned the Women's Movement and of the others, one included reference to an anti-war demonstration (at the same time as the Vietnam demonstrations) and the other to a computer-programmed bureaucratic society of the future.

In the period 1922–78, the content, style of presentation, topics featured, style of story writing and the stories' actual content (place, theme, characters, behaviour suggested as appropriate for male and female and roles and interests ascribed to them) in the genre of magazines read by adolescent girls and described in this chapter as 'romance magazines' hardly changed at all despite a period of considerable social, economic, political and moral change between these years.

Issues of *Glamour* in 1943 and 1951 and *Jackie* in 1978 all contained romance stories, a serial, a reader's true confession, an advice column, an article on beauty, a horoscope, letters from readers and articles on pop stars.

Virtually every story examined in this fifty-six-year period had finding a male partner as the heroine's one ambition, with her work or hobbies of little importance, in fact work was often merely a means of financial support and beauty was the only leisure interest considered worth pursuing. The boy-meets-girl happy ending (leading presumably to marriage) was seen as part of the escapism from work (equated with drudgery), from a inclement world, and from monotony, with a romantic long-lasting glow.

Notes

My thanks to the Acton Society for a small grant which made this research possible.

1 See, for instance, M. Mead, *Male and Female*, New York, William Morrow, 1949; R. Linton, *The Study of Man*, New York, Appleton-Century-Crofts, 1963; W. Davenport, 'Sexual patterns and their regulation in a society of the Southwest Pacific', in F. A. Beach (ed.), *Sex and Behavior*, New York, J. Wiley, 1965.
2 S. Dornbusch, in E. E. Maccoby (ed.), *The Development of Sex Differences*, London, Tavistock, 1967, pp. 214–15.
3 R. E. Sears, E. E. Maccoby and H. Levin, *Patterns of Child Rearing*, Illinois, Harper & Row, 1957; J. Kagen and H. Moss, *Birth to Maturity*, New Haven, Yale University Press, 1983.
4 A. Oakley, *Sex, Gender and Society*, London, Temple Smith, 1972, p. 56.
5 R. Linton cited in Dornbusch, op. cit., p. 195.
6 H. Barry *et al.*, 'Cross cultural survey of sex differences', *Journal of Abnormal Social Psychology*, 55 (1957), 327–32.
7 E. Hilyard, R. C. Atkinson and R. L. Atkinson, *Introduction to Psychology*, 6th edn, New York, Harcourt Brace Jovanovich, 1975, p. 95.
8 G. Noble, *Children in Front of the Small Screen*, London, Constable, 1975, pp. 8–19, 115, 207, 225.
9 J. Curran, *Sex Role Differentiation in Popular National Sunday Newspapers*, D305, Social Psychology, GB, Milton Keynes, Open University, 1976, p. 36.
10 See Table 9.1.
11 M. Marshall, *Libraries and Literature for Teenagers*, London, André Deutsch, 1975, p. 152.
12 W. Lipmann, *Public Opinion*, London, Macmillan, 1972, pp. 59–70.
13 F. Fearing, 'Human communication', *Audio Visual Communication Review*, X, 3 (1962), 78–108.
14 J. King and M. Stott, *Is This Your Life?*, London, Virago, 1977, p. 90.
15 C. Cannon, 'Comics for young girls', *Spare Rib*, November 1972.
16 For further discussion of *Jackie*, see Angela McRobbie, '*Jackie*: an ideology of adolescent femininity', in B. Waites, T. Bennett and G. Martin (eds), *Popular Culture: Past and Present*, London, Croom Helm, 1982; and P. Hoggart, 'The commercial literature of schoolchildren', *Media, Culture and Society*, 3, 4 (1981).
17 S. Sharpe, *Just like a Girl*, Harmondsworth, Penguin, 1978, p. 119.
18 C. Adams and R. Laurikietis, *The Gender Trap*, book 1, London, Virago, 1976, p. 61.
19 L. Corner, *Wedlocked Women*, London, Feminist Books, 1974, p. 6.
20 G. Orwell, *The Road to Wigan Pier*, London, Penguin, 1936.

10

Restyling masculinity: the impact of *Boys from the Blackstuff*

Richard Paterson

The drama series *Boys from the Blackstuff*, transmitted in the autumn of 1982 with wide-ranging effect, is particularly pertinent to the general study of the influence of television. The series dealt with the impact of unemployment on a group of Liverpool men and their families, focusing on male anxieties and the undermining of traditional notions of masculinity, and gave rise to a range of public effects greater than can be accounted for by the relevance of the subject to Britain in the 1980s. Looking at the series as a text, as a media event, as a production and as a basis for audience association, how did this come about and why did the series pass so rapidly and successfully into the national culture in so many different ways.

To understand the effect of television programmes on an audience is much more complicated than either survey methods or textual analysis would indicate, though both of course have much to contribute. The viewer is a private person placed within his or her social, sexual, ethnic or family group but also thoroughly imbued with a number of public contemporary issues and conversant with a number of ideological discussions and television conventions. He or she is confronted by a television text suffused with meanings. There is no necessary link between the intended reading of that text, with its narrative and genre conventions and codes, and any particular viewer's attitude at the moment of viewing. Furthermore the influence and effect of a programme does not end with its viewing – the proliferation of secondary discussion of it alters perspectives all of which have their effects. This is particularly the case with television series whose reputation is built up through review and word-of-mouth comment. The series or serial becomes public much more easily than the single play or TV movie.

Boys from the Blackstuff earned considerable critical acclaim. At the 1983 Edinburgh Television Festival, Jonathan Miller compared it with *Ulysses* as a major art work of the twentieth century. Five of the six contributors to the *Listener* articles published to coincide with the drama debate at the same event identified it as important in some way.[1] *Boys from the Blackstuff* became a television event. After favourable reviews at the time of its first transmission[2] (on BBC-2 in October/November 1982) the series was repeated unusually quickly on BBC-1 (in January 1983). It was the subject of numerous interviews with writer Alan Bleasdale on such programmes as *Nationwide* (BBC-1) and *Riverside* (BBC-2); and part of one edition of the BBC-2 programme *Did You See . . . ?* was devoted to the Liverpool audience's reaction to the series. One of the episodes ('Yosser's Story') was shown at various television festivals, and the series gained a number of awards.

Boys from the Blackstuff was not unique in its coverage of contemporary issues. There is a strong tradition of committed drama on British television which dates back to the *Wednesday Play* and *Armchair Theatre*, best remembered by plays such as *Cathy Come Home*, *The Spongers* and *United Kingdom* which focused on contemporary social problems and became the subject of public debate and discussion. For academic and critical discourse *Boys from the Blackstuff* stands in that tradition, an exemplar of that sort of drama. However the variety of response from different sections of society to the series is more interesting than its critical acclaim, though more baffling to explain: the take-up by the Liverpool football crowd, for example, of various lines from the series ('I can do that!', 'Giz a job!'), the popularity of the Yosser song in Liverpool, the incidence of head-butting in Liverpool, the use of the series in the trade union movement and its endorsement by Liverpool City Council. The series became a symbol within the national culture differently appropriated by different groups. Its discourse became part of other discourses in wider social and political fields and in the representations which television circulates. The series was art television, expressing an author's views;[3] it invoked the art of Liverpool (from the Beatles to the Liverpool poets); it touched common-sense understandings about the life of unemployed men and their families in the 1980s.

*

Boys from the Blackstuff is a realist drama. Using melodrama with tragedy and comedy, the series raises questions about masculinity, femininity and (un)employment within the domains (and ideological problematics) of the family, workplace and community using particular representations of gender and class, in narratives set up around an opposition of power and powerlessness at a particular historical conjuncture. The complexity of text that this indicates begins to explain the varying uses to which the series has been put. It is at once entertaining and depressing and has forged a mythology of the reality of unemployment. It engaged with current social problems and though not offering solutions, offered moral lessons. The complex architecture of implicit discussion which underlies the series is crucial to understanding its influence. It offers identification and understanding, elements of the personal and the political, shock and entertainment.

It is necessary to analyse the way in which the text works and to attempt to match it to viewers' understandings. For some audiences the series may have been taken as a piece of art television emanating from an author where identification is with the writer's view on the question of male anxieties and other themes raised by the programmes, leading to both political reflection and an appreciation of the dramatic construction of the story. For other audiences the series may have been viewed as good family melodrama, an experience of identification or of 'voyeurism', the watching of males undermined within their families. This chapter relies heavily on a limited range of interviews[4] in its account of the wider social impact of one series; this limitation points to the necessity for more adequate research techniques to account for television's diverse influences. However, an attempt is made here to bring together aspects of textual analysis and audience response within a wider sociopolitical frame of understanding.

On an analysis of the text, *Boys from the Blackstuff* works as a melodrama about men. The story-line is based on a group of characters who had featured in an earlier TV play, *The Black Stuff*. In that story the group was away from Liverpool in Middlesbrough when, at the initiative of Yosser Hughes (who wanted to be 'rich and famous'), they did a 'foreigner' that led to them losing all their savings and their jobs. At the end of it all the character elements developed in the series were present.

The Black Stuff was produced in 1978 by the BBC Regional Drama Unit, which had in the late 1970s produced a number of important and innovatory plays and series including *Licking Hitler*, *Gangsters* and *Empire Road*. Alan Bleasdale, the author, was commissioned to write a further series of plays developing the characters. Production was dependent on the use of new lightweight video cameras (because of financial considerations), but when their introduction was delayed one of the, by then, six stories was produced on film in 1980 as a separate play, *The Muscle Market* (about the boss), using different characters. The five-play series was finally commissioned in 1981, just after the eruption of riots at Toxteth in Liverpool and in other British cities. A change in the social atmosphere induced by ever-growing unemployment in Britain was reflected in the scripts.[5]

The five plays were 'Jobs for the Boys'; 'Moonlighter'; 'Shop Thy Neighbour'; 'Yosser's Story' and 'George's Last Ride'. The style varies slightly across each story. Elements of surrealism are introduced in the last two stories but it is the melodrama which gives the series its impact in all but the first play. Melodrama is sometimes taken as a critical category that devalues. In a critical context it delimits a narrative form that deals with personal actions (and particularly emotions and passions) within a constraining and threatening social order. As Dave Kehr has pointed out, 'it is an emotional treatment of emotion, using abrupt reversals in plot, wide swings in tone, and an intensively subjective *mise-en-scène* meant to enforce the strongest possible identification of the audience with the character'[6] and, as Pam Cook has argued, the contradictions of the discourses deployed in melodramas often lead to an excess in the text.[7] The narrative implications of melodrama as a form are key to an understanding of how male anxieties are handled in the series.

The series' coherence relies on an understanding of the 'boys' as a group. Textually their relationship to one another's lives is established by the inclusion of reference in each of the plays to the other characters.

Each story centres to varying degrees on the home and the 'workplace', firmly set within Liverpool. The emphasis is on the home life of men. Melodrama inflects ideological discourses into the domain of the personal. In *Boys from the Blackstuff* the status of the man and the male order are in crisis – masculinity is undermined.[8]

In the first story we are introduced to the 'boys' one by one, signing on at the Department of Employment. The titles come up over a poster proclaiming 'Thirty Years of Progress in Social Security'.

The next scene sets up the enigma which is resolved in this story but reverberates in later parts. An investigator at the Department of Employment and the desk clerk let it be known that they are suspicious of Chrissie's activities; a fact quickly confirmed when Chrissie receives instructions for a job the next day. The gang Chrissie collects (while followed by the investigators) includes Loggo and Snowy Malone. Snowy is the political activist son of George Malone and represents the political theme of socialism, as well as pride in craftsmanship. His commitment is set against Loggo's humorous put-downs ('You're an offence under the Noise Abatement Act'), and Chrissie's matter-of-factness ('When you're scared you think about yourself and yours'). Yosser's arrival with his three children asking 'Giz a job, go on, I know you've got one, giz it, I'm ready' offers a tragi-comic interlude before the ill-managed swoop by the investigators. Snowy dies as he attempts to escape down a rope attached to banisters which give way – the voice of politics dies. The male group is shown as broken by unemployment, unable to obtain self-respect through work, unable to interpret its own circumstances.

The second story – 'Moonlighter' – features Dixie working as a security guard at the docks while still claiming unemployment benefit. His manhood is constantly undermined and his family is in trouble. His sons have lost hope with life; his wife is left a nervous wreck by a Department of Employment investigation of her job delivering leaflets; and finally his male self-esteem is impugned when he ignores a robbery at the docks.

'Shop Thy Neighbour', the third story, has the strongest feminine statement in the series. Chrissie and his wife Angie argue endlessly because of the lack of money and food. As counterpoint to their life we are offered a comparison of the emotional and material existence of Miss Sutcliffe, head of the Department of Employment investigation squad. The story centres on the impairment of masculinity (both of Chrissie and the leather-jacketed investigator). Angie asks Chrissie, 'Why don't you stand up for yourself, fight back!' as the despair of unemployment and its impact on relationships and family are mapped out.

'Yosser's Story' opens with a surreal dream sequence. Yosser walks into a lake with his children, and sees his wife with her lover, Chrissie, Loggo and George float by in boats, before waking in a sweat. The story follows Yosser's loss of self-esteem and identity through a number of situations, before his children are finally taken into care. From 'I'm Yosser Hughes, they're my children, they're staying with me' to 'I'm wet' when asked who he is. His hapless struggle to provide for his children is overwhelmed by the failing support systems of the welfare state – his identity is battered, his dreams are shattered. After his children have been forcibly taken, he finally attempts suicide only to be rescued by two policemen. The despair of the narrative interspersed with black comic interludes (as he talks to the priest . . . 'I'm desperate, Dan') centres on impaired masculinity, overwhelmed by the state and his uncaring wife.

The final story, 'George's Last Ride', draws the threads of the previous stories together, and while showing the caring community in the decaying Liverpool landscape, indicates the inapplicability of old solutions in a situation of ever-increasing unemployment. George's death – the death of a caring socialist stalwart – evokes nostalgia for an earlier age and earlier struggles; but no new nostrums are offered as the mood of the story changes to madness in a pub taken over by the unemployed workers spending their redundancy money and ends with Chrissie and Loggo wondering 'What's gone wrong?' while retaining the ability to laugh ('Beam me up, Scottie').

Primarily the underlying discourse is concerned with the effect of unemployment on men and with the male role in the family. A secondary discourse is that of community breakdown – the new order is destroying community cohesion. The Liverpool landscape acts as a metaphor of decay, realized in the *mise-en-scène*. The old order and its rationale – care, community, socialism – are giving way to a new order of cynicism and madness (cf. Bleasdale[9]). The comments of several interviewees in the interviews conducted in Liverpool by John Archer for *Did You See . . . ?* focused on the political edge of the series (even though it was denied by Alan Bleasdale). John Nettleson, an unemployed worker:

> He's actually made a thing that's been a little taboo . . . . And he like took the lid off the box, and then he wants you to know what the bloody hell is going on in this town . . . . All the conditions are there, you know, and these people are characters that I know. I can relate to all of them.

The narrative throughout uses the characters in their domestic and working lives to play with themes of masculinity and what it means to be male. A major focus is the death of the ideals of the man as breadwinner and of the mores of community and socialism as sites of resistance. This is an implicit mode of castration with complex psychic underpinnings and consequences for both signification and identification. While the question 'Has this man a right to rule a family [like ours]?'[10] is played out textually, the loss inflicted by unemployment on men leads to the impossibility of any real sense of closure in the narrative. Progressive disillusionment is shown to lead to inner violence and the impotent gesture. Thomas Elsaesser has noted how 'melodrama . . . seems capable of reproducing more directly than other genres the patterns of domination and exploitation existing in a given society . . . by emphasizing so clearly an emotional dynamic whose social correlative is a network of external forces directed oppressingly inward'.[11]

The series supplied a framework, not provided elsewhere, to describe what is happening in people's lived experience, allowing personal expression and discussion of problems. Alan O'Toole, unemployed:

> Since the series has been on, people have been saying, yes, I've been at some time or another, as desperate as Yosser, or feeling stripped of dignity as Chrissie . . . he's given us words to communicate with each other about our own experiences.

Common-sense understandings contain some elements of good sense which can be drawn out if a framework is provided. The melodramatic representation of the plight of male characters in the community focused both a personal and a political sense of anger, previously unexpressed.

A local vicar, the Reverend Jim Garnet, thought that 'people can identify with that particular area in Yosser's life . . . a number of life stories here can correspond with that and the problems he faced' – the story provided a point of personal reference and at the same time an exploration of contemporary reality and a survey of the wider world.

The central theme of impaired masculinity also offered identification and emotional release. An unemployed worker: 'The suffering they have to go through, especially if they are married like.' John Nettleson: 'The anguish inside the family. I mean, that woman hiding behind the door terrified by a knock.' The Reverend Jim Garnet: 'I think Yosser was a man without a function and society in the past has put so much on a man's function and not a great deal on the fact that he's a human being and he's valued simply because of that.'

The excesses in the text through narrative and its realization are invariably deflected into jokes, music or action. There is no smoothing over of contradictions in an attempt to make the viewer feel whole. The text is agnostic (hence at one level its critical reputation) but strident too (hence its popularity with the Kop), and imitable (for example, the 'gest' of head-butting).

The comic interludes of the series are important in offering counterpoints to the overwhelming despair. Bleasdale himself considered that 'there *are* funny moments in all the episodes, but the basic tone *is* depressing . . . . We're talking about people's *pride* and position, and when they've got no position their pride comes into question. And you can't do that like *Carry on Dole*.'[12] The black comedy is based on the long tradition of Liverpool humour – it offers a catharsis at key points in the narrative (and for a Liverpool audience, in particular, underpins the narrative's coherence). It is present even in the opening wry exchanges in the first story (Loggo in the Department of Employment: 'You've already made me miss me golf lessons'). In the scene in the confessional in 'Yosser's Story' the priest and Yosser talk:

YOSSER: I'm desperate, Father.
PRIEST: Call me Dan.
YOSSER: I'm desperate, Dan.

The comic interjection relieves the ever increasing tension of the story – the 'told' of the joke and its telling disarms, before the tension is again raised when Yosser head-butts the partition in total desperation. The joke-thoughts act as a means of siphoning off the excess. The comedy disrupts the social discourse in play.[13]

As Adrian Henri commented:

> I think that is, particularly, a Liverpool tradition, which the poets at least have as well, where you can say something and you make people laugh but you can make people cry and you can make people think at the same time. And I think that's part of the local sense of humour and a local way of talking.

But negatively the joke-thought (the comic) can be seen to neuter anything.

Discourses of masculinity, within the domain and ideological problematics of family life, are evidently an important factor for viewers. Traditionally man is understood as the provider in a marriage; representations of the castrating effect of the mental stress of unemployment create particular identifications and an emotional release for male viewers. Reaction to the series varied according to region and experience (particularly of unemployment), by class, race and sex. Identifying with the characters implies a positive feeling. The *Blackstuff* appears to have provided characters as 'social figures' and enabled critical engagement and identification although the privacy of television watching (or at least its domesticity) clearly undermines easy political engagement. However the social negotiation of meaning through mutual aid in decoding must contribute to a sharing of meaning, and significantly for the argument of this chapter, to the propagation and spreading of the symbols, slogans, themes which it bears.[14]

Another effect of the series was to generate among some activists a renewed assertiveness and a belief in the importance of fighting unemployment. John Nettleson: 'What this series has done for me, it's made me more resolved to say, get off the floor and fight back.' Alan O'Toole: 'On the whole, the series left me with . . . more determination to change things. I don't know how it affected employed workers . . . maybe it gave them more sympathy for the unemployed and more determination to fight for the right to work.'

Certainly the public re-expression of motifs from the series was rapid. Billy Butler, disc jockey on Radio City: 'Yosser Hughes only existed for six weeks and is now part of Liverpool folklore. I mean, to be part of Liverpool folklore, you exist at football matches . . . and within two weeks of that series being on, Yosser Hughes was a Kop character.' A different exploitation was attempted by a pop group, the 3-Ds: 'Everybody was sort of saying giz a job, you know . . . and it was a little catchphrase . . . it needs to be in a sound, because you can't just walk around saying giz a job.' And of course there were imitations of Yosser's head-butting, the proliferation of Yosser jackets, and the establishment of a new mythology of being male in Liverpool in the 1980s.[15] These representations and their take-up should not be seen in isolation from other aspects of the artifice of the series. The distinctive music of the melodrama (saxophone, clarinet, piano, drums) is used either to siphon off excess tension or to heighten pathos and tension, particularly in 'George's Last Ride'. The setting of events in Liverpool, its decaying streets and homes, its deserted docks, evokes as do George's memories nostalgia and a sense of loss of tradition. Liverpool is used both as backdrop and actor. The connotations of a community under stress are significantly emphasized by a documentary look aided by the use of video. The fetish objects which exist in the 'real world' which have subsequently taken on aspects of the series (Yosser jackets, slogans, etc.) both acknowledge the lost objects (the masculinity associated with employment, thriving community, etc.) and assert their presence and continuation in the existence of the object.[16] In any reading which touches political and cultural nerve ends there is a complex negotiation between dominant memory as reworked in the representation and the private memories brought to bear which determines different versions of history.[17] Language and social interactions informed by common experience are restyled by contact with the series' rewriting of accepted discourses.

*

Boys from the Blackstuff is a polysemic text; meanings are offered in different ways both within the text and to be read in the text because of the relationship of the viewer to his/her social world and his/her competence in manipulating the various discourses at play.[18]

Scheduling has an effect on the take up of any television programme, both in terms of the audience made available and the expectations associated with different slots and channels. The series was first transmitted on BBC-2 at about 10.00 pm on Sundays against a new series of *Omnibus* on BBC-1 and, but for the first week, ITV's arts programme *The South Bank Show*. Thus although late-night Sunday might be considered an inauspicious time to transmit, the highbrow arts programming on the other two channels would only be certain of a relatively small national audience. Against such competition a melodrama clearly has considerable advantages. The original single play had received little critical attention (it was first transmitted in January 1980, and repeated in July 1981) and so the memory of it could not be relied upon. In the week of the transmission of the first episode, *Radio Times* carried an article, 'Spreading success', about Alan Bleasdale written by Benedict Nightingale,[19] and positive previews of the series were carried in the press. Over the next weeks the initial audience of 3.1 million quickly grew to about 4.5 million, with a drop in the last week (due probably to the starting up of Channel 4). There was a marked difference in regional uptake, with the northern regions providing a much larger share of the audience. On retransmission in early 1983 on BBC-1 on Tuesdays at 9.25 pm the audience ranged between 3.2 million and 7.9 million. The series was, then, never a ratings blockbuster, but still achieved influence and popularity.

The plays could be taken as entertainment, serious art television or family drama articulating a number of contemporary concerns. A variety of readings of the text was possible. It is interesting to compare the findings of Katz and Liebes, whose research into the understandings of *Dallas* held by Jews of different ethnic background, shows various interpretations.[20] Obviously it is highly likely that any programme will be differentially appropriated according to class, age, sex and region. The evidence available points to viewers identifying with different elements in the series, a significant factor in its widespread influence and effect at a cultural and political level. There is a differential interpellation of the subject in the narrative and within the aesthetic modes in use. Also there is a differential take-up or comprehension according to pre-existing understandings of the social, political and cultural discourses in play. The publicly visible effects of the series depended in part on the level of identification with the characters in the text – but it gave rise also to debates in other social spaces which can be seen as emanating from the series discourse, and to the widespread use of series symbols and motifs.

All individual understandings are constructed within publicly defined discourses. Discourses are constantly renovated and can pose political alternatives where none previously existed. It is important to remember the timing of the appearance of the *Blackstuff* in gauging and understanding the public response. Drama previously had been singularly unsuccessful in reviewing unemployment or registering the threats to accepted notions of masculinity (one exception was the sitcom *Shelley*).

The dynamics of the evolving representation of unemployment (particularly on television) and of the emotions and feelings associated with it have to be explained through an understanding of audience 'gratifications' at the social and cultural level as well as that of the individual. The individual works with the material he/she has within his/her repertoire of understanding, and what is on offer is read through that competence. The materiality of practice offers the possible use and reuse of statements in many domains or fields of understanding; and connections can be engendered on many levels.

The power of conversation to continue to transmit the generically ordered discourses of the *Blackstuff* seems to have had an effect. The cultural resonances in many distinctly class-specific areas of the national culture were more than a television-effect, and were crucially amplified by conversation.

As a series of plays *Boys from the Blackstuff* interweaves and reworks a set of discourses around the relationship between the personal and the political. As Bleasdale said,[21] the stories do not 'know all the answers'. What was invoked was a set of common-sense understandings of British labourism and a memory of its struggles and achievements, set within the tensions created by family life and the problematics of masculinity and femininity, all worked out through the narrative conventions of melodrama. The multilayered focus of the texts led to a variability of audience response; and despite the invariable male point of view, this could be inhabited in different ways and provided a narrative space which either sex could occupy.

At the level of individual responses there were a number of different uses and ways of identifying with the series. The uses and gratifications approach exemplified by the work of Denis McQuail and colleagues delimited media/person interactions under three headings: diversion, gratification and personal reference.[22] Criticisms of this approach, particularly its individualistic, empiricist and static-abstraction conceptualization, with mass communication treated in isolation from any other social process, must be borne in mind when examining individual responses among the audience members.[23] But these individual responses are indicators of wider social responses, and the pressures and contexts within which they occur – furthermore it is not gratification so much as use which is of particular interest in this case, most specifically the social reuse of imagery and motif initially expressed in the mode of melodrama. The social meaning of this genre is understood by an audience, so that escape into a fantasy world, although an individual response, becomes unlikely. The forgetting of worries or emotional release through identification ('diversion' in McQuail's schema) become available positions. More interesting are the variable uses to which the programme was put in mutual aid, both in watching in the domestic situation, and in the reuse of TV images for new political ends or for psychological support through public display.

Current research has no understanding of how individual and social responses work through the textual inscriptions of the subject, or of the complex psychic modes operative in any identification – these areas can only be briefly referred to here. A subject's own identity (and viewing experience) is achieved by the process of differentiation 'marking out separations between itself and its own surroundings in order that it may find itself a place in the signifying chains'.[24] What that place is depends on the individual's formation in language (and the further problem of an ever-evolving linguistic order informed by competing discourses), and on the way the text works both to bring together discourses within a problematic and to interpellate the subject. Crucially in the *Blackstuff* the terms of inscription are 'masculine' and the questioning of masculinity as heretofore understood.[25] With the *Blackstuff* there was a breach in representations of masculinity that struck a local and a national chord.

The greatest significance of this series was its transcendence of simple media/person interaction and the domestic viewing situation, to become a symbolic phenomenon in a national and political way. Television is traditionally grist for gossip – but when that gossip becomes politicized and leads to actions beyond the bar and the bus conversation, the individualist explanation must be supplanted by a social one. Conversation is 'gratification' for McQuail, as is the establishment of a vicarious relationship with characters, but though this was one aspect of viewer response it provides an insufficient account of the Blackstuff phenomenon. The initial 'family viewing' pre-existed the public events; the public discussion created secondary meanings which reverberated in the everyday. The series had a public and private existence – the dilemmas of the undermined group of men became 'exposed' publicly. Styles of masculinity became a shared public question and led to public expression in slogans and clothing – a social echo of television, amplified in the political conjuncture.

To summarize the argument: the working out of discourses within the narrative and the social subjectivity of viewers leads to a variety of effects in the private domain, ranging from self-assessment, to voyeuristic survey of contemporary problems, to display in public.

The public after-life of the series (in newspaper reviews, articles, education, etc.) has drawn out its concerns with the personal problems posed to male workers and their families by growing unemployment, both in media and in political discourse. Television has thus acted out an intervention role in the national culture – showing the plight of Liverpool's unemployed – and has carried out its public service role in allowing the expression of an author's point of view.

Criss-crossing the text itself and the mind of the viewer simultaneously are a number of important issues and debates in contemporary British society. The public reception of the series reflected on a number of these; the private (and in some ways potentially oppositional) implications of the series vary from its function as a marker of despair, as an evocation of lost times and lost causes (a nostalgia), as a manifesto of desired change in the economic situation, as a barometer of male style.

The series effected a change in the 'dominant memory' (and popular memory) of being unemployed in Britain in the 1980s. The questioning of the dominant political understandings challenges prevailing notions of social justice, while the effects of unemployment on men and women, as represented in the series, alter the understood notions of masculinity and femininity. Following feminism's concerns in the 1970s with representation of women engaged with gender representation came now representations of undermined men – masculinity denied by unemployment – to strike a chord in 1980s Britain. What have been taken up differentially across a variegated public are these very problematic elements of 'masculinity'. The take-up of macho elements (head-butting, Yosser jackets) is indicative of a released repression. So is the series' critical acclaim and its new concern with the way men are represented. Media event, political event, personal viewing – there have been an array of influences on the national culture caused by the transmission of *Boys from the Blackstuff*, but the key one at all levels has been the new focus on masculinity.

Notes

1 'A loss of nerve' by Jonathan Powell (28 July 1983); 'The con of social realism' by Roger Gregory (4 August 1983); 'Relevance is relative' by John Arden (18 August 1983); 'Where are the new voices?' by Michelene Wandor (25 August 1983).

2 The favourable reviews ranged across the 'quality' and 'popular' press, e.g. Herbert Kretzmer (*Daily Mail*, 9 November 1982), 'it has been . . . a lovingly observed drama of people for whom the work ethic is still paramount and who feel themselves degraded by enforced idleness'; Chris Dunkley (*Financial Times*, 17

November 1982), 'there is compassion there and even love, but it is the almost cruel ability to keep them at arm's length which makes him [Bleasdale] such a valuable and different writer'; Sean Day-Lewis (*Daily Telegraph*, 2 November 1982), 'it made the unimaginable horribly real'.

3 Cf. John Caughie, 'Rhetoric, pleasure and "art television"', *Screen*, 22, 4 (1981), 9–31.

4 All comments are taken from the transcript of interviews conducted by John Archer in Liverpool for *Did You See . . . ?* Selections are reprinted in R. Paterson (ed.), *Boys from the Blackstuff*, BFI Dossier 20, London, British Film Institute, 1984, pp. 48–58.

5 See Bob Millington, 'Making *Boys from the Blackstuff*: a production perspective', in Paterson (ed.), op. cit., pp. 4–24.

6 Dave Kehr, 'The new male melodrama', *American Film*, 8, 6 (1983), p. 44.

7 Pam Cook, 'Melodrama and the women's picture', in Sue Aspinall and Robert Murphy (eds), *Gainsborough Melodrama*, BFI Dossier 18, London, British Film Institute, 1983, p. 22.

8 The term masculinity is understood as neither a static nor a unified system of interlocking representations and discourses about men. The different meanings which are constructed and recognizable vary according to the historical and class context of use. (See Jeffrey Weeks, *Sex, Politics and Society*, London, Longman, 1981, p. 41 and Michele Barrett, *Women's Oppression Today*, London, Verso, 1980, p. 252.) The commonly accepted notion of masculinity to date has tended to emphasize male 'power', while 'manhood' has been synonymous with the ability to maintain one's family.

9 See Paul du Noyer, 'England today – uglier by far', *New Musical Express*, 13 November 1982, p. 17.

10 See Geoffrey Nowell-Smith, 'Minelli and melodrama', *Screen*, 18, 2 (1977), p. 115.

11 Thomas Elsaesser, 'Tales of sound and fury', *Monogram*, no. 4 (1972), p. 14.

12 du Noyer, op. cit.

13 Cf. Terry Lovell, 'A genre of social disruption', in Jim Cook (ed.), *Television Sitcom*, BFI Dossier 17, London, British Film Institute, 1982, pp. 19–31.

14 Cf. Elihu Katz and Tamar Liebes, 'Mutual aid in the decoding of *Dallas*: preliminary notes from a cross-cultural study', in P. Drummond and R. Paterson (eds), *Television in Transition*, London, British Film Institute, 1986.

15 Roland Barthes, *Mythologies*, London, Paladin, 1973 (first published: Paris, Editions de Seuil, 1957).

16 Juliet Mitchell, *Psychoanalysis and Feminism*, Harmondsworth, Penguin, 1975, p. 84.

17 Popular Memory Group, 'Popular memory: theory, politics, method', in Richard Johnson *et al.* (eds), *Making Histories*, London, Hutchinson, 1982.

18 Cf. David Morley, 'Texts, readers, subjects', in Stuart Hall *et al.* (eds), *Culture, Media and Language*, London, Hutchinson, 1980, p. 167.

19 *Radio Times*, 237, 3074, 9–15 October 1982, p. 19.

20 Katz and Liebes, op. cit.

21 du Noyer, op. cit.

22 Denis McQuail, Jay G. Blumler and J. R. Brown, 'The television audience: a revised perspective', in Denis McQuail (ed.), *Sociology of Mass Communication*, Harmondsworth, Penguin, 1972.

23 Philip Elliott, 'Uses and gratifications research: a critique and a sociological

alternative', in Jay G. Blumler and Elihu Katz (eds), *The Uses of Mass Communications: Current Perspectives in Gratifications Research*, Beverly Hills, Sage, 1974.

24 Ros Coward and John Ellis, *Language and Materialism*, London, Routledge & Kegan Paul, 1977, p. 98.

25 J. Laplanche and J. B. Pontalis, *The Language of Psychoanalysis*, London, Hogarth Press, 1980: 'a subject's identification viewed as a whole are in no way a coherent relational system. Demands co-exist within an agency like the super-ego, for instance, which are diverse, conflicting and disorderly. Similarly, the ego-ideal is composed of identifications that are not necessarily harmonious', p. 208.

Part 4

Media and culture

Introduction

This section consists of exploratory essays examining another aspect of the media – its role as a cultural agency – that has been neglected in mass communications research. Taken together, they shed light on the relations between the media and cultural élites, the attempts of media institutions to manage, measure or predict popular taste, the social and economic relations influencing cultural trends, and the ways in which media absorb elements of popular culture and thereby shape the cultural consumption of the British public.

Philip Elliott and Geoff Matthews have taken the important theme of the early BBC's relationship with the music industry and examine the processes of interaction between technical innovation and the creation of institutional machinery for handling musicians. The BBC entered a minefield of corporate relationships with great care and tact, first permitting the world of music to dictate technical standards, then, as the professionalism of broadcasting production and the improvement of technology caused the weight of relevant expertise to swing from the extra-institutional to the intra-institutional, modifying its relationship to the music industry. An accommodation thus came to be effected in which musicians accepted the BBC's role as principal patron of the world of music.

David Chaney examines another key aspect of the cultural development of the BBC – its reorientation towards the general public. He shows how a patrician style of Reithian management (graphically illustrated by the decision to deny R. S. Lambert, the editor of the *Listener*, the circulation figures of his magazine in the first five years of his editorship) was modified by creative attempts on the part of some members of the BBC in the 1930s to involve listeners in programme production. This gave way, in turn, to a new orientation to audiences as an aggregation of consumers and the forging of a new relationship based on the measurement of consumer choice through the development of market research. In this way, Chaney argues, the BBC moved away from participant democracy towards 'market democracy', from pioneer attempts to enlist audiences as colleagues to serving them as consumers in the style of the commercial cinema and the press.

The way in which 'market democracy' evolved in the record industry is examined by Simon Frith in his chapter on its corporate development between the 1920s and 1960s. Gradually, in a welter of company take-overs and industrial 'shakedowns', control over the selection of music for recording became distanced from the sources of music: publishers and promoters gave way to corporate management. Decisions on 'popularity' began to revolve around 'statistics, inoffensiveness, professionalism, efficiency'. Thus popular music was transmuted by stages into the organizational structure of a commercial mass medium.

People's knowledge of scientific culture is largely derived from the media. In the concluding chapter in this section, Roger Silverstone takes a single science programme, *The Death of the Dinosaurs*, and examines in detail how methods of production, professional instincts, and the conventions of documentary narrative structure popular scientific knowledge. He shows how TV documentary not only selects from and organizes complex areas of debate but, in the process, structures scientific discourse.

11

Broadcasting culture: innovation, accommodation and routinization in the early BBC

Philip Elliott and Geoff Matthews

Because media research has developed in the age of television, relatively little attention has been paid to questions about the impact of a new medium on the culture.[1] Television was a striking innovation but in cultural terms its introduction was less revolutionary than that of the two media which preceded it, film and radio. The organizational framework for television was already set by the experience of operating sound broadcasting. Notoriously, the television pioneers in Britain were regarded as mavericks by their colleagues in the radio establishment. Only thirty years before, however, the radio pioneers had been working entirely in the unknown without any established colleagues to guide or direct them. Similarly, television content was able to incorporate forms developed by other media. Radio broadcasting was already providing a variegated service in the home. The cinema had developed narrative conventions within an audio-visual medium. It was through these two earlier media that the concept of such a service and the scope of such conventions were defined.

The obverse of this argument, that television was culturally derivative, is that the media to study for cultural innovation are the cinema and radio. The two early industries differed in the scope they allowed for creative innovation. Early film-makers were largely dependent on marketing their product. Film developed out of the existing entertainments of vaudeville and the fairground where an audience was available for a technological novelty. The development of the cinema was a relatively slow process of film-makers discovering what forms and content would provide them with a separate audience of film-goers. Radio developed the other way round with the manufacturers of the distributive technology, radio sets, looking for content with which to fill it, broadcasting. Broadcasters were thus to some extent insulated from the immediate problem of finding an audience for their particular production. In other words the early broadcasters enjoyed relatively more creative autonomy. This is not to deny the innovative achievements of many early film-makers but to point out they were achieved against the odds. Film lacked the hothouse of a single organization which not only forces the pace of development but allows the process to be clearly observed.

The broadcasters were also much closer to the cultural élites of the time.

Such ties can be seen in the middle-class professional and managerial origins of the early broadcasters, in their use of material from the established arts and in the interest which the existing élites in these areas took in the way their arts were reproduced over the radio. The radio pioneers had thus more reason to be self-conscious about their cultural and social role than the pioneers of the film. They are the subject of this chapter, which seeks to examine the process of cultural innovation in one field within radio broadcasting, music. This innovation happened in relationship to contemporary developments in the cultural field itself so that broadcasting had a selective impact on the field as a whole.

As broadcasting itself became established, so it developed its own mode of organization, technical resources, occupational categories and cultural forms. In a surprisingly short space of time both the output and the production processes became more routinized. Only five years elapsed between the foundation of the British Broadcasting Company and the resignation of the first cadre of broadcasting executives. By that time 'broadcasting' was established both as a technology and as a cultural form. The priorities of the broadcasting leadership changed from the promotion of broadcasting as a social function to efficient administration. This had inevitable consequences for cultural innovation. Occupational categories and responsibilities became more precisely defined. Cultural forms became more predictable. The technology became better understood and it was more closely attuned to programme production. Though much has happened since, this early period offers a unique opportunity to study the interactive processes of organizational and technical development, their relationship to existing cultural practice and the ways in which new forms of such practice developed.

The 'idea of broadcasting'

Eric Barnouw has vividly recreated the pre-war years of continuous wave communication in the USA when the occasion of picking up a Fessenden music and voice test was 'a miracle never to be explained'.[2] That sense of the miraculous and unprecedented long persisted and is an important element in the initial development of a broadcasting praxis. In Britain the vision of the first group of executives in the broadcasting company and the part they played in developing the 'idea of broadcasting' has to some extent been overshadowed by the commanding figure of Reith as he played the role of publicist for himself, the company and, later, the corporation. Nevertheless, the others (Eckersley, Arthur Burrows and C. A. Lewis) all had important and different contributions to make to the concept of 'broadcasting'.

They shared the same awe of the incredible. In his account of his years in radio, starting with adolescent imitations of Marconi's experiments in electric wave communication, Eckersley recalled how, as late as 1923, he could still be possessed by a powerful sense of the miraculous. He described how 'when I first heard . . . the BBC transmit an opera, Humperdinck's *Hansel and Gretel* . . . I sat for three hours . . . rigidly clamped by head telephones, completely absorbed, oblivious of discomfort . . . . I had been to the opera without going to the opera. Broadcasting, I realised, would let me join in events without my having to drag my body all over the place.'[3] Cecil Lewis wrote in the following year: 'It never ceases to be a marvel to me how the great symphony concerts go along the roadsides, all over the hills, through the towns, brushed by trees, soaked by rain, swayed by gales . . . and are suddenly loosed out like a gushing fountain into the homes of millions of people.'[4] The illustration Burrows chose was 'the nightingale projected across starry skies and windswept mountains to a Swedish home, as well as to thousands of houses in the crowded cities of this country'.[5] Lewis explicitly pointed to the lesson for broadcasting of his illustration, the symphony orchestra, when he wrote:

> The sound of the great orchestra contrasted so forcibly with our little band of seven in the studio, that it came as a revelation of what the future of broadcasting might be. It made us more confident of success and carried us forward to those days when we should have great conductors and orchestras in our own studios.

Before 1922, Eckersley, Burrows and Lewis had all come to a view of the future of wireless in broadcasting, an idea which put them ahead of their times. Eckersley, from the vantage point of the Writtle Station, which began transmitting in March 1921, broke free from the narrow horizons which wireless in the hands of the scientists imposed. He was transformed from a scientist who saw the public utility value of electric wave transmission into one who saw the possibility of incorporating electric wave transmission into everyday life. Arthur Burrows's approach was defined by his position as a public relations counsel of the 'new' Marconi firm. He was attracted at first by the publicity value of telephony and then by the suspicion that there might be a market for wireless receivers in the UK. In accordance with his training as a public relations official, Burrows saw his task as fashioning an organization that would provide the service that a varied range of many publics would require. As early as 1918 he clearly foresaw a *broadcasting* future.

The contribution made by Lewis stemmed from an avant-garde conviction that from new technology would emerge new modes of expression. He brought to the company a constructive artistic tradition that valued the 'new' as the material of artistic experimentation. Lewis's interest was in 'the art of the microphone', his faith that artistic creation would flourish in those milieux that were peculiarly products of their own times.

The first eighteen months of the company was a period in which the idea of electrical wave communication which would play a limited role in society was set aside in favour of the idea and reality of 'broadcasting'. The British Broadcasting Company was registered in December 1922 and received its PO licence in January 1923. London 2LO Station broadcast its first programme in May 1922. There was a transitional period of several months, until the company opened the Savoy Hill Studio, in which the company broadcast from the old 2LO Studio in the cinema of Marconi House. By the end of 1923, the company was putting out five and a half hours of programmes daily. From the autumn of that year and throughout the following year, the company opened a series of low-powered 'relay' stations. In May 1923 it began experiments in distributing programmes, originating in London, to these low-powered stations via telephone. In the course of 1924 the creation of a network of relay stations made it possible for between 60 per cent and 70 per cent of the population to receive a programme. The aim of making a broadcast programme available to a truly national audience was brought a step nearer when planning commenced in December for a high-powered transmitter station. In the summer of that second year, the decision was also made to broaden the scope of broadcasting. The company established first a drama department and then in August an education department.

The decision in 1923 for comprehensive broadcasting, one which enmeshed the full range of existing cultural interests – variety, drama, politics, public information, sport, education and religion as well as music – was not one taken on the spur of the moment. It was a decision shaped by the experiences and the reflections of three of the original broadcasting company executives in the two years before 1922. The two years were marked by the opening of the Western Electric Pittsburg Station in November 1920 and the boom in broadcasting in the USA which followed. In Britain there was a new phase of growth in 'amateur' telephony. The interest shown by the press encouraged those who suspected that there was a market for receivers in this country to test the interest of the public in broadcasting. It was this period which saw the emergence of 'the idea of broadcasting' from its telephony integument.

During the course of 1924, the second year of broadcasting, Burrows, Lewis and Reith published their syntheses of eighteen months' experience in an attempt to impress the public with their vision of what had been done and of the way ahead.

Their writings conveyed their shared sense of having initiated as much in the realm of ideas as in the realm of practice. The task of creating broadcasting was indivisibly theoretical and practical. Reith expressed this dual demand, at once to theorize and act, when he wrote: 'We were overwhelmed by the needs of the moment, but at the same time plans had to be formulated, not for the present but for the future; it had to be determined if possible where this service was to lead, how best it might be developed.' In a chapter headed 'Uncharted seas', he wrote of the sparseness of the original terms of reference and of the irrelevance of all previous experience. 'There were no sealed orders to open. The commission was of the scantiest nature . . . . A broadcasting service was expected and had to be initiated and developed . . . . There was no precedent, no store of experience to be tapped, no staff ready to hand with mettle proved in a similar field.'[6]

As Reith saw it, the first staff defined as well as executed their task. Reith wrote: 'Almost everything depended on the personality of those to whom, almost by chance, the service had been committed.'[7]

Lewis found different words to express the same view of the company's origins. He remembered the task of founding broadcasting as peculiarly without points of reference from any task previously undertaken in society. Lewis wrote: 'We had to deal with an entirely new set of circumstances of unparalleled difficulty.'[8] 'There we were, a round half-dozen people, with the whole company's organisation to set in motion, confronted with new and difficult problems on every side, with no precedents of past experience to go upon.'[9]

Burrows, likewise, saw the original staff as peculiarly 'without precedent to work upon'. As a Marconi public relations counsel, he was well placed to foresee the 'broadcasting' possibilities of electric wave communication. In his writing he remembered the gaps which separated the public from those who through long association with the wireless field had guessed at its broadcasting future. The few, said Burrows, had 'a desire to demonstrate to the public the extraordinary, but in the majority of instances the unsuspected, possibilities of broadcasting'.[10]

In 1924, Reith wrote of the first eighteen months:

> We had no precedent . . . . Rightly or wrongly we took a comprehensive view of the possibilities of broadcasting . . . . Had we then been officially informed . . . that we were to confine ourselves to the transmission of concerts, then the service would . . . have been limited to that . . . . No such intimation, however, was received . . . . In setting aside the limited conception, one contracts for an indefinite and continuously growing influence. The service would either be conducted within clearly defined and narrow limits, or else there would be no limits at all . . . . Assuming that the service is still to extend in many directions and that a wider range of subjects is to come within its scope . . . and that millions of people are listening, the influence is obvious . . . . It is not musical taste only which is likely to be affected.[11]

Thus the original cadre of broadcasting executives collectively held the view that theirs was a field ahead of its time. Each of them was persuaded of the need to develop a practice unparalleled in previous experience. Eckersley became the engineer bent on spreading the service to the whole nation. Burrows became the programme organizer who saw broadcasting in terms of the quality and range of programmes that would sell sets to a variety of publics or audiences. From Lewis came the inspiration that the unfamiliar resources of the microphone, the studio, the echo chamber, the possibility of appeal to one sense only, were not constraints but the sources of a new art. Their practice was guided by bold projections of the type of organization that national coverage, increasing hours of regular broadcasting and an increasing audience with developing tastes would require. It led to the development of new functions and the employment of new categories of personnel. The modernist tradition that a new medium of communication would generate a new art and a new public contributed to the foundation and development of 'Sound Effects' in 1924. The formation of 'Balance and Control' in 1926 was a product of the belief that the studio, the microphone and the broadcasting chain required an unprecedented mode of organization, coupled with an act of obeisance to the musical establishment and to traditional concert-going audiences, to win them over to broadcast listening.

In finding out what broadcasting required, the founders had only their own understanding of their everyday work experience to guide them. Though they did not use the term, they were undertaking the invention of a communications praxis. Each of the major groups, schedule-builders, engineers and producers, were constantly involved in the early 1920s in major revisions or re-understandings of their tasks. The programme organizers came to understand that broadcasting was a new communications environment with implications for all communications interests. The three books published towards the end of the first eighteen months of the company's life, intent on characterizing broadcasting, are powerfully informed with that understanding.[12] Likewise, the engineers, who grappled with the problems of reproducing music and dramatic sound, came round to the view that the studio must be treated as part of an artificial sound reproducing system. Sound produced in the studio was conditioned by the acoustic of the studio and mediated through microphones of variable characteristics. Only at the end of a broadcasting chain was it received through the two ears of the listener.[13] The complex variables that affected the performance *as heard by* the listener was also a field beyond the competence of artists. From that understanding emerged the argument that as well as the new functions of programme-building, and microphone and studio engineering, there was the function of managing or 'faking'[14] programme-specific sound whether that sound was musical, dramatic or variety. Thus the two specialized studio staffs were as necessary to the founding of 'broadcasting' as such other articles of faith as the schedulers' programme building, the producers' concepts of 'pure radio' and 'the art of the microphone', and the engineers' devotion to the echo chamber and ideas like variable 'artificial echo'.

After 1927 the self-conscious originating role of the first executives became relatively less important. The period in which the first corps of executives attached priority to defining the fields of programme-building, of studio and microphone engineering and of the management of programme-specific sound, ended with the resignations of Burrows, Lewis, A. G. D. West and Eckersley. That sense of the new-fangledness of everything done in broadcasting and with it the need to build a new organization in novel conditions came to an end as electrical communication became normalized in the world of the first national electricity grid (1927–33), of electric gramophone records (from 1925) and of sound-on-film movies (1927–9). Broadcasting became less unique and the vision of broadcasting as an enterprise of undreamed-of possibilities became less convincing. In the late 1920s the accent was less on pioneering, leadership and origination, and more on the administrative task of making efficient use of the resources of a large organization. The departure of Burrows, Lewis, West and Eckersley, the winding up of the Production Research Section and the fall into relative disfavour of Lance Sieveking, the experimental drama producer in the late 1920s and early 1930s, marked the end of one era and the opening of a new one. But by the time this change from innovation to consolidation took place, broadcasting was established as a cultural form.

Musicians and broadcasting

Broadcasting originated and developed in an environment of specialized cultural élites. The world of classical music was initially the most important in defining and realizing the possibilities of the broadcasting medium. Subsequently, other specialisms such as religion, education, variety, sport and finally news and current affairs were incorporated. An influential minority among the musical entrepreneurs, critics and leaders of corporate music bodies in Britain showed interest in the technical facility of broadcasting. This was as much a result of changes in the world of music as it was of the intrinsic capability of the new technical facility but the coincidence of the two was extremely influential for the development of broadcast music.

We have chosen to look very broadly at the currents of change and ideas affecting the world of classical music in the post-war years in order to assess the reasons the various music interests had to exploit the possibilities of the new medium. The interest the individual cultural specialisms had in integration with broadcasting varied according to the complex of circumstances in which they found themselves. In an age of growth and development in the press, the political establishment of this period had in the daily newspapers a relatively adequate means of reaching their constituencies. In contrast, musicians, for reasons set out below, found the concert hall a failing means of reaching a national audience. The progressive tradition of popularizing 'good' music and the post-war circumstances in the concert halls combined to push musicians towards a full and rounded accommodation with the broadcasting organization. This relationship was not achieved without some friction on both sides. One consequence was the development of a new occupation specific to broadcasting to be responsible for the output not simply in engineering terms but in terms of its quality. Thus the Balance and Control Section within production was important as a strategic device. It eased the accommodation between the organization of electrical engineers and a cultural group which had misgivings about the effects of mechanization on its art.

The company became known in its first five years because of the thrust supplied by music interests who quickly saw in the infancy of broadcasting an opportunity to extend their audiences. The broadcasting company was the beneficiary of a movement in classical music which began before broadcasting commenced. It was the collective ambition of a number of musical entrepreneurs to establish a musical culture in Britain. The foundation of the Promenade Concerts in 1895 marked the origins of a movement to popularize 'good' music and raise the standard of orchestral performance.[15] The movement introduced the 'sandwiching' of new works by English and foreign composers among more familiar works and the effort to replace the deputizing system by permanent all-the-year orchestras. It anticipated the classical music programme-building policy of the company and its decision, from the inauguration of the Music Department, not to allow deputizing but to contract orchestral players only on a part- or full-time basis.

The links between the movement to popularize classical music through low-price concerts and annotated programmes and the broadcasting of 'good' music were both institutional and personal. What Robert Newman and Henry Wood did to establish new audiences for orchestral music, Percy Pitt, in alliance first with Hans Richter and later with Thomas Beecham, did for opera. They and their successors became involved in music broadcasting. Pitt became musical director at Covent Garden in 1907. In association with Richter, he was responsible for the first production of *The Ring*. He served in the same capacity for Beecham's Opera Company in 1915–16 and for its successor, the British National Opera Company (BNOC). With Beecham's orchestra he was involved through the war years in 'almost non-stop opera seasons', mainly in West End theatres to audiences of soldiers on leave, and girl clerks from government offices. Opera reopened after the war to a public newly educated to opera.[16] The BNOC, directed by Pitt, was the only entirely new opera initiative between the liquidation of the Beecham Company in September 1920 and the first opera broadcast in January 1923. Pitt's company opened in February 1922 at Bradford and went on to further seasons in Edinburgh and Liverpool. But attendances did not rise for BNOC performances at Covent Garden. Pitt and his orchestra, with the memory of the boom opera years of the war still fresh and their recent experience of opera publics in provincial cities still vivid, were confident of the existence of a national audience for opera. They were looking for the right means to reach it.

Developments in the gramophone field had already indicated that here was a new supplementary if not direct channel of musical communication. Percy Scholes, as the editor of *Musical Times*, quickly recognized that the British Broadcasting Company was the Gramophone Company's opportunity writ large. The editor and critics of the *Musical Times* were well placed throughout this period to take a broad view of the movement to popularize 'good' music and to see early the opportunities of the 'new musical media', as Scholes termed gramophone, cinema and broadcasting.[17] It is significant that when the Gramophone Company (later His Master's Voice) in the wake of the wartime boom in gramophone records, opened its education department in 1919 to promote the acceptance of the gramophone as a means of musical education, the company commissioned Percy Scholes to write a propagandist handbook.[18] Scholes, it seems, was peculiarly sensitive to the place of new media in the task of widening the audience for music. He recognized the propagandist role of annotated programmes and instructional handbooks and the part 'missionary societies for music' might play in any movement that sought to enlarge and improve audiences for music.[19] He was already convinced of the importance of the gramophone as a new musical medium, so it is not surprising that he became the first music critic of the British Broadcasting Company on 16 June 1923. Two years later he followed up his handbook *Listening to Music* via the gramophone with *Everybody's Guide to Broadcast Music*.[20] With so early an involvement in the organized 'propaganda' for 'good' music,[21] it is not surprising that he saw the inauguration of the *Radio Times* as the birth of 'a weekly journal that *the* most ardent and sanguine worker for music of the beginning of the century never expected to live to see'.[22]

Not that everyone was so enthusiastic about the new medium and its publicity organs. Institutional opposition to broadcasting music came not from artists or orchestra members but from musical agents and concert hall owners such as Chappell & Co., and Powell & Holt Ltd. Chappell were the iessees of the Queen's Hall, and Powell & Holt the agents of the London Symphony Orchestra (LSO). William Boosey of Chappell & Co., managing director of the Queen's Hall, refused to allow artists under his control to accept broadcasting engagements.[23] Harold Holt advised and represented Melba in her refusal to let her performance of June 1923 be broadcast.[24] Powell suggested to the directorate of the LSO that the engagement of conductors who also broadcast would lower receipts from the orchestra's concerts. The directors replied that 'the public would always prefer the atmosphere and the live element of the concert room and that in their opinion broadcasts would create a keener desire on the part of the public to hear the music at first hand'. In the context of these pressures, the LSO took its first steps along the new path of broadcasting and recording. The post-war period gave the orchestra a formative experience of the new music market-place. By the beginning of the autumn/winter season 1920/21, the orchestra was losing money heavily. In September, the orchestra concluded its first three-year contract with Columbia. In the summer of 1922, United Artists hired Covent Garden as a first-release movie house and the orchestra members became pit-players for screenings of Douglas Fairbanks's *Three Musketeers*. The LSO gave broadcast performances as early as February 1924 and a forward company of six players of the LSO performed as a broadcasting ensemble at least as early as September 1923.[25] It seems that orchestral members were not to be resisted in their readiness to make use of the new means of communication. As Captain Fraser put it to the Crawford Committee three years later, 'Mr Boosey states that he does not allow them [his artists] to broadcast, but the fact remains that most of them do so regularly.'[26]

One result of the downturn in the concert music market was that Percy Pitt and BNOC crossed over to the newly incorporated British Broadcasting Company. Filson Young, another journalist-musician influential in the foundation of music broadcasting, credited Pitt with the achievement of convincing the musicians of the potential of broadcasting.[27] From his long experience of entrepreneurship in concert music, Pitt was able to persuade them that the coming of broadcasting had created a new market for music and that co-operation with broadcasting did not mean any loss of control over the quality of the musical product.[28]

Provincial musicians outside Pitt's orbit of influence also took advantage of the opportunities of the new medium.[29] Dan Godfrey, the son of Sir Dan Godfrey, leader and conductor of the Bournemouth Symphony Orchestra, became Manchester Station Director, and converted Hallé members, including their leader, T. H. Morrison, to music broadcasting during the course of 1923.[30] In conformity with a decision that each station should possess a separate director of music, the company appointed Mr Braithwaite from the musical department of its headquarters as Musical Director at Cardiff. Mr Braithwaite had a distinguished musical career, being the youngest Wagnerian conductor, having conducted this composer's operas for the O'Hara Opera Company at the age of 23. He had also been conductor of the Carl Rosa Opera Company and sub-conductor of the BNOC. C. A. Lewis urged musicians to see their engagements to broadcast as part of a shift towards music-making on a new basis. Putting the point materially, he wrote: 'Don't forget that we [the Broadcasting Company] are the biggest concert organisation in the country. Perhaps we may be a sideline to you now, but – who knows – we may be bread and butter to you later.' Lewis saw broadcasting as a major and not just a supplementary channel of musical communication.

The quality of broadcast music

The integration of the concert musicians into the structure of broadcasting entailed 'accommodations' by both sides. On the musicians' side, accommodation was predicated on the existence of the progressive elements just discussed, who recognized the rise of new audiences and who had, before the coming of broadcasting, explored new ways of reaching them. On the broadcasting side, accommodation required, first, that the quality of music through microphone and receiver should bear comparison with what was achieved via the gramophone and, second, that the company should organize the supply of music on the scale that broadcasting required.

In 1920 and 1921 there were several ventures, some individual and some organized, in music broadcasting. There were 'concerts' from the Nederlandsche Radio-Industry of The Hague and gramophone recitals by amateurs.[31] The enthusiastic use of the air for 'tests' involving gramophone records and requests for 'repeats' gave rise to a fear at the Post Office that the grant of a broadcasting franchise to a commercial company would license the use of the air as a medium for entertainment rather than as a utility. The response of Burrows, with his journalistic and public relations background and training, was quite otherwise. To Burrows, the spontaneous use of the air by telephony buffs as a medium of musical entertainment at once defined the needs of the public and the path along which broadcasting must travel. Cecil Lewis (1924) characterized Burrows as a journalist 'educated to give the public what it wants . . . . He is always to be found putting himself in the place of the man in the street and trying to look at things from the point of view of the masses.'[32] Of course, the telephony buffs, able to afford and experiment with novel equipment, were not really 'the masses'. They were simply another among the complex of factors which decided the level at which broadcasting made its entry to the culture. In this age before 'pop music', 'popular music' meant popular classics.

The start of regular broadcasting was accompanied in May 1922 by a shift in Marconi research away from the problems of telephoned speech and audibility over great distances towards a total system for the better reproduction of the higher musical frequencies. This involved changes of wavelength and the adaptation and redesign of the circuit and microphone. The focus of attention of Burrows and the engineers at the Marconi Station in the second half of 1922 was on the faithfulness with which the system reproduced particular musical instruments or voices. The engineers' log and Burrows's letters of report to head office reveal that certain instruments showed up the limitations of the broadcasting technology. In October, the engineers' commentary on programmes noted that listening to the piano over the air was like sitting right under a very tinny instrument. This was to become a commonplace observation. At the end of the year, Burrows commented that the wireless piano had 'all the tinny effects long associated with it'.[33] The high frequencies of the violin gave rise to similar distortions. Referring to the combination of a Dickens reading and a violin recital that made up a demonstration programme from Bristol, Burrows recorded soberly: 'While the speech quality was such that every word could be understood, the quality of musical reproduction was not good.'[34] Marconi 'demonstrations' showed as convincingly to opinion leaders as they did to Arthur Burrows and the Marconi engineers that the wireless had not yet arrived at a point at which it could give pleasure to musically minded listeners. The editor of *Musical Times* wrote of a violin transmission that 'to say that I heard a violin solo would be to state the case feebly. The sound magnified and brassy rather than stringy, bored its way into my skull in a manner suggestive of a surgical operation.'[35] After hearing the violin via the wireless, Scholes advised his readers that they might write off wireless as a serious medium for musical communication for several years to come.

This made the task of the research arms of the big electrical firms urgent. By the autumn of the year, changes in wavelength and adaptations of the circuit had been made. These narrowed down the search for the obstacle to music broadcasting to 'the present system of microphones'.[36] To the three big electricals already committed to funding a broadcasting venture from the sale of sets, with the music publics in London and in the Midland and northern cities as their potential market, the perfection of a music microphone became a condition of success. Burrows and his staff, their time divided between their publicity work and the new technical venture, were prey to fears that they had overcommitted themselves to broadcasting, so much so that they feared the risk of having 'burned their boats'.[37]

All three companies gave research priority to solving the technical problems of music broadcasting. The logjam around the broadcasting of music of a pleasing rather than novelty value was finally broken when Western Electric Company opened a rival London station on 8 November 1922 and brought into use the stretched steel diaphragm microphone developed in the USA. This assured Western Electric's place as the third of the Big Three in the Broadcasting Company. For Burrows, who had felt himself at times disproportionately committed to the new venture, some weeks of Western Electric's nightly music broadcast must have been reassuring. Western Electric's microphone patents, available to the prospective company, brought the London wireless music market, which had for some months evaded 2LO, within the company's reach. Eckersley, the chief and only engineer of the BBC in February 1923, recollected Reith welcoming him with an anxious first question: 'Is it true that the Western Electric microphones are better than the ones we are using at the 2LO studios?'[38]

The breakthrough was demonstrated with striking clarity with the broadcasts of the BNOC operas from Covent Garden in January–February 1923. The Western Electric technicians themselves were uncertain of the outcome. But the sense of having achieved with the opera relay something more than had been dreamed of is captured in Lewis's account:

> I well remember the occasion . . . . We all assembled in a little room on the top floor of Marconi House, where a loud-speaker stood on the table. Suddenly, with a loud click, it was thrown into circuit, and a confused babel of noises was let loose. At first indistinguishable, it soon became apparent that we were hearing the talk and rustling of programmes in the auditorium. Finally, there was a burst of clapping, which died down to dead silence, and was followed by two sharp raps; a second later the huge orchestra had leaped into its stride, swelled up to a great crash of brass and cymbals, which could be heard all down the corridor at Marconi House.
>
> Our excitement was immense. The broadcasting of opera was an assured success: that could be said after listening for a few moments. The sound of the great orchestra contrasted so forcibly with our little band of seven in the studio that it might come as a revelation of what the future of broadcasting might be.[39]

Lewis's sense that the interests of electrical engineers, musicians and the organizers of a new industry had merged in the single event was confirmed by that same editor of *Musical Times*, Percy Scholes, who only months before had written off the merger of music and electrical science as years away:

> I sat by a friend's fireside and heard two acts of *Aïda* and a couple of *La Bohème* with Melba bringing down the house, and I am convinced that the invention which a year ago seemed like a futile toy is about to create something like a revolution in the musical world.[40]

The discovery of the music microphone was a critical point in the transition from the engineering of broadcasting to broadcast engineering. The attention gradually shifted from the technology to the output. The broadcasting studio was at its inception predominantly a test laboratory. The first broadcasting ventures at Writtle originated as light relief for a research and development team who saw their tasks as radio telegraphy, rather than broadcasting. C. A. Lewis in his description of the 2LO Studio at Marconi House disclosed a scene in which broadcasting was the secondary, and the testing of microphones the primary, goal. He wrote: 'There were four microphones in this studio and . . . the engineers could not leave them alone. They tapped them, they shouted at them, coaxed them and whispered to them every minute of the day . . . . And insisted on silence while they were doing it.'[41] In January 1922, Burrows, the official charged with programmes, drew the attention of the Marconi Company to the need to distinguish between the conduct of broadcast concerts according to 'what I will term professional style as distinct from the Engineers' Programme work with which we have been hitherto accustomed'.[42] Burrows distinguished with precision between the problems of technical development and those of broadcasting: 'We have to face problems requiring solutions by acoustical rather than electrical experts.'[43]

In time these problems became obvious to those outside as well, especially those who wanted to see broadcasting selling radio sets. Major Binyon, one of the directors of the company, wrote to Reith, the general manager, complaining that the broadcasts were not faithful to the sound of the dance band. The complaint prompted two answers from Reith. First, that on the matter of the sound balance of instruments, the company had already evolved a studio technique and that he proposed to embody the embryonic method in a permanent organization. This was the Balance and Control Section. Second, that research was under way to discover the studio technique that would reproduce both the instrumental sound and environmental sound elements that composed music styles both in studios and on outside broadcasts. This resulted in 1925 in a report to the directors by A. G. D. West, the head of Engineering, in which he acknowledged the discovery of new music programme values and of the beginning of the search for a technique that would maximize these values in programmes. 'After . . . a satisfactory microphone (the magnetophone) was evolved . . . then it was begun to be realised as a result of the popularity of certain transmissions from outside halls that in these cases much more pleasing and natural effects were obtained with just a certain amount of echo effect.'[44]

Later, in 1927, West recalled that from this discovery had emerged a 'studio technique'. 'The chief point in the development of studio technique is that it is desirable to transmit all kinds of programme material with the acoustic environment that is most suitable to it.'[45] Larger studios had been commissioned and the amount of drapery reduced but the marked difference in quality between studio and concert hall sound remained.

The practical task that faced the company engineers was to seek out the design properties of outside halls and incorporate these in the design of future studios. The terms of reference of the research engineers were to identify and reproduce in the studio 'any effect between that of a draped room and that of a Cathedral with the full realism of an outside broadcast transmission'.[46]

The engineers' search led them to the scientific work of Professor Sabine of Harvard University, undertaken before broadcasting began, on the design properties of concert halls. Professor Sabine's critical step was to co-ordinate his measurements of the reverberation times of halls 'with the opinion of musicians qualified to give their opinion from a musical point of view'. As West put it, 'the American investigation worked out curves for a desirable reverberation for various types of music from the point of view of members of the audience'.[47] In the first of his articles on 'A tour round Savoy Hill' in 1927

West made clear that, as part of the company's effort to please the listener, the engineers had come into line with programme producers. The engineers had seized upon reverberation time from the work of Sabine as a way of penetrating the engineering conditions of musical values.

Acoustical conditions became of crucial importance to the microphone engineer because the microphone, unlike the ears of the musically trained listener, was unable to reject the distortion caused by concert hall conditions. Moreover, Sabine's investigations into the properties of halls depended on identifying the sound *which sounded right to the musical ear*. This meant the engineers came to favour the institutionalization of 'the opinion of musicians qualified to give their opinion from a musical point of view'[48] as the standard through which engineers might co-ordinate their measurements of conditions.

The engineers' report on acoustics was submitted in December 1925 and the institution of the Balance and Control Section followed early in the new year. Engineering support for the setting up of a balance and control section followed naturally as a body of music-engineering theory matured. Acoustics at this time was an inexact science. As the *BBC Handbook* for 1928 put it:

> It is a difficult enough matter to measure the characteristics of a microphone, to find out how it deals with the various musical frequencies in the conversion from sound into electrical energy. It is a much more difficult matter to obtain any definite information on the effect of environment – of studio or hall – on musical broadcast transmission . . . . So far results have been judged mainly by ear (the musician's) without any adequate scientific conception of what they represent.[49]

The engineers followed in the tradition of Sabine in taking, as their standard of reference for their investigations, the opinion of a section of trained musicians. To quote the 1928 *BBC Handbook* again:

> They [the Balance and Control Section] are, primarily, musicians, but know enough of the engineering side to appreciate the technical limitations of the equipment . . . . Microphones, amplifiers, transmitters and telephone lines are not yet perfect, and the musician has of necessity to model his arrangements to compensate, if possible, for the difficulties which the engineer has not yet been able to overcome.[50]

Eckersley remembered Balance and Control as

> a special section of the BBC staffed by musicians who had some technical knowledge . . . . A member of the section has to rehearse the orchestra and judge the 'balance' in the reproduced sound. In my day the balancer listened to headphones. The players were moved about until the resulting sound in the headphones was, in the judgement of the balance expert, satisfactory.[51]

The development of music-engineering theory meant the engineers supported the new section. The formation of the Balance and Control Section, staffed by musicians, played a crucial role in bringing about an accommodation between the world of classical music and an organization hitherto dominated by electrical engineers.

The role of the music critics

The opposition to music broadcasting continued from the London concert-giving organizations, Messrs Chappell and the trustees of the Central Hall, Westminster. They feared that the wireless would replace the concert hall as the principal music medium. The opposition of the concert hall organizations served as a forum for those who were apprehensive that the interests of music were about to pass into the hands of a commercial or state monopoly dominated by electrical engineers and administrators whose values were not musical. William Boosey, the managing director of Chappell's, indicated his fears of the consequences of the domination of engineers in the new organization when he wrote: 'Mechanical music and music broadcasts are revolutionaries . . . . Music must not, shall not, be all mechanical.'[52]

This fear was shared not only by critics of the BBC like Boosey, but also those like Filson Young who saw potential in the new medium.[53] The Balance and Control Section was the key response to this difficult charge. The solution provided by this device was theorized by progressive music critics like Filson Young and Percy Scholes. Filson Young in particular became ready to push musicians into finding common ground between the music and the engineering cultures. Sabine had showed engineers a way of working with musicians. Filson Young (journalist, composer and friend of Percy Pitt) performed the same service in reverse. He suggested to musicians a way of bringing musicians' interest into an adaptive experimental relationship with engineering research and development.

Filson Young was part of 'the great educative movement' in music[54] to extend the audience for classical music and was particularly influential in seeing how broadcasting could contribute to it. In his evidence to the Crawford Committee in January 1926, Filson Young identified himself as a musician of the new generation who accepted that the old forms of music sound practice offered no guidance in the new technical, social and economic conditions of the post-war period. Young saw the new generation of musicians confronted with the task of reconstructing music sound practice to take account of engineering practice. In a challenging paragraph, Filson Young set out the radical tasks facing musicians and broadcasting. 'The BBC has therefore not sufficiently recognized that this business of conveying . . . entertainment to an audience of invisible millions is an entirely new thing, requiring a new technique, both in the performers, and in many cases in the thing performed.'[55]

Filson Young's thesis was that the broadcasting organization's ambition to communicate the full repertoire of classical music surpassed what the existing technology was capable of.

> With regard to music, I think it will not be denied that all the BBC has aimed at has been to take musical performance as it exists already in the concert rooms . . . and, by means of the microphone, transmit it to as many people as possible. Now, in my opinion, that policy can only have a very limited scope. Here we are on technical ground.[56]

The inescapable fact is that some instruments are suitable for reproduction and some are not. But the music that we like to listen to, and that sounds well before it is transmitted, is composed of the sounds made by all the instruments including those which are unsuitable for broadcasting . . . . At present the BBC broadcasts every kind of music and every kind of instrument, irrespective of whether it is suitable or not.[57]

If music were broadcast before improvements in music engineering, it might threaten musical culture and the aural cultivation of the new music audience of millions. The danger of this practice was that 'the whole broadcasting system becomes a system not of elevation and education but of degradation'.[58] In other words, 'the degradation of people's ears will go on if they get accustomed to hearing loudspeakers instead of orchestras'.[59]

For Filson Young the central concern of the broadcast-music critic was to ensure the transmission to the new wireless audiences of the high aural culture of the concert hall unimpaired.[60] Filson Young's charge that the company was 'feeding the microphone with [musical] substance it cannot stomach' was the basis of his claim that it should entrust its musical conscience to Percy Scholes and himself.

Though the receiving apparatus was just as much an instrument of music culture as the microphone, the commercial set manufacturers employed no music critic. In his oral evidence, Young made clear his views that the receiver manufacturers could be relied on to supply only the lowest standard sets that the overall market would bear. To Young, who saw the possibilities of wireless as an instrument to extend and deepen musical education, the subjugation of innovative and sensitive engineering to commercial interests was the worst of all possible new worlds. The committee asked him whether the receiver manufacturers might not be expected to play a part in the great task of conveying the musical cultural inheritance to the millions. Filson Young replied:

I am afraid that waiting for the manufacturer to improve his instrument is not enough for me. The manufacturer has not improved his instrument really as much as he might have improved it, because he is satisfied with the low standard which people accept for music, and all he cares about is to sell his instrument; as long as they are good enough for people to buy, they are good enough for me and you.[61]

By contrast, the authority structure of the broadcasting corporation gave Filson Young the space to make a realistic appeal to artistic values. His idea was that the broadcast critic was to institutionalize a wholly new and necessary dimension in the organization of cultural engineering. In this system the artists should be more powerful than the engineers and executives. Filson Young's proposal was to strengthen artistic authority at the point of production. Those in charge of mediating the old arts in a new setting would have to learn to take account of the same broadcasting factors as Filson Young had done: the level of technical development (the engineers' interest) and the level of education of 'the vast invisible audience' (the executives' interest). Filson Young rounded off his written submission by advocating that

> as an organisation . . . the BBC should be simplified, and its artistic policy controlled more by artists and less by boards and committees. Otherwise, with its ultimate control freed from all commercial interests, I think it should be allowed to continue its monopoly and be encouraged to develop broadcasting as a separate art.[62]

Filson Young developed this argument at the oral hearing. His concern was not whether the broadcasting authority should be a government body or a public corporation but with 'the *artistic* direction of broadcasting in whomsoever's hands that broadcasting is. It comes then to the *personality* of those artistically responsible for broadcasting' (emphasis added).[63] In his view, that personality should be artistic in its values rather than technical or bureaucratic.

Young concluded that if, as he believed, the idea of completely faithful reproduction was still far distant, then there was a place at the musician's side for a phased translation of the corpus of the musical inheritance to the new medium. This would take account of, and match, the music performed to the method of reproduction employed. His analysis required that 'all music performed by broadcasting should be specially chosen, arranged and performed, with a view to its suitability for the particular method which is being employed'. To achieve the phased translation of the musical culture to the wireless medium meant broadening the scope of the original engineering organization. His favoured solution was 'the re-scoring . . . of a large portion of orchestral music, with a view to its transmission by wireless'. As he admitted, this 'involves the permanent employment of a staff of copyists'.[64]

The chief engineer's reply to the committee on Young's proposal showed a more traditional engineering approach. Eckersley accepted that the company was a music-broadcasting organization, but more important it was a research and development organization for music engineering. 'We suggest', Eckersley argued, 'that this policy may result in a false satisfaction upon the part of those responsible for reproduction and that development towards what all visualise as the ideal (i.e. perfect transmission and reproduction) will be retarded.'[65] He also pointed out that it was not practical to employ a taskforce of musicians to rescore '300,000 hours of transmissions of music a year'. Many years later, Eckersley was prepared to single out Filson Young as 'the only one of us who could truly be described as having the cultural outlook'.[66] In the same paragraph in which he paid tribute to Filson Young, he recognized that 'the company undoubtedly saw itself as a cultural force . . . . The unfortunate thing was that the idea of becoming a cultural force was so uncultured.' Filson Young was the exception. This exchange brings out clearly the contest for control over broadcasting between the various interests, artistic, engineering and administrative, which was being played out underneath the general enthusiasm for the new medium which promised so much. Through intermediaries like Scholes and Filson Young and through mechanisms like the establishment of the Balance and Control Section, radio and music were able to reach an accommodation which made the new organization, the British Broadcasting Company, the heir to the leadership of 'the democratic movement in Music'.

The seven years between 1923 and 1930 was the period during which the company reached this accommodation. They were marked by first the introduction of the music microphone, then the foundation of a department of Music under Pitt, and finally the formation of the BBC Symphony Orchestra in August 1930 at the end of this period. In 1927, the first year of the corporation's existence, Messrs Chappell surrendered their control of the stronghold of the Queen's Hall and their responsibility for the promotion of the Promenade Concerts there, an event of considerable symbolic importance.

During those years, the broadcasting organization's conscientious discharge of its role as the great power and patron of the world of music stilled the fears expressed by Boosey and others that the interests of the high-class music culture were about to pass into insensitive hands. Throughout, the company and the corporation treated the musical establishment with the respect which such an establishment felt it deserved. The establishment of the Balance and Control Section was an important mark of that respect. Broadcasters accepted the unique importance of the musicians' skills and expertise and institutionalized the mechanism to allow musicians to control the quality of their finished product. The arrangement became unstable, however, as broadcasters acquired greater self-confidence and organization, and began to reserve to themselves such powers of control, but initially it played an important part in convincing musicians that broadcasting would treat them with seriousness, respect and even deference.

Conclusion

The musicians who adopted broadcasting as a new way of reaching a wider public were also moving over to a medium which had access to new sources of funds, first through the company and then through the licence fee. The other ways tried by the musicians of the 'popular movement' to reach larger audiences had met with only temporary success. Over time all had proved financial failures. Thus Beecham's orchestra and opera company, which had played to packed houses in the West End in the war years, finally went into liquidation in September 1920.[67] This was after a successful season in 1919–20 which Beecham hoped would win the company the backing of Covent Garden and enable them to perform in a 'theatre more directly associated with opera'. The Covent Garden syndicate however was not persuaded that opera would pay and refused. As economic conditions worsened even the Promenade Concerts ceased to pay their way. In 1927 they too were rescued by broadcasting.

By this time the Crawford Committee had pronounced, the company had been incorporated and broadcasting was established. As Briggs notes[68] this was the view of Lord Clarendon, first chairman of the Board of Governors. It is not surprising that the immediate priority of Reith and the other broadcasting executives changed from promoting the idea and potential of broadcasting to more mundane matters of organizing and administering the service. The change was marked by the departure of the first cadre of executives whose work has featured so prominently in this chapter.

Balance and control raised some particularly difficult issues under this new regime. The device had a continuing value in soothing artistic sensibilities but it proved to be a difficult function to measure and define. Over the next twenty-five years no less than four committees and inquiries took on this task and made a series of pronouncements on the types and grades of operatives who were involved, the duties they should be expected to perform and the way in which the occupation should be characterized, as part of Programmes or Engineering. The situation was complicated by parallel developments in Drama and later in other departments, which produced more employees with the same title but doing slightly different jobs. The committees provide a fascinating index of the relative power of different groups within the corporation, administrators, engineers, musicians, dramatists and the balance and control operatives themselves, and the values they represented. In the early period, discussed in this chapter, balance and control was favoured by the broadcasters' aim to establish radio as a culturally respectable medium. The growth of this new occupation, peculiar to broadcasting, provides a good indication of broadcasting's point of entry into the culture.

This study has focused on a period when organizational and technical developments within broadcasting interacted with changes occurring in the world of music. It may well be that there are other periods, in the more recent past, in which the coincidence of developments in sound engineering and changes in the music field would allow historians of communication to make similar studies of cultural change. Forty years on, in the mid-1960s, Glenn Gould, prompted by the commercialization of stereophonic music systems, reviewed the broad lines of advance in the music world.[69] He looked particularly at the impact of a more active audience, equipped with the means to blend into a musical whole fragments of music performance taken from many sources. These speculations were prompted by the coming of four-track tapes, stereophonic dials allowing control over the details of music balance and tempo, and devices for adjusting reverberation according to the play-back environment. The way in which he anticipated a new generation of listeners would exploit audio-engineering innovations was akin to the adolescent telephony experiments of the pre-broadcasting age. Gould hoped for an advance to new thresholds of musical self-education from audiences blending their own Beethoven from diverse subjects. His essay formed part of the 1960s avant-garde's search for a new music and for audiences freed from opera managements', concert agencies' and record companies' control over what they might listen to. Our tale of accommodation and incorporation in early broadcasting suggests Gould's projections were likely to be idealistically utopian. Nevertheless this period appears to offer another coincidence between technical, organizational and cultural change.

254 *Impacts and Influences*

The studies by American sociologists of work and occupations in the commercial music world have already yielded valuable insights into the dynamics of cultural innovation.[70] Edward Kealy, for example, has traced the 'real rock revolution' to the transformation of the sound mixer from technician to artist. Kealy focused on the sound mixer as a figure whose role in shaping the aesthetics of musical art has been little understood or appreciated. The sound mixer is the distant heir of the balance and control man in music broadcasting, occupying a similar point at the interface between art and modern technology. In a valuable study, Kealy uncovered the forces which, from the mid-1960s, increased the sound mixer's part in decision-making, with resulting consequences for musical aesthetics.

His study, like our own, shows how a focus on the changing form and content of the occupations involved in the collaborative process of production in television, theatre, film or radio, can illuminate the artistic and cultural impact of the media.[71]

Notes

1 Briggs however includes an aside in the course of a brief discussion of the cultural consequences of radio in the introduction to the first volume of his history, remarking that 'the beginning of a popular revolution in musical appreciation was generally conceded'. See A. Briggs, *The History of Broadcasting in the United Kingdom*, vol. I, *The Birth of Broadcasting*, London, Oxford University Press, 1961, p. 16.

2 Stanley Manning in 1912 equipped with a De Forest audion picked up a snatch of speech and music, part of a Fessenden test. 'When I heard it I thought I was going crazy . . . . I called several people, and they heard it, so it was real.' John Fetzner in Indiana on a night in November 1913, when he listened in to time signals from Arlington, was 'suddenly startled to hear violin music bursting forth from the mike . . . as far as we were concerned a miracle never to be explained'. See E. Barnouw, *The Tower in Babel: a history of broadcasting in the US*, vol. 1, *To 1933*, New York, Oxford University Press, 1966.

3 P. P. Eckersley, *The Power behind the Microphone*, London, Jonathan Cape, 1941, p. 30; hereafter cited as *Power behind Microphone*. According to Howard Rosenthal, 'the matinee performance of *Hansel and Gretel*, 6 January 1923, was broadcast by the recently founded BBC over station 2LO; this was the first opera broadcast from a theatre in Europe': H. D. Rosenthal, *Two Centuries of Opera at Covent Garden*, London, Putnam, 1958, p. 415. However, there is a disagreement among the sources; see also H. M. Dowsett, *Wireless Telephony and Broadcasting*, London, Gresham, 1924, p. 64, and the *BBC Yearbook*, London, BBC, 1930, p. 160.

4 C. A. Lewis, *Broadcasting from Within*, London, Newnes, (February) 1924, p. 68; this book was described by the author in an introductory note as 'simply the first year's work and the future possibilities seen through the eyes of one who has been intimately connected with its development'.

5 A. R. Burrows, *The Story of Broadcasting*, London, Cassell, (July) 1924, p. 110.

6 J. C. W. Reith, *Broadcast over Britain*, London, Hodder & Stoughton, (September) 1924, p. 23.

7 Reith, op. cit., p. 24.

8 Lewis, op. cit., p. 48.

9 ibid., p. 26.

10 Burrows, op. cit., p. 69.

11 Reith, op. cit., p. 24.

12 Lewis, op. cit., Burrows, op. cit., Reith, op. cit.

13 Eckersley, *Power behind Microphone*, p. 109.

14 Termed 'putting through' in the *BBC Handbook*, London, BBC, 1928, p. 113.

15 The *Musical Times* observed that the Promenade Concerts of 1896 'gathered to themselves an audience of a quite distinctive kind. One's impression was that it consisted in some considerable measure of music lovers, who despite their unmistakeable keenness, one did not see at concerts other than those of this informal autumn series.' Cited in P. A. Scholes (ed.), *The Mirror of Music*, vol. I, London, Novello & Co. and Oxford University Press, 1947, p. 195; hereafter cited as *Mirror of Music*.

16 Rosenthal, op. cit., pp. 398, 412.

17 Scholes, *Mirror of Music*.

18 P. A. Scholes, *Listener's Guide to Music: with a Concert-Goer's Glossary*, London, Humphrey Milford, 1919; hereafter cited as *Listener's Guide*.

19 See the entry for 'annotated programmes' in P. A. Scholes, *Oxford Companion to Music*, London, Oxford University Press, 1938, p. 36; hereafter cited as *Oxford Companion*. The phrase 'missionary societies for music' occurs in P. A. Scholes, *Everybody's Guide to Broadcast Music*, London, Humphrey Milford and Hodder & Stoughton, 1925, p. 223; hereafter cited as *Everybody's Guide*.

20 Scholes, *Everybody's Guide*; a title enlarged as 'including a simple description of the various forms of music, and of the orchestra, a short account of the history of music, some advice on the enjoyment of broadcast opera (with a list of published *libretti*) and a discussion of what constitutes good music and a good musical performance'.

21 Scholes used the term 'propaganda' with reference to the Queen's Hall Promenade Concerts: see Scholes, *Oxford Companion*, p. 208.

22 ibid., pp. 122ff. P. A. Scholes began to contribute weekly articles on broadcast music in autumn 1923: see Scholes's entry in S. Moseley, *Who's Who in Broadcasting*, London, Sir I. Pitman, 1933.

23 Briggs, op. cit., p. 277.

24 Rosenthal, op. cit., p. 418.

25 The LSO broadcast took place on 9 February and 22 April 1924. See H. Foss and N. Goodwin, *London Symphony Orchestra*, London, Naldrett, 1954, p. 109. For the ensemble see *Radio Times*, 1, 28 September 1923, p. 28.

26 Crawford Committee, Supplementary Memorandum, p. 6; cited in Briggs, op. cit., vol. I, p. 345.

27 'It was Pitt . . . in the most exciting period of the musical history of broadcasting in England [from 1923] . . . who managed gradually to win the world of virtuosi to the microphone, which they had hitherto unanimously reviled. It was not until he had done this that broadcasting began to be taken seriously both on artistic and economic grounds.' Filson Young, *Shall I Listen: studies in the adventure of broadcasting*, London, Constable, 1933, p. 76.

28 'He put broadcasting on the musical map and raised the dissemination of music by this means from being part of a miscellaneous entertainment to a policy and a great educative movement in art . . . . Everyone trusted him . . . he acquired a position

of authority with regard to opera work that not even a genius like Sir Thomas Beecham had achieved . . . . So working in the background in the difficult world of stars and prima donnas, he was content to take an inconspicuous place so far as the public was concerned. But on the other side of the fireproof doors, he was the man who never failed. The work of Sir Thomas Beecham and of Covent Garden could not have been done so well without him.' Filson Young's obituary of Percy Pitt, *Radio Times*, 9 December 1932, p. 748.

29 That there were other worlds beyond London and even the big cities is attested by the career of Dan Godfrey (1868–1939). P. A. Scholes in *Mirror of Music* (London, Novello & Co. and Oxford University Press, 1947) describes him as 'one who was not a "great" director, and yet accomplished much for music in this country'. The *Musical Times* of March 1894 reported: 'Bournemouth has engaged Mr Dan Godfrey Jun. as municipal music director and will spend £5000 on a band.' In 1896 the prospectus of winter concerts said: 'It is proposed to augment the existing string orchestra at the Winter Gardens to thirty-one and give a series of high-class orchestral concerts during the forthcoming season . . . Beethoven, Schumann, Mendelssohn.' The *Musical Times*, June 1911, reported a dinner given to Dan Godfrey in London by 'an influential gathering of musicians', 'well-known musicians from all parts of the Kingdom'. Speaking at the dinner Sir Alex Mackenzie 'recalled when there were only three orchestras in the country . . . . Bournemouth was the first provincial town orchestra during 18 years. Sir Dan Godfrey achieved a record only equalled at the Crystal Palace; he had given no fewer than 965 classical concerts and we heard brought forward the chief productions of Britain.'

30 Burrows, op. cit., pp. 157ff.

31 See Burrows, op. cit., p. 57 and H. M. Dowsett, op. cit., p. 58. Lewis wrote of the period, 'the air was full of music': op. cit., p. 21.

32 ibid., p. 150.

33 Commentary from 'Notes on a broadcast of 1.11.22' and note from Burrows to R. M. White (Burrows's superior in the Marconi Company), 18 December 1922, from the Marconi Company Archive; hereafter cited as MCA.

34 Burrows, *The Story of Broadcasting*, p. 68.

35 Scholes, *Mirror of Music*, p. 795.

36 Letter from Burrows to R. M. White, 18 October 1922, MCA.

37 That Burrows saw the future of his new career hanging in the balance on the development of more efficient music reproduction is suggested in the attention his letters to head office give to this issue, as 'I am most nervous that this question of transmitting quality [of music] shall be handled as quickly as possible': Burrows to C. O. Simpson, 30 June 1922, MCA. He referred once but briefly to his anxiety during the first six months following the opening of the London Station when a breakthrough to music broadcasting was in sight but still unachieved, when he wrote: 'We in London well remember, too, that as no permanent appointments had been made, and we had no desire to burn our boats, the broadcasting duties were carried out for some six weeks in addition to our ordinary office routine.' Burrows, op cit., p. 69.

38 Eckersley, *Power behind Microphone*, p. 62.

39 Lewis, op. cit., pp. 32ff.

40 Scholes, *Mirror of Music*, p. 795.

41 Lewis, op. cit., pp. 29ff.

42 Letter from Burrows to R. M. White, 31 January 1922, MCA.

43 ibid., p. 100.

44 A. G. D. West, 'Report of experiments carried out by the BBC Research Department in connection with studios and halls', 22 December 1925, BBC Written Archive Centre, Caversham, Reading, p. 5; hereafter cited as 'Report'.

45 A. G. D. West, 'A tour round Savoy Hill', 4 parts, *Wireless World*, February–March 1927.

46 West, 'Report', p. 1.

47 ibid., p. 3.

48 ibid., p. 1.

49 *BBC Handbook*, London, BBC, 1928, p. 207.

50 ibid., pp. 312ff.

51 Eckersley, *Power behind Microphone*, p. 111.

52 W. Boosey, *Fifty Years of Music*, London, Ernest Benn, 1931, p. 195.

53 'Journalist and musician, war correspondent of the *Manchester Guardian* (Boer War), Literary Editor of the *Daily Mail* 1903–4, Editor of *Outlook*, Editor of *Saturday Review* 1921–4. Connected from 1926 with the BBC Programme Branch, in advisory capacity, devising the "Foundations of Music", the Bach Cantata series and various experiments in the presentation of opera.' Moseley, op. cit.

54 Phrase from Filson Young's obituary of Percy Pitt, *Radio Times*, 9 December 1932, p. 748.

55 Filson Young, written evidence submitted to the Crawford Committee, no. 26, para. 4, BBC Archive Acc. 44182 or R4/2/3/6; hereafter cited as 'written evidence'.

56 ibid.

57 ibid., para. 6.

58 ibid., para. 8.

59 ibid., para. 10.

60 This was P. P. Eckersley's summation of Filson Young's theory in his comments for the Crawford Committee on the evidence of Filson Young, BBC Archive Acc. 44182 or R4/2/3/6; hereafter cited as 'comments on evidence of FY'.

61 Transcript of Filson Young's oral evidence to the Crawford Committee, BBC Archive Acc. 44182 or R4/2/3/6.

62 Filson Young, 'written evidence', para. 17.

63 ibid., para. 9.

64 ibid., para. 11.

65 Eckersley, 'comments on evidence of FY'.

66 Eckersley followed this up with the view that the possible approaches to broadcasting were two: either administrative or artistic. 'The artist man asks, is it good or bad art?' Eckersley, *Power behind Microphone*, pp. 54–7.

67 Rosenthal, op. cit.

68 Briggs, op. cit., p. 16.

69 J. Culshaw, 'The mellow knob or the rise of records and the decline of the concert hall as foreseen by Glenn Gould', *Records and Recording*, 10, pt 2, 1966, 26–8.

70 E. R. Kealy, 'From craft to art; the case of sound mixers and popular music', *Sociology of Work and Occupation*, 6, 1 (1979), 3–20; R. R. Faulkner, *Hollywood Studio Musicians*, Chicago, Aldine Atherton, 1971; R. R. Faulkner, 'Dilemmas in commercial work, Hollywood film composers and their clients', *Urban Life*, 5, 1 (1976), 3–33.

71 Other works consulted in the writing of this chapter were: W. L. G. Legg and E. T. Williams, *Dictionary of National Biography, 20th century (1941–50)*,

London, Oxford University Press, 1959; R. Elkin, *Queen's Hall, 1893–1941*, London, Rider, 1944; T. Russell, *Philharmonic Decade*, London, Hutchinson, 1945; S. Sadie (ed.), *The New Grove Dictionary of Music and Musicians*, London, Macmillan, 1980.

12

Audience research and the BBC in the 1930s: a mass medium comes into being

David Chaney

1

The creation of the Listener Research Department in the BBC in 1936 has usually been treated as a natural development in a progress towards increasing public accountability: natural in a sense that it is consistent with the consultative forms of mass democracy. I shall argue that the development is more adequately understood as part of the process of broadcasting becoming a mass medium: as such it was indeed part of concurrent changes in political form but these were not necessarily leading to greater public participation or accountability. I shall not be concerned with whether we should try to determine media influence or effects because I am less interested in the 'success' of research than that it was developed as a bridge to public opinion. The reason for concentrating on the 1930s is that innovations in the conceptualization of public as audience were being sought and developed, innovations which were subsequently subsumed in the allocation of resources to propaganda by governments caught up in a world war at the end of the decade.

In the course of the inter-war years politics became 'massified' in three senses: first, in the sense that it became populist in tone, although another way of putting this would be to say that it was sensationalized through personalities rather than issues; secondly, that to some extent it became independent of parties; and thirdly, that constituencies became both national and atomized, in the sense that a following for a politician or a cause could transcend 'natural' constituencies and exist in most social divisions although tending to be expressed as a personal choice rather than being mob or crowd will. This version of massification is not the same as massification in popular entertainment, which tends to be used to refer to a combination of audience size with centralized production facilities, although there are a number of important analogous developments such as shifts in the nature of the charisma, and in the role of spectacular sites for the transformation of reality such as both Nuremberg and metropolitan picture palaces. Perhaps the most important common ground in the institutionalization of massification in politics and entertainment was the use of a language of democratic endorsement as a display of legitimacy. In both institutions the popular will became a matter of gross consumer choices mobilized by organs of public opinion while remaining unreliable and unpredictable.[1] I shall argue that listener (audience) research marks the acceptance of a language of consumerism to index modes of political participation.

A concern with audience taste was not new to the 1930s, however, but was part of a long tradition of managerial concern with popular entertainment (for contrasting examples see Lowenthal,[2] Dunae[3] and Zurcher and Kirkpatrick)[4], a concern that has generally stemmed from seeing popular culture as threatening and something which 'responsible opinion' ought to attempt to control. There is by now quite a large literature on the continued attempts throughout the nineteenth century to create 'rational' leisure habits among the working class[5] and such a moral panic over wasting time is closely analogous to outrage at the content of popular entertainment. One interventionist strategy has been to try to create more worthwhile alternatives – much in the spirit of the salvationist query of 'Why should the devil have all the good tunes?' Unfortunately, however well-intentioned, such strategies have rarely been successful in their own terms and therefore reformers have gone for more direct forms of intervention and control. As well as legislating for illegitimate content, an approach which by definition gives the forbidden an alluring status and is in general ineffective while inevitably contravening the dominant liberal ideology, there have been two main modes of control. The first is structural in that there have been attempts to control the sites of popular entertainment, the best example being film censorship, which was initially effected through licensing buildings for exhibition rather than particular types of film. The second mode of control is institutional and works through setting up semi-autonomous bodies to direct the production of popular culture as in the example of the BBC. As these methods are indirect a rhetoric of freedom and choice remains uninhibited and a respect for popular taste is ostensibly preserved.

The public monopoly of the BBC is usually presented as an archaic survival of earlier moral concerns until it learnt to adapt to democratic necessity, in part through creating the machinery of listener research. I shall argue that if we wish to understand the wider political significance of processes of massification we must look more closely at the presuppositions both within the corporation and held by commentators in other media about the implications of 'discovering what people do want'. The working-out of accountability as it related to responding to audience wishes up until 1939 was not in two contrasting stages, pre- and post-listener research, but it is reasonable to assume that this innovation signalled new modes of participation. If only because, as we well know, in the post-war world of broadcasting, statistics on attendance and involvement, etc., have become the predominant constraint on policy-making.[6] I would not want to suggest, however, that these shackles were or even could have been anticipated by those who campaigned for audience research in the 1930s.

I do not want to deny that the restricted social world from which the BBC had drawn its appointments had imposed severe blinkers upon the corporation's ability to respond to popular taste. For example, Silvey has noted that one of the first effects of listener research was the shocking – to corporation mandarins – discovery that the world at large dined before eight pm.[7] It is also true that the managerial élite at the BBC derived its view of public opinion and the corporation's response to this public from methods 'distorted in favour of the opinions of articulate and powerful interest groups'.[8] It does not seem to me, however, that abrogating certain modes of élitism is necessarily to replace ideological blinkers with greater social truths. As pictures of the world the statistics of audience choices and behaviour are as 'ideological' as any sources of information they replaced.

It is important to note at this stage that there were pressures in relation to most social institutions in the 1930s such that the discovery of social facts was encouraged from a variety of viewpoints. For example, the British Medical Association undertook a survey of levels of nutrition in 1939 and although it set a standard below that used for Scottish convicts estimates indicated that up to 20 per cent of the population fell below it. Other initiatives in the field of social research were the commencement of a series of broadsheets dealing with issues in public affairs to be published by Political and Economic Planning (PEP) in 1933. Later in the decade the New Fabian Research Bureau was set up and several universities set up survey research teams to conduct studies of living conditions in their localities. This range of social research can be seen as an extension of the type of work undertaken at the end of the previous century. The innovation in the USA of studying public opinion, associated with Dr Gallup, as well as the social-anthropological innovation of studying community life, took some time to cross the Atlantic. Britain lacked a tradition of market research and there was certainly nothing comparable to the studies of comparative effects and appeals of different media initiated in American universities in the 1930s.[9] There was, above all, in addition to these more professional studies of social conditions the climate of documentarism in journalism, films and literature which embodied what has been called 'the cult of fact'.

2

It may seem unpromising to concentrate upon radio in British society because British broadcasting was officially under the monopolistic control of the BBC and a history of relevant research should be simply a history of competing attitudes within the corporation. There are two reasons why I believe this presumption to be mistaken. The first is that effective attitudes to decision-making were not restricted to corporation employees. Although the BBC and, in particular, Reith received more than their fair share of hagiographical tributes, the chorus of praise in the 1930s was not uniform or consistent. Quite pungent questions about the presuppositions of corporate paternalism were posed with consequential questions about how else broadcasters might respond to perceived public taste. This more general discussion of BBC policies was often initiated by ex-employees of the corporation, but was not exclusively restricted to such interested parties. A second reason why this presupposition would be mistaken is that part of the hidden history of broadcasting in the UK is the story of BBC endeavours to suppress competition that it felt to be either ideologically unreliable or commercially injurious or both. There were two main types of competition in the 1930s for the BBC: schemes to transmit programmes through wired networks and schemes for overseas stations to broadcast in English being sponsored by advertising revenue from British companies.[10] The attitude of the corporation and 'establishment opinion' in general to these competitors was very much that the BBC's 'good work' would be undermined by the anarchy of uncontrolled broadcasting. It is still true, though, that decision-making within the corporation was throughout the decade affected by suspicions about the 'latent' popularity of this 'illegitimate broadcasting'. In the response to these pressures I am less interested in fractures within a (self-described) intellectual mandarinate between 'commercials' as opposed to 'patricians' than in how a wider constituency began to respond to a key question posed by R. S. Lambert: 'But it has yet to be proved whether broadcasting as a form of popular entertainment can permanently be run by a bureaucracy.'[11]

The several answers to Lambert's question initially differed in their interpretation of the phrase 'form of popular entertainment'. One would be whether what was broadcast was *genuinely* popular? It would be put in this way because it could be argued that when there is a monopoly any provision must get an audience, but present choices may not be what would have been freely chosen. This is, however, an infinite regress as whatever the choice open to members of an audience it is possible to argue that some further option would have commanded real collective enthusiasm. It was therefore argued at the time, and has since become a key element in debates about the accountability of public services, that it is part of broadcasters' responsibilities to attempt to lead, in ways they think creative and constructive, aspects of public taste rather than slavishly follow what has been established to command popular support. This interpretation of 'form of popular' is difficult to legislate for because to dismiss it too quickly might imply endorsement of the interventions of the exponents of moral outrage, while acceptance has usually meant that sensitivity to the public has vacillated between institutionalized arrogance and gross surveys of audience attention and liking. To argue that the main advantage of bureaucratic organization of broadcasting is that a breathing space for a creative élite can thereby be provided assumes a rather pessimistic interpretation of 'popular'. A more positive interpretation of 'form of popular' was embarked upon uncertainly and ambivalently in the early 1930s under the aegis of the BBC and this turned upon understanding 'form' as a relationship between broadcaster and listener so that 'popular' became a mode of participation.

One of the clearest theorists of this third interpretation was Hilda Matheson, herself an important figure in the history of broadcasting as she is often credited with creating the broadcast talk as an informed, even controversial, medium of discussion and commentary in the later 1920s. She left the BBC still fighting to establish her initiatives although her subsequent book is not in any sense a polemical criticism of the corporation.[12] She is instead describing what radio can and cannot do well given the constraints of technology and taste, etc. In relation to public opinion she argues that radio is inevitably changing politics because it both personalizes issues and events (taking the ordinary listener to the heart of occasions otherwise closed to him or her) and, almost paradoxically, because the commentary provided is more objective than that available through other forums of public opinion such as newspapers. Both virtues are possible because 'the main business of explaining news [is] in the hands of a few individuals possessing the rare combination of first-class knowledge, the right voice and the right personality'.[13] Even without such luck, however, Matheson appreciates (in a way that also anticipates Mass-Observation) that the combination of 'objectivity' and personalization dramatizes public events and perhaps promotes identification which 'may help to make the modern state work'.[14] It is intriguing that in this respect she mentions the function of broadcasting in a revolutionary society such as the Soviet Union thereby pointing to a very different measure of response to that provided by a survey of listening habits.

I have noted that Matheson's solution to problems of controlling the dramatic potential of broadcasting for politics is a responsible élite who can be trusted to act on behalf of public opinion, although she recognizes that it is also essential that its members possess 'a progressive understanding of the listening audience, not as a bundle of "average listeners", but as a public of infinitely varying elements'.[15] In this and another contemporary article Matheson is groping towards an account of broadcasters' responsibilities which is quite different from the combination of moral smugness and pride in technical efficiency formulated by Reith: 'it is not enough to press for this or that formal concession, the inclusion of some particular bulletin, an extension of rights to certain programme hours. What counts is microphone effectiveness.'[16] Such a concern with effectiveness within the canons of broadcasting can become a craft pride in self-imposed standards and thereby collapse back into what can be heard as institutionalized arrogance. Maurice Gorham has told a characteristic story to illustrate the ambivalence:

> I remember attending a Programme Board – I think it must have been the Silver Jubilee programmes – where Colonel Dawney, then Controller of Programmes, mentioned that the BBC's efforts had been highly appreciated by press and public, and added, 'But of course that is not the final test. The real criterion is what we ourselves round this table think of our work.'[17]

At its most sensitive, however, the sense of responsibility to democracy transcended institutional rhetoric within the corporation and became a concern with the language of political discourse in popular democracy. As a concern with language this was often expressed as a debate over whether national broadcasting would lead to the destruction of regional dialects or whether the BBC had a responsibility to use only correct language. Although lessened in intensity, that debate has not disappeared but now no one seems to expect that the BBC has a responsibility to teach all children a standard English so that they should be able to 'communicate across the country', as Maine proposed in 1939.[18] In fact, Maine's argument that a standard way of speaking will encourage children 'to regard speech merely as a useful means of ordinary communication and not at all as a flexible instrument of thought and emotion'[19] treats standardization in a way that is analogous to criticisms of political massification. If democratic participation is to mean something more than uniform access to the vote then political expression will have to be flexible and variable. We have not yet solved what such a politics might be like but at the level of broadcasting it would certainly not take the form of equal expression for all legitimate points of view (cf. Pateman's discussion of the representation of political debate[20]).

A slightly more prosaic formulation of accountability can be developed over the extent to which the corporation felt it necessary to explain or justify its policies and practices to the electorate who ultimately paid its bills. In a striking polemical paper published in 1935, Raymond Postgate[21] attempted to tackle this version of accountability. His criticisms focused on three main headings: BBC accounts and financial returns, which were amazingly bald and an important indication of Reith's disdain for any form of parliamentary control; labour relations within the corporation, a whole series of absurd rules and prohibitions and generally oppressive practices which culminated in the scandal over Lambert and 'the Mongoose case' and were rightly condemned in Parliament; and the attitudes which informed the decision to build and design Broadcasting House. Although the last heading may seem the least important, I think Postgate is right to seize upon it. The arrogance which made the absurd decision to build a broadcasting centre in Central London, and which then chose a completely unsuitable site, and selected incompetent surveyors so that the building had to be absurdly shaped to local constraints, and incompetent architects and designers so that some studios were unusable from the beginning and the building as a whole was too small and had to spill into adjoining sites, culminating in Broadcasting House being principally an administrative centre tricked out with pretentious and ill-advised mottoes and statuary, is of a piece with the arrogance behind inadequate accounts and disastrous relations with employees. The misplaced hubris of Broadcasting House is particularly informative because apart from Postgate's isolated criticisms, the predominant contemporary response was to praise the technological complexity of the operations conducted therein and to stress the good fortune which had so mysteriously but providentially made this incomparable organization of equipment and resources available to the 'British People'.[22] This is, of course, part of a tradition in which the BBC has been the object of smug self-congratulation amongst those in British public life.[23] This combination of complacency and trust in an administrative élite is precisely the direction which paternalism was encouraged to take.

The version of accountability that the corporation would have stressed in the 1930s can, I think, be summarized under three headings: the defence of standards; raising taste; and stimulating interests. In relation to each of these the corporation saw itself as having responsibilities to 'the public' so that rather than measure existing taste it was more important to attend to how taste could and should be developed.

The interdependence of paternalism and education in most discussions of public broadcasting has been confusing because radio's ability to stimulate borrowing from public libraries, the promotion of interest in hobbies such as gardening and cooking, the rapid spread of and importance attached to schools broadcasting, and other activities (for an early study oriented to these aspects of citizenship see Jennings and Gill[24]), is not the same as didacticism. I shall therefore discuss some aspects of policies of cultural intervention more fully. Before doing so, however, it is as well to be clear about the constraints within which such policies were embarked upon. Lambert reports that an early 'Aids to Study' pamphlet included

a pictorial diagram showing the growth in membership of working class organisations – trade unions, co-ops and working men's clubs during the past half-century [but] . . . the censorial blue pencil was struck through that part of the diagram showing the figures of trade union membership. We were not allowed to print evidence of the growth of this dangerous movement.[25]

I shall discuss three aspects of cultural intervention policies in slightly greater detail as they are interestingly illuminating about the corporation's sense of responsibilities to audiences before quantifiable research techniques. The three aspects are: broadcasting to schools; BBC publications; and adult listening groups. In each case the general corporate disdain for market research was superseded by a recognition that effectiveness was dependent upon a commitment to discovering audience response, although the forms of 'discovery' differed between each area and were certainly not limited to market research. Therefore although Briggs was correct in concluding that 'the schools broadcasting department of the BBC had been forced to concern itself directly with the sociology of its listening public in the schools before the BBC as a whole examined the sociology of its listening public in their homes',[26] the sociological concern was interestingly co-operative. (I think it is relevant to note at this point that when Sir Stephen Tallents, Controller (Public Relations), came to prepare a record of BBC initiatives in various forms of audience research at the end of 1935 they were overwhelmingly based upon educational broadcasting.[27])

The BBC embarked upon a programme of broadcasting for schools from the earliest days and while the usual sources stress the dedication of those officials whose initial responsibility it was, this dedication was allied to a recognition that children could not be treated as an audience in abstract. Lecturers, scriptwriters, etc., were encouraged to spend time in schools so as to get the feel of what their listening public could reasonably manage. This sort of sensitivity allied to opposition within some parts of the teaching profession and to the necessity of persuading councils and other bodies to commit funds to the provision of reception facilities in schools, meant that the service provided had to be researched and justified in ways that were never true of general broadcasting. Indeed this was so much the case that it was found useful to conceive of schools broadcasting as a permanent experiment in which teachers co-operated with producers to develop topics and styles of teaching appropriate to the new medium. It was on this basis that schools broadcasting recruited a wider audience throughout the 1930s, that 'listening-end work' had to be combined with and could not be arbitrarily subordinated to the prejudices of the transmitting end.

If there was a degree of institutional hostility amongst local authorities and teachers' organizations to the intervention of the BBC in schools, it was as nothing to the hostility shown by other publishing corporations to BBC publishing ventures culminating in the furore over the birth of the *Listener*. As Briggs has noted, Lambert did not have the same approach to listener research as Gorham (they were respectively editors of the *Listener* and *Radio Times*), in that Lambert was less concerned with the commercial acceptability of programmes or his journal than with promoting a climate for the educated appreciation and discussion of broadcasting.[28] It is relevant that Lambert worked for the Workers' Educational Association and that he initially joined the BBC to help develop its work in adult education. Once again we are coming across this distinction between those who were concerned with relating the organization of programming to the interests of specific groups and those who wanted to respond to the tastes of the audience in general. The rationale used to justify BBC publications was that they grew out of broadcasts that were not 'really' intervention by a government body in a free market (documentary film-makers for the Empire Marketing Board and then for the GPO had to tackle very similar criticisms); and however much that might in practice be stretched it led to the sort of decision reported by Lambert who for the first five years of his editorship was not allowed to see any circulation figures for the *Listener*.[29] But however absurd this is by itself it is undoubtedly intensified when it is realized, as Lambert further reports, that through these publications the corporation had a medium for publicity, propagandistic self-aggrandisement and, above all, revenue from advertising which 'yielded from ten to twenty per cent of the Corporation's whole revenue'.[30] It was precisely because of these reasons that circulation managers engaged in sophisticated market research from the earliest days and used their knowledge of market tastes as leverage to influence programming.

The other side of corporation attitudes to accountability is brought out in the history of listening groups as part of a programme of adult education. The first programme of training for leaders of listening groups was undertaken in 1929 and by 1930–1 there were over a thousand groups in existence. Although the BBC had announced a commitment to adult education some years earlier, it took the existence of such groups and the setting-up of machinery of collaboration between the BBC and the Central

Council for Adult Education before an adequate schedule of talks and accompanying literature was announced. It is not appropriate in this context to assess the real adequacy of the provision of broadcasting time or the accompanying back-up facilities, but rather to note that this was a form of public broadcasting – with associated facilities for feedback – that is very different from monitoring set use in private houses. It is true, as Lambert notes, that a shift in attitude was represented by the change in name for such groups from discussion to listening groups,[31] but at their best Siepmann's description is reasonable: 'it is in some ways a parliament of listeners, and incidentally by far the most democratic element in our broadcast service, for here you get a really intimate relationship between the needs of listeners and the fare provided for them'.[32] In this case the initiative to provide a new framework for assessing audience needs could not be sustained (the reasons, given a shift from participation to public relations, are summarized by Briggs[33]); much of the steam had gone by 1934 and the programme was eventually overwhelmed by the war.

Two papers by Cardiff[34] and Scannell[35] have investigated programming policy in the 1930s, particularly those programmes which related to the constitution of the contemporary political agenda, and have concluded that in the course of the decade there was a significant shift away from 'participation' to 'management'. By participation I mean the commitment amongst certain corporation staff to adding the facilities of radio to the pool of knowledge of social conditions and opportunities for discussing the reasons for and possible cures of those conditions. This commitment does not mean a radical cell but people who, working through a responsibility to the microphone, were led to radical practice. In terms of the programme of talks this meant that speakers were encouraged to be informal and not to assume that a seriousness of topic required pompous delivery. The rationale for this approach was that radio was conceived as a bridge of accessibility over which the private listener was introduced to the public world of citizenship; educational certainly, but education committed to enhancing the individual's ability to participate rather than just receive wisdom. An approach that was enhanced through a realization that neutrality did not mean an uncontroversial voice governing every programme, but rather that neutrality means encouraging controversial contrasts between programmes – letting listeners state their own synoptic views through a series of programmes.

This style of broadcasting shifted in the course of the decade to what can be called a management approach. Cardiff and Scannell set out various reasons for this and various ways in which the change was effected but in general it can be summarized as the development of an institutional voice speaking on behalf of the public; so that instead of linking the multitude of publics Matheson conceived, the corporation developed a national stance incorporating a more abstract sense of the public at large. In practice this approach involved a retreat from direct experience: both a withdrawal from a more documentary style of social reporting and a relegation of working-class voices to the category of quaint local colour. This process was matched by a trend towards a self-consciously serious mode of address: expert speakers were not chivvied to make their material accessible but were allowed to dictate the terms of address. 'The dismantling of Talks signified the end of experiment, of *possibilities*, and the decisive arrival of corporate thinking, of rationalisation, of planning and policy.'[36] The process through which the corporation came to see itself in practice as well as ultimate function as speaking on behalf of the nation was not therefore just a matter of articulation but was also organization – both within the corporation and over the distribution of resources between London and the regions. And finally the management style was also displayed through the increasing preponderance of introducers, chairmen, etc., who through scene-setting appropriated the voice of rationality to hold the ring for controversy.

3

The initial pressure within the corporation for some form of research into audiences was particularly associated with Val Gielgud and the Drama Department. As he said in a memo on 12 May 1930, he and others in his department 'are more and more exercised in mind concerning our ignorance of the true reactions of our programme public'.[37] He goes on to point out pungently that there is no point in remembering 'the cabman's wife in Wigan' (a common contemporary corporation point of social reference), if the only access to her views is what a member of the Programme Board thinks they might be. Gielgud also makes the point in his memo that correspondence either to the corporation or in the national press could not be relied upon as a barometer of response. Although often acknowledged, the practice of producers, both throughout the 1930s and in the post-war years, has been to welcome correspondence as a response as substantive as they can lay their hands on. A further interesting feature of this initial memo is that it attempts to deal with what were to be common objections to audience research: autonomy, and method. The first heading refers to the public's rights (or even ability) to say what has been successful in broadcasting terms: 'I do not suggest that popular opinion is or should be the last word as to whether our programmes are or are not good and should not be continued in any particular form.' This common recognition of a necessary if at least a limited autonomy for broadcasters was sustained throughout the decade as was the concern with method. Briefly, no one was at all clear how to proceed, what to ask about or what could either legitimately or economically be discovered. Therefore discussion was riddled with prejudices, such as the remarks that come in a generally favourable comment by Cecil Graves on Gielgud's memo: 'I entirely agree that any form of questionnaire is not worth while. It is against the psychology of the British public to answer questionnaires. They are always put in the wastepaper basket.'[38]

The terms of the debate about listener research (LR), as audience research was known in the BBC in the 1930s, were set by the granted inadequacy of procedural knowledge; a recognition that broadcasting stations overseas did seem to be able to benefit from forms of LR and that we should be able to learn from their experience; worries about cost, which recurred throughout the decade; a persistent distrust of statistics particularly as to their suitability for assessing what were felt to be aesthetic responses; a desire for reliability, which clashed with a commonly voiced desire for impressionism – it was often said that a skilled sympathetic investigator talking to a few intelligent and responsive members of a community could discover more than a more widespread enquiry; a lack of knowledge in the intellectual community about methods of social research so that sympathetic dons were eagerly courted but were not usually very helpful or appropriate; and a deep uncertainty over whether LR should properly be concerned with knowledge of the listening publics in general and/or with knowledge of more specific responses to programmes or types of programme. There was, for example, a persistent uncertainty within the corporation whether research was restricted to studying audience habits or could discover their tastes.[39]

The most persistent sponsor for some form of research was Gielgud and the Drama Department, although he was enthusiastically supported by Matheson and then Siepmann from Talks, suggesting the clear association between commercial success and good broadcasting which was so strongly resisted. Indeed Gielgud, having complained that 'nothing handicaps me more than the non-possession of anything in the nature of a thermometer which would correspond in the theatre to the acid-test of box office returns',[40] was led to appeal on the air on 8 and 9 March 1934 for listeners to write and say 'candidly' what they 'feel about the whole question' of their 'real requirements'. Although these appeals were surprisingly successful in eliciting correspondence from listeners, Gielgud could not, of course, treat these letters as more reliably representative than unsolicited correspondence and the experiment was not repeated.

The decision actually to embark on a form of LR did not stem from this intermittent pressure group within the corporation – although members of this pressure group did constitute the initial Listener Research Committee and support the first research proposals – but rather grew out of other administrative changes. These were the flurry of promotions, resignations and repostings that occurred in 1935 which have been described by Briggs,[41] and particularly as they relate to the earlier break-up of the Talks Department. Briggs relates the reshuffle in 1935 to the administrative restructuring in 1933 which formulated 'a crucial distinction' between administration and programming.

The significance of this is that the clarification of problems of management implied in the restructuring opened a space for the effective management of the public images of the corporation. This became clear when Sir Stephen Tallents was appointed Controller (Public Relations) in the summer of 1935[42] on a par with three other controllers (Programmes, Engineering and Administration). It seems to have been clear to Tallents that one of his duties would be to resolve the issue of LR and a memo from Major Atkinson (a long-term members of the internal pressure group for LR) on 2 August 1935 was dismissed over the next fortnight by an agreement to leave the matter for Tallents's arrival. Press comment was also clear; for example, in the *Manchester Guardian* of 9 July 1935 Tallents's appointment was announced with the comment that 'he will aim at bringing the public and the broadcasting authorities into closer touch. He will ask the listener what he wants and reflect his views.' The innovation of LR was therefore embarked upon as part of the extension and formalization of the management of public relations by the corporation.

It is not only the function of the position Tallents was employed to fill that is important but also the interests and record of the man himself. Briefly, Sir Stephen Tallents was a member of the traditional British establishment through family, education, military service and career, etc., who had become convinced of the need to use the facilities of contemporary communication to broadcast the virtues of British institutional structures. He is perhaps best remembered for his sponsorship of the documentary film team assembled under the aegis of John Grierson first at the Empire Marketing Board and then at the GPO. His concern with dramatizing issues for public concern and moulding public opinion was not confined to film, however, but extended to more conventional forms of public relations. A week before his appointment to the BBC was announced he had been the first public servant to be awarded the cup of the Publicity Club for London for his services to advertising. Although in the end mistaken, the *World's Press News* shortly after his appointment was encouraged to speculate that he would launch the BBC into advertising in order 'to make the public more fully appreciative of the good points of the broadcasting service' (11 July 1935).

The climate of strong links between advertising, public relations and LR was not confined to the inception of LR, however, but persisted until the direct determination of policy by the state during the war. I can point to three aspects of these links which are relevant. The first is that organizational alliances were quickly formed with the research sections of other public corporations and advertising agencies. For example, Fox, a market researcher, was co-opted on to the BBC's LR Committee from the research section at the GPO and Pat Ryan, Tallents's second-in-command at the BBC, had previously been publicity manager for the Gas, Light and Coke Company; it is also relevant that Silvey himself was recruited from the London Press Exchange and there was a characteristic scheme in 1938 to exchange information between the BBC's Listener Research Department, the London Press Exchange and the Walter Thompson Agency.[43] It is also relevant that Tallents should, for example, think it reasonable to approach the Radio Manufacturers' Association and the Radio Valve Manufacturers' Association in June 1937 for supplementary finance to help the research effort. Given the history of the advice and co-operation the BBC had received from academics it is not surprising that in the second half of the decade there is a turn to commercial research models but the latter certainly encouraged the second aspect of these links – what I shall call the guiding metaphors of the research process. To set out all the instances of this aspect would take us into too fine a degree of detail, but an appropriate illustration is provided by the draft of an early talk by Silvey.[44] In clarifying the purposes and aims of LR he utilizes an analogy between the BBC and a department store with listeners being seen as equivalent to customers, so that the purpose of market research is effectively to anticipate customer demand. It is true that Briggs suggests that Reith, still Director General, would not have been pleased with such imagery, but there is no record of any reproof and the work of the LR was increasingly being endorsed at all levels – even by personal memos from the Director General himself.[45] Thirdly and most importantly the uncertainties from the previous years over what sort of research the BBC should or could undertake were resolved by Tallents and Silvey in favour of research projects concerned with market conditions rather than particular programmes' effectiveness and/ or success; that is, the world to which broadcasting should adapt rather than policies or aims of broadcasting which research should seek to develop.

I do not think it is necessary to set out the steps by which Tallents and a small group of enthusiastic collaborators first exploited the General Advisory Council's endorsement to set up a Listener Research Committee and then a few months later to employ the BBC's first professional researcher (the period from his appointment is in any case very adequately covered in Silvey's book[46] and there is also Pegg's admirable survey of the several types of research undertaken in 1936–9[47]). There are, however, two further aspects to the style of research which the corporation embarked upon which are relevant to my general interpretation of the research effort as public relations and audience management. The first is that the new medium of television, partly I suppose because it was not associated with the more traditional corporation mandarinate and partly because the new facility was committed to a policy of entertainment more fully than ever radio had been, collaborated with the initial research projects and was strongly associated with the research effort right up to the outbreak of war. It is interesting in this context that the television planners were prepared in 1938 to encourage a research study to investigate whether viewers found scheduling and sequencing useful, whereas such techniques were anathema to Reith and only came into standard broadcasting after the war. Secondly, the general concern with habits and interests of listeners combined with a distrust of elaborate statistical techniques (as well as an inability to afford them) meant that Silvey's efforts were often directed to barometers of taste that were closely analogous to Mass-Observation's panels of respondents: a type of research that culminated in Silvey's scheme for a continuous survey in wartime which was particularly similar to the Mass-Observation research framework. A connection that nearly received organizational blessing occurred in February 1938 when Silvey proposed Tom Harrisson and the Bolton team to conduct some research for the corporation but this seems to have been squashed by the North Region Public Relations Office.

I think it is too easy to organize those initially involved with Listener

Research and their efforts into a consistent narrative. Not only was the relevance of research accepted only cautiously and grudgingly, but those concerned were not consistent about what they hoped to do or what, indeed, could be accomplished, and there were certainly some bizarre expectations – given the methodology and resources available – of what research could accomplish. For example, the Controller (Programmes) asked his second-in-command to write to Silvey on 31 August 1937 to see if the latter could discover material relevant to planning 'the most suitable time for Saturday Night Music Hall'. But the legitimacy of research was gradually accomplished culminating in the clear recognition of the utility of research in planning an effective broadcasting service in wartime conditions. Under the pressure of very pressing needs to manage the terms of public interests and participation, research came directly into its own. On 20 September 1939 the DPP issued a memo referring to 'the invaluable assistance of Silvey's Listener Research' in 'evolving a more or less satisfactory service for listeners' in wartime.[48] After the pressures of the next six years, the post-war service reopened buttressed by confident and unquestioned interdependence with audience research.

Describing the corporation as becoming more responsible for the management of political debate does not mean that in any simple sense policies become more conservative. Reithianism had always leant heavily towards the status quo and the bureaucratic neutrality of the corporation had never meant that a responsibility to provide a platform for the full spectrum of political debate had been recognized. But there is a crucial difference between inspiring and helping to bring into being new channels of political participation and a self-conscious respectability which directs a range of responsible opinions at a listening public. The general move away from creative responses to sectional interests towards an attempt to cater to the general audience as a mass of individual listeners can be seen in retrospect as exemplifying certain forms of democratic participation. It is illuminating in this respect to realize that the policy of the Arts Council has been to increase the potential audiences for artworks of various kinds rather than to increase the number of people making art.[49] Sociological research which quantifies responses within the general audience is consistent with this representation of democratic participation but is not part of understanding alternatives.

4

In conclusion it is reasonable to ask what of research initiatives in relation to other mass media? The press is interestingly different in that certain statistics, particularly circulation figures, at least as they contributed to gross income, had been crucial for a paper's survival from earliest years. It is also relevant that the reliance upon advertising, which developed in the middle of the last century, had initiated a concern with statistics of comparative success that really took off in the circulation wars of the 1930s. But in a major sense the traditional economic competitiveness of newspapers meant that for informed commentary the problem was not the accountability of a cultural monopoly so much as the responsibility of a democratic institution. Responsibility was used in two senses, first a responsibility not to pander to readers' grosser tastes by trivializing and sensationalizing public events, and secondly a responsibility to protect a certain conception of political citizenship – as a PEP report put it in 1936, 'the capacity of British journalism to pull its weight in the coming struggle against "totalitarian" tendencies'.[50] In relation to both senses there was a persistent concern over whether the management of the press (owners, editors and journalists) could be trusted to uphold its responsibilities, a concern which could not really be helped by statistics on audience taste.

In fact the problem of bias in relation to the press came to be posed very clearly in the 1930s. A weak and vacillating leadership on the social democratic left became more obsessed with defending the reasonableness of its gradualism than with developing the militancy of rank and file organizations shown in struggles by the unemployed and underpaid to resist local exploitation. As well as the failure to organize a mass movement three other features of the press were used as evidence of anti-democratic tendencies: increasing concentration of ownership in the hands of individuals and groups opposed to working-class interests; a trend towards sensationalism in style and content amongst the popular papers including the *Daily Herald* as the circulation war intensified in the course of the decade (see the appendix to the report of the post-war Royal Commission on the Press[51]); and the success of the Nazis in capturing political power through, as they boasted, intensive use of propaganda to distort their electoral base and deny power to well-organized socialist parties. It was in this context that a PEP report came to formulate a programme for research only taken up thirty years later: a concern with the agenda-setting function of the press.[52] It was argued that the ability to formulate an agenda for public opinion came through three powers: of initiative; of exclusion; and of presentation. Unfortunately the best that the PEP reports could come up with in response is the sort of solution formally embodied in the BBC's monopoly – a combination of legal constraints with 'exacting professional standards which will give a higher status and greater independence to journalists'.[53] A corporate solution undoubtedly does give greater independence to media professionals but that is not necessarily the same thing as opening public opinion to public participation.[54]

In relation to the cinema the status of research in these years is even more confused. I have noted that films were always an occasion for moral disquiet and there are research reports detailing potential hazards such as that published by the National Council on Public Morals in 1917. This type of content analysis similar to that used in studies of the press bias persisted alongside straightforward commercial concerns with audience size and composition, etc. There was even in Britain an inter-war article on the sociology of the cinema, although its author, A. Hauser, unfortunately begins from a presupposition about the massification of the audience: 'Nothing but that they pour into the cinema unites them, and they pour out again and re-dissolve, just as shapeless as when they were stuffed into them.'[55] Given this starting point it is unsurprising that Hauser decided that the diversity of response is uncharacterizable and that he remained content with pompous generalizations about art forms and popular taste. The lack of a sociological contribution to the conceptualization of the meaning of entertainment in different life-styles meant that approaches to audiences were contained within commercial considerations. Rowson's papers on social research and films make elevated claims – 'my paper today is a pioneer effort in the scientific investigation of the social and economic problems of the people's amusements and recreations, and perhaps also in the still wider field of the economics and philosophy of leisure'[56] – but despite this they remain couched within a series of questions which, as he admits, are essentially based on 'trade concerns'.[57]

The commercial problematic of social research and films, outside the outraged efforts of moral reformers, does not contradict my general thesis about the contribution of audience research to the forms of massification in politics and entertainment. Tom Harrisson, of Mass-Observation, has put the point with characteristically candid naïveté: 'one of the reasons social research has come into being is because, under modern economic and administrative conditions, it is difficult for any "high-ups" to keep in close or sympathetic touch with "low-downs"'.[58] Citizenship in mass politics and consumerism are equally democratic and equally effective as ways of stabilizing potentially disorderly collectivities.

It is intriguing that one of the most radical attempts to rethink the position of audience members, in conditions of mass distribution, in the production of popular entertainment came from outside the social sciences and in relation to the massification of publishing. I do not want to discuss the intricacies of F. R. Leavis's own position or his influence on other intellectual commentators, but, recognizing the uniqueness of her book, I will discuss some aspects of Queenie Leavis's research on popular audiences.[59] The purpose of Mrs Leavis's work was to show that 'the impartial assessor . . . can hardly avoid concluding that for the first time in the history of our literature the living forms of the novel have been side-tracked in favour of the *faux-bon*'.[60] The reason being that communities have been replaced by cities 'composed of units whose main contact with each other outside the home is in the dance-hall, the cinema, the theatre, social but not co-operative amusements'.[61] This project meant that Mrs Leavis could never be content with critically reading popular fiction, however closely, nor with interviewing a sample of readers, because they were not competent to discuss what they could not experience. She had therefore to examine instead the mechanism of literary production for the contemporary market-place to discover why there had been a transformation of '*the relation . . . that exists between novelist and reader*' (emphasis added).[62] It is not necessary in this chapter to set out the gross inadequacies of Mrs Leavis's methodological practices such as her extraordinarily cavalier inference of causal relationships from minuscule evidence. What is interesting is that her concern with relations of literary production was based upon an assumption of the existence of several publics so that meaning and significance could not be exegetically inferred from the text alone. (It is, of course, a separate although fascinating question why this conclusion did not figure on the subsequent agenda of either those associated with *Scrutiny* or students of textual criticism in general.)

I have explored some aspects of the process through which the audiences for national mass media became consumers with the consequence that research could be seen as a version of democratic participation. The BBC is a particularly intriguing opportunity because the rhetoric of public service makes the relevance of social research to effective accountability difficult simply to endorse or reject. The kernel of this chapter is the argument that the mobilization of public opinion through the language of social research in post-war democracies has emphasized choice rather than participation. If democracy means some effective degree of control over the circumstances of life by the person in the street then mass democracy has been illusory. I have used the example of public broadcasting to argue that one meaning of 'public' in this context – that is, responsible or accountable to the audience – is analogously illusory in its reliance upon audience research as measures of choice. Alternatives which work through the mobilization of specialist constituencies collaborating with producers and representatives are possible political forms for popular democracy; although the forms of public discourse which will then develop are possibly less likely to be rational and/or respectable in terms of managerial concerns with leading public opinion.

Notes

1 C. Seymour-Ure, 'The press and the party system between the wars', in G. Peele and C. Cooke (eds), *The Politics of Reappraisal 1918–1939*, London, Macmillan, 1976.

2 L. Lowenthal, *Literature, Popular Culture and Society*, Englewood Cliffs, NJ, Prentice Hall, 1961, chapter 3.

3 P. A. Dunae, 'Penny dreadfuls: late nineteenth-century boys' literature and crime', *Victorian Studies*, 22, 2 (1979).

4 L. A. Zurcher Jr and R. G. Kirkpatrick, *Citizens for Decency*, Austin, University of Texas Press, 1976.

5 P. Bailey, *Leisure and Class in Victorian England*, London, Routledge & Kegan Paul, 1979.

6 For example, see M. G. Cantor, *Prime-Time Television*, London, Sage, 1980, chapter 4, and S. Hood, *On Television*, London, Pluto, 1980, chapter 2.

7 R. Silvey, *Who's Listening: The Story of BBC Audience Research*, London, Allen & Unwin, 1974, pp. 62, 65.

8 M. Pegg, *Broadcasting and Society 1918–39*, London, Croom Helm, 1983, p. 98.

9 P. F. Lazarsfeld, *Radio and the Printed Page*, New York, Duell, Sloane & Pearce, 1940.

10 See M. Gorham, *Broadcasting and Television since 1900*, London, Dakers, 1952,

chapter 6, and R. H. Coase, *British Broadcasting: a Study in Monopoly*, London, Longman, 1950, chapters 4 and 5.

11 R. S. Lambert, *Ariel and All his Quality*, London, Gollancz, 1940, p. 150.

12 H. Matheson, *Broadcasting*, London, Thornton Butterworth, 1932.

13 ibid., p. 93.

14 ibid., p. 97.

15 H. Matheson, 'Listener research in broadcasting', *Sociological Review*, 27 (1935), 410.

16 H. Matheson, 'Politics and broadcasting', *Political Quarterly*, 5 (1934), 193; cf. J. C. W. Reith, *Into the Wind*, London, Hodder & Stoughton, 1949.

17 M. Gorham, *Sound and Fury*, London, Marshall, 1948, p. 52.

18 B. S. Maine, *The BBC and its Audience*, London, Nelson, 1939, chapter 4.

19 ibid., p. 77.

20 T. Pateman, *Television and the February 1974 General Election*, BFI Television Monograph no. 3, London, British Film Institute, 1974.

21 R. Postgate, *What to Do with the BBC*, London, Hogarth, 1935.

22 See, for example, H. Brittain, *The ABC of the BBC*, London, Pearson, 1932, chapter 2, and W. Goatman, *By-Ways of the BBC*, London, King & Staples, 1938, passim.

23 Coase, op. cit., especially chapters 6 and 7.

24 H. Jennings and W. Gill, *Broadcasting in Everyday Life*, London, BBC, 1939.

25 Lambert, op. cit., p. 53.

26 A. Briggs, *The History of Broadcasting in the United Kingdom*, vol. II, *The Golden Age of Wireless*, London, Oxford University Press, 1965, p. 190.

27 BBC Written Archive Centre, Caversham, Reading (hereafter cited as BBC WAC), Listener Research File (hereafter cited as LR file), 20 December 1935.

28 Briggs, op. cit., p. 292.

29 Lambert, op. cit., p. 108.

30 ibid., p. 167.

31 ibid., p. 74.

32 Quoted in S. A. Moseley, *Broadcasting in my Time*, London, Rich & Cowan, 1935, p. 140.

33 Briggs, op. cit., pp. 218–20.

34 D. Cardiff, 'The serious and the popular: aspects of the evolution of style in the radio talk 1928–1939', *Media, Culture and Society*, 2, 1 (1980).

35 P. Scannell, 'Broadcasting and the politics of unemployment 1930–35', *Media, Culture and Society*, 2, 1 (1980).

36 ibid., p. 27.

37 BBC WAC, LR file, memo from Gielgud, 12 May 1930.

38 BBC WAC, LR file, memo from Graves, 15 May 1930.

39 Pegg, op. cit., pp. 111, 122–3.

40 BBC WAC, LR file, memo from Gielgud, 18 November 1933.

41 Briggs, op. cit., pp. 442–9.

42 ibid.; although on p. 264 Briggs makes it clear that the appointment was in 1935, on p. 448 he implies that it was a year later, 1936.

43 BBC WAC, R34/1/16.3.38.

44 BBC WAC, LR file, 13 October 1937.

45 BBC WAC, LR file, 8 July 1937.

46 Silvey, op. cit.

47 Pegg, op. cit., chapter 5.

48 See also BBC WAC, R34/416/1 (19 September 1939).

49 I am grateful to Nigel Watson for drawing my attention to this parallel.

50 PEP, *The Freedom of the Press*, PEP report no. 82 (22 September 1936), p. 3; hereafter cited as PEP report 82.

51 *Report of the Royal Commission on the Press*, Cmnd 7700, London, HMSO, 1947–9.

52 PEP, *The Press and the Public*, PEP report no. 118 (8 March 1938), especially pp. 10–13.

53 PEP report 82, p. 11.

54 C. Heller, *Broadcasting and Accountability*, BFI Television Monograph no. 7, London, British Film Institute, 1978.

55 A. Hauser, 'Notes on the sociology of the film', *Life and Letters Today*, 1938, p. 80.

56 S. Rowson, 'A statistical survey of the cinema industry in Great Britain in 1934', *Journal of the Royal Statistical Society*, 99 (1936), 67.

57 ibid., and see also in particular S. Rowson, *The Social and Political Aspects of Films*, London, British Kinematograph Society, 1939.

58 T. Harrisson, 'Social Research and the film', *Documentary Newsletter*, 1, 11 (1940), 10.

59 Q. D. Leavis, *Fiction and the Reading Public*, London, Chatto & Windus, 1932.

60 ibid., p. 39.

61 ibid., p. 37.

62 ibid., p. 41.

13

The making of the British record industry 1920–64

Simon Frith

Introduction

In 1956, Edward Lewis, chairman and managing director of the Decca Record Company, distributed with the accounts at his shareholders' AGM his own, privately published, autobiography. It was titled, somewhat obscurely, *No C.I.C.*, and its purpose was to attack the Capital Issues Committee, which had just been set up to supervise capital raising projects involving more than £10,000 or any foreign currency. Lewis's argument was that Decca had flourished because of his special ability to raise money quickly, riskily, and without bureaucratic interference. His story ended with a stirring account of free enterprise: investment, by definition a venturous business, must be rewarded. Lewis presented himself as a buccaneering entrepreneur (the Freddie Laker of his day), up against the stifling tentacles of government meddling and its only beneficiaries, 'the big companies'.

At the time Lewis was writing, Decca and EMI shared equally more than 80 per cent of the British record market. In 1956 Decca itself declared a provisional profit of £1,780,000 on its production of 27 million records and its ownership of the Decca Gramophone Company (which made gramophones), Selecta (Britain's largest wholesale distributor of records and domestic electrical goods), subsidiary record labels like Vogue, and various radar, navigation and precision instrument companies. Decca owned London Records in the USA, companies in Canada, Germany and Italy, and had a turnover of £4.5 million in exports alone. It must have been unclear to his shareholders what 'big companies' Lewis was worried about.

I find Lewis's comments fascinating for a different reason. Rock historians have always interpreted the business history of pop music in terms of the conflict between the major record companies and the independents. The assumption is that musical innovations always come from outside the majors. Independent companies are the outlet for the expression of new ideas and interests, and only when such ideas have been shown to be popular have the major companies used their financial advantages to take them over, to turn them into new, 'safe' products. Innovation in the oligopolistic record industry is only possible because technological changes open gaps in existing market control, and if, in the long run, competition means creativity (the more the sources of capital, the more chance of musical progress), in the short run the music business is intensely conservative, more concerned with avoiding loss than risking profit, with confirming tastes than disrupting them. Records are made according to what the public is known to want already.

According to this argument (which has been applied most systematically to the history of the American popular music industry) the only people who notice or encourage changing musical demands are entrepreneurs operating outside the existing music business structure.[1] Such independents can only make money by creating or servicing new markets and they are, therefore, by necessity, the only real risk-takers, the only genuine cultural entrepreneurs. As their risks pay off, they are joined by other petty businessmen who are equally able to compete in this small-scale scene, and there is, for a moment, a burst of musical creativity, industrial innovation and market competition. Eventually, though, returns are sufficient to attract the big companies and the new practices are routinized, the independents bought out, absorbed, driven off by unfair competition – hence the rise and fall of rock'n'roll in the mid-1950s, progressive rock in the late 1960s, punk at the end of the 1970s.

The suggestion implicit in this, the standard account of pop history, is that musical creativity is sapped not by profit seeking but by *big* profit seeking, by the concentration into too few hands of the means of musical expression. The problem is not art versus commerce, but big business versus small business, and the heroes of this version of musical change are the independent entrepreneurs (rather than the musicians themselves): small-label bosses like Sam Phillips of Sun, Berry Gordy of Tamla Motown, Chris Blackwell of Island, maverick publicists and packagers like Malcolm McLaren of the Sex Pistols.

What is fascinating about Lewis's autobiography, then, is that even in 1956 the boss of Decca (one of the obvious 'villains' of British rock history) saw himself as an independent, as a risk-taking, innovating pirate. The reason for this inappropriate self-image lies, I believe, in the fact that Lewis was not a music business person who had become a successful capitalist but was, rather, a successful capitalist (a stockbroker) who had become involved in the music business. This informs his understanding of such terms as 'risk', and his autobiography, read carefully, is an enlightening account of the problems and possibilities of music as commodity. It is, further, a way into an explanation of *why* the British music industry works the way it does.

Rock commentators take the 'blandness' of pre-Beatles British pop for granted and 'show biz' has been a routine term of rock critical abuse for years, but as the history of pop since the Beatles makes clear, the relationship between commercial intention and cultural effect is not straightforward.[2] The questions remain: how was pop music constructed as a mass medium in Britain and what is the impact on society of a record industry? The story of this industry in Britain has never been examined critically and my own research has so far been tentative and patchy.[3] I think it is possible, nevertheless, to make some general points and that is the purpose of this chapter.

Boom

Decca itself began as Barnett Samuel & Sons, musical instrument makers who were established in 1832 and made the first-ever portable gramophone, the Decca Dulcephone, in 1914. Edward Lewis became involved in the company in 1928: he was the broker who handled the stock flotation when the Samuel family sold out and the 'Decca Gramophone Company' went public. In assessing the prospects of the new company Lewis noted the leaping shares of other record-player makers (the price of a share in the Columbia Graphophone Company, for example, rose from 11 shillings in 1923 to a peak of nearly £20 in 1929), but he also realized that 'a company manufacturing gramophones but not records was rather like one making razors but not the consumable blades'.

Lewis entered the music business at the moment when its consumer logic was changing: if people had previously bought records in order to have something to play on their gramophones, they were now buying gramophones in order to play records. The 1920s had been a boom time for all companies involved in music making and selling but almost all the numerous British companies issuing discs (Edison Bell, Vocalion, Crystalate, Metropole, Dominion, Duophone, Filmophone, Broadcast, Homochord, Radio, Sterno, etc.) had got into the business through involvement in the new electrical hardware. They were companies based on gramophone or gramophone parts manufacture; their profits were dependent on innovations in the techniques and quality of sound reproduction generally; their record-making activities were an aspect of the marketing of record players and radios. Even the record consumer magazines, *The Gramophone* and the *Gramophone Critic*, carried columns on 'Your Gramophone Shares'.

The British record industry began, then, as part of the electrical goods industry; it was not under the personal or financial control of the established pop musical world of song publishers, theatre owners, agents, promoters and performers. At the same time (and for the same reasons) its musical policies, the decisions about what songs and performers to record were *entirely* dependent on the judgements and tastes of the 'live' music entrepreneurs: record companies competed to issue records by successful stage performers, and versions of the latest show hit or dancefloor craze appeared on every label. The companies were not interested in promoting new numbers or performers, in initiating new styles. In these boom years pop seems to have been regarded as necessary, like advertising, but not significant. For most companies the important part of the catalogue was the 'serious' music. The assumption (articulated in the pages of *The Gramophone*) was that the long-run success of the gramophone industry (once the novelty had worn off) would depend on people building up libraries of *permanently* valuable classical music.

Slump

The year 1928 was the last of the record sales boom. As the recession bit into people's leisure income, as consumer habits changed with the spread of radio and the development of talking pictures, so the record industry found itself in desperate trouble, trouble charted most graphically by the *Talking Machine News*, the trade paper for gramophone and record retailers (records were then sold exclusively in electrical goods shops, distributed by the electrical goods distributors). From 1930 *Talking Machine News* was obsessed by retailer morale and sales gimmicks – like the 'film/record tie-up', precursor of what was to come in the 1970s.

The music business slump was, paradoxically, Lewis's music business opportunity. He began looking for a record company to buy just as the record companies themselves were looking urgently for capital support. In 1929 Lewis put together his own holding company to buy Duophone and then used Duophone to take over Decca. Decca shares did not reach their 1929 value again until 1945 and for at least the first three years of Lewis's management the books only balanced because there were still enough profits in making record players to cover the losses on records. Nevertheless, it was in the slump years that the British record industry took on its familiar shape: as the small companies went to the wall, the big companies built up an irreversible monopoly.

In 1932 the Columbia Graphophone Company and the Gramophone Company merged to form EMI (which thus ran the HMV, Columbia, Parlophone, Regal-Zonophone and MGM labels). Both companies had been operating since 1898 and both had extensive American interests. Columbia had begun as a branch of the American Columbia Gramophone Manufacturing Company and had retained these links even after it came under British control, in 1922. The Gramophone Company was linked to the RCA-Victor Talking Machine organization (and Louis Stirling, who became the managing director of EMI, had also built up a large shareholding in Chappells, Britain's largest music publishing and concert promoting company).

Stirling's EMI set-up became a model for Lewis at Decca. The task was to cover every base in terms of both musical and commercial activity. In 1934 Decca bought the UK rights to the German Polydor label simply in order to have a classical list. In 1937 Decca took over Crystalate, a company which made cheap records for Woolworths, simply in order to have its own plastics manufacturer (and recording studio complex). But Lewis's own first priority was an American connection and in 1932 he bought the British Brunswick business for £15,000. This subsidiary of the American Brunswick Radio Corporation had become successful in Britain in the 1920s as a deliberately all-American label, issuing only American recordings, but by the end of the decade its parent company was in difficulty, being taken over firstly by Warner Brothers and then by the American Record Corporation (ARC), the subsidiary of another Hollywood company, Consolidated Films. In his negotiations with ARC, Lewis was quick to appreciate the possibilities for expansion opened up by the collapse of record sales in the USA itself (100 million records sold in 1928, 10 million records sold in 1933) and in 1934 he bought Warner Brothers' New York record manufacturing and pressing plant and set up his own American company, Decca, Inc.

The international deals of both EMI and Decca were necessary for their survival – in Britain record sales reached their lowest level in 1937–8 – and reflected too their shared interests. Decca gave EMI the right to press and distribute Decca records in Asia, Australia and South America in return for Decca's right to press and distribute Parlophone and Odeon records in the USA and Canada, and in 1937 Decca and EMI jointly took over the record business of the British Homophone Company. By then the two companies manufactured virtually all the records issued in the UK (the only independent record-making plant available to the remaining small labels was owned by the Oriole Record Company, which was founded by D. M. Levy in 1931 and survived until its take-over by CBS in 1964). In 1940 the power of the EMI/Decca duopoly was finally consolidated when Decca took over Selecta Gramophones (the leading national record distributor) and Dowes of Manchester (the leading northern record wholesaler). The only other large distribution organization, the Jackson Talking Machine Company, was already a subsidiary of EMI, and from then on the record companies did their own distribution – there were no significant independent operators.

Competition

The slump in record sales ended with the outbreak of war, but by then the structure of the British record industry was fixed: EMI and Decca controlled the infrastructure of the music business, the processes in which records were pressed, packaged and distributed, and they were, at the same time, tied into an Anglo-American control of the international music market.

In his autobiography, Edward Lewis attributes Decca's extraordinary growth in the 1930s to his skill in bringing off a succession of take-overs and mergers. For most of the decade the company was, in fact, unprofitable and its expansion was, thus, completely dependent on loans – such 'risks' (whether taken by bankers or fellow electrical goods entrepreneurs like Jules Thorn) were what Lewis saw as the essence of creative capitalism. But obviously these financiers supported Lewis because of their positive assessment of Decca's commercial strategy, and Lewis's real achievement in the 1930s was to set the new rules of record market competition which ensured Decca's eventual victory.

These were not simply matters of commercial practice. In the 1920s, when records hardly differed as musical products from company to company, price competition had been the obvious way to an increased market share. The assumption was that consumers would, by and large, go for the cheapest version of the latest hit song (which was why the Woolworths/Crystalate deal was so successful) and Lewis's immediate move when he took over Decca was to reduce its record prices. But in the recession, in the competition for a declining market, when the problem was to get people to buy records at all, the limits of the equation of record market choice and economic rationality became obvious. Decca's sales tactics changed accordingly.

Firstly (and partly to keep the goodwill of the retailers, who made less money from cheaper records) Lewis began an unprecedentedly aggressive sales campaign – pushing Decca releases in front page displays in the popular press, organizing elaborate shop window shows. Secondly (and as a direct effect of such campaigns) Lewis became aware that the crucial asset of a record company was not the hit song but the big star, the performer who had large sales on every record released. The shift in emphasis was obvious in the *Talking Machine News*: in the 1920s record company advertisements were ·organized around song titles or musical styles; in the 1930s the selling point became the artist. And it was not enough just to invest in existing big names, to sign up the already popular live performers, it was also necessary to work on artists as *recording* stars, and in this work record company bosses like Lewis could take advantage of their independence of the usual music business assumptions. Recording stars could be created from scratch, and one clear effect of the record companies' 1930s policies was the increasingly direct relationship posited between the record producers and consumers. 'Public taste' was no longer mediated through publishers or promoters but, rather, through the retailers – the only other people in the music business for whom Lewis had any concern.

Decca's 1930s commercial policy – the initial price cutting followed by aggressive selling and the making of recording stars – was extremely costly. It meant heavy expenditure at a time of falling revenue, it involved high risks as the advance costs of record making and selling rose, and only companies with real (EMI) or paper (Decca) capital survived the resulting competition. In the long run, though, the returns on record selling were raised equally – successful records sold far more copies than previously. In 1931 Decca signed Jack Hylton for an unprecedented advance which included 40,000 shares in the company, but his success – an early release sold 300,000 copies – enabled the company to raise its record prices – Hylton's guaranteed sales freed Decca from the constraints of price competition. Similarly, when Lewis started Decca, Inc. his first move was to hire Jack Kapp from Brunswick as recording manager. Kapp brought Bing Crosby with him and Crosby's sales made certain Decca's US survival.

Radio

Both Hylton's and Crosby's stardom derived from their popularity as radio performers, and radio, the most important musical medium in the 1930s, was central to the new processes of record selling and star making. It was radio, for example, that made American performers (as well as American songs and styles) part of British pop, and it was radio that gave record companies a means to develop their own stars – Lewis describes how 'six months' hard work' on Radio Paris's 'Sunday Decca Hour' ensured huge record sales for

Arthur Tracey. This was not just a matter of the record companies exploiting radio. Radio stations were equally interested in records – as a form of cheap programming, as a source of radio performers. Radio producers no longer had to recruit artists from stage shows or dance halls – the radio/record tie-up was an alternative path to musical success; the traditional powers of pop, publishers and promoters, could be by-passed altogether.

Perhaps the most symptomatic figure in the radio/record relationship in Britain was the BBC presenter ('the first disc jockey'), Christopher Stone. Stone became interested in the record business in 1923 when his brother-in-law, Compton Mackenzie, launched the *Gramophone* (with the assistance of Walter Yeomans, head of the HMV Education Department). The *Gramophone* was designed to 'encourage the recording companies to build up for generations to come a great library of good music', and Stone ran the magazine's London office.

In 1924 Mackenzie was invited, as a record expert, to present a regular Gramophone Hour for the BBC. Stone took the show over in 1927 and changed its emphasis from classics to pop. It was soon obvious to record dealers that a play on Stone's Tuesday slot had an immediate and dramatic effect on sales. As explanation, Stone quoted Sir John Reith: 'Good material can stand advertising, and broadcasting is an advertising medium unexcelled.'[4] The record companies began buying plays on the continental stations.

The immediate problem for the BBC was to prevent record plugging (there were already rules about song plugging). Stone's record choices were vetted, his comments had to be scripted in advance – he wasn't allowed to 'express the slightest preference for one record over another' – and he was discouraged from even saying what labels records were on. His conclusion was that record show presenters should be paid by the record companies, as their 'accredited announcers', rather than by the BBC:

> Actually the trade in popular songs is in comparatively few hands, just as the recording of them also is. The writing of such amiable amenities of daily life is nothing. The marketing of them so as to bring in remuneration to author and middleman is the problem.[5]

Stone made great efforts to solve this problem. He was a reviewer (for the *Daily Express* as well as the *Gramophone*), a broadcaster (for the BBC, for the Gramophone Company with Radio Rome, for Decca with Radio Paris), and even a performer – 'doing a lightning tour of gramophone recitals in the big towns on behalf of the Columbia Graphophone Company', appearing at the London Palladium. In 1933 the *Talking Machine News* offered their retailer subscribers a weekly window bill: 'Christopher Stone selects for you the latest records.' Underneath would be Stone's pick of 'the twenty best sellers from the current lists of the manufacturers'.

Christopher Stone was the first pop personality in Britain to be made by radio and his influence reflected a general shift in cultural power – from Tin Pan Alley to Broadcasting House. The music publishers spelt out the effects of radio in their evidence to the Crawford Committee on Broadcasting in

1925, claiming that the BBC had reduced music sales, shortened the commercial life of a hit song from twelve to six months, and caused a decline in musical performance, both public and private. The committee's response was that if sheet music sales were down, record sales were up. The problem was to adjust copyright deals to take account of recordings.

This was to evade one of the points raised by the publishers. The issue was not just their falling share of music business income, but also who was to decide what the public wanted. The rise of radio meant a change in the organization of popular music – from the publisher/showman/song system to a record company-dominated star system.[6] In 1933, for example, the BBC changed its song-plugging rules – dance programme producers now dealt directly with the band leaders rather than with the venue managers. Dance programmes were organized less and less as 'transparent' broadcasts of live events, more and more as specially designed radio shows. The judgement (and judges) of what was a good number, a good performance, shifted accordingly. The 'popularity' of pop music became measured by record sales and radio plays – it now meant the popularity of a particular *performance*. The BBC had no equivalent to the USA's *Hit Parade* programmes (and the importance of *Billboard*'s charts in America partly reflected the mass production there of juke-boxes), but in 1934 the *Gramophone* did start carrying lists of the top melodies in Britain. There were three charts: the top six songs, based on trade returns of sheet music; the ten biggest selling records; and the ten tracks featured most often in the previous week's radio shows. The point of these lists (which ran from 1934–6) was explicitly promotional – they helped organize the sale of records, they were guides to the tastes that mattered commercially.

Taste

Christopher Stone once suggested that 'the broadcaster's job is to provide the equivalent of a bath and a change for the tired man's and the tired woman's mind'. His own musical tastes were 'wide' but his programmes were, in the language of the time, determinedly middlebrow. He did not play the 'hot American dance music' that appeared on the Parlophone label, for example. These records, which appealed to the 'sophisticates of the West End and the University', were, in the words of the *Talking Machine News*, played incessantly in 'the nigger-ridden community where jazz seems to be the be-all and end-all of existence, yeah, even in the "dives" of Gotham and the night haunts of Mayfair and the Tottenham Court Road', but they were not suitable for Stone's listeners, whose 'jazz' tastes were trained by Jack Payne and Henry Hall, by the BBC's dance bands.[7]

Ronald Pearsall has argued that the BBC's middlebrow culture reflected a deliberate attempt 'to make classical music popular and popular music classical'. The idea was to educate the masses 'into good music', and the relations of class and taste between the wars were so tight that the BBC, a middle-class organization, inevitably expressed middle-class musical values.[8]

But this was not just another aspect of the Reithian view of broadcasting. The record industry was also run by the bourgeoisie and most of its staff had even less experience than the BBC's producers of popular culture or popular tastes.

British record companies seem to have begun operations with two assumptions: first that pop music was worthless; second that its worthlessness made it commercially exploitable. Jazz, suggested the *Gramophone* in 1926, was an entertainment like Hollywood cinema or advertising – it created the needs it fed and its popularity depended on its ability to slither over the surface of the emotions. Three years earlier the magazine had commented that

> every month new and more exciting dance tunes are produced which, as they weary us, we discard for newer and still more exciting ones. For it is notorious that jazz tunes, admirable as they are, do soon become a burden . . . . The gramophone is most convenient; no need to be too careful of the life of the records, you can wear them out and get the latest.[9]

The *Talking Machine News*, the retailers' paper, was aware of the implications from the start. In 1921 its editor commented that

> it is more than probable that it is the light and popular music of the moment that pays [record companies] best and that it is through the profits on such records that others of a higher and more classical description are made possible. In which case real music lovers have cause for thankfulness.

The implication was that the record dealers themselves were 'real music lovers' but had to sell pop to make a living. The advantage of 'light songs' was that 'they are easily tired of, for none of them live, and the records being scrapped newer ones are soon demanded, whereas a classical record is often kept carefully for years'. The disadvantage was that wrong judgements about fickle public taste could land dealers with stock that would *never* sell (the recession caught many retailers with unsold and therefore unsellable piles of dance tunes). Either way, assumptions about the musical vacuity of pop were built into the record industry's commercial tactics.

In the 1920s it was still argued that musical education was a way to increased record sales – hence HMV's Education Department and its support of the *Gramophone*. The record companies saw themselves as analogous to book publishers: their long-term success depended on improving general standards of musical literacy. In July 1922 *Talking Machine News* carried an editorial entitled 'How dealers can improve public taste'. The editor recommended his readers to take up the Gramophone Company's offer of a 'free school for dealers', with tuition in such subjects as 'the foundations of a knowledge of musical works', and how to advise customers and 'guide their tastes in the right direction'. Seven years later the paper was arguing that

> it behoves us, then, to see to it that both our wireless and our gramophone concerns are under the control of sane bodies with some sort of cultivated musical perspective, in which event the two, working side by side, will be able to

accomplish much on the matter of relieving us from the terror of an age made demented by incessant syncopation.[11]

Control

Talking Machine News was one of the victims of the recession, and while the BBC maintained its 'sane' and 'cultivated' control of popular music broadcasting, the emphasis of the record companies in the 1930s moved from educating the masses to servicing them. Pop tastes were still disdained, but aggressive salesmanship, the emergence of the EMI/Decca duopoly and the development of the pop star system made these tastes manageable. In this context the BBC's principles came to be seen as a constraint on efficient record selling – 'public service' was not the same thing as 'giving the public what it wants'. Record makers and sellers became an important source of the populist demand (orchestrated by papers like the *Daily Mail*) for more 'entertaining' programmes – especially on Sundays, when listeners tuned, *en masse*, to the record-company organized shows on Radio Luxembourg and Radio Normandy.

Scannell and Cardiff have argued that the BBC move from the public service to the light entertainment use of pop music began in the late 1930s.[12] It was accelerated by the provision of the Forces Network during the war and by the formal adoption of the lowbrow Light Programme after it. From the point of view of pop history, what mattered most about these changes was their result: by the 1950s the power of radio to orchestrate tastes and sell pop records was, in Britain, as it had been for many years in the USA, at the disposal of the music business. In the 1950s Decca and EMI were able to realize the profits of the power they had built up in the 1930s.

The recession ended for the record industry with the war. From 1940 there was more money spent on leisure and people spent more of it on entertaining themselves – public shows were scarce. Decca and EMI were soon engaged too in military projects (like the development of radar) and the resulting stress on the profits of technology continued after the war with the development of hi-fi. Decca, for example, pioneered 'full frequency range recording' and issued Britain's first long-playing records, in June 1950. There followed un unprecedented sales boom (Decca's turnover increased eightfold between 1946 and 1956) but while there were some business rearrangements (Decca, Inc. was sold to MCA; London Records was set up to market Decca's British records in the USA, its American licences in the UK), the basic structure of the British record industry remained unchanged.

By the end of the 1950s the only new record companies were Philips (with 12 per cent of the UK market) and Pye (with 6 per cent). Both companies were subsidiaries of successful electronics firms (and thus had the necessary base for record manufacture and distribution), neither had 'alternative' musical policies. Otherwise there were about twenty-five small labels, issuing records pressed by the handful of small-scale 'outside' manufacturers (like Oriole). Most of the resulting discs had specialist appeal (folk, jazz, spoken word, train and bird noises) or filled a specific commercial niche (like Woolworths' imitation hits); none made an impact on the charts. Such was the power of the pop establishment that even when a new market was revealed (by the emergence of teenage culture and the success of American rock'n'roll records) the majors were able both to meet the new demands (EMI signed Cliff Richard, Decca took Tommy Steele) and to integrate the new styles into the existing structures of pop production, pop promotion, pop programming.

It was rock rather than rock'n'roll or skiffle that changed the organization of British pop power, and, ironically, it was the very success of British rock (the Beatles signed to EMI, the Rolling Stones to Decca) that proved to be the undoing of the British record business. The power of EMI and Decca was challenged not by British independents but by increasing competition (for both sales and artists) from foreigners. The cosy international deals that enabled Decca and EMI to profit from the success of American pop in the 1950s were destroyed by the international success of British pop in the 1960s. When the next recession came it was the big American (and European) companies which benefited from the terms of intensified competition. The tactics that Edward Lewis had developed in the 1930s – sales drives, star making, a taste management that depended on huge advance expenditure – finally rebounded. At the end of the 1970s Decca was taken over by Polygram, the German-based organization which had by then replaced EMI as the 'largest record company in the world'.[13]

Impact

In this chapter I have suggested that the British record industry was formed by the specific conditions of the 1930s recession. Companies had to struggle to survive and most did not (hence Edward Lewis's subsequent embattled self-image). The resulting organization of British pop was shaped by the competitive necessities of this struggle and, particularly, by the central position radio acquired in successful music marketing. The 1930s, in short, meant a decisive shift in the organization of popular musical culture. Music had long been a commodity, but the form of that commodity was now irrevocably altered – from live to recorded performance, from sheet music to disc, from public appearance to public broadcast – and its control passed from one set of institutions (music publishers, music hall and concert promoters, artists and agents) to another (record companies, the BBC, stars and managers). In the future, changes in musical taste and style, whatever their source, would be mediated through the record business.[14]

Numerous questions remain. I have said little, for example, about the effects of the record industry on the content of pop music. What was involved in the replacement of Gracie Fields by Vera Lynn as Britain's most popular singer? (Gracie Fields was Britain's biggest pop star in the 1930s, but her appeal derived from a style and persona developed on music-hall stages in the 1910s and 1920s – these were simply reproduced in her film, radio and studio work. Vera Lynn was a much 'purer' radio and record star.) What does it matter that Jack Hylton, Jack Payne, Henry Hall, were Britain's biggest dance band stars? (Payne openly despised jazz; Hylton sought to replace it with 'symphonic syncopation', saying, 'to my mind it represents a pleasing combination of harmony, melody and rhythm in such a way that the musical cravings of any normal person are satisfied. In the dance-hall or on the gramophone record alike, it makes a subtle appeal to our British temperament. It is fast becoming a truly national music.'[15])

While there is not space to explore these issues fully, I want to conclude with a general point. The effect of record company control of popular music was twofold: on the one hand, the people who determined what music was recorded were no longer directly connected to the sources of that music (as, in different ways, both publishers and promoters had been); on the other hand, the popularity of pop music began to be defined in new ways – in terms of statistics, inoffensiveness, professionalism, efficiency. Jack Payne's words have the necessary ring:

> In all my show business ventures it is my aim to base programmes on a policy of something for everybody, rather than deliberately attempt to satisfy the demands of specialist groups. I have been broadcasting for something like twenty-one years, and all this time, orienting my programmes to the tastes of listeners as evidenced by the BBC Listener Research section and my own organisation's post-bag, I have been building up, modifying and improving a policy which I now believe meets the tastes of the large majority of listeners. Of course it pays, financially and ethically.[16]

In the 1930s music became a mass medium; songs and tunes and performers and performances became *malleable*. From their manufacturers' point of view pop records expressed nothing. They were simply packages of entertainment. Their purpose was to sell and the sale justified the product – meant the music paid 'financially and ethically'. The paradox, of course, was that pop became so malleable a form that it could be used by its consumers for their own ends too. Cheap music had a power that would, eventually, become a matter of dispute.

Notes

1 For this argument see, for example, R. A. Peterson and D. G. Berger, 'Entrepreneurship and organisation: evidence from the popular music industry', *Administrative Science Quarterly*, 16 (1971). For a more detailed critique of this approach as applied to American pop history see S. Frith, *Sound Effects*, London, Constable, 1983, chapter 5.

2 See S. Frith, *The Sociology of Rock*, London, Constable, 1978.

3 I am waiting for the promised study by Mark Hustwitt.

4 Quoted in C. Stone, *Christopher Stone Speaking*, London, Elkin, Mathews & Marrot, 1933, p. 117.

5 C. Stone, op. cit., pp. 196–7.

6 For a bitter commentary on this shift see William Boosey, *Fifty Years of Music*, London, Ernest Benn, 1931. Boosey was chairman of Chappells (and the

Performing Rights Society, which had 40,000 composers on its books in the 1920s). He fought to prevent his acts broadcasting. Chappells were important concert hall promoters, and Boosey, who also had links with Moss Empires, believed that the BBC was driving promoters out of business in unfair competition (he handed Chappells' sponsorship of the Proms over to the BBC in 1927). Boosey saw the 1930s music business as a struggle between publishers and record companies, between composers and performers. He accused record companies of 'feeding off the enterprise of others' – they could sell records without having to meet the expenses of 'making music'.

7 *Talking Machine News*, January 1929.
8 R. Pearsall, *Popular Music of the 1920s*, Newton Abbot, David & Charles, 1976, chapter 1. And see Paddy Scannell, 'Music for the multitude? The dilemmas of the BBC's music policy, 1923–1946', *Media, Culture and Society*, 3, 3 (1981).
9 *Gramophone*, April 1923. Christopher Stone writing under the pseudonym James Cackett.
10 *Talking Machine News*, November 1921.
11 ibid., April 1928.
12 See Scannell, op. cit., p. 257, and P. Scannell and D. Cardiff, 'Serving the nation: public service broadcasting before the war', in B. Waites, A. Bennett and G. Martin (eds), *Popular Culture: Past and Present*, London, Croom Helm, 1982.
13 See Frith, op. cit., chapter 13.
14 See Scannell, op. cit., pp. 258–9. Perhaps the most intriguing aspect of this is that British pop was clearly dominated by American sounds but these sounds, from jazz to rock'n'roll, were always mediated through the peculiar sensibilities of the British record industry and radio set-up.
15 J. Hylton, 'The British touch', *Gramophone*, September 1926. And see J. Payne, *This is Jack Payne*, London, Sampson Low, Marston & Co., 1932, pp. 83, 109.
16 J. Payne, *Signature Tune*, London, Stanley Paul, 1947, pp. 65–6.

14

Narrative strategies in television science

Roger Silverstone

Introduction

Television science documentaries have the following characteristics. They have beginnings, middles and endings. They contain a selection of material – interviews, demonstrations, illustrative and dramatic sequences, graphics, commentary, music – ordered in such a way that the programme as a whole will entertain and inform its audience. The facts which they present are carefully chosen, the result of detailed research, and are in general accurate. The specialists selected to speak, to argue a particular position in a controversy or explain a technical aspect of their work, also have been carefully chosen, on the basis of their representativeness, their distinction and their ability to communicate.

The commentary introduces them and establishes the significance of what they do or what they are about to say. Their contributions will be placed in a context which the programme defines as appropriate, and if they are criticized or contradicted then such criticism will be presented responsibly and in the belief that the cause of truth is thereby served. A programme's leading ideas will reflect the *ad hoc* interests of the producers or will appear as the result of editorial response to suggestions from outside or to perceptions of amorphous or focused public interest. In a series such as *Horizon*, there is a premium on clarity of exposition, on professional and technical competence and on variety of subject matter and treatment. Commitment, honesty, careful research are each taken for granted as essential. The demands for balance of opinion in a single programme, though formally required, are less in evidence than they might be in matters of political controversy. But while the science documentary may take a line unreservedly critical of its subject and contributors, it is clear that a series such as *Horizon* will not and cannot consistently antagonize the scientific and intellectual community upon which it depends for its stories.

In any one series of programmes, some will succeed and be considered good or important television, both by producers, their administrative superiors, and/or their audience; others will be judged weak either because they were not deemed sufficiently interesting, because they failed to convince, because the chosen contributors were inadequate or insufficiently charismatic, or because they were poorly shot or confusing. Many of the judgements which professionals make of each other's work are at root based on 'gut' feelings (as are many editorial decisions), the 'gut' being the location of the intangible, incoherent and apparently inexpressible feelings that properly responded to can make the difference between success and failure. These judgements are also more often concerned with matters of form than with matters of content.[1]

If this brief account is a more or less accurate representation of the kernel of science documentary practice, then all that might subsequently be required is to illustrate through a discussion of the intellectual and technical effort of production how it works out in practice. Why, then, as for example in this chapter, the insistence on a close scrutiny of the form and content of a programme, or as elsewhere on an equally close scrutiny of the making of such a programme?

The first part of the answer is relatively straightforward. Science, technology and medicine are of vital importance in the lives of every member of contemporary society. For the most part our knowledge of them is gained from television and from the other mass media. Hence television's treatment of science, the how and the why of it, may be as important an issue as science itself.

The second part of the answer, consequent upon the first, is perhaps more difficult to settle. A close concern with the television programme as a text to be analysed, and with the production as a process to be explained, have as their aim the penetration of what is often taken for granted and as such unchallenged in the work of television. There is no suggestion here that the makers of television science programmes are particularly complacent about their activities – some are, many are not – but like members of any fairly self-contained professional community, their vision will be bounded, as their practice is limited, by all manner of constraints. Of some of these they will be aware, of some not; some will be resisted and some accepted. Their perspectives will be defined, broadly but significantly, by the institutional and cultural context of their work, and the accounts of it which they offer, often not incompatible with the one which I began, beg questions which they themselves cannot or will not answer. These are questions of the relationship of a television documentary account with reality; of the management of meaning; of the implications of consistent or inconsistent patterns of judgement across programmes; of the compromises inherent in the process of film-making; of the relationship between film-maker and subject, between film text and literary text, and between the specialist and the popular; and of the relationship between television science and its audience. I hope that this chapter will begin to face some of these questions in a relevant and useful way.

Issues

Science does not come to television naked. I mean two things by this. The first is that science, in the popular knowledge and fantasies of it, derived as much from fictional as factual sources,[2] is itself highly charged.[3] Television takes science and technology seriously; the BBC has a Science Consultative Group to advise and comment on matters of programme policy; the *Horizon* series has been running since 1964 (though originally it was a magazine programme) and it is widely regarded as a flagship of BBC documentary output. Science is imbued, both in academic and everyday discourse, with a powerful, ideological significance – as a panacea or as a tormentor. We may be encouraged to reject knowledge unless it is scientific, or to be suspicious of rampant scientism as a dimension of oppressive bourgeois ideology.[4] Science is indeed part of, and contributor to, the ideological coherence of contemporary society, and like every facet of that ideology it is increasingly open to challenge.

The second is that science writing, the presentation of the results of scientific activity, and its public face, is itself a process of literary and intellectual endeavour. It has its own rhetorical and narrative strategies, designed to inform, of course, but also to enforce and reinforce the authority and objectivity of its results and conclusions, as well as the material anonymity of the experimenter-author. The scientific paper persuades;[5] it is selective rather than exhaustive;[6] it manifestly fails to represent the activity of science;[7] it is presented, usually, as a successful quest for knowledge, 'une aventure cognitive'.[8] The scientific paper has a particular lexicon[9] and range of metaphor;[10] it incorporates through citation both an implicit knowledge and a claim for status;[11] it makes assumptions about its audience and incorporates these into its text. It is through the scientific paper, but also through the informal talk of scientists,[12] that science gains its public face. And it is in the semi-popular journals like *New Scientist* and *Scientific American*, and through the public rather than the private talk of scientists, that television embraces its views of science, and from them begins its own work of mediation.[13]

I have already suggested that individual science producers working in television may be more or less aware of this context of their work. As creative workers they are as varied a group as one might expect. But the texts which they produce, be they brief items in a magazine programme devoted to gee-whiz technology or full-length documentary films on particle physics, are the outcome of a conscious and unconscious negotiation with the public face of science, and with the particular constraints – economic, bureaucratic, political and aesthetic – associated with the making of television programmes.

In this chapter I wish to present an account of one full-length documentary, principally through an exploration of it as a text, in other words as a motivated construction of image, sound and extra-filmic discourse. I will want to persuade the reader that such an account, flawed as all efforts at interpretation must be, and never conclusive, is a suitable way of making sense of the work done by television in the presentation of certain aspects of science. The stress will be on the how of meaning rather than the what of meaning; on the way in which a television documentary constructs meanings rather than what those meanings are. Above all I will want to show how through the various dimensions of narrative and narrative framing which I intend to discuss, a coherent, plausible and arguably compelling film is constructed. The film chosen provides good, but not exhaustive, examples of strategies which television adopts in its construction of science. No single case study can do more than set the terms of reference for future comparative work.

Of course in presenting an analysis in such a manner, to argue that a television documentary is a construction in no way poses the same kind of critical challenge to established orthodoxy as the suggestion that science itself is in an important sense a literary or social construction.[14] It can be assumed – though some practitioners will dispute it – that all television has an equivocal relationship with something which might be called reality. My intention is not, therefore, to attack the straw man of factuality, but to demonstrate through what kinds of artifice such a text is constructed and to indicate some of the implications of that. And it must be said at the outset that my concern will be much less with the accuracy of the reports of scientific matter than with the way in which generally accurate references and explanations are framed and given weight and plausibility.

The programme chosen was broadcast on BBC-2 on Monday 16 November 1981. It was repeated on BBC-2 the following Sunday. Running time was 45 minutes 51 seconds. It was called *The Death of the Dinosaurs*.[15] It was a remake of a programme transmitted earlier in the USA as part of WGBH's *Nova* series and called there *The Asteroid and the Dinosaur*. The remaking consisted of the addition of entirely new sequences, the restructuring and editing of the original sequences and the rewriting of the commentary. It was shot on film and not on videotape. To all intents and purposes it was an entirely new film, with some material included that had been previously used in another similarly focused film.

It was chosen for analysis from among the twenty-five *Horizon* films in the 1981–2 season because it illustrates clearly most, if not all, of the various elements which, from a careful study of a large number of science documentaries (including those in the 1981–2 season of *Horizon*) appear to be important. It contains discussions of geophysics, climatology, palaeobotany and palaeobiology. It presents science in dispute and does so in a self-consciously dramatic and attractive way. It reached an audience of 4.6 million (8.8 per cent of the total possible audience in the UK) and recorded a BBC Appreciation Index of 78.[16] This was the largest audience recorded for any single *Horizon* programme during that season. The programme was screened a third time during the summer of 1982 as part of a brief season of *Horizon* on BBC-1.

The programme

I offer in this section an account of the programme. It cannot substitute for the full text as transmitted and it can only be treated as an *aide-mémoire*.

The programme had been preceded by station announcements trailing it, both the week before and immediately before transmission. It was accompanied by a full-page article in *Radio Times*.[17]

Horizon titles and music open the programme,[18] and as the commentary introduces the film there is a zoom towards a still of the earth as seen from space: 'Sixty-five million years ago something very strange happened to the planet earth. Seventy-five per cent of all the species living there were wiped out. What caused this catastrophe has until recently been a total mystery. Yet had it not happened, it is possible that man might never have appeared' (2).[19]

Stills (paintings) of dinosaurs follow (3–8) as does a brief excerpt from a feature film showing Raquel Welch and friend hiding from two battling dinosaurs (9–29). The commentary reiterates the mystery of the dinosaurs' disappearance and disabuses us of our beliefs in them as essentially violent and menacing.

We are then introduced to a tiny mammal known to have been alive at the time of the extinction (30, 31); a model of a shrew-like creature held in full frame. Then a tilt from claw to head of *Stenonychosaurus*, a small, evolutionarily advanced and intelligent dinosaur (32, 33). Dr Dale Russell (palaeobiologist, National Museum of Canada)[20] stands beside the model and explains its significance (34–42): 'It was bipedal, carnivorous; it had binocular vision and an enlarged brain; in other words these animals were as intelligent as our own ancestors.' Dr Russell suggests that not only were the dinosaurs at the time of their extinction remarkably successful but that had they survived, 'I think it's rather unlikely that our own species would have appeared on the surface of the earth ultimately'.

The commentary reaffirms the significance of their disappearance and introduces the inquiry into how and what we know about it. As the camera zooms out from the fossilized head of *Triceratops* (43, 44), then to a photograph of revealed geological strata (45), and to a church tower (46), we are told in voice-over commentary that the fossil record is the key, that the Cretaceous–Tertiary boundary marks the time and that Gubbio, Italy, is where 'a possible answer was found'.

Dr Walter Alvarez (Professor of Geology, University of California) is seen walking along a country footpath towards camera (47, 48). The significance of the setting is established through microscopic views of forams, tiny sea-creatures whose distribution is said to be important for the solution of the problem (49, 53). Kneeling beside an outcrop of rock he identifies the separate Cretaceous and Tertiary limestone beds and the half-inch clay layer between them. The distinct evolutionary status of each of the limestone beds, Alvarez suggests, is indicated by the different quantity and size of the forams present in each deposit: 'The clay layer, right here, marks the boundary between two different geological periods' (50–5).

A section of the rock has been extracted and preserved in lucite. We are shown it in close-up (56) and then introduced, via an establishing shot of Berkeley campus (57), to Walter Alvarez's father, 'Nobel prize-winner Luiz Alvarez', (Professor of Physics, University of California) who, sitting beside his desk in his office, explains the recent history of the sample of rock, of how his son had explained its significance to him and also of his son's ignorance of how long the clay layer took to be deposited – a crucial measure in understanding how swift the extinction of the dinosaurs was (58–64).

A sequence of graphics and models follows illustrating the formation of the earth (65–7) and the significance of iridium, an element now falling on the earth at a known rate, and which could be used to indicate the speed at which the clay was deposited at the time of the extinction. The commentary voice: 'Alvarez decided to measure how much iridium there was in the clay and calculate how long it had taken to form. But that's not quite how things turned out.' The image is of earth from space with tiny dots passing from screen left to right (67).

We are introduced to two of Alvarez's colleagues at Berkeley, Dr Helen Michael and Dr Frank Asaro, and to an extended sequence of the procedures involved in measuring the amount of iridium in a sample of clay: from pestle and mortar, to test-tube, to container, in preparation for 'an extremely sensitive technique called Neutron Activation Analysis . . . samples were bombarded with neutrons produced in [Berkeley's nuclear] reactor's core', and to the traces as measured on an oscilloscope. 'The results surprised everyone' (68–79).

Dr Frank Asaro (University of California, Berkeley) explains, in vision and standing next to a bank of controls (80), that they found iridium in large quantities, and Luiz Alvarez, at his desk again, is asked how this measure was to be interpreted (81–3). He explains that his first hypothesis was a shower of iridium from an exploding supernova (a dynamic model of a star-field and a painted still illustrate his words (84–5)). He goes on to say why this hypothesis was rejected (86). They tested for the presence of plutonium 244 (graphic of exploding star (87)). As the explanation progresses in commentary there is a full visual sequence (88–92) of the apparatus and the mechanics involved in the testing, ending with a shot of an oscilloscope screen (93) and a bank of controls (94).

Further stills of a cliff face (95, 96) followed by a mid-shot of Dr Helen Michael (University of California, Berkeley) speaking to camera accompany a discussion in commentary, in voice-over and voice in vision, of the search for the iridium in the clay layer (97, 99) (98 is a still shot of the trench which was dug to generate the samples). Having measured the unexpectedly large amounts of iridium in the clay layer of Montana, their suspicions of sample contamination were aroused. Shots of material being ground in a mortar accompany this account (100). Marion Sturz tells to camera the story of how the source of the contamination was finally discovered – in her platinum wedding ring hardened with iridium. As she talks she continues to grind material in her mortar (101–7).

Luiz Alvarez explains to camera (108) that this reveals the sensitivity of the techniques, but the commentary insists (109), over an animated map, that 'the iridium layer is real'. The quest for an explanation continues. A shot (110) of Alvarez working at his desk. Frank Asaro to camera introduces, but without naming, the currently favourite hypothesis (111).

That too 'comes from space', says the commentary over an animation of flying rocks in space (112), followed by a close-up of a shiny mottled surface full frame. Dr Robert Hutchinson (Natural History Museum, London) crouching beside a slice through a six-ton meteorite identifies its origin and its significance: 'It's especially rich in iridium' (113–17). Voice-over commentary explains how it might be possible for an asteroid some six miles wide to hit the earth 'with devastating effects'. A series of graphics and a photo of earth from space, culminating in images of flames and finally an aerial shot of Meteor Crater, Arizona, illustrate the account (118–29).

Dr Eugene M. Shoemaker (United States Geological Survey) crouches beside Meteor Crater, Arizona, and in the longest single shot (130) of the film (containing a zoom in and then out again) he offers an explanatory hypothesis to camera of the pattern of events following the crash of a meteor on earth some 25,000 years before. His concluding metaphor is of a nuclear explosion. Two shots of just such a happening follow (131, 132).

The commentary asks: 'Is this really what happened 65 million years ago?' as aerial shots of the earth and a map of the identified crater sites around the world appear (133–6). The suggestion is that no crater site has been found to meet the requirements of Alvarez's theory. The commentary suggests, therefore, that the asteroid may have landed in the sea (136).

Dr Fred L. Whipple (Smithsonian Astrophysical Observatory, Cambridge, Mass.) stands beside a large globe (137–9), and uses it to demonstrate and explain his theory of where the asteroid fell. He suggests that it fell at a weak point in the earth's crust, on a mid-ocean ridge, and that the result of the impact would not be a crater, but a volcanically produced island.

Over images of a close-up of the globe and of volcanic flames, Whipple explains, with the commentary's support (140–4), that Iceland was the product of the impact, and that geologists confirm that it is the approximately correct age for his theory. The sequence ends (145, 146) with two shots, one of the globe showing Iceland, the other of volcanic flames.

But then Luiz Alvarez, to camera, indicates that Whipple is mistaken (147). As his son, Walter, has reported: 'At the time of the extinction, Norway and Greenland were firmly tied to each other and there wasn't any ocean there for the asteroid to fall into.'

Graphics illustrate this (148, 149) and commentary suggests that maybe the crater is elsewhere.

Dr Cesare Emiliani (Professor of Geology, University of Miami) is introduced standing beside a map of the ocean floor (150–7). He explains to camera where in the sea he thinks the asteroid fell and why there is no evidence of its impact: 'A portion of the ocean floor since then has disappeared under the continent.'

A shot of an H bomb exploding (158) accompanies the commentary's indication of what the effects of this impact might have been. And we return to Dr Luiz Alvarez (159–64), at his desk, referring to a book on the explosion of Krakatoa, and to its usefulness in helping him calculate the amount of debris likely to have been introduced into the earth's atmosphere. Stills from the book accompany his discussion, but reference in commentary to red sunsets for a period of two to three years afterwards suggested that the scientists needed more information. Three images of sunsets (165–7).

An experiment is filmed at the California Institute of Technology (identified in commentary). Dr Thomas J. Ahrens (Professor of Geophysics, CIT) and Dr John D. O'Keefe (geophysicist, CIT) talk through a sequence in which the effects of high velocity impacts are measured (168–89). There are shots of an 'old naval gun', flashing red lights, and slow-motion images of the impact interspersed with shots of flames, with graphics of asteroid movements culminating in a shot of a nuclear explosion, with the earth from space and with heavy red-tinged clouds.

Luiz Alvarez is at his desk (190 and 206) and he explains the significance of the loss of light, the consequence of the impact and the cause of the clay layer formation. The food chains are disrupted because of the substantial interruption of photosynthetic activity. A sequence (191–205) explains how photosynthesis works, and what happens when it is interrupted or stopped by the denial of sunlight. Images of a field and leaves of grass introduce a series of shots in a laboratory where plants are deprived of light under experimental conditions. Their absorption of carbon dioxide is illustrated by reference to a dial and a pen trace. The sequence ends (203, 205)[21] with images of leaves dying, their decay effectively speeded up as a consequence of delayed action photography. The voice-over commentary suggests that 'without sunlight, the plants wilt and the green chlorophyll gradually disappears'. The plants have indeed wilted but the commentary points out that they have done so after only ten days of darkness, and that Alvarez suggests that the cloud would have stayed up for much longer. Pictures of desert rocks accompany the commentary's question (208): 'The world laid waste . . . . Is it really possible?'

Dr Emiliani, outside now (209) and standing beneath some trees, takes up the account. He does not think such a period without light was possible, for it would have involved the entire collapse of the biosphere and no time (some 65 million years) for the higher animals subsequently to develop as they did.

To a desert next, and to Dr Leo Hickey (palaeobotanist, Smithsonian Institute, Washington) who is actively investigating the fossil record: 'One type of evidence might resolve the debate', the commentary suggests. Hickey is seen uncovering fossils to the astonishment and enthusiasm of his associates who are sitting beside him (210–15). He doubts that such a black-out ever occurred: 'Looking at the plant evidence across the Cretaceous–Tertiary boundary here, we see no evidence of an asteroid impact' (216).

As the sequence with Hickey at work continues (a close-up of hands and fossil 217–19), the commentary announces its dispute with his findings:

'Nevertheless, half the plants did become extinct. Something must have happened. And although Hickey doubts it, others still believe there was an asteroid – and it did collide with the earth.'

The image of the earth from space reappears (220). Radiophonic music and the commentary suggest, and Dr Emiliani spells out (221), the explanation: that since the asteroid landed in the sea, a considerable amount of water was thrown up with the dust and that this water rained back fairly quickly, in so doing clearing most of the atmosphere.

More stills of the earth with and without dust, followed by a shot of moving clouds, allow the commentary to restate what Emiliani has just suggested (222–5), and as the images of clouds continue, it introduces a further implication of Emiliani's theory – 'a greenhouse effect' (226). Emiliani, to camera and still standing beneath the trees (227), explains that a rise in surface temperature was the cause of the extinction.

A sequence of sunbathers follows (228–32) and over it the commentary explores how it is that some mammals, human beings included, can survive major changes of temperature, but that others, such as alligators, as Emiliani points out (223), referring to the summer daytime temperature and humidity in Florida, cannot. A sequence of alligators and elephants in the heat follows (234–44). A fall in temperature is tolerable; a rise is not. 'All in all', the commentary suggests, 'when the temperature rises, big means vulnerable' (245–6), and since dinosaurs 'were not exactly on the small side' (a still painting of a *Triceratops* (247)), Emiliani's theory is 'at least worth considering'.

A cut to a drilling operation at sea (248–51), and the commentary's question of whether there is any evidence that the sea temperature did rise 65 million years ago. 'One way to find out is to drill into the ocean floor' (249–50). Dr Nicholas Shackleton (Godwin Laboratory, Cambridge) is introduced (252–4) and the commentary explains what he is looking for – forams (microscope shot of forams (256)) – and how (various shots of microscopes, glass apparatus, controls and pen traces (255–62)). The inquiry is into evidence for changes in the temperature of the sea through the proportion of different oxygen isotopes in the forams' shells. The temperature rise was, Shackleton suggests to camera (263–4), 'probably of the order of two or three degrees. And it seems to have been pretty fast. And it probably didn't last very long.'

The commentary suggests that this does not prove Emiliani's theory to be correct but that further evidence to be found in the movement of isotope ratios indicates a 'massive decrease' in the productivity of the oceans (267). The shots are of apparatus and moving pen traces (265–9).

Both Shackleton (270) and Emiliani (271) summarize to camera what they think might have happened. It was the heat and it affected adversely the larger animals and the animals which lived in the surface oceanic water.

A painted still of a dead dinosaur (272) and a photograph of an early mammal follow (273). It was the mammals who survived because of their small size. The commentary provides a summary as the camera dwells on the full fossilized skeleton of a dinosaur in a museum. Children look on (274–8). 'Much of this is still, of course, conjecture . . . . Nevertheless, the idea that a collision with an asteroid caused the extinction of the dinosaurs is at least being considered seriously by an increasing number of scientists' (274).

The final question follows, as the sequence continues: 'What would have happened had the asteroid not collided with the earth and the dinosaurs had not disappeared?' (278)

Dr Dale Russell is reintroduced. Standing beside a fossil dinosaur he talks to camera (279) and introduces his museum's model of what an intelligent dinosaur would look like, had they survived as a species. Music accompanies the camera's tilt from toes to head (280–1). Russell identifies the creature's various significant characteristics and defends the charge, raised in the commentary, of anthropomorphism (282, 283). A repeat tilt (284) provides the image as the commentary concludes: 'So, perhaps if it were not for a chance collision with an asteroid, creatures very like this could be ruling the world today, just as they did all those millions of years ago.' The frame is frozen with a close-up of the head of the model. The opening music returns and the credits roll.

Narrative

The narrative of a television programme, even of a documentary programme, has no necessary relationship with the world to which it refers. That relationship is merely sufficient. There will never be, nor has there ever been, an exact replica of a story told on television presented in any other medium or in the so-called real world. Of course elements within it can be checked against their appearance in other texts – the pages of scientific journals, the transcripts of interviews or simply 'what everyone knows' – but the narrative as a whole with its distinct beginning, middle and end is the product of a particular kind of aesthetic work. It refers to a series of events which in documentary are explicitly granted the status as real, independent of the act of narration. The narrative is constructed, even in its uniqueness, on the basis of conventions and rules which are generally applicable, recognizable and effective. If it was not, we would be unable to understand it.

In order to make some sense of how a television documentary narrative does its work we need to make a number of elementary, albeit sometimes questionable, distinctions. The first is between form and content; the second is between story and plot.

It is quite impossible to distinguish conclusively form and content; every item of content provides a form for more content; every expression of form is itself content for another form.[22] Both notions involve the reification of process, change and interdependence. No classification will do less. But in the analysis of narrative the distinction is useful if only to suggest the double valency of the elements which comprise it. A documentary film is both a structure – complete, self-regulating, transforming[23] – and a set of references outside itself. An opening sequence, for example, will demand of its audience that they bring to it a competence in the recognition of words and images which will allow them to be meaningful; such expressions as 'a vital problem for mankind' or a reference to 'this time last year', such images as the flashing lights and the beady technology of a laboratory, will depend for their understanding, their initial impact and their cultural status, on a set of references fixed to content, and which lie outside the range of purely formal analysis. But equally those elements function within the coherence of the text itself – the television programme or series of programmes – as units of a structure and as such subject to and contributing to that intrinsic coherence. They will establish a setting for the events which follow, frame the way in which the text is to be understood, inaugurate an argument and the narrative's quest. These elements will have a formal status which is analytically but not substantively independent of their status as units of content.

The second distinction is between story and plot and it is a familiar one in the analysis of narrative.[24] The story is what is told. The plot is how it is told. The story is the sequence of events in their actual chronological order; the plot is the unique arrangement in one telling of them. *Cinderella* is a story which has been told many times, but the plot which Walt Disney constructed, though recognizably the same story, is particular. Many people can tell the story and account for the death of the dinosaurs, but the television programme which I shall shortly be discussing in detail presents it in just one way.

Of course such a distinction appears to be more immediately relevant to narratives of fiction. But in so far as documentary texts are narratives which, if not fictional, are necessarily constructions, then this distinction remains crucial. It is necessary to extract from the complexity of the television narrative the various dimensions of its story-line, and the frames which are defined for it through them. And it is necessary to explore the ways in which the story is expressed, the various aspects of the different rhetorics which are involved in the presentation of meaningful images and sounds.

Let me illustrate and explore these two sets of distinctions by referring to the pre-title sequence of *The Death of the Dinosaurs*. It consists of three shots: a long, slow zoom towards an image of the earth photographed from space, followed by two paintings of dinosaurs in what might have been their natural habitat. There is a zoom in, then out, from these two images. A whining crescendo (from Khachaturian's Symphony No. 1) provides the background music. The commentary is as follows:

Sixty-five million years ago something very strange happened to the planet earth. Seventy-five per cent of all the species living there were wiped out. What caused this catastrophe has until recently been a total mystery. Yet had it not happened, it is possible that man might never have appeared. Among the victims of this catastrophe were the most powerful and dominant animals of the time – the dinosaurs. Their extinction, and our emergence, may be linked by a catastrophe that changed the world.

A great number of things are going on here. First of all it is clear that both the image and the commentary refer to and define the context through which the audience is being asked to interpret the film it is about to see. Commentary references to mystery, catastrophe, victims, extinction, emergence, all define a frame for the following narrative (both story and plot) and for the science which it will treat. This framing in verbal imagery is reinforced by the unearthly (though now quite familiar) view of earth, and the familiar (though unearthly) view of dinosaurs, and by the music. It is defined in terms of the most fundamental and fundamentally archaic questions to which science, in its heroic mould, is perhaps expected to attend. These references, a function of the content of the opening sequence, lock the following text into a resonant context defined for it outside the film by the world of traditional stories and mystical beliefs.

It is worth pointing out something quite obvious here; that a framing of this kind, indeed any directing and relatively unambiguous framing, is bound to exclude alternatives. We are not invited, for example, to relate this supposed catastrophe to the potential catastrophe that our species is in the process of manufacturing for itself, either through nuclear proliferation or atmospheric pollution. The producer considered these possibilities but rejected them.

However, in addition to such a frame which invites the viewer to place both the programme and the reported theories and experiments in a specific extra-filmic and ideological location, this pre-title sequence initiates the narrative as such. It begins a story, modelled consciously or unconsciously on traditional forms of story-telling; it inaugurates an argument, modelled on our conventions of rational discourse, and it initiates a complex discourse with distinct and distinctive rhetorical strategies. The first two are aspects of story. The third concerns plot.

In a previous paper[25] I made a distinction between two different ways of presenting story, and following Northrop Frye (1971), I called them the mythic and the mimetic. This formulation was crude and I would like to refine it. The mythic refers broadly to the kinds of aspects of narrative which echo forms of story-telling in pre-literate, oral culture and which have been preserved in most simple narratives, even literary ones: heroic, fragmented, episodic, dependent on a categorical logic and a loose but effective chronology, they are the product of communication which is restricted by what its speakers and listeners can remember at one hearing, and which are dependent on a community to recognize the restricted nature of its formulae, clichés and stereotypes. Such communications, often associated with ritual or more secular assertions of cultural potency, express directly or indirectly the essential problems of humanity in terms which the society which presents them can recognize and understand.

Many writers have noted the recrudescence of such forms in the products of modern electronic media; and I have discussed their implications fully elsewhere.[26] The recognition of so-called mythic or pre-literate forms of expression in contemporary broadcast texts does not imply that through them our culture has fundamentally regressed (though in a certain sense it is regressive), nor that they appear unaffected by the millennia of literariness, through writing and printing,[27] which have transformed most of the world's cultures irrevocably. As Walter J. Ong suggests,[28] these texts represent a 'secondary orality', the compromised result of the intrusion of an audio-visual and hence essentially oral/aural, technology into mechanical, literary and print-base culture. We do not need to look far to see evidence of this in the drama of film and television, nor much farther, as I hope to suggest, in science documentary. One fundamental dimension of narrative framing therefore, and one of the sources of tension in science documentary, is provided by the deeply embedded tradition of story-telling. Its presence is a function of the new technology of film and television, but also, and consequently, of a whole series of more or less well-grounded assumptions about an unseen audience and about what makes a chosen issue appealing or popular.

The mimetic, as its name implies, refers to the representational aspect of a documentary programme, both through the image which guarantees fidelity to a perceived and experienced world, and through the forms of literal explanation which commentary and informed voices offer as a further guarantee of honesty and truth. But there is a further dimension to the mimetic, at least as far as television documentary is concerned, and that is that every literal image or accurate report is both a selection (of course) from an infinity of possible images and reports and is also part of the overall effort of the text to persuade. In J. L. Austin's terms[29] a documentary film is not a locutionary but a perlocutionary act; not simply a matter of sense and reference but an attempt to convince, persuade or deter.

There are a number of conventional forms through which the mimetic might be expressed. The story might follow the model of a lecture, a demonstration, a speech or a written argument, essentially word-driven according to the perceived norms of rational discourse and governed however loosely by a structure derived from classical rhetoric.[30] Or it might follow a model set by extra-filmic discourse, for example the chronology of a day's events, or the passage of the seasons. These ways of framing and constructing a documentary film are perceived to be, and are generally believed to be, natural (and neutral) and as such a legitimate way of presenting information about the world. They are of course conventions, and as such essentially taken for granted by literary culture. In so far as a film is part of literary culture as well as oral culture, it will define for itself a particular, though frail, compromise between myth and mimesis, between the heroic and the naturally historic forms of story-telling.

In a schematic way the distinction between the mythic and the mimetic can be presented thus:

Mimetic: representation – literalness – clarity – information – argument·
Mythic: dramatization – fantasy – power – entertainment – story

Every programme, I suggest, appears as the result of a negotiation between these two, as each producer/director in the management of his or her programme must continually make decisions of inclusion, exclusion, stress and emphasis, which bear materially on one or the other of these competing narrative frames.[31]

The significance of the distinction lies in the suggestion that in the persistence of mythic forms, television adopts, but adapts, forms of traditional story-telling which link its products directly, and I believe fundamentally, with man's archetypal capacity for telling stories.

The discourse of the narrative appears through the various aspects of the rhetoric of television which any given programme exploits: the stylistic and formal repertoire in sound and image through which television expresses itself. Rhetoric – the art of persuasion – is in documentary concerned with the successful replacement of reality by images. In so far as it is successful then television is a magical art, and even mimesis must be a source of wonder.[32]

Primers exist[33] to instruct the neophyte in the artful techniques of television and film production, how to frame and light an image, how to maintain the line, how to cut a film and edit it. I would like to identify three dimensions of television's rhetoric which do not necessarily coincide with these pedagogically oriented categories in order to draw attention to the particular ways television's art manifests itself in a programme such as *The Death of the Dinosaurs*. I will call them image, look and voice.

By rhetoric of the image I refer to the various ways in which the visual content is presented: for example, in the visual metaphors of science: the white-coated scientist, the close-ups of test-tubes and pipettes, the traces on an oscillograph. Science in the real world may or may not be a visually appealing activity; producers often complain, for example, that there is nothing to film in an area of science to which they are directing their attention. This is quite a complex complaint, of course. It refers not just to the lack of moving and visually interesting images (dinosaurs don't move, for example), but also the lack of a story, or the failure to find articulate or expressive scientists to tell it. But the demands of the image in turn require that science, collective, methodical, stuttering, dull as often as not, and rarely unequivocally successful, be transformed. This transformation is significantly image-led.

But clearly the images of science as such will only comprise part of a film which has as its ostensible aim a treatment of science or scientific issues. The practical activity of science itself may well disappear in a film which, in concentrating on the social or political issues, will find images of its effects. And it will always be contextualized through images which have a much wider rhetorical currency: establishing exteriors, illustrative cut-aways, images of non-specific activity and so on.

By rhetoric of the look, I refer to the way in which sequences are shot and cut together. I am aware that the distinction between image and look is an ambiguous one, for no image appears without being framed in a particular way. Nevertheless the distinction is worth pursuing for through it we can recognize the ways in which an interview, for example, is presented – as the result of a whole series of deliberate and motivated decisions which affect the size of the shot, the angle of the camera, and the length of the sequence. A shot from below will have a very different connotation from one that is shot from eye-level. Zooms, pans and tracks turn a static image into a dynamic one. A hand-held rather than a fixed camera, and above all the lighting of a shot, are further aspects of the look as it is constructed through the camera, and which materially affect the way in which an image is presented. The juxtaposition of images, the various techniques, both optical and mechanical, which affect the image as shot in a particular way – slow mixing, wiping, split-screening for example, as well as the introduction of titles or subtitles, are all part of the look imposed during editing. They too are relevant in making sense of the way in which a documentary text is constructed.

Each frame, each sequence is an instruction, and not just a statement, as Christian Metz[34] would suggest; not just 'Here is a dinosaur' or 'Here is a laboratory', but 'Look at this dinosaur, this laboratory in this way.' The consistency with which a particular rhetorical style is adopted in the making of science documentaries in general has profound implications for the way in which the viewer will come to accept its truth and authority. And it is at this level of rhetoric that deliberate change – that is, a deliberate attempt to instruct the viewer to look in a different way – is particularly hard to achieve.

Finally in rhetoric of the voice I include all those strategies of plausibility and persuasion which are spoken, either in commentary or as a result of interview, either in vision or in voice-over. Here the terms of classical rhetoric provide a framework, and I will discuss them on pp. 313 ff. below, in relation to *The Death of the Dinosaurs*.

The commentary, where there is one, will argue a case, dominating and reinforcing the perlocutive image and seeking closure as all good arguments do. The lack of a commentary does not mean, however, that the film becomes an open text, only that it might become, by virtue of the innate ambiguity of the image, less closed. Further there is no suggestion that all science documentaries argue a particular line, tyrannically unswerving and admitting of no contradiction. Most will include some contrary evidence if only to discount it; others will seek, in the manner of the BBC's own stated ideology, to present a balanced view and refuse judgement, closing the film with a request or a question for the audience themselves to decide upon. But even in these cases, of course, the narrative in general, and the voice in particular, defines and excludes, and thereby provides a logic of its own. Scientific matters, whatever their complexity, are rarely didactically treated. They are often referred to social, political or moral issues and as such contextualized in a way which is crucial for our understanding of them.

Two points need to be made immediately. The depiction of the closure demanded by television documentary, itself a function of the narrative and its rhetorical expression, needs qualification. Firstly because no television narrative ever succeeds entirely, neither in the judgement of those who make it, their colleagues, nor in the judgement of the lay audience who see it. There are unevennesses, sequences that don't work well (I'm using the rather intangible language of the producers themselves here), questions that remain unanswered, links that fail to convince. Equally there are the inevitable unresolved contradictions in the presentation of an issue which I have characterized in terms of the opposing narrative forces of the mythic and the mimetic, which professionals might see in terms of the differences between story and information, between film and journalism, or between the subjective and the objective.[35]

The second point is a more general one, but it is often at the forefront of academic consideration of the presentation of documentary material on television. It derives very much from an appreciation of the narrative of its programmes. It concerns their ideological status and the cultural closure which, in the programmes' broad consistency, they are presumed to effect.[36] Science documentaries are far from being immune to such considerations. Jones, Connell and Meadows suggest that this closure is substantially a function of the way in which the programmes accept the primary definition of the science which they treat from the scientists themselves. Television frames its science in accordance with the frames provided by established science, and it does so because both programme-makers and scientists occupy the same ideological space 'though there are times when they may take up differing positions within this space'.[37] This is certainly true, though equally certainly it is a trivial and vague truth. Of course those who produce programmes for an established broadcasting organization will occupy the same ideological space as those who have succeeded as scientists, and it will certainly be in their interests to appear to occupy it. But such a generalization masks the conflicts, contradictions and persistent strains not just between scientists and their mediators but also within the broadcasting organization itself as Young Turk producers fight (in an albeit limited way) the ideological constraints built into the system.

It is true[38] that scientists are not generally treated to the same kind of public cross-examination on television as the politicians are; the questions asked of them are generally open-elicit, and rarely followed by probing supplementaries. Scientists are asked for information, and information is judged to be essentially ideologically and politically neutral. Science is assumed not to be the site of the same essentially contested reality as the political one, and television still appears to be in the largely unproblematic business of opening windows.[39] But it is also true that every one of these taken-for-granted assumptions can be challenged – and they often are, even by the producers themselves. And it is also true that the construction of windows is a delicate and complex matter.

The Death of the Dinosaurs: the mythic narrative

There are two dimensions to any mythic narrative: a chronology of heroism and adventure and a logical structure of concrete categories. The first, archetypally expressed in the various forms of folktale, provides the narrative with its momentum; the second, recognized since the work of Lévi-Strauss on myth, provides the narrative with a base in experience and ontology. In identifying both dimensions in the science documentary *The Death of the Dinosaurs*, I wish to make a number of points. Firstly that a television science documentary such as this crucially depends on forms of narrative which are themselves entirely familiar both within our culture and cross-culturally; secondly that this is so despite explicit and implicit claims to be presenting objective, true and neutral accounts; thirdly that the presentation of factual material within a frame which is entirely identified with fiction and with fantasy has important repercussions for our understanding of the place of television documentary, and television generally, in our culture. It has, of course, profound implications for the popular understanding of science.

The heroic narrative, as one might expect in an oral text which depends for its effect on a single telling, is extremely simple. Following the model provided for the folktale by Vladimir Propp,[40] and subsequently elaborated, developed and amended,[41] its basic functional elements are as follows:

1 α/a   *The initial situation*: the setting and the problem; the how and why of the extinction of the dinosaurs some 65 million years ago. The quest for a solution is inaugurated by:

2 B   *Dispatch*: the first scientist, Russell, acts as the dispatcher, identifying more precisely what the implications of that extinction are for man, and in so doing commits the narrative to finding an answer to a vital question: 'And had the dinosaurs not vanished in that cataclysm of 65 million years ago, I think it's rather unlikely that our own species would have appeared on the surface of the earth ultimately';

3 ↑   *Departure*: the unnamed hero(es) – at this stage we, the audience, fill the space to be occupied by the heroes of science – are dispatched abroad.

4 C   *Consent to counteraction*: with the discovery of Walter Alvarez at Gubbio, Italy, a hero is identified and a commitment to the search is undertaken. Luiz Alvarez picks it up.

5 D.E.F.   *Qualifying test* (1) (D: first function of the donor; E: reaction of the hero; F: acquisition of magical agent): 'A possible answer' is suggested in the forams on either side of a clay layer separating the Cretaceous–Tertiary boundary

6 D.E.   *Qualifying test* (2): and then in the deposition rate of iridium which Luiz Alvarez, as hero, identifies as being potentially important as an indication both of the rate of deposition and the origin of the clay (and hence the cause of the extinction). Other helpers appear: Asaro, Michael, the associated technology.

7 F (−)   *Failure of qualifying test* (2): the magical agent, Neutron Activation Analysis, fails to indicate any significant results. 'But the iridium layer is real'; the knowledge identified in 5 above (D. E. F. (1)) encourages Alvarez, as hero, to continue the search.

8 H   *Main test*: a new theory, this time of the arrival of a meteorite into the earth's atmosphere. A number of helpers are now co-opted by the narrative (not necessarily by Alvarez himself, of course): Hutchinson, Shoemaker, Whipple (who comes closest to becoming, by virtue of his erroneous theory, the villain in the narrative), Emiliani, 'this rather rare book' on the eruption at Krakatoa, Ahrens, O'Keefe and the laser gun. The theory is tested with the help of supporting evidence (and the dismissal of untenable theories) plus analogical modelling.

9 I ±   *Result of main test*: inconclusive. Alvarez posits a major blocking of the sun, with consequent fundamental damage to photosynthesis. Not sufficiently negative for the narrative to stop there.

10 o   *Unrecognized arrival of the hero*: Luiz Alvarez's last appearance in the narrative (206). 'We don't know how long our supposed cloud would stay up, but we've always said a few years or several years.' His place as hero taken by Emiliani.

11 M.N.Q. *Glorifying test* (M: difficult task; N: solution of difficult task; Q: recognition of the hero): the new hero, Emiliani, suggests and completes a theory. His opposer is Hickey and he is helped by Shackleton.

At this point, I suggest, the fundamental ambiguity of the narrative is at last clearly stated, for having let Emiliani and Shackleton present their arguments, and having done so within a narrative framework which itself has established closure through the sequence of its functional units, the commentary attempts a qualification. On the one hand functional closure is reinforced by the paintings of dinosaurs which marked the opening of the narrative and by a qualified ('he believes') though undisputed acknowledgement of success in the commentary: 'It was a small temperature rise that lasted for only a few years but was sufficient to kill entire species, he believes. Among those that survived were our ancestors, the early mammals. Their small size enabled them to withstand the heat.' On the other hand the commentary attempts a retraction: 'Much of this is still, of course, conjecture. There are many questions yet unanswered. Nevertheless, the idea that a collision with an asteroid caused the extinction of the dinosaurs is at least being considered seriously by an increasing number of scientists.'

12 T.   *Return and transfiguration*: ignoring the commentary's hesitation, the narrative closes with the image of the dinosaur transformed towards man. Russell, the initial dispatcher, presents a model of what might have been; not the solution to the problem, but the possible consequence of there never having been an extinction in the first place.

Again following Propp, I can present the actorial structure as seen in Figure 14.1.

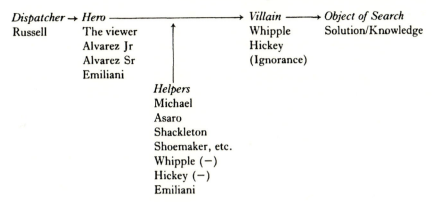

Figure 14.1 The actorial structure in *The Death of the Dinosaurs*

A number of points are worth making again briefly. First of all it is not until the appearance of the first Alvarez that the role of the hero is filled by the text itself. Until that point, the heroic space is left empty. We, the audience, are invited to undertake the quest; we are interpellated[42] both through the opening commentary identifying the mystery and by reference to our culture's collective fantasies through the extracts from *One Million Years BC*. By the time both the Alvarezes have appeared the narrative has asked us to identify with them, and through them with the process of science itself.

Secondly the progress of the narrative is in part a mimicry of the supposed activity of science – the building up of an argument and the piecing together of the elements of the quest – and is expressed as if it happened that way. The immediacy of the image, the directness of the demonstrations and the juxtaposition of the segments – Gubbio, California, Montana, Arizona; Alvarez, Michael, Shoemaker, Whipple and so on – slot into the heroic narrative structure in a way that belies the effort at its construction.

It follows from this that the structure itself, and the expectation it brings with it to be able to follow a rattling good story, has a semantic significance all of its own which is independent of the content it carries. In this the narrative finds its closure. So when the commentary, the voice of the text, urges caution, suggests a balance or a compromising footnote, the weight of the narrative and the anticipation of its resolution is in fundamental conflict with that caution. The power of the film which is in the audio-visual power of a traditional and entirely familiar narrative structure compromises the literal (and literary) caution of the spoken word. And of course vice versa.

The final, perhaps obvious point, arises from this. The programme is made because of, or on the back of, a story. The film focuses on the problems of understanding the death of the dinosaurs, and the science appears only in so far as it illuminates those problems. The programme is not in the business, say, of investigating forams, supernovas or neutron activation analysis and enquiring into their relevance for science or the world at large. What this amounts to is a simple observation about how television works. It is television and not science which defines the frame.

The second aspect of the mythic narrative concerns its logic, an organizing structure of concrete categories which provide both the building blocks of its own narrative and a way in which that narrative grounds its material in the fundamental experience of a culture. These categories, as I have suggested elsewhere,[43] focus on the organization of space and use familiar and everyday images to present a textual expression of the basic ordering capacity of mankind.[44] Specifically, the logic provides the frame for a presentation of science which is grounded in an articulation of a series of simple oppositions: nature and culture, mind and body, life and death, male and female, man and animal. I have noted the references in commentary to the significance of the content of the programme for understanding the origins of mankind, itself a classically mythical preoccupation.[45] Indeed it is clear that the images – of the earth from space, of the paintings of the dinosaurs, of the explosions, fire, wild animals, in slow motion, and of micro-technology – are powerfully evocative of aspects of the world both different from, and a challenge to, everyday experience.

What follows is both schematic and summary.

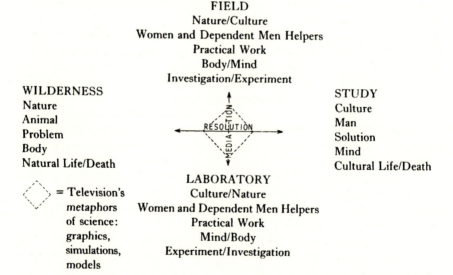

Figure 14.2 The mythic logic in science in *The Death of the Dinosaurs*

The disentanglement of the structure shown in Figure 14.2 should not obscure its basic simplicity, nor should any of it be a surprise. The model of the mythic logic of a narrative such as this must work with categories that are entirely understood and acceptable, unconsciously if not consciously, by the culture which receives it. In its movement through the structure, the narrative, with its beginning in the wilderness and its conclusion in the study/museum (active and passive expressions of cultural domination over nature), tells its own story and with these categories explores the broadly philosophical dimensions of the text. (See Mauss, note 32.)

The basic geographical code, Wilderness–Study–Field–Laboratory, is expressed directly in the images of the programme. It begins in outer space and moves immediately to archaic nature before arriving at the museum where the implications of the problem of the dinosaurs' extinction are spelt out; then again to the wilderness (44, 45) before undertaking a circular path from field to study to laboratory and museum, interrupted by occasional excursions through simulation and modelling, back into the wilderness (natural or man-made) in images of nuclear explosions, supernovas, starfields, flames. The wilderness, essentially macrocosmic in this film, is presented quite negatively both as destructive and as the source of the problem for the narrative to solve. It is pure nature, as opposed to the pure culture of the study and the museum, where man's domination over nature is expressed in thought or in the products of thought and classification.

It is here that the significant acting units of the narrative are to be found: the dispatcher Russell in his museum surrounded by models and restorations of long-dead species, and the dominating hero of the search, Luiz Alvarez, in his book-lined office, sitting at his wide desk in the heart of the Berkeley campus in California.

Mediating between the relative purity of nature and culture are the locations which are defined as field and laboratory, each expressing a different version of the conjunction of nature and culture in scientific activity: the field where nature still dominates against the intrusion of man in his efforts of discovery and experiment (Walter Alvarez; the digging in the Montana hills; Meteor Crater; Hickey with his fossils); the laboratory where culture dominates against the intrusion of nature in the efforts of controlled experimentation (neutron activation analysis; the demonstration of photosynthesis; the analysis of marine deposits by Shackleton; the testing of high impact velocities). These are the elements of the dominating code, dominating, I suggest, by virtue principally of the demands of a visual medium to *place* its action, and by the primary filming decisions as to where any and every sequence must take place.

Subsidiary levels of coding are the technical, the social and the physical. Each adds a dimension to the significance of place established through the geographical code.

The social code concerns the placing of man and animal: the masters of the wilderness – untamed, threatening, the subject of myth and fantasy; and man in his post-Baconian environment – rational, dominating, cerebral, controlling, even when, as in this case, he is only modestly successful in his theoretical thinking. This juxtaposition is stated at the outset of the film, and it is at its strongest in the opening and closing frames where Russell is placed beside his models. Alvarez, the hero, never leaves his desk. He is surrounded both in reality and in the film by helpers, including his son, only waiting for ideas 'which none of us could knock down' (Asaro, 111). These helpers are the lesser men, and also women, who occupy the more marginal, though it might be argued also the more productive, positions, either in field or laboratory – the worker ants. These status distinctions, variously upheld in science and variously accepted in a text such as this one, are useful as explorations of that boundary which marks the human from the animal and with which all societies in their different ways are concerned. In our society, of course, science is a main focus of that concern. To separate man, in general and in the particular, from animal, the text places a number of marginal beings: helpers who are less than men measured by the exacting standards and status of the theoretical physicist, and women, inferior in any case in a chauvinist culture, each of whom has no place either in the study or, except as a victim, in the wilderness.

In relation to their positive contribution to the solution of the mystery it is quite clear that the text treats field and laboratory differently. There are three sequences of scientists actually in the field: Walter Alvarez at Gubbio who identifies the problem and then goes to his father for help; Shoemaker at Meteor Crater who describes the effect of a meteor landing on earth; and Hickey, digging up botanical fossils, who refuses to accept the Alvarez thesis – an objection which is discounted by the film. Each is weak narratively, and Hickey is positively unhelpful. On the other hand those who work in the laboratory, men only, except Michael and Sturz who are shown to have failed in their attempts to measure the amount of iridium in the clay layer, have a more positive function narratively. Their work (Shackleton, Ahrens, O'Keefe) moves the argument and the tale along.

The two exceptions to this are Whipple and Emiliani, and they prove something of a problem, for Whipple, standing beside an enormous globe, offers a theory which is summarily rejected but does so in an environment closer to a study than a laboratory, and Emiliani, first beside a relief map and then under Miami trees, are both anomalous. Indeed, each of them has claims to be hero. It is Whipple's idea of the meteor's puncturing of the earth's crust that, were it to have been acceptable, would have completed and confirmed Alvarez's view of the meteor's significance. It fails. Whipple is granted the status of thinker (hence his location away from the laboratory) but an unsuccessful one. Emiliani, however, develops, apparently more constructively, the Alvarez hypothesis, and from the point of view of the text, gets the final theoretical words. His placing outside, close to nature, is only justifiable in terms of the content of what he is saying – an argument about the effects of water vapour in the atmosphere, the consequent rise of surface temperature and the negative effect on large reptiles and mammals; and by the evident heat and humidity in Miami at the time of the filming. As potential hero, of course, he is not bound by place in the way a modest helper might be expected to be.

Neither the physical code (life:death; physical:mental) nor the technical code (active:passive; problem:solution) are particularly intrusive in this text. It is clear that the wilderness is the place for, and the source of, life and death, both natural, and that the study is the potential source both of cultural life (in the form of successful theory) and cultural death (the frequent reference to, leading to images of, nuclear explosions). Field and laboratory are both the places for the transformation and the control of nature, and, to a degree, of our understanding of the matters of life and death. The wilderness is physical as opposed to the study which is mental. Both laboratory and field combine the two.

In the technical code the same opposition holds; the wilderness as problem, the study as solution, the wilderness as actively producing, the study as passively producing, with the laboratory and field transitional and transformational.

It seems important to say that my argument is not that the programme *The Death of the Dinosaurs* is *about* life and death, or nature and culture, or activity and passivity, but that it uses these very simple oppositions as a way of expressing its own particular narrative truth,[46] and it does so, almost essentially, in an unconscious way. The power of the narrative exists in these juxtapositions and transformations. Its work is relatively subtle. Perhaps more obvious is the way in which an advertisement for a gleaming product of modern technology will place a car or a washing machine, naked, in a desert, beside the sea or on top of a mountain. To point it out methodologically is only to reveal some of the conditions for the possibility of meaning, not the meaning itself. The status of the analysis is identical to that of a linguist in relation to natural language who will not add to the meaning of a given spoken or written text, but seeks only to explore its potential to create meaning.[47]

That we are dealing with plural meanings, and therefore with the demand that the analysis will be sensitive to that plurality, now becomes abundantly clear. The mythic, in chronology and logic, provides one, albeit central, dimension to the narrative. It does, in common parlance, generate the story. A parallel dimension of the text is provided by its argument, and by the mimetic. This is the subject of the next section.

The Death of the Dinosaurs: the mimetic narrative

If the mythic in television documentary pulls the viewer towards fantasy, then the mimetic pulls him or her towards reality. It does so by a label 'documentary'; and it does so in the image which in its presence seems to guarantee fidelity to a separate and unmediated reality; and it does so through a narrative form, essentially word-driven, which defines an argument or a logic which by its very invisibility is recognized as natural. Television documentary science is no exception to this. Nor is *The Death of the Dinosaurs*.

Science in our society, and in conventional views of it, is a supremely rational activity.[48] It has access to truth by virtue of its ability to follow rules of procedure, by its techniques and technical language, and by open communication within specialist communities. Scientific propositions conform to facts.[49] A science documentary must claim the same, but it does so with neither the specialist community, the language, nor with the same kinds of rules. Its audience is potentially universal; its language is the intangible but restricted language of television, and its rules are the rules of narrative and of common sense. Television's texts are therefore not true but plausible, and television must persuade us, each time it speaks in its programmes, of its authority. It does so through the structures of its argument, through its rhetoric.

The forms in which classical rhetoric were structured have, as Richard Lanham has pointed out,[50] governed

> a good deal of writing and speaking not specifically rhetorical. Its structure has influenced the way we think and argue, of course, in every instance where we argue a case . . . . We tend to take it as an inevitable pattern of dialectic thought. In fact, there seems no more reason to regard it as an inevitable form for an argument than there does to regard beginning—middle—end as the only form for a narrative.

A television documentary, as I have suggested, argues a case and does so both by reference to a form of argument, and through its ability in the image to present reality to all intents and purposes transparently. This is what I have called the natural history of documentary narrative. The form may be argument or description; if the latter, the text may follow the pattern of the seasons or the natural sequence of a journey or classification. In *The Death of the Dinosaurs*, there is an argument, and I want in this section to examine how it is constructed.

Broadly it conforms to the six steps in the arrangement (*dispositio*) set by classical rhetoric. An *exordium* or introduction sets the story in a compelling way. *Narratio*, where the outline of the problem is presented, and *divisio*, where the material is divided into manageable parts or sequences, follow. *Confirmatio* (confirmation) and *refutatio* (refutation) appear to establish the validity of the arguments and the case being offered, and the invalidity of the opposing case. This is followed by the *peroratio*, or summing up.

In *The Death of the Dinosaurs* the *exordium* consists of the pre- and immediately post-title sequences: shots of the earth from space, the paintings of the dinosaurs and the sequence from the feature film. The commentary reinforces the picture's eloquent invocation of great themes and powerful fantasies. The sequence of the tiny mammal and Dale Russell in the museum provide the *narratio*: the implications of the massive extinction are identified and the problems for solution are established. The bulk of the film, the various theories, tested, confirmed, rejected, the conflicting hypotheses of Alvarez, Whipple and Emiliani, provide the *confirmatio* and *refutatio* (or seek to provide it), and Russell is given the job, supported by commentary, of the *peroratio*, with the return to opening themes. The magical 'So' in 'So, perhaps if it were not for a chance collision with an asteroid, creatures very like this would be ruling the earth today, just as they did all those millions of years ago' (284) forecloses any objection, and assumes in a neat rhetorical tactic that the issue is settled, and that the previous argument has led naturally to this one conclusion. Of course the programme has done nothing to identify the specific evolutionary path that dinosaurs might have taken were they to have survived, nor to consider the enormous complexity of any evolutionary strand over a period of 65 million years. A great deal is buried, rhetorically, behind the word 'perhaps'.

If the viewer is asked by the mythic narrative to be its hero, then the mimetic narrative asks him to be magistrate;[51] a judge of the testimony of expert and commentary voice. The viewer is in the place of the crowd for a classical oration. Television seeks to sway the multitude in the process of informing it, though the multitude is unlikely to be aware of the significance of that ambition.

Let me present, in summary form, an account of the framing arguments in *The Death of the Dinosaurs* (Figure 14.3). Like so much on television this framing logical structure is both remarkably simple and remarkably effective. It mirrors the Popperian view of how science itself is undertaken[52] (1. below = P_1; 2. = TT_1; 3. = EE; 4. = TT_2; 5. = P_2). In so doing both in its form and in its content the television text appeals to science for arguments and proof that it cannot by itself provide, just as science, in its own way of doing things, appeals to empirical evidence. Its close parallel with the mythic narrative chronology is obviously worth noting, and that too echoes the practice of presenting science, even in specialist papers.[53]

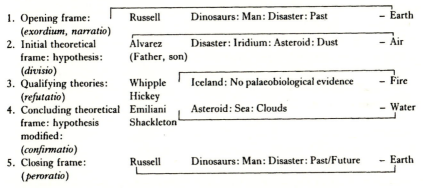

1. Opening frame: (*exordium, narratio*)	Russell	Dinosaurs: Man: Disaster: Past	– Earth
2. Initial theoretical frame: hypothesis: (*divisio*)	Alvarez (Father, son)	Disaster: Iridium: Asteroid: Dust	– Air
3. Qualifying theories: (*refutatio*)	Whipple Hickey	Iceland: No palaeobiological evidence	– Fire
4. Concluding theoretical frame: hypothesis modified: (*confirmatio*)	Emiliani Shackleton	Asteroid: Sea: Clouds	– Water
5. Closing frame: (*peroratio*)	Russell	Dinosaurs: Man: Disaster: Past/Future	– Earth

Figure 14.3 Mimetic logic of science in *The Death of the Dinosaurs*

At the risk of some repetition: opening commentary and Russell establish the context of the problem, the way of its solution, its implications and its focus. The 'very remarkable dinosaur', *Stenonychosaurus*, makes the link between the reptile and the human, by virtue of its intelligence, just as the paintings make the link between present and past, and the extracts from the feature film between reality and fantasy. The extinction is presented as the consequence of a chance event, and there is no discussion of the possibility of this initial assumption being incorrect.

The first theoretical frame is defined by the two Alvarezes, son and father, firstly in the identification of the mysterious clay layer between the Tertiary and the Cretaceous coincident with the time when the dinosaurs were presumed to have been made extinct, and secondly through a series of hypotheses suggested by the Nobel physicist; iridium, supernova, asteroid, earth or sea landing, are the elements to be tested and confirmed or refuted. At each stage hypothesis and 'the real mystery' are measured against what is already known; for example, the commentary can suggest, without blushing, that 'the iridium layer is real' (109).

The alternative theories are presented: the first, Whipple's, summarily refuted; the second, from Hickey, summarily ignored. Emiliani and Shackleton are given the task of presenting a revised theory, and the one which the narrative, at least, accepts.

Russell provides the peroration, returning to the initial themes and a model of the consequences of the alternative scenario. The reference, now scientific and legitimated by the narrative, is to what might have been. Science too has its fantasies.

In its progress the narrative generates one major inconsistency and one contradiction. The inconsistency lies in its discussion of the impact site of the asteroid and of Whipple's suggestion that it landed in the sea, across a continental ridge. Whipple failed to account for the effects of continental drift and so his argument is refuted, but the narrative mistakes the refutation of his suggestion of site for a refutation of the whole Whipple theory. Alvarez, bolstered by evidence from Krakatoa, talks subsequently about the amount and the effect of dust in the atmosphere, and no further reference to the specific effects of a sea landing is made until Emiliani reintroduces it (220), with false novelty: 'The key was that the asteroid fell into the sea.'

The contradiction concerns Hickey's refusal to accept Alvarez's theory because 'there is no evidence of an asteroid impact' from the palaeobiological evidence. The commentary immediately counters: 'Nevertheless, half the plants did become extinct. Something must have happened. And although Hickey doubts it, others still believe there was an asteroid – and it did collide with the earth.'

This sequence is a forceful example of the way in which a television narrative will present what might appear to be a balancing element, but in such a way as to neutralize its effect. Many studies of news and current affairs have analysed the ways in which unconscious political bias is effected in this way. Here it is an intellectual argument which, simply by ignoring the force of counter- or contrary evidence, rhetorically achieves the coherence and consistency which the medium demands.

The Death of the Dinosaurs: varieties of rhetoric

Image

Before discussing the specific images of science in *The Death of the Dinosaurs*, I need to say something of the film's contextual imagery.

This is a film about dinosaurs. And dinosaurs are extinct. In setting out to make such a film, this appeared to be the primary problem, and it forced the film-maker to effect reconstructions and simulations of as great a variety as possible to fill the screen with interesting images. This is a film therefore with a high proportion of iconic images and visual metaphors.

The icons consist of the paintings, extracts from other films, models, globes, maps, graphics; background for voice-over commentary – wallpaper in television's own parlance. The dominating visual metaphor is of the nuclear explosion, which both echoes the scientists' own words to describe the kind of impact the meteor would have had (186) and anticipates them (158).

The presence of such icons and metaphors reflects two aspects of television documentary discourse, the first generic and therefore subject to change, the second more substantial. The first reflects the great anxiety about the 'talking-head', the presence on the screen, in mid-shot or close-up, of a man or woman talking to one side of the camera and to an unseen interviewer. It is believed that such images should be carefully restricted. Very few scientists are thought to possess the magnetic personality sufficient to hold an audience, and hence the search for images which will illustrate and possibly reinforce what they have to say. The second reflects a much more basic assumption, that seeing is believing, that a visual illustration properly executed can say more than a thousand words, and that images themselves are likely to be remembered when what they are supposed to illustrate has long been forgotten.

The second set of non-specifically scientific images concerns the establishment of context. The external shot of a laboratory or a campus precedes the entry of the cameras inside. In *The Death of the Dinosaurs* this is used relatively little. Only two sequences are established in this way. Both Walter Alvarez and Luiz are established initially by wide shots which contain church or bell towers, first at Gubbio and then at Berkeley. Otherwise each of the scientists talks to camera and does so without formal visual introduction. They are placed on location, as it were, either in the field or in the laboratory. Consequently, the visual narrative gives the impression of speed and of a dialogue actually taking place between the protagonists.

So to specific images of science. They can be characterized in three ways.

(a) *Anthropomorphic images*: scientists do science and scientists talk about science. On television scientists will have to be seen doing both, though mostly they will be seen talking. Where they are placed, therefore, as I have already suggested, assumes some considerable significance. *The Death of the Dinosaurs* affords a clear example of the different roles television provides for scientists:

    (i)   *scientist as thinker*, surrounded by the products of his thought, or of the thoughts of others, and seated at his desk, where thoughts are produced (Luis Alvarez);

    (ii) *scientist as technician*, surrounded by equipment and placed in the laboratory, the scientist is master of mysterious and powerful apparatus (Ahrens, Michael, Asaro, Shackleton);

(iii) *scientist as labourer*, surrounded by manifestly uninformative nature, the scientist with simple tools can produce information as a result of physical activity (Walter Alvarez, Hickey, Ahrens);

(iv) *scientist as demonstrator*, surrounded by audio and/or visual displays, the scientist can teach (Whipple, Emiliani);

(v) *scientist as interpreter*, surrounded by the meaningful (to him) natural world, the scientist can authoritatively decipher it (Shoemaker, Hutchinson).

Each of these roles, of course, suggests a different aspect of the scientist as hero (or occasionally as anti-hero), the abiding impression of him which is reinforced both by the general failure of television to challenge or cross-examine him and by the imposition of a context which both frames and echoes his unchallenged competence as a specialist in our society. Science as a consequence of this particular set of images is presented as a highly individualistic affair, undertaken by men (principally) who are articulate and successful (even if, as in Whipple's case, they are shown to be wrong; indeed, even Alvarez refers to Whipple as 'the great comet expert' prior to excluding his contribution as inadequate). Scientists do not generally have families, warts, stammers, bad tempers or difficult colleagues; they are neither stupid, glamorous, unreasonable or depressed. They are almost always disinterested.

(b) *Technomorphic images*: science is a technical activity and television assumes that it cannot be undertaken successfully without sophisticated technology. Here our culture's general enthusiasm for the biggest, the newest, the most expensive is given free rein. Such technology must be made visible, and often, as I have suggested, scientists are placed beside a particularly impressive bit of it while they talk to camera. Under such circumstances its function and its workings are not always clearly explained.

In *The Death of the Dinosaurs* there are two sequences in which samples of clay are being tested, firstly for iridium, then for plutonium 244, in what is identified as Neutron Activation Analysis (73–8; 88–93). In this case the commentary does say something to identify the process and its working:

> To measure it an extremely sensitive technique called Neutron Activation Analysis was used. Carefully prepared samples were taken down to Berkeley's nuclear reactor. Here the samples were bombarded with neutrons produced in the reactor's core. The neutrons excite the atoms in the clay. Later, as the atoms decay, they give off gamma-rays. The pattern of gamma-rays reveals which elements are present. The results surprised everyone.

The images are of a big close-up of some brown powder being transferred into a container, that container being placed in a larger container with a label *Caution, Radioactive Material* attached to it and towards which the camera zooms. Next the scientist is seen carrying a container through a pink-lit room and then through a green-lit chamber before passing it on, silently, to another white-coated figure. The camera pans down to the deep blue of what we are referred to as the 'reactor's core'. The following shot is of a control panel being activated, a shot of the gently rippling water surrounding the core and a pattern on an oscilloscope with one line significantly longer than the other.

A sequence such as this privileges the objects and technology and provides an account of what these images are to signify. The relationship between image and word is essentially arbitrary. A sentence such as 'The neutrons excite the atoms in the clay. Later, as the atoms decay, they give off gamma-rays', for example, bears no significant relationship to the pictures which show gently rippling water surrounding a metal object. Equally we are not told here or anywhere else in the programme what gamma-rays are, how they are used to measure the presence of iridium, or how accurately. (The technique is referred to as 'extremely sensitive'.)

Given the lack of such information, which I am not suggesting is necessarily illegitimate from the point of view of the producers, and given the lack of any information which will allow the viewer to judge for himself or herself both the significance of the images and the weight of the commentary, we might be forgiven for suggesting that the burden which this sequence carries is of a more fundamental order; that it signifies, as do many similar sequences, something quite simple: that science can be visually appealing, that we, the lay audience, are not expected to understand it or judge it, and that it depends crucially on machines as mediators.

(c) *Semiomorphic images*: the third set of images which television produces to illustrate science are those of its products, its own texts. They are, principally, of two kinds: images of readings, for example on the oscilloscope just mentioned, and images of final texts, for example a page from a textbook or scribbled equations on a blackboard. Clearly television's own graphics, while not science's own and motivated with a mission to explain, are also semiomorphs. But here their function is more directly associated with the logic of the mimetic narrative. These can be called second order representations. First order representations are minimally mediated and along with whatever commentary accompanies them are expected to be self-evident. The image on the oscilloscope is just such a representation; a pen trace (262) purporting to measure isotropic ratios in forams is another.

It is quite clearly impossible for television to explain in detail the precise significance such readings have for science, and it is quite clear that any explanation which a scientist offers as to their significance will be accepted as trustworthy and we, the viewers, will accept television's account of it as trustworthy also.

Indeed the mere appearance of such literal manifestations of the result of scientific activity has, I suggest, another function. It is through such images that science is transcribed as *Science*; and as *Science* it is, in these images, its own hieroglyphs, an arcane, inaccessible and potent activity.

Look

The documentary look is a look at its object, fixing the object rather than putting its look into play, the object looked at but only itself looking on; the figures of the drama exchange and reverse looks, the figures of the documentary are looked at and look on. Within the conventions of documentary, the objectifying look is part of the support of truth and neutrality.[54]

There is nothing so artful, so motivated, as the construction of the documentary image to be real. From this manifest paradox arises the possibility of a rhetoric of the camera's look. It is, of course, theoretically impossible to separate look from image; the how from the what of television's visuals. It is equally impossible to offer a complete or convincing account of such visuals without a sophisticated theory of perception or, equally plausibly, a sophisticated theory of language, the unconscious and the construction of the symbolic.

This very brief discussion therefore depends on a separation of look and image which reflects the practices of film-making, above all the series of technical and aesthetic decisions summarized in the question: 'How are we going to shoot it?' It also leaves open the question of the best theoretical way to make sense of otherwise crude and naïve observations about the implications of the way an image is presented for the screen. Crucially the problem is that of the management of emotion. Images are not amenable to the same kind of rational analysis as words, and even they, of course, are infinitely plural. Images, even of the most prosaic kind, will have a resonance which, as single shots or in sequences, will touch members of an audience in powerful and individual ways, ways which may have very little to do with the intentions of the producer or director who selected them.

In deciding how to shoot a shot or a sequence of shots, the following seem to be material:

(a) lighting and camera angle
(b) size of shot
(c) movement of camera
(d) montage (juxtaposition of edited shots).

(a) In the case of lighting and camera angle, the nuances of expression are slender; decently lit exteriors, balancing light and shade, sensitively lit interiors, with filling or back light. The camera will be steady, held at eye height, and its movements, a pan or a zoom, lead the viewer's eye in a particular direction. Such naturalistic images, however difficult to achieve – the sun might be high in a cloudless sky or the interviewee's glasses may be reflecting a spotlight – are the standard fare of documentary practice and they are rarely other than taken for granted. The nuances of light and shade and of camera angle seem like the nuances of intonation in a spoken text.

But equally there are many sequences which leave this ideal, the mellow exterior or comfortable interior, for something more pointed. Even here, of course, there is no way in which the sense of the natural is breached, because the content of the image is still that of the real. Nevertheless we are aware of faces lit from below (the horror of sunken eyes) or of an atmosphere created by a scene under- or backlit.

Much of the camera's look in *The Death of the Dinosaurs* has the natural feel about it, but there is one sequence in particular which is worthy of notice (68–73). It begins with a high shot of a scientist arriving at a bench. The shot is generally underlit and the single light source appears to come from above – the top of the head and papers on the bench are well lit, as is one side of the piece of apparatus. The second shot is of material being ground in a crucible, in normal light (apparently daylight), and this is followed by a close-up of a hand emptying the sample from a test-tube into a bowl. Here the light returns to the harsh semi-darkness. The next shot is a tight close-up of the scientist's face in full profile; light picks out the line of her face, of her glasses and of wisps of her hair. The sequence is completed with a shot of hands and crucible again in contrasty light and shade.

There is no question that this is a dramatically framed and lit sequence, and one can only speculate on the motives of cameraman and director in shooting it in this way. But the result is clearly a heightening of an otherwise mundane activity in a way which attempts to make dramatic capital of a simple scientific operation.

(b) Since, as I have suggested, the shot is an instruction to look in a particular way, the size of the image becomes important, and especially the close-up which becomes a kind of italicization, a stress and an emphasis. Christian Metz in his discussion of the close-up recognizes its simply descriptive element, but also argues that the close-up has, often, a powerful symbolic significance which it gains rhetorically from its relationship to what is absent: 'one of the main ways in which an object is transformed into a sign, in the cinema, is by selectively representing one part of the object . . . thereby choosing the meaning one wants to give it over and above the representation (but through it)'.[55] The close-up is the cinematic synecdoche; the part for the whole, the metonymy of film. In television science documentary, the images of science as scientist (close-up of face or hands), of science as machine (close-up of switches, dials, test-tubes), of science as symbol (close-up of print-outs or printed pages), are all synecdoches and all examples of the way in which the close-up can be seen to have this double valency, both literal and symbolic.

In *The Death of the Dinosaurs* close-ups are used to introduce intelligent dinosaurs (33) – head, claws, eyes – a sequence which fragments the coherence of the body in a way which is often perpetrated on the bodies of women in mass-mediated images. There are subsequent close-ups of the eye-sockets of a fossilized *Triceratops* (43), of the clay layer between the Cretaceous and the Tertiary (51ff), of Luiz Alvarez holding a fragment of the rock embedded in lucite (59ff), of hands grinding clay in a crucible, of the first interview with Asaro (80) where the camera is positioned high and to the right, of Luiz Alvarez's hand writing at his desk. There are close-ups of the controls of machines and of oscilloscope screens, of hands managing delicate equipment, and so on.

The close-up is used on faces, on parts of the body, on bits of machinery; it is used at the end or beginning of a zoom as a way of drawing the viewer into or extracting him from a detail of the object or scene in vision. None of this is surprising, though it might be important to note that in, for example, an interview, the size, angle and indeed focal length of the lens chosen can have profound effects, and can significantly transform the image as real.

(c) There are four principal camera movements: the zoom in which the elements in the lens move so that the size of the image can be increased or decreased; a pan and a tilt in which a stationary camera can either move horizontally or vertically; and a track in which a moving camera, either on a dolly or hand-held, can follow or create movement or action. Each, of course, is a particular request for the viewer's attention, and each technically has a function in film practice. Each allows a single shot to develop without cutting into it. Each generates a visual narrative of its own.

From the point of view of what has already been said, the zoom in to the close-up is particularly interesting, for that movement provides potentially a bridge from the literal (the full-frame context) to the symbolic (the close-up fragment), so that the movement to close-up is at the same time a focusing for sight (description) and emotion (sign). The zoom out is the opposite. For example, in *The Death of the Dinosaurs*, the longest single shot (130), of Shoemaker sitting on the rim of Meteor Crater and speaking to camera about the likely effects of a major asteroid impact, contains both a zoom in and out. It is preceded by an aerial shot of the crater and is framed initially with Shoemaker sitting right of centre and talking to camera left; on his immediate right (camera left) a dead and possibly scorched tree stump balances his posture and acts as a metonym of the great heat of the explosion some 25,000 years before. The crater extends behind. Shoemaker is asking the viewer to construct an imaginative picture of his own: 'Picture yourself standing about twenty miles from here about 25,000 years ago.' The shot is held until the line, 'In fact it grew so bright that you will be on the verge of being scorched', at which there is a slow zoom to a mid close-up (framing head and shoulders and allowing for demonstrative hand movements). Shoemaker continues his piece to camera, and just before he returns to the 'you' of his imagined audience, the camera begins a slow zoom out to its original position. The camera seems hand-held throughout.

The camera movement is a simple one and it allows the viewer, having seen the context of his utterances, to concentrate more on the man who is uttering them. The assumption seems to be that a close-up here provides less distracting visual information for the viewer, though clearly this is arguable since the size of the framed image (the screen) and the amount of visual information being transmitted is identical in each case. But it is instructive to note that the camera movement approximately coincides with Shoemaker's own secondary focusing; the repeated reference to the 'you' of the audience. The camera takes literally the instruction to become involved in the spoken text and provides a physical and visual initiative for the viewer to follow in thought.[56]

There is a similar example (211) in the sequence where Hickey finds a fossilized leaf. A close-up of the splitting of the rock becomes a zoom and a tight close-up as the voices of those involved express surprise and wonder. The fossilized leaf in tight close-up becomes metonymically of considerable significance: as a representative of 'the laurel family', as a fragment of the buried past, and as a piece of evidence to discount the Alvarez theory.

(d)   Representation A and representation B must be so selected from all the possible features within the theme that is being developed, must be sought for, that their *juxtaposition* – that is the juxtaposition of *those very elements* and not of alternative ones – shall evoke in the perceptions and feelings of the spectator the most complete image of the theme itself. . . .

Our films are faced with the task of presenting not only a narrative that is logically connected, but one that contains a maximum of emotion and stimulating power.[57]

Serge Eisenstein, working in the silent cinema, conceived a theory and practice of the management of emotion through the juxtaposition of the visual image. When we talk of the power of film, even in the days of sound, it is most often the image to which we are referring.

A detailed analysis of the juxtaposition of images in *The Death of the Dinosaurs* is impossible here, but I can make an elementary distinction which might be helpful. There is a difference between the juxtaposition of shots in order to build up a sequence which has a particular literal, narrative or visual consistency, as, for example, the sequence (57–64) which presents Luiz Alvarez's first appearance and which begins with an establishing shot of the Berkeley campus, followed by a mid-shot of him in his study, a close-up of the sample of rock being held in his hand, and then an alternation of mid-shot and close-up of face; and the juxtaposition which marks the end of that sequence and the beginning of the next, where the cut is between Alvarez in his office and a brightly animated graphic of the formation of the earth. Although the second image seems called for in the commentary, it does not have the same necessity as those of the previous sequence. It is a shock. And from the point of view of the syntagmatics of the film text, it is an indication both of the total (paradigmatic) freedom that the director has in selecting images, and the consequent impossibility of constructing a viable linguistics of the film or television text.

There is a third possibility in the relationship of shot to shot which acts as a variation of the conjuncture/disjuncture pairing just described. It can be characterized in terms of metaphor, where either the image is presented as a vehicle of a previously stated theme in commentary, as for example at the end of the Shoemaker sequence where his reference to a mushroom cloud is followed by an image of just such a cloud; or where the words provide a vehicle for a previously identified theme in the image, as for example later in the film (205–7), when Luiz Alvarez is speculating on how long the dust cloud would remain in the atmosphere: 'We don't know how long our supposed cloud would stay up, but we've always said a few years or several years'.[58] This is voice to camera. The next shot is of a red sky and desolate landscape. The sound is of the wind, and it is not until the following shot of a further landscape that the commentary intones: 'The world laid waste.'

Consideration of montage in such a way, once again, has as its consequence the blurring of the distinction between image and look, and it does so quite necessarily for judgements on the efficacy of a particular juxtaposition depend centrally on appreciation of the content of the image and not just on the mere fact of juxtaposition. In his or her relation to a documentary television programme such as *The Death of the Dinosaurs*, it is unlikely that a lay viewer will make much of such a distinction. Only analysis requires it, and then only provisionally.

Voice

It will come as no surprise that a text such as that of *The Death of the Dinosaurs*, in the construction of its argument (both in commentary and in contributors' voices), will both exemplify and depend on the measures of persuasion defined in classical rhetoric. The words are spoken to a large and indiscriminate audience. The programme must convince this audience not only of its authority to speak, but of the correctness of its arguments, the adequacy of its description, and the truth of its analysis. Scientists in their interviews will, to a greater or lesser degree, seek to persuade the questioner of just this, and the programme as a whole must do likewise. There is a premium therefore on coherence and consistency, both of which extend, of course, right into the heart of documentary discourse, and not just to the spoken word.

At once there is a paradox and it is one to which I have already referred. It is the paradox of balance, and it is well known in classical rhetoric. A BBC producer is enjoined, particularly in matters of contention (and this is indeed only where it matters), to provide a balanced view in order for the viewer to be able to decide between competing accounts or policies. While this may be possible in a political debate, and it is sometimes possible in television science, it is nevertheless difficult given two factors: the first being an ideological demand to present science authoritatively and therefore not fundamentally or irresolvably in dispute; the second the cultural imperative to tell a good story which requires a clearly defined resolution – a good ending. No single programme can do both, but even those that do push a particular line – and the producers in these cases of course believe themselves to be entirely justified by the evidence in so pursuing it – must nevertheless bow to demands for balance. Hence what I suggest is the principal rhetorical figure in the spoken argument of television science: *apophasis*.

Apophasis is a kind of irony, a saying of one thing and the doing of another, which in a sense is built into the whole structure of paradox, but it has a specific manifestation in a pretence to ignore what is really affirmed. This is crucially done in the sequence which I have already discussed, where Leo Hickey's contrary evidence, included and discussed, is nevertheless simply ignored. At the risk of some repetition (a good rhetorical strategy itself), let me comment on the interchange (214–17).

Leo Hickey: About fifty per cent of the forms that characterize the Cretaceous are extinct, but the basic plant communities that characterize the Cretaceous, and the dominant plants within those communities, remain the same.

Commentary: So where is the devastation an asteroid would produce? Leo Hickey doubts it actually happened.

Leo Hickey: Looking at the plant evidence across the Cretaceous–Tertiary boundary hère, we see no evidence of an asteroid impact.

Commentary: Nevertheless, half the plants did become extinct. Something must have happened. And although Hickey doubts it, others still believe that there was an asteroid – and it did collide with the earth.

The half empty glass has become half full; the opportunity for an alternative and competing thesis is eschewed, and the seriousness of Hickey's objection is unacknowledged. No evidence is presented to challenge Hickey's position. The narrative can proceed. The viewer can be persuaded.

Little would be served by listing the various rhetorical tropes and identifying their presence in a text such as this one. Having established the basic framework which television in turn establishes for argument, it is quite clear that those classical artifices will continually appear, particularly those which are involved in presenting balance and paradox (*alloiosis*, **antanagogue**, *anthypophora, climax, sermacinatio*), emotional appeal (*anacoenosis, apodixis, aporia, apostrophe, diabole, epiplexis*) or the use of example and the citation of authority (*analogy, anamnesis, apodixis, apomnemonysis, exemplum*).[59] I have already noted, following Metz, the significance of metaphor, metonymy and synecdoche as fundamental and overarching rhetorical tropes which are ever present in image and text of such a film. I might add irony to these three.

The presence of these figures in a text of television science is, however, crucially significant, and this can be explained by reference to the work of Chaim Perelman, and in particular to his consideration of the distinction between demonstration and argumentation.[60] A demonstration 'is regarded as correct or incorrect according as it conforms, or fails to conform, to the rules. A conclusion is held to be demonstrated if it can be reached by means of a series of correct operations starting from premises accepted as axioms.' The truths of science, its current sociology notwithstanding, depend on adequate demonstration: 'once we have accepted the framework of a formal system and know that it is free from ambiguity, then the demonstrations that can be made within it are compelling and impersonal'.

Not so argumentation – dialectical reasoning founded on opinion and concerned with contingent realities: 'an argumentation is always addressed by a person called the orator – whether by speech or in writing – to an audience of listeners or readers. It aims at obtaining or reinforcing the adherence of the audience to some thesis, assent to which is hoped for.' It presupposes a meeting of minds, a disposition of the audience to listen, mutual goodwill and, of course, a common language. The truths of television, no less, depend on the plausibility and effectiveness of its arguments.

Perelman's distinction cannot hold absolutely, for science has its rhetoric, and television its demonstrations, but even if it is a matter of degree rather than an absolute, the differences are marked and clear. Whatever the image, and the combination of images and words of television, do to the presentation of science, a major transformation is effected by the words alone. This transformation and the presuppositions upon which it depends both define and are defined by the particular context within which television as a whole operates. I have discussed it elsewhere in terms of the concepts of plausibility, community and legitimation,[61] which together identify, I believe, the elements of the particular ideological field which in cultural and social relations has television at its centre.

Conclusion

This essay is an attempt at the deconstruction of a television science documentary. In it I have tried to identify the various ways in which an infinitely complex text generates its meanings in its search for plausibility, consistency and persuasiveness. I have suggested that it is a text deeply embedded in traditions of story-telling and argument, but I have not considered specifically the wider issues of ideology and culture which such an analysis raises and even presupposes, and which any study of a television programme such as this must face. These issues will be discussed elsewhere.

The analysis defines the ways in which a television documentary incorporates, and in that incorporation transforms, material from another extra-televisual reality, and equally it generates pointers to the kinds of questions about those processes' ideological and cultural status. I would maintain that no analysis of production, reception or more broadly of signifying practice can afford to ignore the detailed structure of the texts of the communication, just as no study of speech can afford to neglect the form and content of what is being said. The reverse is equally true.

Science, from this point of view, has little special status. It is subject to the processes of television, and these processes work, to a significant extent, irrespective of content. They also work in a social environment in which science is already tarred with the brushes of popularization. But equally science illustrates very clearly, by virtue above all of its unmediated inaccessibility, the various strategies which in turn make up these processes of television, and which, of course, are crucial in making sense of the kind of science television communicates.

Notes

This paper arises out of research undertaken with the support of the Joint Committee of the Science and Engineering Research Council and the Social Science Research Council. It was first published in *Media, Culture and Society*, vol. 6, no. 4, 1984, and is reprinted by kind permission of Sage Publications Ltd.

1 Two points. This summary, uncontentious though it may appear, refers principally to *Horizon*, and is based on the analysis of the texts of programmes but also on extended periods of participant observation with the *Horizon* unit during 1981–3. In an analysis such as will be presented in this chapter I have occasionally drawn on evidence and inferences derived from that participant research. Secondly, although basically concerned with *Horizon*, I have undertaken interviews with science producers of other programmes and watched them at work. Inevitably such a description would change – though I doubt significantly – from one series of programmes to another.

2 George Gerbner, Larry Gross, Michael Morgan and Nancy Signorielli, *Television's Contribution to Public Understanding of Science: a Pilot Project*, Philadelphia, Annenberg School of Communications, 1980.

3 Cf. Jacques Barzun, foreword to S. Toulmin, *Foresight and Understanding: an Enquiry into the Aims of Science*, London, Hutchinson, 1961.

4 R. G. Dunn, 'Science, technology and bureaucratic domination: television and the ideology of scientism', *Media, Culture and Society*, 1 (1979), 343–54.

5 Charles Bazerman, 'What written knowledge does: three examples of academic discourse', *Philosophy of the Social Sciences*, 11 (1981), 361–87; G. Nigel Gilbert, 'Referencing as persuasion', *Social Studies of Science*, 7 (1977), 113–22 (hereafter cited as 'Referencing'); Steven Yearley, 'Textual persuasion: the role of social accounting in the construction of scientific arguments', *Philosophy of the Social Sciences*, 11 (1981), 409–35.

6 G. Nigel Gilbert, 'The transformation of research findings into scientific

knowledge', *Social Studies of Science*, 6 (1976), 281–306 (hereafter cited as 'Transformation'); Karin D. Knorr-Cetina, *The Manufacture of Knowledge: An Essay on the Contextual Nature of Science*, Oxford, Pergamon, 1981.

7 P. B. Medawar, 'Is the scientific paper a fraud?', *Listener*, 12 September 1963, 377–8.

8 A. J. Greimas, 'Des Accidents dans les sciences dits humaines: Analyse d'un texte de Georges Dumezil', in A. J. Greimas and E. Landowski (eds), *Introduction à l'analyse du discours en sciences sociales*, Paris, Hachette, 1979, pp. 28–60.

9 Bazerman, op. cit.

10 D. O. Edge, 'Technological metaphor', in D. O. Edge and J. N. Wolfe (eds), *Meaning and Control: Essays in Social Aspects of Science and Technology*, London, Tavistock, 1973, pp. 31–60; J. Gusfield, 'The literary rhetoric of science', *American Sociological Review*, 41 (1976), 16–34.

11 Gilbert, 'Referencing'.

12 G. Nigel Gilbert and M. Mulkay, 'Contexts of scientific discourse: social accounting in experimental papers', *Sociology of Science Yearbook*, 1980, pp. 269–94; John Ziman, *Public Knowledge: An Essay Concerning the Social Dimension of Science*, Cambridge, Cambridge University Press, 1968; hereafter cited as *Public Knowledge*.

13 There is deliberate irony in my use of terms here, for it will be clear as the chapter proceeds that I use, indeed must use, similar narrative strategies, of course transmuted to an exclusively literary and 'scientific' text, as those which I identify as being central in the televisual text. As many students of narrative have suggested, at a very simple level of structure, there may be a kind of unity in all acts of narration.

14 Knorr-Cetina, op. cit.; B. Latour and S. Woolgar, *Laboratory Life: The Social Construction of Scientific Facts*, Beverly Hills, Sage, 1979.

15 *The Death of the Dinosaurs*. Written and produced by John Groom. Film editor: Michael Casey. Transmitted: 16 and 22 November 1981, BBC-2.

16 The Audience Appreciation Index, constructed by the Broadcasters' Audience Research Board, is derived from a 6-point scale of appreciation submitted to a daily panel of *c.* 1000 viewers who report on their week's viewing. A value ranging from 100 to 0, with a high A.I. indicating a high level of appreciation, is constructed for each programme. The index is calculated by treating the scale points 6, 5, 4, 3, 2, 1, respectively as scales of 100, 80, 60, 40, 20, 0 and taking a simple average. An A.I. of 78 is high for *Horizon*.

17 *Radio Times*, 14–20 November 1981, 6–7.

18 Roger Silverstone, 'The right to speak: on a poetic for television documentary', *Media, Culture and Society*, 5 (1983), p. 142 (hereafter cited as 'The right to speak').

19 The numerical references are here identified single shots and are taken directly from the post-production script which the BBC has kindly provided.

20 References to identity, in brackets in the text, appear as superimposed subtitles on lower screen.

21 Shots 204 and 207, as listed in the post-production script, do not appear in the transmitted version of the programme.

22 Cf. Claude Lévi-Strauss, *Structural Anthropology*, vol. II, London, Jonathan Cape, 1976, p. 131. 'For [formalism] the two domains must be absolutely separate, since form alone is intelligible, and content is only a residual deprived of any significant value. For structuralism, this opposition does not exist. There is not something abstract on one side and something concrete on the other. Form and content are of the same nature, susceptible [to] the same analysis.'

23 Cf. Jean Piaget, *Structuralism*, London, Routledge & Kegan Paul, 1971, pp. 3–16.

24 Cf. Seymour Chatman, *Story and Discourse: Narrative Structure in Fiction Film*, Ithaca, Cornell University Press, 1980, pp. 15–43; cf. Boris Tomashevsky, 'Thematics', in Lee T. Lemon and Marion J. Reis (eds), *Russian Formalist Criticism: Four Essays*, Lincoln, University of Nebraska Press, 1965, pp. 66–78.

25 Silverstone, 'The right to speak'.

26 Roger Silverstone, *The Message of Television: Myth and Narrative in Contemporary Culture*, London, Heinemann, 1981 (hereafter cited as *The Message of Television*).

27 Cf. Jack Goody, *The Domestication of the Savage Mind*, Cambridge, Cambridge University Press, 1977, and Elizabeth Eisenstein, *The Printing Press as an Agent of Social Change*, Cambridge, Cambridge University Press, 1979.

28 Walter J. Ong, *Orality and Literacy: the Technologizing of the Word*, London, Methuen, 1982, p. 11.

29 J. L. Austin, *How to Do Things with Words*, London, Oxford University Press, 1975.

30 Cf. Ronald Primeau, *The Rhetoric of Television*, London, Longman, 1979, pp. 53–4.

31 Cf. Norman Swallow, *Factual Television*, London, Focal, 1966, p. 131: 'What the producer wants is the largest audience he can get without lowering his standards. All the pitfalls of the professional populariser lie before him, and he has done his work well if he holds the attention of a big audience without forgetting the respect of those who work in whatever science or art he has chosen to handle. This is a thin tightrope, and he may fall off it during the public performance. For it is as disastrous to be cheap and superficial as it is to be pedantic and obscure.'

32 Cf. Marcel Mauss, *A General Theory of Magic*, London, Routledge & Kegan Paul, 1972, pp. 141–2: '[Magic] is still a very simple craft. All efforts are avoided by successfully replacing reality by images. A magician does nothing, or almost nothing, but makes every one believe that he is doing everything and all the more so since he puts to work collective forces and ideas to help the individual imagination in its belief.'

33 For example, Gerald Millerson, *The Techniques of Television Production*, London, Focal Press, 1972.

34 Metz, op. cit., p. 405.

35 Swallow, op. cit., pp. 176–208.

36 Greta Jones, Ian Connell and Jack Meadows, *The Presentation of Science by the Media*, Leicester, Primary Communications Research Centre, 1977, p. 52.

37 ibid.

38 Cf. Carl Gardner and Robert Young, 'Science on TV: a critique', in T. Bennett *et al.* (eds), *Popular Television and Film*, London, British Film Institute, p. 178.

39 Cf. *Report of the Committee on the Future of Broadcasting* (chairman Lord Annan), Cmnd 6753, London, HMSO, 1977, p. 354.

40 Vladimir Propp, *Morphology of the Folktale*, 2nd edn, Austin, University of Texas Press, 1968.

41 Ernst Ulrich Grosse, 'French structuralist views on narrative grammar', in W. V. Dressler (ed.), *Current Trends in Text Linguistics*, Berlin, Walter de Gruyter, 1978, pp. 155–73.

42 Cf. Louis Althusser, *Lenin and Philosophy*, London, New Left Books, 1971.

43 Silverstone, *The Message of Television*; and 'A structure for a modern myth. Television and the transsexual', *Semiotica*, 49 (1984), 95–138.

44 This ascent to the rarefied atmosphere of a philosophical anthropology should not be misunderstood. Man's capacity to create, and dependence on creating, order is an obvious but intangible point of reference for any analysis of culture. It grounds, of course, Lévi-Strauss's structuralist enterprise, though not unequivocally. It is the latter's demonstration of the effectiveness of our species' ability with concrete logic which underlies my arguments in this section.

45 Mircea Eliade, *Myth and Reality*, London, Allen & Unwin, 1964, and *Myths, Dreams and Mysteries*, London, Fontana, 1968.

46 Cf. James M. Redfield, *Nature and Culture in the Iliad, the Tragedy of Hector*, Chicago, University of Chicago Press, 1975, p. xiii: 'There is the truth achieved by the poet *vis-à-vis* his material as he brings it to a formal intelligibility. This truth is not much like the truth of science; it is more the kind of truth we mean when we say that a man is true to himself or to his vocation.'

47 While the parallel is formally exact, the scientific status of the results is clearly not identical; for natural language has so far proved more amenable to formal and structural analysis than have the distinctly more complicated and uncertain languages of television.

48 Cf. Ziman, *Public Knowledge*, and John Ziman, *Reliable Knowledge: an Exploration of the Grounds of Belief in Science*, Cambridge, Cambridge University Press, 1978.

49 Cf. Chaim Perelman, *The New Rhetoric and the Humanities: Essays on Rhetoric and its Applications*, Dordrecht, D. Reidel, 1979, pp. 9–15.

50 Richard A. Lanham, *A Handlist of Rhetorical Terms*, Berkeley, University of California Press, 1968, p. 113; cf. Primeau, op. cit., pp. 21ff.

51 Jane Scannell has encouraged me to see the role of the witness and of testimony in the presentation of documentary on television.

52 Cf. Neil Ryder, *Science, Television and the Adolescent: a Case Study and a Theoretical Model*, London, Independent Broadcasting Authority, 1982, pp. 34ff.

53 Cf. Bazerman, op. cit.

54 John Caughie, 'Progressive television and documentary drama', *Screen*, 3 (1980), 30–1.

55 Christian Metz, *The Imaginary Signifier*, Bloomington, Indiana University Press, 1982, p. 195.

56 There is an instinctive element to this kind of zoom, one which, my own observation suggests, some cameramen and some directors have and some do not. For the movements in and out are often done as a response to an ongoing interview, and depend on an acute sensitivity to what is being said. Technically it allows a smooth transition from wide shot to close-up, and consequently the option of including the movement in the final film, or cutting out the movement altogether.

57 Serge Eisenstein, *The Film Sense*, London, Faber, 1943, p. 14.

58 Perelman, op. cit., pp. 91–100.

59 Cf. Lanham, op. cit.

60 Perelman, op. cit., pp. 10–12.

61 Silverstone, 'The right to speak', pp. 145–52.

Conclusion

Telecommunications and the fading of the industrial age: information and the post-industrial economy

Anthony Smith

We can see around us many of the elements of a great change. We know that the present wave of unemployment will eventually be followed by new and different kinds of work. But we do not know whether there will ever be enough work again. Large numbers of production and service activities are being transformed into computer-based activities – turned from a physical to an information mode. Even within the long recession of the 1980s certain areas of the economy and society are enjoying an unprecedented and rather uncanny boom, and most of these are connected with entertainment, the cultural sector or the storing and exchange of data. In other words, as so often in this country, it is painfully clear that much energy and skill is being, and has long been, deployed in public and private sectors without the commensurate rewards coming in and reaching society as a whole.

This chapter is an attempt to provide a glimpse of what has happened and it is based on two hypotheses. The first is that these burgeoning information industries are gradually establishing a dominating position. The second is that the different nature of information as a commodity (whether in entertainment, industry, commerce or education) has not been fully grasped by the political parties and by the institutions of our society. They have not realized that with the change to an economy dominated by information there must be a parallel change in the way we handle political and economic issues, in our perception of value, in our creation of priorities among social needs – in short, in *all* our political concerns.

The opportunities and tragedies of a modern economy arise from the fact that extractive and manufacturing activity has shifted towards the periphery, leaving information activity increasingly in command of the heights. Where industry was once the natural focus of politics, the place where political programmes and ideologies were tested, it is now in the fields of culture, the media and education that the main contest occurs. Success in the modern information economy comes to the society which has most developed its intellect-intensive industries, for it is in these that the greatest scope for added value lies.

Moreover it is from this information/media sector (including those parts of manufacturing which support it) that the society as a whole can be steered, and it is in those institutions where the *character* of the society is being fashioned that real ideological choices have to be made. There are no correct political solutions to the problems of this era any more than to those of previous eras, only a new series of debates; our politics, however, still revolve around ancient debates concerning the role of the state versus the free market, falsely posed questions of freedom. Perhaps we have not yet grasped the essential nature of the change in society which cable, satellite and the new telecommunications as a whole are offering us.

The regulation of information and the trades and industries which handle it have always been a major concern of the state. The Canadian writer Harold Innes (who is really the father of modern discussion about the media and communications) left virtually as his testament a work (*Empire and Communications*) which shows how each form of government which has evolved is at root an apparatus for storing and processing information. Bureaucracy was a substitute for armed power and extended power beyond the personality of the monarch and his court. Education and religion have been principal areas of state policy, because as centres for the imparting of ideas and knowledge and representations of society, they are potentially rival centres of authority. The long argument of the sixteenth and seventeenth centuries about the divine right of kings became inextricably enmeshed in the simultaneous argument about the control of printing and, in England, regulation of this equipment was considered by some to be *the* essential justification for the divinely based royal prerogative. For if the production of text ceased to remain above Parliament, invested in kingship itself, power would begin to rest upon mere opinion, upon endless irrevocable schisms. The long argument about freedom of the press has never ended, for no society has ever finally resolved the question of when a piece of text ceases to be the just concern of government.

In our own time the term 'information' has been stretched to encompass a considerable range of materials, from entertainment to industrial and commercial and scientific data. There is good reason for this deliberate distortion of meaning. In the past few decades all these forms of material have come to depend upon the same physical contraptions – computers, tapes, telecommunications systems. Material which was once associated with different arts and industries, even with different physical senses (music, film, novels, magazines), has come to depend upon the same branches of electronics for reaching the public. Furthermore, much of the phenomenon which we label information may be an emanation of economic activities which were not previously thought to have anything to do with knowledge or culture; banking was once a physical activity dealing in material substances – metal and paper – but has today been reduced largely to the manipulation of computer data and is thus aspiring to the condition of information, into digitized messages passing along wires.

It is not surprising that a society such as ours where so many economic activities are becoming dependent upon or are turning into information functions is approaching a new kind of industrial revolution. If this is so, one would expect a new and appropriate view of the state and of political life to emerge. The new contraptions which are the basic equipment of this new stage of society are all, at root, dependent upon the state for regulation, that is, for their existence and maintenance within a socially and economically responsive framework. That is a necessity of their existence, not an ideological preference: telecommunications, more than roads and railways, are becoming the nervous system, the veins, arteries and heart of a society all at once. They employ resources of air, electromagnetic spectrum or space which belong either to the nation or to the international community or, in a sense, to the cosmos.

The devices, however, which we use today to store and send messages (between people or just between computers) are not like Victorian mechanical inventions which need merely to be made safe for the public or subjected to economic competition. They are parts of a vast reticulation of interconnections, the construction of which began in Queen Victoria's day and which will continue for generations to come. They are not discrete objects but part of an interdependent national and international resource. To examine them while dominated by moral and emotional beliefs in one form of 'enterprise' rather than another is to misrepresent to oneself the nature of this whole historic evolution.

It is now twenty years since economists (and others) started to notice the increasing importance of 'information' as a sector of the economy. In the early 1960s Fritz Machlup coined the phrase 'knowledge economy'. A decade later Daniel Bell began talking about 'post-industrial society'. Japanese telecommunications officials at the same time started popularizing the phrase 'information society' in analyses of their own situation. As the hardware of the new information technology started to flow into government, into the newspaper industry, into an increasingly broad sweep of industrial and service functions, politicians in several countries began to import the new terms into the political language, but without noticeably adjusting their ideological framework. The widespread discussion of 'de-regulation', for example, which has spread – terminologically, at least – from the USA to Britain, is an old debate about government and private enterprise extended into new industries. Despite attempts by journalists and popular sociologists to emphasize the fundamental structural alteration in society implied by a transition from 'industrial' to 'post-industrial', the terms of the political discourse have not shifted very greatly.

Americans have adopted the term 'de-regulation' to identify a particular debate concerning their new national policies towards telecommunications. They borrow much fervour from the instinctive belief that de-regulation has something to do with the traditional spirit of enterprise and free competition. We too are tempted to intertwine these two sets of aspirations. In fact, the USA is having a particularly intense debate at the time of writing (1986) because it has a special problem. The main institutions which it employs –

and will continue to employ in order to control its telecommunications activity in the private sector (in the USA, as in the UK, most tele-communications provision is actually within the public sector, having to do with government itself and defence especially) – were created during the period of the New Deal. The American Federal Communications Commission (FCC) is a structure which arose from a desire to implement an anti-cartel trust-busting ideology; the FCC is used to supervising vast corporations in the private sector, which have, today, to undergo a complete capital reorganization, a reseparation of parts. It is natural, therefore, for the USA to adopt the term 'de-regulation', when it undertakes actions which in Europe would go by the name 'regulation'; the USA is recasting its institutions, is creating a certain amount of new competition but, on the whole, is simply reassigning different parts of various private (but publicly supervised) bodies. However, the US government has been preparing since the early 1970s for a great change of scale in telecommunications. Contrary to popular belief in Britain, business activities in this sphere are controlled by a myriad of regulations, which are changing rather than being eliminated.

Most of the hard statistical work which affirms that we are reaching a special information stage in the evolution of western economies has been carried out in the USA and Japan. It centres on the hypothesis that half of all (US) economic activity consists in the processing of knowledge rather than physical goods. While at the beginning of the century US Department of Labor figures show that about a fifth of the workforce was thus occupied, figures in the last few years indicate a proportion of more than half. Something rather more than 'white-collar workers' is implied by this categorization. The new work is more than traditional clerical work; it involves manipulating and transmitting data via computers, actually displacing various forms of physical production activity. A bank clerk and a railway booking clerk are now superficially indistinguishable, operating, as they do, the same machine. The blue-collar workforce has long been shrinking; society is actually losing a significant proportion of a social class whose aspirations, mores, and general social consciousness have lain at the root of many of the historical changes of the century. The new information workers perform the same roles in totally different industries and their needs and aspirations must generate new social and industrial alliances.

Why is this change occurring? What role does information, thus crudely heaped together into a single term, actually play in the economy? What might be the consequences, not just of a long-noticed decline in the traditional working class, but of the evolution across the economy of a mass of 'information workers' – who do not as yet *feel* themselves to belong to the same social or economic grouping? Certain prevailing myths about this group have to be cleared away and, happily, some recent statistical work on the US workforce published by a British economist, Charles Jonscher, working at Harvard University's Department of Economics, enables us to do this.

The first myth is that education accounts for a large proportion of this growing element within the workforce; in fact, personnel working in education and research represent only 10 per cent of the information workers and the number has been falling as a proportion over the course of a generation. The second myth is that government and the administrative bureaucracy account for the phenomenon. Not so. US government, at all three levels – federal, state and local – has indeed been growing in numbers employed and has also been growing as a proportion, but still represents less than a tenth of the new information workforce. The third myth is that the information produced by this sector is something to do with the new markets for entertainment and educational materials. The Harvard studies indicate that information produced for 'final consumption' (i.e. printed and broadcast media and education), while it has been increasing prodigiously, still represents under 6 per cent of the total output of the information sector and actually fell as a proportion in the thirty years from 1942 to 1972.

The information workforce consists in fact of an organizational group whose members collect, arrange, co-ordinate, monitor and disseminate information about activities taking place within the production economy. They are mainly servicing production. They are accountants and managers, advertisers and brokers, clerks and administrators, buyers and sellers of goods and services. They have arisen as a vast proportion (80 per cent) of the total information workforce because of the way the economy itself is evolving. Changes have taken place in the number of units of production and in their mutual relationship, in the levels of differentiation of production, in all the interrelationships and inputs entailed in a modern economy, such as to require a whole host of new information activities. What Alvin Toffler calls the 'Third Wave' is a *result* of specialization, of increasing consumer sophistication, of automated efficiency in production. The very processes which have reduced the physical production workers have resulted in the creation of this new army; the task of co-ordination which follows in the wake of increased technical efficiency in production and distribution involves a multiplication in the quantity of transactions internal to the economy.

It is hardly surprising that in recent years it is this information infrastructure which has attracted a fresh wave of efforts in the field of automation. The new information technology results from the prudent attempt to increase efficiency in a sector which has been relatively remote from automation since the development of the typewriter. We may today confidently expect this effort to account for an increasing proportion of our total economy. The growth of the information workforce has been on a scale which suggests that it probably further inhibits efficiency in production methods and is an appropriate new target for large-scale investment. The information society, therefore, is one in which the swollen information workforce is progressively *reduced* as a proportion of the total. Indeed, there is data to suggest that it has already levelled off in America; 50 per cent seems to be a rough limit beyond which continued improvement in production efficiency offers less help to general economic performance than improvement in the management of information. The 'information society' as such, emerges from the mechanization of the information sector, and the 'information economy' results from the task of refocusing investment into this area. An array of information technologies begins to be distributed through the society, very much as new production technologies made their way in the last decades of the eighteenth century.

In political terms, the aftermath of this transformation is, inevitably, a society transformed in its drives and tensions, in the disposition of its internal interests. The test of whether a particular society or nation can succeed in exploiting the new opportunities is still, of course, to be precisely formulated, but it must surely depend to a great extent upon the willingness of those responsible for government to grasp the nature and implications of these changes.

Information is not an extractive industry or a production activity in the normal sense of the term. Nor does it consist of a series of separate 'inventions' like the spinning jenny or nuclear power which a country has to 'get into' at a given moment. Information is a resource of a fundamentally different kind and its development and exploitation (as a service and as a consumed good) operates according to different principles, even though it passes through a variety of pieces of equipment which are manufactured goods.

The major advantage of the coming of information technology to our economy does not lie in employment, or in the wealth in the conventional sense, which might emerge from the manufacturing of equipment, the digging up of roads, the launching of satellites. Quite possibly those societies which have been unsuccessful in recent decades in the establishment of industrial wealth will find themselves similarly disadvantaged in these new industries. Britain, in particular, is no more likely to be the seat of a great manufacturing boom in computer hardware or accessories than it has been in the manufacturing of motor cars or computers in the 1960s and 1970s. There is no probable benefit as a result of being 'first' to use any one of the endless sequences of new transmission technologies which are emerging today. The benefits could well accrue to other countries already better geared to modern manufacturing. Britain may do well in some of these areas, but to pretend that the information era is merely industrial society in continuation is to look at the new phenomenon from the wrong end. We have to find ways to create wealth from the *use* of the new hardware; and that wealth has to be greater than the actual cost of the hardware. Otherwise we may be in danger of offering merely a further great stimulus to the Japanese economy. Japan's economy is the one most likely to succeed on the manufacturing side, since it is the society which has been thinking about the nature of information as a commodity longest and at more social and administrative levels – ever since it rode to prosperity on the back of the transistor in the 1950s.

To grasp the kind of opportunity now available entails scrutinizing the end product, information. It is a non-tangible good which arises in vast quantity from the total activity of a society, cultural and moral as well as commercial and industrial. In its traditional manifestations information has always attached itself to a physical substance, paper or celluloid, or stone, or clay tablets, and it has been possible to handle the base substance as if it were the information itself, as if it were a tangible manufactured good. We treat information in its traditional forms as a protected piece of merchandise. For centuries we have surrounded it with copyright legislation, with performing rights controls; we have naturalized it within a manufacturing economy and adopted various legal analogies drawn from normal capitalistic or mercantile systems.

But when information consists merely in a stream of electrical impulses which reach its market in any one of a variety of randomly or freely selected media we have to treat it differently. For one thing the information concerned may never be intended to be absorbed by a human mind; it may be destined simply for the attention of computers. It belongs in no fixed abode but may wash around the globe, recognizing no nationhood at all. It might not, in due course, even belong in any particular human tongue but may turn up on request in the language determined by the receiver. Information in the form to which it aspires in the information age has no physical substance; moreover, it becomes increasingly misleading to employ even analogically the concept of information as a physical good.

One Canadian telecommunications manager (Gordon Thompson of Bell Canada) uses music as an appropriate analogy. After all, we are used to hearing people hum songs to themselves without feeling that they have stolen something. Indeed, the frequency with which people use a composer's music adds to its value and its value to society is precisely that people wish to hum it. The more people who express the value of a piece of information by using it, the greater is its value to society. The task of creating that perception of the value of a piece of information is itself an information skill. The critic who helps to establish the reputation of a new writer or composer or film-maker is creating value, is adding to a national economic resource. So is the producer who recognizes the tastes and consciousness of an audience, the latent value to be tapped in a new work of culture.

Now, the extent to which a society is equipped to create information and to use it, the extent to which it possesses the skills to evaluate and recognize value in information is the ultimate measure of the potential wealth of a society in the information age. It is foolish to build the value too completely upon the individual personality of the creator of the information, for the value is created through the perception of the value and through the specialists who work with the information months, years, decades, centuries after the act of 'authorship' which gave rise to it in the first place. In this sense, the value in information belongs primarily to whole societies, perhaps to humanity as a whole.

In the information age a society is wealthy according to whether it provides opportunities to those who might create information wealth, according to whether its national values (in the moral sense) are such as to be conducive to the further creation of information wealth, according to whether its workforce feels psychologically able to participate in the mass consultative process by which value is created and added. I am not referring here, of course, merely to cultural and entertainment information but to all forms of research, to all collections of data whether they arise from and are destined to assist general manufacturing processes, or whether they are destined to be directly consumed. In fact, information is never 'consumed' as other goods are; it is added to by those who purchase and employ it. The banking information of a community is a great resource in itself, so is its medical data and its insurance-related data, provided these have been collected, stored, handled and manipulated with skill and accuracy. The better trained in the information skills a community happens to be, the greater the value to society of such bodies of data.

What then are the appropriate duties of government in the information age? Firstly, it needs to ensure that its laws enable information to flow as freely as is consistent with the economic needs of the producers; copyright legislation presently forces information to conform uncomfortably to the needs of an older industrial society. Secondly, it needs to ensure that the benefits of education, in the sense of an ability to handle text, language and data in all their likely forms, is spread as widely and as evenly as possible; the greater the inequalities in the ability to handle information and information equipment, the more handicapped a society is. (By 'handling information' one refers to an intellectual and cultural rather than a merely technical training.) Thirdly, society requires an effectively regulated telecommunications system, owned by government and private interests in combination and constantly subject to increased investment; such a system must be grown slowly and constantly, for it does not consist in any particular or any single technology but rather in all of the wires and cables, all of the radio and microwave and satellite linkages, which began to be assembled over a century ago and which link a society internally and externally. Such a resource can only in practice be governed by the same agencies which govern the society itself, for government itself is but a vast section of the information-processing function of a society. In the last resource there is no such thing as de-regulation, only re-regulation and further re-regulation. Telecommunications policy is not an enemy of commercial freedom, or of political freedom; it is rather the next challenge for democracy, how to open up for public policy discussion the countless issues which construct the nation's telecommunications resources.

In an information economy the state may have to make a series of interventions in unfamiliar areas and may conversely need to withdraw from others. New institutions will be required to inspect, to rationalize (and to keep altering) the respective functions of public and private capital. Indeed, the one essential role of government is to create an appropriate machinery of inspection and control, the essential task of politics being to develop, through debate, society's priorities for the use of an increasingly pervasive resource.

Notes

This essay was first published in *Political Quarterly* (Spring 1983).

Name index

Abrams, Mark 31, 37
Ahrens, Dr Thomas J. 298, 308, 312
Aldgate, Anthony 96
Alvarez, Dr Luiz 296, 297, 298, 307, 308, 309, 311, 314, 316, 317, 318, 322, 323–4
Alvarez, Dr Walter 295–6, 297, 307, 309, 311, 312, 317
Amery, L. S. 70
Anstey, Edgar 76
Archer, John 222
Asaro, Dr Frank 297, 307, 312
Askey, Arthur 165
Asquith, Lord 97, 102, 104, 109
Atkinson 270
Austin 177
Austin, J. L. 303

Baden-Powell 19
Bagehot, Walter 171
Baldwin, Stanley 51–2, 56–7, 58, 60–1, 62, 66, 85, 87, 93, 97, 106, 107–8, 152
Balfour, A. J. 100
Ball, Sir Joseph 67, 69, 94, 152
Bannister, Joseph 17
Barnouw, Eric 236
Barrington-Hudson, Donald 76
Barthes, R. 175
Bartholomew, Guy 67, 77
Bartlett, Vernon 69
Bayley, Thomas 12
Beaverbrook, Lord 28, 66, 97, 99, 102–3, 104–8, 109, 110
Beecham, Sir Thomas 242, 252, 256
Bell, Daniel 333
Benjamin, Walter 184, 194
Benn, Stephen 133
Benn, Tony 116, 130
Berry, Gordon 279
Binyon 247
Birkenhead, Lord 106
Blackwell, Chris 279
Blatchford, Robert 10, 13
Bleasdale, Alan 219, 220, 222, 223, 225, 226

Blumler, J. G. 157, 168, 180
Bonar Law, Andrew 97, 104, 105, 106, 107
Bond, Brian 59
Boosey, William 243, 249, 289–90
Bottomley, Horatio 51
Bracken, Brendan 108
Braithwaite 244
Briggs, Asa 86, 252, 265, 266, 269, 271
Brocklehurst, Fred 14
Brooke-Wilkinson, Joseph 71
Brooks, Colin 49
Bruce Lockhart, Sir Robert 106, 108
Bundred, Steve 120
Burrows, Arthur 237, 239, 240, 244, 245–7, 256
Butler, Billy 224

Cadbury, George 9–10
Campbell, Sir Malcolm 75
Camrose, Lord 76
Canterbury, Archbishop of 178, 179–80
Cardiff, D. 267, 287
Cardozo, Hardol 48
Carpendale, Sir Charles 69
Carvel, John 116
Castlerosse, Lord 109
Cawston, Richard 168
Chamberlain, Austen 61, 104–5
Chamberlain, Joseph 9, 11, 12, 13, 19, 96–7, 100, 110
Chamberlain, Neville 55–6, 57, 58, 59–60, 62, 66, 67, 69, 83, 84, 85, 90, 94, 107, 109, 152
Charles, Prince 168, 188
Churchill, Winston 61, 67, 106, 109, 167
Clarendon, Lord 252
Clarke, Nita 125
Clarke, Tom 98, 103
Clavering, Sir Albert 72, 152–3
Coatman, John 69, 70
Connell, Ian 306
Cook, Pam 220
Cooke, Alastair 194

Subject index